MAKING FACES

Number One:
Texas A&M University Anthropology Series

Reconstruction of the head of Philip II in bronzed resin, with sculpted hair and beard and well-healed eye wound.

MAKING FACES

Using Forensic and Archaeological Evidence

John Prag and Richard Neave

Texas A&M University Press
College Station

Ora, parum fidi, toties aliena secuti,
Grati scripta damus denique conjugibus.

Published in the United States in 1997 by
Texas A&M University Press

First published in 1997 by British Museum Press
A division of The British Museum Company Ltd
46 Bloomsbury Street, London WC1B 3QQ

A catalogue record for this book is available from the British Library

ISBN 0-89096-784-9

Designed by Martin Richards

Printed in Great Britain
by Butler & Tanner Ltd, Frome and London

SOURCES OF ILLUSTRATIONS

Map: Gareth Smith

CHAPTER 1: fig. 1 Peter Dorrell/University of London Institute of Archaeology; fig. 2 after W. His *Johann Sebastian Bach... Bericht an den Rath der Stadt Leipzig* (Leipzig 1895); fig. 3 *Archiv für Anthropologie 25* (1989) 337, courtesy of The British Library.

CHAPTER 2: fig. 7b Lancashire Constabulary; fig. 8b-c Thames Valley Police; fig. 9b South Wales Constabulary; fig. 11b Greater Manchester Police.

CHAPTER 4: figs 1, 10 after M. Andronicos *Vergina: The Royal Tombs* (Athens 1984), figs 55, 98; fig. 2 Archaeological Museum, Thessaloniki; fig. 3 Gareth Smith; fig. 11 Dr Martin Price; fig. 12 Ny Carlsberg Glyptotek, Copenhagen; fig. 13 Archaeological Museum, Thessaloniki/Dr Katerina Romiopoulou; fig. 14 Professor K. Fittschen and Soprintendenza alle Antichità delle Province di Napoli e Caserta, Naples.

CHAPTER 5: fig. 2 Thames & Hudson Ltd; fig. 3 Trustees of the British Museum.

CHAPTER 6: pl. VIa The Knossos Trust through Sinclair Hood; pls VIb, VII after G.E. Mylonas, *Mycenae Rich in Gold* (Athens 1983) figs 41, 20; fig. 1 R.V. Schoder, S.J., through the Mycenae Archive; fig. 2 after O.T.P.K. Dickinson, *Origins of Mycenaean Civilisation* (Göteborg 1977) fig. 7; figs 5, 7 Archaeological Society at Athens; fig. 23 Diana Wardle after C. Doumas, *The Wall-paintings of Thera* (Athens 1992), 162-3.

CHAPTER 7: fig. 1 Professor J.A. Sakellarakis; fig. 4 Athens, National Museum/Professor J.A. Sakellarakis; figs 5, 9 Heraklion Museum/Professor J.A. Sakellarakis.

CHAPTER 8: pl. X and fig. 1 Trustees of the British Museum; pl. XIIa and figs 5, 6 Drents Museum.

CHAPTER 9: pl. XIII, figs 5a-b, 9a,c Trustees of the British Museum; figs 1, 6 Soprintendenza Archeologica per la Toscana-Firenze; fig. 4 Musée du Louvre, Paris; fig. 7 Ny Carlsberg Glyptotek, Copenhagen.

CHAPTER 10: fig. 1 Gareth Smith; figs 2, 7 Bodrum Museum; figs 4a-b, 5 Trustees of the British Museum; fig. 6 Art Museum, Princeton University (Museum purchase, Fowler McCormick Fund).

CHAPTER 11: fig. 1 St Albans Museums.

CODICIL: pl XI a-b, figs 3, 4 University of Utrecht.

All other illustrations were provided either by members of the team or by the University of Manchester (The Manchester Museum, the Photographic Unit of the School of Biological Sciences, and the Department of Medical Illustration, Manchester Royal Infirmary). To all these we offer our thanks.

Contents

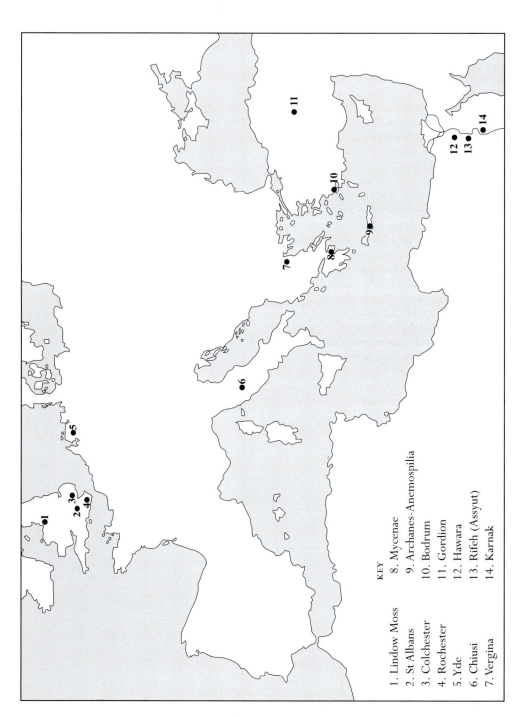

KEY

1. Lindow Moss
2. St Albans
3. Colchester
4. Rochester
5. Yde
6. Chiusi
7. Vergina
8. Mycenae
9. Archanes-Anemospilia
10. Bodrum
11. Gordion
12. Hawara
13. Rifeh (Assyut)
14. Karnak

The findspots of the skulls.

ACKNOWLEDGEMENTS

This book is the story of a collaboration, not only between its two authors – they merely take the credit because their names appear on the title page – but one that has involved many other people from different disciplines, different countries and even different centuries. We owe them all a great debt of thanks, for their contributions have been crucial to the making of the story. It is good that at long last we have the opportunity to thank them all publicly.

First, there are those without whom this book could never have happened, those whose faces we have had the privilege of reconstructing. We are never quite sure whether these people become our patients or our colleagues, but either way we feel that by the end of it all we have got to know them fairly intimately. Their names – where we know them – appear in the chapters that follow.

Close behind these people must be those who now have their remains in their care in museums around the world, who have not only readily given us access to these remains but have in many cases provided help, enthusiasm and support far beyond the call of duty. In England there are Brian Cook, Dr Ian Stead, Dr Judith Swaddling and Dr Dyfri Williams (The British Museum), and Dr Rosalie David (The Manchester Museum). In Greece: the late Professor Manolis Andronicos and his team, and Dr Katerina Romiopoulou, the late Dr Ioulia Vokotopoulou, Dr Aikaterini Despini and many members of their staff at the Archaeological Museum in Thessaloniki; the late Professor G.E. Mylonas, Professor Spyridon Iakovidis, Mrs Eleni Palaiologou and Mrs Phane Pachygianni-Kaloudi, respectively acting ephor and ephor of antiquities in the Nauplia Museum, and their staff (Mycenae); Dr Katie Demakopoulou (National Archaeological Museum, Athens); Professor Yannis Sakellarakis and Dr Efi Sapouna-Sakellaraki (Archanes-Anemospilia, Crete); Dr Nicolas Yalouris, then Inspector-General of the Greek Archaeological Service. In Turkey: Professor Enver Bostançi and Professor Berna Alpagut (Ankara), and Oğuz Alpözen and his staff at Bodrum Museum. In the Netherlands: Dr Wijnand van der Sanden (Drents Museum).

Next, we offer our thanks to those without whom this book would never have come together, our colleagues in a very flexible and wide-ranging team. There are times when we feel we have trespassed on their time and their good nature as well as their knowledge beyond all reasonable bounds of friendship and collaboration. We hope they will forgive us for these impositions, we hope that they will not feel that we have plagiarised or abused their comments, their reports or their goodwill, and that they have found it all as much fun as we have: Dr Jonathan Musgrave, who has been part of the team from the start, assisted at Mycenae by his wife RoseMary; Avril Neave, artist as well as spouse; Danaë Thimme, whose conservatorial skills calmed us and restored our patients on more than one occasion; Dr Elizabeth French, who though never 'officially' a member of the team was a crucial prop and stay in Greece, both in Athens and Nauplia, as well as in England; Dr Bob Stoddart, who examined so many of our patients with a pathologist's perceptive and often gently cynical eye. Here too belong Ray Evans, Denise Smith and Caroline Wilkinson, who share the highs and lows of work in the Unit of Art in Medicine, along with John Hartshorn and Mary Harrison.

Then there are many people who have helped us in innumerable ways in answering questions, providing illustrations, looking in museums, saving us from errors and lapses, doing make-up, literally lending us their hands, feet and ears, and much more besides; the demands we have made have been varied, various and sometimes simply eccentric. Occasionally we have pestered colleagues so often that they may feel they qualify as members of the team rather than in the list that follows: if so, we welcome them, and would assure them that we value their help, and have intended no offence. The list is long, and we hope that no-one has been left out altogether. Some have helped us with a single individual, some with several.

For the Egyptians: Dr Rosalie David, Dr Eddie Tapp, and Professor Ian Isherwood who shared his unparalleled knowledge of diagnostic radiology in some of our other cases too; Dr Robin Richards and Dr Alf Linney, who later also gave help with the milled skull of the Yde Girl.

In the case of Philip of Macedon: the late Dr Frank Howard, Dr Alastar Jackson and Dr Nick Sekunda all gave helpful advice on matters relating to archery and sieges (Dr Sekunda also helped us with Midas later); Mr John Lendrum from the Plastic Surgery Unit and Mr Eddie Curphey of the Facio-Maxillary Unit at Withington Hospital (the University Hospital of South Manchester) advised on injuries to the skull; Dr James Longrigg, Dr Christine Salazar and Professor John Scarborough guided us through ancient surgical practice; Dr Christopher Ehrhardt and the late Professor Al Oikonomides cleared up some historical points; the late Dr Martin Price produced otherwise inaccessible information on Macedonian coins; Ruth Quinn and Julie Wright did the make-up on the two waxwork versions; Dimitrios Mathios gave practical help in Thessaloniki; Dr Jane Cocking provided moral support at a tense period.

We owe the initiative for Midas to Dr Veli Sevin; Professors Keith DeVries and Kenneth Sams, successive directors of the Gordion Project, gave us ready access to their project's discoveries; the British Institute of Archaeology at Ankara and its director and assistant director, Dr David French and Dr Christopher Lightfoot, provided help with permits, advice and hospitality in Ankara and a visit to the site at Gordion; Professor David Hawkins, Dr Oscar White Muscarella, and Dr Dominique Collon offered guidance in Assyrian and Phrygian history (Dr Collon also gave advice on the 'Carian Princess'); Professor Peter Kuniholm shared his unparalleled knowledge of Anatolian dendrochronology; Professor Alan Sommerstein read an early draft; Matthew Neave undertook the photography; Dr Roger Wood's advice in genetics began with Midas but then extended to others as well; and Dr Ali Ahmed quite literally lent us his ears.

Taking the Mycenaeans and Minoans together, we thank Dr Oliver Dickinson for sharing his knowledge of the Aegean Bronze Age so generously and for giving much useful advice in our choice of skulls to reconstruct; Dr Hector Catling and the British School at Athens for obtaining the necessary permits and providing us with habitable workspace during the great heatwave of 1987; the late Dr J.L. Angel for his constructive enthusiasm in supporting our new approach; Malcolm Wiener and Professor Günter Kopcke with whom we argued about the gold masks; Diana Wardle and Dr Lyvia Morgan for sharing their knowledge of Aegean hairstyles – especially the former, who made the beautifully clear drawings which appear in this book; Louise Adkins and David Rawson for redrawing the plans; Peter Clayton for photographs; Sinclair Hood for allowing us to publish for the first time the original painting of the 'mummy' from Mycenae; Dr Tina McGeorge who considered the bones from an anthropologist's viewpoint; Kostas Piteros who provided a much-needed extra pair of hands in Nauplia Museum; Dr Colin Macdonald for hospitality and advice in Crete; Professor Alexander Kontopoulos for allowing us foreigners to work on Greek material that he might well have regarded as his preserve; and Lisa Little-Georgakopoulou who took samples for DNA analysis and made some very perceptive observations.

Dr Judith Swaddling first suggested we work on Seianti, and became a key member of the team, tolerant of both our requests and our procrastination; Professor Marshall Becker and Dr Birgitte Ginge had been working on these remains before we moved in, and generously shared with us the work they had already done (we apologise to them and to other members of the Seianti team for the delay in publishing the full report); Dr David Whittaker with Dr G.J. Thomas provided valuable help on ageing Seanti from her teeth, and Dr John Lilley made a more conventional dental study – both he and Dr Whittaker spent much time on the teeth of the 'Carian Princess' as well.

To reconstruct the 'Carian Princess' was the brainchild of Professor Geoffrey Waywell, who gave us much support along the way, and for further help in her case we also have to thank Professor Sir John Boardman, Dr Susan Walker, Dr John Peter Wild and Dr Dyfri Williams in England, and John and Alison Simpson, Aykut Özet, Mehmet Ozgenç and Harun Özdaş in Bodrum.

Those who invited us to reconstruct the heads described in Chapter 11 probably did not realise how much we should need to call upon their knowledge: Vivienne Holgate at Verulamium Museum, St Albans Museums, Dr Paul Sealey and Christine Jones at Colchester Museum & Visitor Services Division, and Michael Moad at the Guildhall Museum, Rochester, who all tolerated our tardiness and our questioning; and in York Richard Kemp provided useful information while Susannah Addyman allowed us to consult her unpublished thesis as well as discussing problems of reconstruction from a point of view other than our own.

For the Codicil, Professor Peter Egyedi became first the unwitting and then the enthusiastic subject of an experiment organised by the Utrecht group of oral and facio-maxillary surgeons.

In the University of Manchester our respective heads of department have given us support and encouragement, and have even condoned our obsessions: Alan Warhurst and especially Tristram Besterman, successive directors of The Manchester Museum; Dr Robert Ollerenshaw and later George Rogers, directors of the Department of Medical Illustration; the late Professor George Mitchell, Professor of Anatomy; Professor Mark Ferguson, who was instrumental in providing an environment in the School of Biological Sciences in which the work has been able to continue for the last eight years. John Davis, Chief Technician in the anatomy dissecting rooms, gave constant assistance in all matters relating to forensic material. Gareth Smith helped in innumerable ways in the Museum, and Serena Ronan has faced John Prag's scribbles, discs and incomprehensible jargon with equanimity, even enthusiasm. Roz Bratt has over the years given much of her time to Richard Neave's clumsy notes, and even when the occasion demanded stood with her feet in tubs of alginate. We owe a debt of gratitude to several photographers in the University for doing the impossible in recording much of the work: notably Tony Bentley and his associates in the Photographic Unit of the School of Biological Sciences, and Wilf Thomas and Geoff Thompson at the Manchester Museum.

Further afield Helen Clark at the British School at Athens worked well beyond the call of duty in trying to locate photographs of items in Greek museums for us. For permission to quote from the poems of Seamus Heaney, we thank both the poet himself and Faber & Faber Ltd. And then there is Coralie Hepburn, Senior Editor at British Museum Press, who was not at all fazed by our erratic timekeeping, and who remained (outwardly at least) calm, enthusiastic and supportive to the very end.

Several bodies and individuals have provided us with funds or support in kind at various times: The Manchester Museum, the Staff Travel Fund and the Delta Travel Fund of the University of Manchester, the Society of Antiquaries, the Institute of Aegean Prehistory in New York, the British Academy, the Royal Society, the British Institute of Archaeology at Ankara, Mr Clemens Kothe, John and Alison Simpson, and SunMed Travel. Part of this book was written while John Prag held the Visiting Fellowship of the British School at Athens in 1994.

We are heartily and warmly grateful to all these people. Yet despite all this help, freely given and much appreciated, the responsibility for the final product must remain our own, whether it is the actual reconstructions or the opinions we have voiced. Even so, one may wonder how many wives have had to bear with lunch-time discussions of the nicer points of cremation or a dining-room full of half-completed heads? And with husbands whose offspring has spent years, not months, in gestation. To them this book is gratefully dedicated: we hope they will accept it.

Foreword

'It is the common wonder of all men, how among so many millions of faces, there should be none alike.' Sir Thomas Browne was quite right.[1] Faces are fascinating, and they are all different.

Making faces – facial reconstruction – is a slow and painstaking business. The skull is the frame for the face, and to create a faithful likeness of how a person might have looked by reconstructing his or her face accurately upon the skull entails an objective, muscle-by-muscle and feature-by-feature approach. We have taken the art of facial reconstruction forward from the relatively crude and little-known stage it had reached forty or fifty years ago to something that can claim considerable accuracy. Although new techniques such as ultrasonic measurements and computed tomography are yielding ever more precise data, in the three-dimensional reconstructions with which we are concerned we have no doubt that the plastic skills of a sculptor with an intimate knowledge of the workings of human anatomy still remain fundamental. Computers and computer graphics will undoubtedly play an increasing role in facial reconstruction in the next few years and the prospects which they offer are exciting, but at present the technology is still being developed.

What we have tried to do is to produce the recognisable faces of particular historical individuals from their skulls. The reconstruction of a skull found in an archaeological context sets out to achieve the greatest possible accuracy by using all the evidence that the physical remains can provide, and as such it must be seen in its proper historical context. Hence many of our chapters go to some length to set out that context and to pose historical questions. The reconstruction is in fact a three-dimensional report on the skull, and all the more effective for that, but it is usually only one part of a much larger historical jigsaw. Of course the methodology of archaeological reconstructions is not quite the same as that of forensic ones. In a forensic case the aim is simply and quickly to ignite the spark of recognition which leads to the identification of a previously unidentified body. No friend or relative can come forward to identify an archaeological reconstruction, and ancient portraiture in the periods with which we have been dealing does not set out to be an accurate representation of its subject in the manner in which we understand it today (indeed, to use a portrait as a control before the advent of photography might raise more questions than it would answer; we prefer to reverse the process, and if at all to use the reconstruction to check the portrait). It has been very important to face the regular checks and challenges of forensic work, and the fact that the majority of the forensic reconstructions are recognised and identified demonstrates beyond doubt that the technique works. In the end we even succesfully met the ultimate challenge, to reconstruct the face of a living person without knowing in advance who he was.

This book is the story of a collaboration, intended for the general reader with an interest in the ancient world, not a manual for forensic anthropologists. It is true that we have needed to delve into the forensic evidence, and we touch on topics from anatomy and archery to mythology and waxworks, for the cases we have tackled have all raised questions that required us to call upon friends and colleagues in many other fields – that is what has made it all so interesting. Nevertheless it is fundamental that we have approached our subject as a medical artist and an archaeologist and museum curator, and in the last resort we have each relied upon and adhered to the teaching and the rigours imposed by our own disciplines.

It is important to know that we undertook nearly all of the reconstructions described in this book because we saw in each of them a new challenge to the technique which we are developing. The Egyptians first set us off on the trail, and later provided an opportunity to test computed tomography. In identifying the cremated skull from Vergina in Macedonia as that of Philip of Macedon we brought forensic science into an archaeological problem. The skull from the 'Midas Mound' in central Anatolia led us into byways of genetics and of folklore. A group of Mycenaeans raised the question of facial similarity among kinsfolk and are now leading us into DNA studies, all as part of an attempt to unravel the dynastic struggles of the Greek Bronze Age. A Minoan priest and priestess killed during an earthquake gave us experience of dealing with disaster victims that all too soon was put to forensic use. Two bog bodies, their heads distorted and still covered in tissue, required a radically different approach since one could hardly expect to make plaster casts of their skulls. Etruscan Seianti introduced questions that concerned not only the differing approaches of anthropologist and pathologist, but also others related to the beginnings of western portraiture. The 'Carian Princess' in Bodrum combined a historical identification with an adventurous museum display. Altogether they are a fascinating company of faces, and for us they have raised not only technical problems but also the ethical questions that must concern all those who work with human remains.

Faces are fascinating, and faces from the past hold a particular fascination. If the reconstructions help to solve problems that have vexed scholars, we have learned that they also generate interest and answer questions in a much wider context. Sir Mortimer Wheeler maintained that 'archaeology is digging up people, not things'. He meant that it was important to use the artefacts found in excavations to bring to life the people who made and used them. We believe that we have taken his precept a stage further: through the reconstructions one comes another step closer to meeting those ancient people. 'Face to Face with your Past', as the title of one exhibition put it.

CHAPTER 1

The History of Facial Reconstruction

For centuries the remains of the dead have been regarded by some peoples as sacred relics to be revered and preserved, and by others as objects to be feared and avoided. Different societies have dealt with the mortal remains of their dead in many different ways. At one end of the spectrum the corpse was cremated until only ashes and small pieces of bone remained, while at the other elaborate attempts were made to preserve the body for eternity, a practice epitomised by the elaborate rites performed in ancient Egypt. In between lie a host of diverse customs.

For the physical anthropologist, total destruction of the body is a disaster, for it removes the opportunity to discover how these people may have looked – their stature and build, their health and how they died. Fortunately ancient cremation practice was rarely so efficient, and with modern techniques much information can still be retrieved from cremated remains. The process of mummification, be it natural or artificial, allows a great deal of anthropological detail to be gathered, particularly from the skeleton, which is likely to remain well preserved although the overlying tissue and wrapping may obscure details even from the X-ray camera. Despite the best efforts of the embalmers, the soft tissue of mummies is usually brittle and fragile, and therefore less rewarding for the anthropologist and the pathologist because less resilient. On the other hand bodies that have been naturally preserved in peat bogs can provide much information about the soft tissues, yet the balance of the soil acids is crucial: at the very least they can soften the bones so that they become distorted by the weight of the peat pressing down on the body, and at worst they can dissolve the bone altogether, leaving nothing but soft tissue. To lie locked in the ice of the Arctic or of mountain glaciers for thousands of years, like the 'Iceman' recently discovered in the Alps, would appear to be an ideal form of natural preservation, yet this too has its drawbacks, for once it is exposed, scavengers, insects and the bacteria of decay will go to work just as effectively on any fresh corpse, whether twenty-four hours or four thousand years old.[1]

Some human remains were treated in a different manner. The Neolithic inhabitants of Jericho in the Jordan valley normally buried their dead under the floors of their houses, but they also followed a custom of separating the skull from the skeleton, often without its lower jaw, and burying it separately. The absence of the mandible is most easily explained by the fact that on any mammalian skull except the badger's this bone will fall away from the cranium as the soft tissue decomposes. It has been suggested that the crania were detached from the bodies and buried with special reverence in order to preserve the wisdom of the previous generation for its descendants, and it seems certain that we have evidence here for a form of ancestor worship. There are many parallels in the ancient world for according special respect to the severed head or skull. However, in the Levant the practice was raised a step higher: in 1953 the excavators at Jericho found two deposits under the floor of a house in the 'Pre-Pottery Neolithic B' levels (c.7500–5500 BC) totalling nine skulls, on which the faces had been built up over the bone in plaster with shells set into the eye-sockets to simulate eyes. In 1958 another single skull was found at the other end of the site, and similar skulls have been found at other sites in the area (fig.1).[2] On only one of the Jericho skulls is the lower jaw present: on the others the chin has been modelled over the upper teeth, making the heads appear rather squat. Nevertheless the care lavished on making the faces is striking. The excavator wrote, 'Each head has a most individual character, and one cannot escape the impression that one is looking at real portraits...They are not the oldest representations of the human form, nor even possibly the oldest portraits...but they are far more lifelike than any earlier examples.' However, despite their individuality, it is wrong to describe the Jericho heads as portraits in the sense of true physical likenesses. The mere fact that the artist was not concerned to include so important a part of the skull as the mandible suggests that physical accuracy was not of primary importance to him and that the modelled face was a symbolic rather than a figurative reconstruction.

1. *Plastered skull from Jericho, seventh millennium* BC.

The practice of plastering skulls, although it seems already to have been followed by the previous culture at Jericho ('Pre-Pottery Neolithic A'), only had a relatively short vogue among the Pre-Pottery Neolithic B people, and it needs to be seen in the context of the artistic traditions of the Levant in the Neolithic period. At Jericho the plastered skulls were followed by a series of stylised figures in which the head has been reduced to a flat profile but onto which simple yet arresting features were modelled and hair painted; the eyes – the most striking aspect – are again rendered by inserting shells into the plaster. The next stage was to reduce the face to a completely stylised spade-shaped disc, without any attempt to show the features plastically. Meanwhile 'Ain Ghazal near Amman in Jordan, another site where plastered skulls have been found, has recently yielded a remarkable cache of plaster figures belonging to the same period. The bodies and features are stylised, but the heads have much in common with the plaster heads from Jericho: the heads are oversized, with great emphasis on the eyes, which are modelled in the round and vividly painted. It may not be coincidence that these figures are also built up on a frame, this time not onto the bone but over a frame of reeds or rushes. At another Early Neolithic site in the region, Nahal Hemar at the southern end of the Dead Sea, archaeologists have found a most curious collection of skulls whose crania have been decorated with a lattice-work of asphalt strips, and the same site has yielded two painted stone masks.[3]

There is, then, a tradition of modelling and a culture in which the human head has an important focus. It is easy to be carried along by the quality of the most frequently illustrated skull, the only one that retains its mandible, but this is an outstanding and very sophisticated piece of work in comparison with the other plastered skulls and indeed by any artistic yardstick. Yet the fact remains that by working directly onto the skull the artists have retained the correct proportions of the face (except of course in the area of the lower jaw), and even now we get some idea of how the people of Jericho may have looked in the seventh millennium BC. Wittingly or unwittingly they created the first examples of facial reconstruction the world has seen.

Death masks of one form or other have been used in many societies, and perhaps fill some of the part played by the Jericho skulls. However, although they may be realistic and are certainly individual, they are modelled upon the superficial features of the face and thus have more in common with a sculpture created from the outside inwards than a reconstruction founded on the skull. In the same tradition is the practice of taking plaster casts direct from the face as a basis for portrait sculpture; according to Pliny the first artist to do this was Lysistratos in the later fourth century BC.[4] Such is the logic of using the skull as the armature upon which to build a face that it would be very surprising if it had not been undertaken by artists and scientists alike on many occasions since those skulls modelled nine thousand years ago. Perhaps the anatomical models made by the Italian artist and sculptor Ercole Lelli (1702–66) in Bologna fall into this category. He developed a technique of building all the muscles in wax onto the bones of an articulated human skeleton. His models remain in perfect condition and can be seen today in the Anatomical Museum in Bologna. One glance at these remarkably beautiful and accurate anatomical models should dispel the doubts of those who question the words of Galen written in the later second century AD, 'As poles to tents and walls to houses so are bones to all living creatures, for other features take their form from them and change with them.'[5] The models were made to assist in the medical teaching of the day, but when one looks at the exquisite detail that is the hallmark of so much of this work it becomes clear that some of the models of the head and neck must bear a resemblance to the individuals whose bones form the armatures for many of these fine studies. Lelli was only one of a number of skilled artists working in this field: Gaetano Giulio Zumbo (1656–1701) in Florence and Joseph Towne (1808–79) in London are two others whose works are as fresh today as when they were first created.

Not until 1895 was any recorded scientific endeavour made in this field. In that year the anatomist His, who is credited with being the first person to undertake a scientific reconstruction, set out to identify the supposed remains of Johann Sebastian Bach (1685–1750), whose grave had been discovered in Leipzig in 1894 and from which the body had been exhumed. Welcker, a contemporary of His, was also interested in the relationship of the soft tissues of the head and face to the underlying bone structure. Using two-dimensional superimposition techniques combined with soft tissue thickness data which he had gathered and published in 1883, Welcker succeeded in correctly identifying the skull of the German poet and playwright Schiller (1795–1805) by comparing the outline of the skull with that of Schiller's portrait-bust. A year later in 1884 he confirmed the identity of the skull of the Italian Renaissance painter Raphael (1483–1520). Again in 1884, the anatomist Schaaffhausen, working in Jena independently of both His and Welcker, reconstructed the head of a female over her skull. This was a subjective exercise in which the thickness of simulated soft tissue was developed on an intuitive rather than a scientific basis.[6]

From all this it can be seen that although the relationship of the skull to the face was already being explored, no scientifically controlled reconstruction is known to have been undertaken before the work of His in 1895. His's first task was to collect soft tissue thickness measurements using nine midline and six lateral anatomical landmarks, making a total of twenty-one points altogether. These measurements were made by pushing the point of a sharp needle through a small piece of soft rubber. The projecting tip was then located over the selected point on the face and pushed through the soft tissue until it reached the bone, the rubber marking the level of the skin. When the needle was withdrawn the distance from its tip to the piece of rubber could be measured. Data was obtained in this manner from twenty-four male and four female cadavers. His then modelled the flesh over a cast of the skull using the soft tissue measurements to control the development of the face (fig. 2). This work was preceded by a full anthropological examination of the entire skeleton which was presumed to be that of Bach. The validity of the experiment was later confirmed by a comparison between the skull and portraits of the composer painted during his

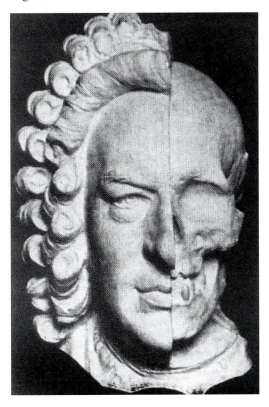

2. His's reconstruction of the head of Johann Sebastian Bach.

lifetime carried out by both His himself and the anatomist Giess. It was confirmed again in the mid-1920s by a complicated system developed by the British biometric school of artists in London.

Following close on the heels of His came Kollman and Büchly, two Swiss whose work has been quoted in almost every paper written on the subject of facial reconstruction. Kollman was an anatomist and Büchly a sculptor: together they began to build upon the corpus of existing knowledge, utilising the tissue-thickness measurements of both His and Welcker and combining them with their own, until they had measurements taken from a total of forty-six males and ninety-nine females. Drawing on these measurements Kollman recommended a precise technical process for the reconstruction of a face upon a skull.[7] This technique was first applied to the skull of an Early Neolithic female aged between twenty and thirty who had lived during the period of the lake dwellings at the site of Auvernier in Switzerland. Kollman produced the basic 'scheme' of the head, which was then completed by Büchly, whose share of the task was, as we now know, very much more difficult, for the morphological details of the face such as the mouth, nose and ears are where most of the problems lie (fig. 3).

3. *Kollman and Büchly's reconstruction of the Neolithic woman from Auvernier in Switzerland.*

Numerous further reconstructions were made by various anatomists and anthropologists of early men such as Pithecanthropus, Neanderthals and men of the Stone Ages. In 1910 Solger, an anatomist working on material from the cave at Le Moustier in France, constructed the head of a Neanderthal adult male. In 1913 the anthropologist Martin and Professor H. von Eggeling in the Anatomy Department at Jena University, working independently of each other, produced different reconstructions of Neanderthals from the same skull. During the same period Louis Masquet, a sculptor working in association with the Belgian anthropologist Rutot, produced a series of greatly admired 'portraits' of early man, utilising the techniques of reconstruction.

In view of the great interest shown in the appearance of early man, it is not surprising that the well-preserved Neanderthal skull found at La Chapelle-aux-Saints in France in 1908, which became the 'type-specimen' for European Neanderthals, should have become the subject of a series of reconstructions made by anthropologists from America, Russia, Poland and elsewhere. The results differed markedly from each other and not unnaturally this brought the whole concept of facial reconstruction into disrepute. Worse was to come. Eggeling had carried out a number of tests and made extensive studies of the relationship of soft tissue to bone, and came to believe that an individual's racial type could be determined by reconstruction. In order to test this theory he measured the soft-tissue thickness of a recently deceased male and made a cast of the head. The head was then defleshed and two casts made of the skull. The skulls and the soft tissue data were given to two sculptors who, working independently, were asked to model the soft tissues of the face. Professor Eggeling anticipated two very similar reconstructions as both sculptors were working within the same parameters. In the event the two reconstructions bore no resemblance to each other, nor did either look anything like the original cast. Eggeling concluded from this that no individual's likeness could be re-created by reconstructing it on that individual's skull. The outcome of Eggeling's experiment had the effect of confirming in the minds of most anatomists and anthropologists that the whole technique of facial reconstruction was unreliable. When we examine the manner in which the test was carried out it becomes clear that neither sculptor actually paid sufficient attention to the relationship of the skull to the face, nor to the soft tissue measurements with which he had been supplied.[8]

There is another aspect to the problem. Inevitably to a professional artist the appearance of the final product is important, and in this instance perhaps became more important than observing the scientific constraints which such work of necessity imposes. But whatever the reason for so unexpected a result, taken together with the disparate results of those who had experimented with the skull from La Chapelle-aux-Saints, Eggeling's experiment effectively stopped any further serious work in this field in Europe for many years. In a scathing polemic article the Czech scientist Suk, a noted adversary of the reconstruction 'bug' that had bitten so many of his colleagues, wrote in 1935: 'All the fossil remains of man which have come down to us are in the form of skeletal bones and can be investigated only as skeletons which can offer us no clues at all for any reconstruction that is true to life.'[9] The Russian palaeontologist Professor Mikhail Gerasimov (1907–70), fully aware of the early work and of Eggeling's disaster, started to develop his own techniques in the early 1920s, making his first serious study in 1924. He developed what today is referred to as the 'Russian method' in which the development of the musculature on the skull and neck is regarded as being of fundamental importance. This is in stark contrast to the American technique, which relies upon the measurements of the soft tissues that lie over the bone. Our own work relies primarily upon the musculature of the face, but the soft-tissue data is also used in order to ensure consistency. During the course of his career Gerasimov reconstructed over two hundred heads of our prehistoric ancestors including Rhodesian man, Heidelberg man and Peking man. He also undertook a large number of historical subjects, such as Ivan the Terrible and once again Schiller, together with some celebrated and successful forensic cases. In 1950 the Laboratory for Plastic Reconstruction was founded at the Ethnographical Institute of the USSR Academy of Sciences in Moscow under his direction. It still exists and plays an important role in the field, though now under the name of the Laboratory of Anthropological Reconstruction at the Institute of Ethnography and Anthropology of the Russian Academy of Sciences in Moscow.[10]

Despite the controversy that smouldered in Europe, others continued to follow the trail. In 1946 the American anatomist Krogman tested the facial reconstruction technique for a second time using the head of a forty-year-old negro and the skills of a sculptress, to whom she handed the defleshed skull and relevant soft tissue data. The conclusion of this test was recorded as follows: 'The restoration was readily recognisable. The entire technique is useful in the identification, via restoration, of an individual represented by skull alone.' Krogman published an account of how facial reconstruction could be carried out in the *FBI Law Enforcement Bulletin* in 1946. The technique which she described represents the 'American School' of facial reconstruction, in which a lattice of connecting strips of clay conforming to the soft-tissue measurements is built over the skull. Krogman's test supported Gerasimov's arguments for the unreliability of the sculptors employed by Eggeling, and reached a much wider audience when her textbook *The Human Skeleton in Forensic Medicine* was first published in 1962.[11] Krogman was not without her critics. Already in 1947 one opponent commented on the experiment, in words that smack of racism, 'I am convinced that recognizable reconstructions would be impossible in the majority of Whites. Certainly one could not expect that a close likeness to a person's appearance during life could be established from the skull alone.' Others wrote of the technique that 'because of the time and talents required in restoring the features the results do not often justify the effort', and that it was 'probably best left to the ample literature of detective fiction'.[12] None would deny that done properly it is a labour-intensive approach but since those words were written in 1958 the results have more than justified the time and effort involved, not least in the world of forensic science rather than detective novels, although there too it has its aficionados, as readers of the genre will know well. An example of the effectiveness of the technique is the Japanese experience, where measurements of the soft tissue published in 1948 based on forty-eight male and seven female Japanese cadavers have since been used successfully in both anthropological and forensic cases.[13] Amongst the most well known and probably most successful exponents of this technique must be B.P. Gatliff, an American medical artist who started working on facial reconstructions in collaboration with the forensic anthropologist Clyde Snow in 1967. Using the tissue measurements of Kollman and Büchly they achieved remarkable results, changing to more modern data as it became available. The collaborative efforts of Gatliff and Snow are well respected in forensic circles in the USA, with an average identification rate of 72 per cent.[14]

There were still those who remained staunch critics of the discipline despite its proven usefulness in forensic investigations. In 1981 this prompted P.C. Caldwell-Ott to formulate a questionnaire for forensic anthropologists, aimed at assessing the value of reconstruction techniques in forensic identification cases. The results showed that her colleagues found the technique as a whole both useful and reliable, and that they preferred reconstructions in three dimensions to those done in only two; the success rate based on three-dimensional reconstructions ran at 59 per cent, that for two-dimensional ones slightly lower.[15]

As facial reconstruction has taken hold around the world in the last twenty-odd years there has clearly been a need for information on the soft tissue thicknesses of a far wider range of racial types if the technique is not to be restricted to a limited number of basically Caucasian peoples. Much new information has become available, on a scale and range that would have been unimaginable a generation ago. Professor Galina Lebedinskaya, a former pupil of Gerasimov who is continuing in his footsteps, has been gathering data from faces of different ethnic groups using the ultrasonic measuring technique already used in many other aspects of medicine. Its importance lies in the fact that it can be used to measure flesh thicknesses on living people. The old technique devised by His, of inserting a pin into the flesh could – naturally – only be employed on cadavers, and changes begin to occur in the soft tissues from the moment of death. Most noticeable is the fact that as the fluids drain away from the face to the back of the head the flesh loses much of its plumpness, with the result that the reconstructions based on cadaver measurements may look less fleshy than did the living subject. Since the late 1970s Professor Lebedinskaya has studied 1,695 individuals, including groups of Koreans, Buryats, Kazakhs, Bashkirs, Uzbeks, Armenians, Abkhazians, Russians and Lithuanians. In the early 1980s new soft-tissue thickness data became available in America for both Afro-Caribbeans and Caucasians. This American material was still based on measurements taken from cadavers. It has been widely used since it first appeared but it too is slowly being superseded by new data taken from living subjects using ultrasonic measuring devices. In 1984 Professor Richard Helmer in Germany published a comprehensive set of measurements for male and female Caucasians through various age ranges using the new measuring technique.

In 1993 Helmer designed a test in which he asked two questions: first, 'Can two independent examiners produce similar reconstructions from the original skull?' And second, 'How good is the resemblance between the reconstructed skull models and the living person?' From Helmer's experiment and from our own experience the answer to the first question is a resounding 'yes'; to the second the answer has to be more subjective, for this depends to a great extent on the skill and experience of the reconstructor, the state of the skull and the amount of background information available, but in the great majority of cases the similarities are very strong.[16]

During the last eight years the technique has increasingly been explored by different individuals throughout the world. No longer are students and researchers working in isolation. The Craniofacial Identification Group, inaugurated in 1988 and enlarged in 1992 to become the International Association for Craniofacial Identification, now provides a forum for the dissemination of knowledge pertaining to many related subjects, of which reconstruction of the human face is only one. Of very great value is the interchange such a forum provides between the different areas where 'craniofacial identification' is employed, from forensic medicine to corrective plastic surgery and archaeology, and between the practitioners of the many different techniques that now form part of the repertoire, from the conventional, traditional medical artist with his (or her) sculptor's training to the newest computer-aided skull identification and video-superimposition.

Facial reconstruction now has a recognised role in the new discipline of forensic archaeology that has evolved beside forensic anthropology, which goes far beyond the mere thrill of seeing what our ancestors looked like. It is helping to provide answers to some of the older archaeological chestnuts, right back to the Neanderthalers who have fascinated both archaeologists and facial reconstructors from the outset, and it provides a fertile area for collaboration between a whole range of disciplines – therein lies part of the excitement.[17] The following pages will show how rapidly the momentum has increased in recent years.

CHAPTER 2

Facial Reconstruction Techniques and the Forensic Evidence

The technique of facial reconstruction was first developed in modern times as a means of identifying skeletal remains thought to be those of specific well-known persons. It had also been used in attempts to demonstrate the appearance of early man. Today it continues to be used in much the same way, with the added dimension of being one of the many techniques of forensic science, and as such it occasionally provides an opportunity for comparing rebuilt faces with the individuals as they appeared when they were still alive. The first reconstructions made in Manchester were of the faces of three Egyptian mummies (see Chapter 3). The results were exciting and dramatic, and inevitably led to requests that we reconstruct the heads of specimens of forensic interest.

Like most people in Britain, we were unaware at the time that similar work was being carried out in the USA, and in order to answer the increasing number of questions being posed on the reliability of the technique, we decided to conduct some controlled experiments before venturing any further down this road. With the cooperation of the Department of Anatomy in the university we selected four cadavers destined for the dissecting class. Their heads were photographed prior to embalming, and the photographs locked in the Professor of Anatomy's safe. Many months later when the medical students had completed their course of dissection, the skulls were made available to the studio in their very-far-from-expertly-handled state. At no time during the course of this experiment did we see the cadavers or the photographs. They were known only by a code number. When the reconstructions were completed they were photographed in their turn, and the original skulls returned to their respective cadavers. All that remained to do was to collect the photographs from the professor, match the faces, and check the code numbers. Just to make things more difficult, we had been given no information regarding the age, sex or ethnic group of the skulls; they were all without teeth and in some cases parts of the bone had been destroyed during dissection. As we were later to discover, this situation mirrored almost exactly the circumstances found in many forensic cases. The object of the exercise was threefold: first, to demonstrate that a different shape of face would result from each skull; second, to see if it was possible, through reconstruction, to link each skull with its undissected face; and third, to check the similarity of the final reconstructions to the original faces. The first two objectives were easily and accurately accomplished; the third is of course more subjective, but the similarities between the faces and reconstructions were obvious to see and could not have been reached by chance. The nature and the source of the original material is such that it would not be proper – or very pleasant – to publish it in this volume, but it has been checked and approved by many of our professional colleagues, who have commented that the likenesses are uncanny.

Such an undertaking is of course not unique, and in the previous chapter we have already touched on a number of other studies of a similar nature, among them Eggeling (1913), Stadtmüller (1922), Diedrich (1926), Gerasimov (1955–68), and Snow and others (1970). A most comprehensive study was undertaken by a team led by Helmer in 1989.[1] Not surprisingly there was no overall consensus of opinion on the results of these various studies. The earlier workers were less optimistic, while Gerasimov claimed total success, and the rest fell somewhere between the two, which is where most informed opinion rests today.

While it is perfectly possible to carry out a reconstruction in a makeshift manner when dealing with just one or two subjects, there comes a time when a proper system has to be established. Certain basic techniques have to be mastered and methods for handling the original specimens devised. One has to evolve an orderly procedure not just for making the reconstruction, but also for carrying out the preparatory work and handling the finished product. As a result of the great increase in work coming into our studio, both forensic and archaeological, the last twenty years have seen the development of a well-proven protocol. One of the many advantages is that the entire staff now know exactly what has to be done when work is required urgently, as is often the case with forensic subjects. The second great benefit is that one knows exactly what is required in the way of facilities and equipment when work has to be undertaken away from the studio. The third obvious gain is that as a scientific exercise one can demonstrate very clearly how the task is carried out, and theoretically another person can repeat the exercise and get the same result. The ability to repeat a process is fundamental to any scientific experiment or technique if it is to be valid, and in the case of facial reconstruction lack of technical knowledge and of manual dexterity are generally the only reasons why the exercise does not succeed. Evidence for this is to be found in the work of some of those who follow the Manchester protocol in a somewhat ritualistic manner, without fully appreciating the relationship between one stage and the next, thereby achieving results that are often wooden or lumpish and lack the individuality and quite simply the accuracy that come from understanding the subject and the methodology.

Each case brings its own problems (and it must be remembered that the *raison d'être* of the work at Manchester has always been to improve and extend the technique), and we shall discuss these as we describe our 'patients' in the following chapters. It would be useful first to outline the methods and techniques of mould-making and casting used and developed in Manchester. As the rest of this book will make clear, they do not pretend to be either the only or the definitive methods for such work. They have, however, been tried and tested over a period of twenty years, during which time we can claim a fair degree of success. They are in truth an amalgam of many ideas and techniques which have all been pooled, some coming from the traditional preserve of the artist and others from dentistry and anatomy. It may be worth noting that sometimes we refer to the skull and on other occasions call it the cranium. Strictly speaking the skull is that collection of bones which form the skeleton of the head, although they are so intimately fitted together that there is no movement between them, with the exception of the mandible or lower jaw. The cranium is the skeleton of the head without the mandible, although in everyday parlance it is often called the skull.[2]

It is a basic principle of the Unit of Art in Medicine in Manchester always to build the reconstruction on a cast of the skull and not on the original skull itself. A number of practitioners might not agree with this practice, but behind it lie at least three very good reasons. First, forensic specimens may well be required for further examination long before the work is complete; second, ancient specimens are often too fragile, and in any case it is a basic tenet of archaeological practice that ancient material, by its nature unique, should not be subjected to any process that may affect its stability and cause irreversible damage; and finally, damaged or incomplete specimens are by their nature too fragile to withstand the stress of supporting a reconstruction, be they ancient or modern. To achieve a satisfactory cast it is vital to take adequate care in preparation, always bearing in mind that it is the safety of the specimen that is paramount. An unsatisfactory mould can be repeated; a damaged specimen is irretrievable. The original is quite simply irreplaceable.

The state of preservation of a skull will vary enormously depending on its provenance and history. Ideally it will be complete with no damage to the more delicate areas such as the nasal bone, and the teeth and mandible will be present. It may or may not be clean and dry, and in the case of forensic material it is essential for the skull to be treated in such a way that it is rendered dry and sterile before it can be satisfactorily handled. It goes without saying that any work of this nature must be undertaken by appropriately qualified personnel working in the correct environment. In the same way we have learned that it is essential when dealing with fragile archaeological remains to have an appropriately qualified conservator as a member of the team. The advice which such a person can give is invaluable – and a great confidence-booster; he or she can clean and consolidate the bone as appropriate, and carry out any conservation work that becomes necessary. Even apparently straightforward tasks like repacking fragile bone in the proper material after work has been completed are much better carried out by someone trained to the task.

There are of course many occasions when the skull is incomplete, badly damaged or fragmented. In such a case the decision as to whether one should even attempt a reconstruction and if so, how to deal with the remains, will depend largely upon the extent of bone loss or damage. It is important to have sufficient of the skull to be able to establish both its vertical and horizontal dimensions. Sometimes this can only be achieved by assuming a mirror image of one half of a portion of the skull. If, for instance, half the maxilla (upper jaw) is missing, we can complete that part of the skull by assuming that the opposite side is its mirror image. While very few skulls are truly symmetrical, the asymmetry has to be extreme before it begins to affect the outward appearance of the face significantly, and therefore any slight error in restoring the missing portions of a skull can normally be accommodated. In the case of a damaged skull it is important to identify the fragments, assess whether there is sufficient material to work on and then decide how to rebuild the skull.

When dealing with modern, forensic material the rebuilding can be carried out simply by joining all the fragments together. The principle is exactly the same as that followed by archaeological conservators in repairing a vase. It can be a time-consuming task and must be done with great care as the slight misalignment of one piece at the back of the skull is likely to result in total misalignment of another area at the front. Therefore it is sometimes better to stick the fragments together with dental sticky wax instead of glue: since the wax becomes flexible when it is warmed, it is much easier to adjust one area or one piece in relation to another. Occasionally one actually has to disassemble a skull again, for instance because further fragments have been discovered, and this too is much easier if the adhesive was wax and not a glue. When the fragments have been reassembled the missing areas can be rebuilt if necessary, again using a wax with a low melting-point which is easily modelled, so that one has a complete skull ready for the next stage.

Such techniques would be totally inappropriate for ancient specimens, where the remains have to be left in the state in which they were found. In most cases the skull will have already been studied, so generally little more than minor cleaning is necessary. As will become clear in the following chapters, ancient skulls are often damaged, and may have been reassembled by earlier workers, which sometimes presents a new set of problems. For example, the old repairs may have become unstable, and there may be large gaps in the skull. Where an ancient skull is still in pieces, it is often possible to rebuild it by making casts in plaster or plastic of the key fragments; some will be too small or too badly distorted to be of any use. Although rebuilding the skull in this manner is nearly always less satisfactory as far as the end-product is concerned, it is in many cases the only way to proceed, and it is much the safest method of dealing with a fragmented archaeological skull. The separate casts can be 'floated' into position over a core of clay or plasticine, and adjusted to achieve their correct relationship one with another.

The correct preparation of a skull, whether it is complete, reassembled from fragments or still in pieces, is critical, for if it is not managed correctly there is a danger of damaging the original specimen or at the very least of making an imperfect cast. The skull, in common with most bones of the human skeleton, does not lend itself to being cast easily. There are many holes, deep undercuts, arches, and thin and delicate areas, together with a lot of fine surface detail, all of which are of vital importance when it comes to building the face, but which create just those hazards for the caster, such as potential air-traps, which an engineer designing a mould for a casting takes great care to avoid.

To cast single fragments of skull, large or small, is normally fairly straightforward where the bone is strong and solid, as is the case with most modern material. A modern cranium can usually be repaired and cast in one piece; sometimes it is even preferable to cast the cranium and mandible together as one item. This makes for a much stronger armature upon which to build a face and is coincidentally easier to store. The only real difference lies in the need to consider carefully the way in which the mandible is attached to the cranium, for just as in nature, there must be space within the temporo-mandibular joint and between the teeth. On a forensic specimen eyeballs may also be fitted before casting if the skull is sufficiently strong and well preserved. Eyes should be approximately life-size, that is about 26 mm (1 in) in diameter, and can be of plastic or plaster – it is of course not necessary to use high-quality false eyes. This has the advantage that one can fit them onto the actual skull, which makes their positioning more certain and accelerates the procedure later.

Taking a cast of an ancient skull needs more care and time. The greatest danger to the cranium is that it may be crushed or that unsupported areas may suffer further fragmentation, and so it is important to provide some support from the inside. The first skull where we had to face this problem was that of King Midas, which was both very fragile and had a large hole in the top. The procedure we devised for dealing with so delicate a specimen is described in Chapter 5. Not only do the holes caused by post-mortem damage (or ante-mortem injury) need to be filled, but so do all the natural orifices of the skull, such as the nasal aperture, the external auditory meatus (outer ear passage) and the foramen magnum where the spinal cord enters the skull, and the orbits: particular care needs to be taken with the orbits so that the borders are not covered, since as we shall see they provide the key to the position of the eyeballs. This too is the moment when eyeballs can be fitted.

Thus far the procedure has been much the same as for a forensic specimen, but on ancient or vulnerable skulls, where the bone is porous or fragile or where the surface is pitted or covered with small undercut areas, it is advisable to protect it from coming into direct contact with the moulding medium, otherwise this will not only run into every minute gap making removal very difficult, but it will also make the bone slightly damp, which may be harmful. The most foolproof method of protecting the bone is to cover it in a thin sheet of aluminium foil: that which we use is approximately seven microns thick. It can be easily burnished onto the skull with a soft cloth and folded over the edges of the bone. With care and practice a complete cranium can be filled and covered in about three hours, and most of the surface details will still be readily visible through the foil. It is not necessary to cover the teeth, as they will be almost impervious to moisture. The silver skull that results is really rather dramatic in appearance. Although from the technical point of view it is not quite the same as working directly on the surface of the bone, if it is done properly details such as suture-lines, cuts, indentations and the details of broken edges will all be faithfully recorded. Bearing in mind that the skull itself will have been studied by specialists, it is only necessary to record the outer surface of the bone to obtain sufficient information for facial reconstruction.

The moulds themselves are generally made of alginate. This material, derived from seaweed, comes as a powder which when mixed with water forms a creamy paste, like porridge in consistency. As with porridge, the thickness of the mixture can be varied to suit the occasion: dentists use a thick mix to take an impression of a patient's teeth, while in a more liquid form it can be poured round an item to invest it. There are numerous different types of alginate, all with different properties. That used for casting skulls is a standard formula with a very rapid setting time. Normally there are about three minutes from the moment the mixing starts to the point when it goes firm, but this can vary with the outside temperature, a point brought home to us rather sharply when we were working in Greece during a heatwave. When set, alginate remains flexible up to a point; it is quite fragile and can tear easily, which ironically is an advantage in that in most situations the mould will break before the specimen. Normally one can expect to get only one cast from a mould: after one use it is likely to have been damaged or distorted.

The best approach to making a mould of a skull is the traditional two-part 'split mould' technique: the mould is designed to be divided all the way round the skull along a line carefully chosen to offer the least resistance when it comes to opening it to remove the specimen. Each half of the mould is made by puddling a reasonably firm mixture of alginate over the surface of the bone to a thickness of about a centimetre, allowing it to flow over any broken edges so that their surfaces are recorded too. The alginate is too flexible to support itself away from the skull, so the moment it has set a supporting jacket of plaster must be layered onto it, a centimetre or a centimetre and a half thick: the two are best segregated by a layer of foil or film, partly to prevent moisture travelling from the plaster to the alginate and distorting it, and partly to make it easier to separate them later. When the plaster has cured, first jacket and then alginate are lifted off the bone, and, with the alginate replaced in its supporting plaster jacket, the final cast can at last be made, using plaster or cold-curing plastic (see Chapter 5, fig. 5).

The two halves of the mould in their supporting cases, looking like the two halves of an open walnut, are now ready to be coated in a first layer of plaster sufficient to ensure that they do not distort or collapse when inverted. As soon as this layer has set but not fully cured one of the two halves is filled with freshly mixed plaster and the other is placed back on top, taking care that the edges are accurately located. The two may now be tied together, and must be rotated continuously to ensure that an even coating of plaster lines the inside of the mould, resulting finally in a hollow cast. As it sets, plaster tends to expand fractionally which helps retain the dimensional integrity of the cast. When the plaster is fully set, the two halves of the mould are opened and the alginate peeled away to reveal – one hopes – a perfect replica of the skull. It only remains to remove minor blemishes, and to check the measurements of the cast against the original to make sure that it is indeed accurate.

The same basic procedures and protective measures are followed for casting the mandible or small pieces of the skull. The problem is of course somewhat simpler because they are small, generally solid, and – except around the condyles of the mandible – offer fewer opportunities for undercutting. There is generally no need to go through the elaborate procedure of making a jacket for the alginate, since the quantities involved are much smaller: a simple box made of clay or card will provide adequate support for a two-part mould.

It matters little what technique is adopted to mount the skull, provided it is such that the whole head appears to be in a natural position when completed. The conventional 'Frankfurt plane' has the line between the lower orbital margin and the external auditory meatus (lower edge of eye-socket to ear-hole) parallel with the ground, but this sets the head in a very formal position, and there are occasions when a more relaxed pose is more suitable, with the head bent forward slightly or tilted to one side.[3] This has to be decided now, for it cannot be altered later.

Up to this point, apart perhaps for the setting of the eyes and the fitting of the mandible, the process has been almost entirely a technical one, but now some

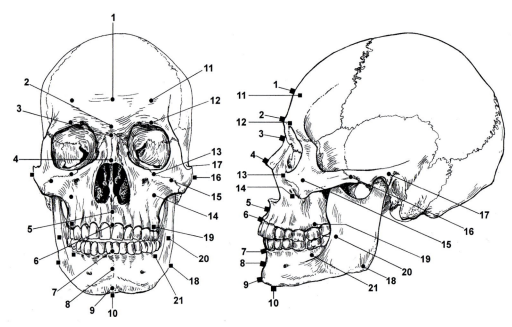

Facial Tissue Thickness of American Whites* (in millimetres)

Measurement Midline	Emaciated male (3)	Female (3)	Normal Male (37)	Female (19)	Obese Male (8)	Female(3)
1. Supraglabella	2.25	2.50	4.25	3.50	5.50	4.25
2. Glabella	2.50	4.00	5.25	4.75	7.50	7.50
3. Nasion	4.25	5.25	6.50	5.50	7.50	7.00
4. End of Nasals	2.50	2.25	3.00	2.75	3.50	4.25
5. Midphiltrum	6.25	5.00	10.00	8.50	11.00	9.00
6. Upper lip margin	9.75	6.25	9.75	9.00	11.00	11.00
7. Lower lip margin	9.50	8.50	11.00	10.00	12.75	12.25
8. Chin-lip fold	8.75	9.25	10.75	9.50	12.25	13.75
9. Mental eminence	7.00	8.50	11.25	10.00	14.00	14.25
10.Beneath chin	4.50	3.75	7.25	5.75	10.75	9.00

Bilateral

11.Frontal eminence	3.00	2.75	4.25	3.50	5.50	5.00
12.Supraorbital	6.25	5.25	8.25	7.00	10.25	10.00
13. Suborbital	2.75	4.00	5.75	6.00	8.25	8.50
14.Inferior malar	8.50	7.00	13.25	12.75	15.25	14.00
15.Lateral orbit	5.00	6.00	10.00	10.75	13.75	14.75
16.Zygomatic arch, midway	3.00	3.50	7.25	7.50	11.75	13.00
17.Supraglenoid	4.25	4.25	8.50	8.00	11.25	10.50
18.Gonion	4.50	5.00	11.50	12.00	17.50	17.50
19.Supra M2	12.00	12.00	19.50	19.25	25.00	23.75
20.Occlusal line	12.00	11.00	18.25	17.00	23.50	20.25
21.Sub M2	10.00	9.50	16.00	15.50	19.75	18.75

*Adapted from Rhine and Moore, 1982; revised 1984. Prepared by J. Stanlet Rhine, Ph.D. and C.Elliot Moore, II, PhD., through the cooperation of J.T. Weston, M.D., Office of the Medical Investigator, State of New Mexico.

1. Table of measurements for flesh thickness, after J.S. Rhine and C.E. Moore, Forensic Anthropology: Maxwell Museum Technical Series 1 (1984).

fundamental deductions and decisions have to be made regarding the age, sex and ethnic group of the subject, together with his or her possible body build. These are all factors which affect the final appearance, for the next step is to fit the pegs which indicate the overall thickness of the soft tissues that cover the bony skeleton of the skull. Some clues are provided by other information that may have been gleaned from the rest of the skeleton, from any surviving artefacts and from the circumstances of burial.

Measurements of flesh thickness over the skull have been taken for almost a century now: the first set, published by Kollman and Büchly in 1898, was based on 145 individuals, and they were the only figures available to us when we first started doing this kind of work. The collection of such information is a long, slow and painstaking process, which is why, even today, there are relatively few sets of data from which to work. Broadly speaking figures exist for Japanese, Caucasians and Afro-Caribbeans. As we have seen, further material has recently been gathered by Helmer in Germany and Lebedinskaya in Russia using ultrasonic probing. These new figures are replacing the traditional measurements taken from cadavers, and particularly those of Helmer represent the most accurate and up-to-date information now available.[4] These are the ones which we now always use, but because they take into account a number of variables beside the simple one of sex they are complex and cover several pages, so we have illustrated the simpler table devised by Rhine and Moore in the early 1980s (fig. 1).

There is always a number of variables to be taken into account, and so there are different sets of figures for the two sexes, and for obese and emaciated people as well as for 'normal' individuals. Having selected the set which is most appropriate to the subject, the skull is marked with the twenty-one (or if one is using Helmer's measurements, thirty-four) anatomical points at which the measurements are taken, and at each point a small hole is drilled in the plaster, into which pegs of 3 mm (⅛ in) diameter wooden dowel are set which project to the distance indicated on the table of measurements. The outer limits of the face to be reconstructed are now fixed in space. The medial and lateral canthus of the eyes — their inner and outer corners — are also marked with a copper pin so that they can be easily located at a later stage. One or two pegs are normally fitted projecting from the nasal aperture to provide some scaffolding for the nose, although as we shall see these cannot indicate its precise measurements (fig. 2).

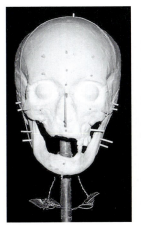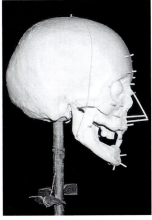

2. Cast of a skull with pegs inserted to mark the soft tissue thickness and the general shape of the nose.

Now the fun really begins. Using a Cornish pot clay with a fine grog the main muscles and muscle-groups of the face are built up over the skull. Initially we used the standard grey modelling clay favoured by so many artists, but the pot clay is much more manageable and has a body and strength well suited to this kind of work. It is important to start with no preconceived ideas about how the face will look, because as it grows from the surface of the skull outwards it will pass through several different stages, each of which may seem very plausible or implausible, but none of which actually gives any true idea of the final appearance.

It is important to note the position and strength of the muscle-insertions as they give an indication of the strength of the muscles, which in turn gives an idea of their bulk: for example, well-marked and prominent muscle-insertions on the base of the skull indicate a strong neck. The exact dimensions of a muscle are not critical, as it is the thickness of the soft tissue that finally determines the fatness or thinness of the face, but their position, direction of pull and approximate strength are crucial to the reconstruction process. Otherwise it would just be a matter of covering the skull to the level of the top of the pegs with layers of clay, paying scant regard to much else. In fact the difference between a sensitive and accurate reconstruction and a wooden, lumpish one stems largely from the attention given to these points.

Over the years an order for building the muscles on the skull has developed which seems to provide the most logical progression. We make no apology for using the anatomical names for the muscles of the face at this stage as there is no other clear way to refer to these different structures. We have provided a simple key at the end of the book (see p. 231), while those who wish to pursue the complexities and form of each structure in greater detail will find them in *Gray's Anatomy* or in any one of the many comprehensive textbooks that now exist on anatomy.[5] Those who find the anatomical description too technical can simply skip the next two paragraphs.

First the big temporalis muscle is built onto each side of the upper skull following the area of its origin on the bone to its insertion on the mandible. It is both satisfying and ultimately rewarding to spend some time just shaping the muscle and indicating the direction of the muscle bundles. The second big muscle to be applied is the masseter on the side of the cheek, arising from the zygomatic process of the maxilla and the zygomatic arch, and inserting on the mandible. It is these two large muscles – four if one counts the two on the other side of the face – that start to change the appearance of the bony skeleton of the head. There follows a succession of smaller muscles: the buccinator, which is basically the cheek muscle, is blocked in and provides support for the orbicularis oris which forms the lips. Some fibres run from the buccinator to form part of the orbicularis oris as do fibres from several other muscles. Indeed so complex is this area in respect of what starts and finishes where that it would be unrealistic to attempt a detailed anatomical reconstruction of this part of the face. Instead one makes an idealised model, looking much as it does in many anatomy textbooks. The orbicularis oris is therefore treated as a basic sphincter muscle (a ring of muscle which contracts to keep an orifice closed) joining onto other muscles in a relatively simple way and overlying the upper and lower teeth and some of the upper and lower jaw. The mouth slit around which the fibres run is placed about one-third of the way up the upper incisors, the width of the mouth being determined by the outer borders of the canine teeth. The distance between the inner borders of the iris (not that between the pupils, as was formerly thought) also corresponds to the width of the mouth, so on skulls where the teeth are missing this can be used to assist in establishing its dimensions. The muscles can now be developed further by adding those used to convey facial expression: the levator anguli oris, the levator labii superioris, the zygomaticus major and minor, the depressor labii inferioris and the depressor anguli oris. Many of these muscles are quite delicate, and it is important to remember that in life such structures would be surrounded with fat, nerves, blood vessels and the like, and that the

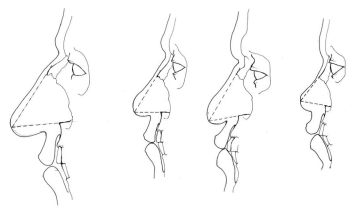

3. Drawing to show how the general shape and size of the nose are determined.

spaces between them would not be empty, so some support has to be provided under those that appear to stretch from one point to another like a strap in order to prevent them from collapsing when they are covered later.

A rough indication of the general shape and size of the nose can be added at this stage, bearing in mind that the width of the nasal aperture in the skull is approximately three-fifths of the overall width of the nose itself. Taking a line at a tangent to the distal or lower third of the nasal bone and projecting it down until it bisects a line projected outwards along the direction of the anterior nasal spine will give the approximate distance that the nose projects from the surface of the skull (fig. 3). Surrounding each eye is the orbicularis oculi muscle, which like the orbicularis oris of the mouth is a sphincter muscle, and has a slit or fissure between the upper and lower eyelids. The angle at which this fissure lies in relation to the skull is clearly indicated at the orbits, for at the inner canthus it is related to the lacrimal fossa (the hollow in the bone where the lacrimal gland is situated), and at the outer to a tubercle or small protuberance that can just be seen or felt on the inner border of the orbit. Thus even the angle at which the eyes appear to slant, be it upwards, horizontally or downwards, can be determined from the skull.

As all these muscles are built up over the skull their shapes and contours will develop, determined by the bone to which they are attached or over which they lie. The muscles which cover the point of the jaw are then blocked in in a relatively

29

simplistic manner. Neither a skull nor a head float unsupported in space, so at this stage or earlier the neck is built to give proper balance to the whole reconstruction. It should be stressed that at this point the reconstruction is not intended to be a detailed anatomical model. There are those who argue that to model the underlying structures in such detail is unnecessary as they will all be covered up once the head is completed. Of course this is true. However, this methodical approach is the most logical and foolproof way of ensuring that the face grows from the surface of the skull outwards of its own accord and according to the rules of anatomy, and reduces to a minimum the possibility of subjective interference by the artist (fig.4).

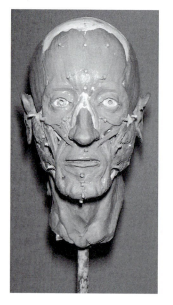
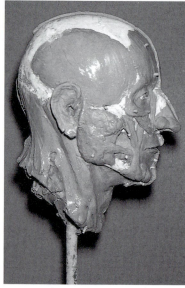

4. Partly reconstructed face with the muscles in place.

5. (Right) Strips of clay representing the soft tissues being laid over the muscles.

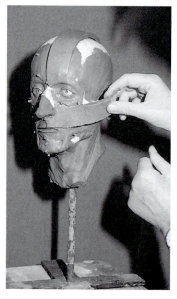
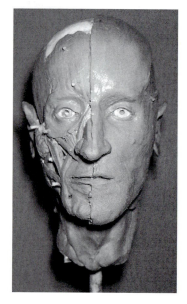

6. (Far right) Partly reconstructed head: half the head is still bare of its final layer of covering tissue, showing the muscles underneath.

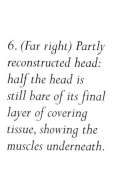

The speed with which the skull changes from an uncompromising skeletal shape into something immediately recognisable as a human face never ceases to surprise, perhaps because all other stages through which a face normally passes after death operate in the reverse direction, be it through anatomical dissection or natural decay. Facial reconstruction should not be confused with figurative sculpture. Where the figurative sculptor builds a head upon an armature of metal or wood, for the medical artist the armature is the skull itself, and although both share certain routine techniques, facial reconstruction is up to this point a purely technical exercise based upon well-documented anatomical rules. One has none of the sculptor's problems of establishing the shape and the proportions of the head, of ensuring that the spatial relationship between different parts of the face is correct or that a line in the jaw or a cheek is in harmony with its neighbour. All these are established by the most accurate of armatures for a face, the skull itself. The great Roman doctor Galen understood this basic principle. We have already quoted his words, but they are so fundamental that bear repeating here: 'As poles to tents and walls to houses, so are bones to all living creatures, for other features naturally take their form from them and change with them.' Indeed, the aphorism has often been quoted in this context, by the great sixteenth-century anatomist Andreas Vesalius and by many others since, but it is worth adding the piece of practical advice from Galen's next paragraph which is usually omitted from the quotation: 'Since, therefore, the form of the body is assimilated to the bones, to which the nature of the other parts corresponds, I would have you first gain an exact and practical knowledge of human bones. It is not enough to study them casually or read of them only in a book.'[6]

In taking a reconstruction on to the next stage, however, one steps briefly outside the strict confines of science. At this point art and science blend before separating again at the end of the process. It is the stage where all the precisely calculated anatomical modelling is covered up by a layer of clay, laid over its surface to simulate the outer layers of subcutaneous tissues and skin. In the early work we used to build this layer slowly with small pellets of clay; we have now learned that it is much quicker and we believe more accurate to apply this layer as wide strips of clay, allowing them to mirror the form underneath but always using the measurements to guide their thickness (fig. 5). This ensures that the hand of the artist does not and cannot influence the final shape of the head and face. The measurements still rule supreme.

There are two useful advantages that come from using strips of clay rather than pellets. Should it be necessary for any reason to demonstrate later how the face is controlled by the structure which lies beneath, one can strip away some of the layers of clay to reveal the muscles still in place underneath. Second and perhaps more interesting is that by building the final covering layer on one side of the head only one can demonstrate how closely it resembles the anatomical side where the muscles are still plain to see (fig. 6). Exactly the same phenomenon can be observed on a cadaver which has been dissected so that the underlying structures are exposed on one side only. Only when this covering is complete can all the features be seen in their proper proportions on the reconstruction. Until then the nose will probably look too big, the mouth will protrude too much and the face will look very angular with a rather pointed jaw. All this alters dramatically within about an hour, at the end of which a face has emerged which will remain fundamentally unchanged during the final steps.

The final modelling of the superficial features is very important for it is these that can bring a face to life. Here too the way in which they come to be represented depends a great deal upon what has been built up beneath the surface. The shape of the eyelids and surrounding soft tissue depends upon the shape of the bony orbit and the positioning of the eyeball, the inner and outer canthi and the orbicularis oculi muscle. The only aspects which are not determined by the underlying skull are the form of the palpable crease on the upper eyelid and the inner canthus. Therefore the artist must use his experience to render these features together with the shape of the eyebrows in a way which harmonises with the rest of the face. The shape of the nose does not of course really depend upon muscles for its shape, for it is formed primarily from bone and cartilage. A nasal aperture on the skull that is long and narrow means a nose that is long and narrow, and a wide aperture entails a wide nose. As we have described, its overall profile is described by the line at a tangent to the lower nasal bone and its length can be determined by extending this line to meet one drawn out from the nasal spine at the nasal aperture. However, the triangle formed by these lines is only a guide, and the exact shape of the nose as it is formed by the cartilage is less certain. One normally knows what to expect, for this guide is a fairly reliable one, but experience and a certain practical common sense play a part too. Noses can be fairly idiosyncratic features, but it is as true here as with any other feature formed from soft tissue that unless there is evidence on the bone one cannot make assumptions about the unusual or the bizarre.

Apart from the ears, the mouth is probably the most speculative feature in any reconstruction. There is evidence for its width and the width of the filtrum (the hollow above the upper lip), but there is no real guide for the shape of the vermilion of the lips, although the degree of fullness of the lips reflects the amount of prognathism of the upper and lower jaws. In the end it is a matter of using all these clues to create a mouth that is in harmony with the rest of the face.

So far as the ears are concerned there is little that can be said. The position of the external auditory meatus (the ear-hole) will indicate the level of each ear on the skull, and the shape and projection of the mastoid process can influence the extent to which the ears stick out, but it is all very vague. Fortunately ears are not normally important in recognition: identifications done for the police using facial mapping have confirmed that, perhaps rather unexpectedly, no one ever really looks at ears provided that they are normal and complete.

Working in clay it is possible to build all these features over the top of the underlying muscle structures, which have in their turn been built over the skull. Each successive layer has to be directly influenced by its predecessor, and so the face will have grown outwards from the surface of the skull of its own accord and with the minimum of interference from the builder. When all the features have been completed and the surface of the skin smoothed off, the reconstruction proper is finished. What happens next depends upon the original object of the exercise. Aside from the individual's state of health, in the case of an archaeological reconstruction there may be information concerning hairstyle, headgear, *modus vivendi* and even character which one wishes to include. Age can be indicated by the addition of folds, creases and wrinkles, but these can also be relevant where the person is known to have spent much time out of doors and so to have habitually screwed up his (or her) eyes against bright sunlight. In other words it is perfectly acceptable to use the basic reconstruction as a vehicle upon which the individual's lifestyle may be drawn. If on the other hand the reconstruction was carried out for forensic purposes then a different approach is more appropriate. Here the aim is to spark off a recognition, so anything that might distract or confuse, such as the speculative addition of creases and wrinkles, is out of place. In a forensic case the reconstruction is a means to the end of identification of a missing person; in an archaeological or historical context it is a three-dimensional report on all the research conducted on the person whose face has been reconstructed, and is therefore virtually an end in itself.

In this book we are concerned with the reconstruction of faces on ancient skulls, where for obvious reasons it is impossible to compare the final results with an accurate image of the individual when alive. However, in order to demonstrate the validity of the work on ancient skulls it is necessary to look briefly at some of the forensic work undertaken on modern skulls. Apart from the controls described earlier in this chapter, until very recently reconstructions undertaken for forensic purposes provided the only opportunity to compare the results with photographic records of the deceased.

There are a number of caveats to be borne in mind when considering the whole question of the success of an attempt to identify an unknown body using facial reconstruction. Such reconstructions are usually publicised through the news media and through posters, but there still remains the fundamental question of who actually sees the reconstructed head or face. Despite the best efforts this must depend largely on chance: just because a body is found in the south of the country does not necessarily mean that it did not originate in the north and vice versa. It therefore follows that the exercise will not be successful if the reconstructed image is circulated in the south while those more likely to recognise it live in the north. Again, not everyone reads the newspapers, or watches television news programmes. Not infrequently those whose remains are found in circumstances where such investigations become necessary have had few friends and may have lived a wandering and irregular life. Furthermore it is not always in the interests of those who do recognise a reconstruction to respond. These are only a few of the reasons why a face may not be recognised, so it is hardly surprising that the average success rate in most countries is between fifty and sixty per cent, regardless of the techniques employed: in Manchester the figure is no different.

As we have already suggested, there are too many variables for a reconstruction based only on the skull to be completely accurate, and it can never be regarded as a portrait. As a general rule what seems to happen is that one creates a face which is very similar to the kind of face which the individual had when alive. In terms of the forensic application such a reconstruction will become just one part of the story: it is in effect a specialist report done in three dimensions which contributes to the whole forensic investigation. As with any report it can only be as accurate as the information which it contains, and if incorrect or false information is included then the report – in this case the reconstruction – will be flawed, as happened in the case of a body found just outside Great Harwood in Lancashire.

In the small hours of 19 March 1988 a passing motorist stopped to investigate what appeared to be a tailor's dummy burning on the side of the road near Dean Clough Reservoir. On investigation it turned out to be the body of a man who had died from blows to the head and chest and who had flex tied round his neck. Despite the fire there was still a considerable amount of detail on the face which gave a good indication of the type of nose and mouth, but it would not have been acceptable to have shown the charred and lacerated remains to the public. Even so it has been contended that the face would have been recognisable as it was, and that there was no need to have had it reconstructed. Such arguments are based on a lack of appreciation of the rigid logic upon which the technique is founded. Just how inescapable are the rules imposed by the skull and how little freedom there is for the artist's imagination was made abundantly clear in this particular case, for some of the information which was to be included in this three-dimensional report turned out later to be simply wrong. The dead person, we were told, was around twenty-two years old, was Malay or Chinese, and male. The circumstances of death and discovery meant that establishing the sex did not present problems, but age and ethnic group can be very much more difficult. However, the reconstruction that was broadcast on national television showed the dead person as a young man of Southeast Asian type. Taken with the background story, the similarities of facial structure, such as the proportions of the face and the shape of the nose and mouth, were so close that despite differences in the eyes and in the forehead creases (for which the skull provides no evidence) the victim had been recognised by a member of his family within twenty minutes of his television appearance. His name was Sabir Kassim Kilu. As it turned out he was nearer forty-six years old and was of Indian

7. The Great Harwood case: the reconstruction and the actual victim.

race (fig.7). Thereafter formal identification was of course carried out using conventional forensic techniques.

The case highlights the problem of the rate of success in forensic reconstructions to which we referred earlier. On this occasion an extensive police investigation in the area where the body was found had revealed nothing, nobody recognising the face. It was not until the case received national coverage that the face was seen by the relevant person: the corpse had been transported in the boot of a car from Leicester to Lancashire, where it was dumped on the roadside. Those responsible for his death were subsequently arrested, tried and convicted.

Another case where the same problem could have arisen had there been no other evidence was that of the young Finnish nurse whose skeletalised remains were found in the woods of Blenheim Palace in Oxfordshire in 1983. The reconstructed face bore an uncanny resemblance to the photograph of a young woman in a passport found shortly afterwards some two miles distant in an abandoned rucksack.

8. The Finnish nurse: the reconstruction, her passport photograph, and another photograph showing her somewhat plumper.

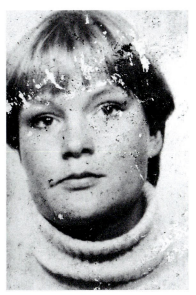

35

What was particularly interesting was that in the rucksack was another photograph of the girl which showed her somewhat plumper than in her passport; but because the skull underneath the faces in the two photographs was the same, there was no doubt at all that they portrayed the same person (fig.8). In this case the reconstruction was not directly responsible for the recognition, but it gave considerable support to the decision that the details of the dentition on the skull be sent to the dentist of the passport holder in Finland. A few days later the identity was confirmed. Sadly her assailant has never been caught.

A textbook case, the stuff of fiction, was undoubtedly that of Karen Price, the teenage girl whose body was found in 1989 by workmen laying new drains, wrapped in an old carpet and buried in a grave at the back of a house at Fitzhamon Embankment in Cardiff. The body had lain undisturbed for nine years. Considerable care had been taken by the police to ensure that all the forensic details were complete before the reconstruction was started. Dr David Whittaker at the Dental School of the University of Wales in Cardiff had established her age with great precision at about fifteen and a half years, and made some very shrewd observations regarding the dentition, noting on the one hand slight defective formation of some of the teeth, and on the other the fact that some of her fillings had probably been done outside the United Kingdom. The skull was in perfect condition, unlike so many specimens, and unusually there remained an almost complete head of hair. The skull was cast and the rebuilding of the head was completed in two long days. The case was accompanied by considerable publicity, including what was fast becoming the customary television appearance on 'Crimewatch UK'. Within about ten days she had been recognised by two separate individuals in different parts of the country; David Whittaker's perceptive examination of her teeth proved extremely useful in confirming their identification when compared with Karen Price's dental records (fig.9). Ultimately her killers were brought to justice and condemned for murder, almost exactly a year after the screening of the 'Crimewatch' programme. The manner in which this came about was yet another of the many twists to this tale. Not only had the television programme jolted the memories of two people who had cared for the girl, and thus led to her identification, but it had also resulted in one of the killers, who happened to have watched it too, being persuaded to give himself up to the police.

Unfortunately success of this nature is not guaranteed. One of the saddest and most poignant cases which serves to emphasise this fact must be that of the one remaining unidentified victim of the King's Cross Station fire in December 1987. Although the body had been very badly burned, there were nonetheless still numerous clues about his face that could be gleaned from the remains, particularly around his nose and mouth. An extensive dossier was compiled outlining his height, age, state of health and more besides. He had undergone major neurosurgery in which a cerebral aneurysm in his brain had been clipped. This had required the removal and replacement of a large piece of bone on the side of his skull. He had a full set of artifical dentures, upper and lower, which displayed some technical idiosyncrasies. Somewhere there are detailed notes on this man's medical and dental treatment. Somewhere his name has been recorded along with many other personal details, sufficient to make a positive identification. Somewhere there will be radiographs and almost certainly a photograph. But without a name none of this can be followed up. The reconstruction and the whole story received wide coverage. Despite the concentrated efforts of many people over many months, and at least one false trail which only proved to be a blind alley some two years later, the one victim whom all the investigators thought they would be able to identify most easily because of his very distinctive medical history remains stubbornly anonymous — so far: even ten years later a chance remark at a lecture has produced another possible lead.

Not always is the skull in perfect condition. In some cases it may have been deliberately damaged in an attempt to foil recognition, on other occasions it is the

9. Karen Price: her reconstruction and a photograph taken in life.

manner of its discovery that causes the damage. Spades, mechanical diggers and agricultural ploughs are no respecters of the fragility of human remains. A case where a deliberate attempt was made to prevent the victim being recognised is sometimes referred to as 'The Headless Body Reconstruction'. The decapitated body of a male was found at Wyre Street under the railway arches of Piccadilly Station in Manchester in December 1993. Needless to say there was nothing that we could do at the time, but three months later the head was found in a shallow pit just off the M6 motorway at Cannock in Staffordshire by a dog being taken for a walk. The body had meanwhile been kept in cold storage, unlike the head which had been buried. What made things particularly difficult was that one of the assailants had mutilated the face and skull with a meat cleaver or machete, smashing the skull

37

into over a hundred separate fragments. Such damage can be repaired with care but where some of the bone is missing vital evidence can be lost. Due to the severity of the damage and the manner in which the remains had been recovered, all the bone that forms the mid-portion of the face was missing (fig. 10). Thus all the evidence for the shape of the nose, the inner corner of the eyes and the upper lip are absent, and further, the overall integrity of the proportions of the skull were slightly compromised as it was not possible to reassemble properly some of the larger pieces since they had separated along the suture lines. Sufficient of the hard palate and upper molar teeth could be relocated to ensure that the vertical proportions were about right, and fortunately the mandible had not suffered too badly. The missing

areas could only be replaced by eye, building onto the existing bone and extending it until the skull was complete. Given the amount of missing bone there seemed little likelihood of a successful outcome to this particular exercise, but as is usually the case when we are called upon to do forensic work, this was the last chance. The last chance proved the lucky one. Many people thought they recognised the face. In the event there were seventy-six names to follow up, all different. Almost in the last moments before the investigation was to be abandoned the final name was checked out, and it tallied with the reconstruction. Ironically it had been one of the first received: there had after all been nothing about the body to suggest that it was of that of a foreigner, but the name in question, Adnan Abdul Hameed al-Sane, was indubitably foreign, and as such had very properly been left to the end of the list as the least likely subject. The dead man proved to be a millionaire Kuwaiti businessman who

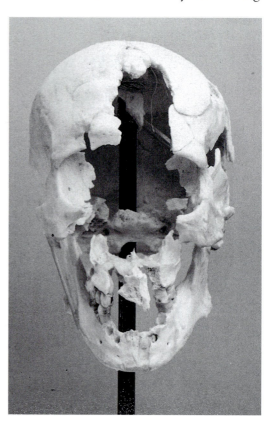

10. The skull of the Wyre Street murder victim repaired from fragments.

lived in London and who had last been seen alive there the previous December on the day before his decapitated body turned up in Manchester (fig. 11). His killers had clearly worked very hard to prevent his ever being seen again in any form or manner, but to no avail. Aside from the feeling of gratification at a job well done, for us there was the additional satisfaction of knowing that if a recognisable reconstruction could be made from Mr al-Sane's mutilated remains, then we could feel confidence in the reconstruction of the Minoan priest on whose fire and earthquake-damaged skull we had worked in 1987–8 (described in Chapter 7).

It is worth reporting a similar case which came to a successful conclusion virtually as this book went to press. A partly decomposed body was turned up during ploughing in Hampshire in 1996, but the ploughshare had cut through the body and the skull, reducing the latter to 140-plus fragments. These were painstakingly cleaned and restored into a virtually complete skull on which a face could be reconstructed for the police and in due course identified. It would seem that despite all the limitations and uncertainties surrounding facial reconstruction and the inevitable hostile criticisms that the subject sometimes attracts, as a means of

11. Reconstruction of the Wyre Street victim, and a photograph of Adnan al-Sane.

achieving recognition when all other attempts have failed, it can and does work when the right person sees someone whom they knew well. With this in mind we can start to look at and assess the results of some of the historical reconstructions with greater understanding and certainty than would be the case if the technique had never been tested.

Earlier in this chapter we said that until recently only forensic work provided the opportunities to assess the accuracy of the technique. Modern technology has now made it theoretically possible to reconstruct the head of a living person while having no idea of what that person actually looks like. Medical scanning techniques such as computed tomography (CT-scans) can be harnessed to computer-controlled milling machines to cut a replica in styrene of the skull of a living person upon which one can then rebuild a face in the conventional manner (see Codicil, pp. 228–30). Alternatively, using a technique called selective laser sintering, the CT-scans can be harnesssed to a computer-guided laser beam which recreates the skull by polymerising a powdered plastic. Such computer-controlled machines are of course doing the work which we used to do by hand, working first from traditional X-ray photographs and later from CT-scans, but they are much quicker and more accurate than the early hand-made models, which were after all designed for a different use altogether, that of aiding a surgeon to plan a corrective operation.

Computer technology increasingly touches every aspect of modern life and facial reconstruction is no exception. Techniques already exist where an optical laser scanning system can gather all the data on a skull in a matter of minutes and reproduce it as a three-dimensional image on the computer. A face can be stored on computer in the same way.[7] By matching the soft-tissue measurements it is possible to wrap the scanned image of another individual's face over a scanned skull. This process naturally requires very sophisticated software and equally sophisticated equipment. There are a number of other problems which need to be taken into account: for example, the face wrapped over the skull must be of roughly the same age as the skull, and must fit all the other known criteria. The fundamental difficulty in using the computer in this way is that it can no more answer the problems of the unknown than any other technique, for while it alters the shape and the dimensions of the scanned face it cannot change its basic morphological features such as the nose, the mouth and the eyes. The computer is probably quicker than the medical artist and changes can be made more rapidly, and one might add somewhat cynically that the result will be more readily accepted as accurate simply because it is a computer-generated image. Without doubt in time all these problems will be overcome. For the present, however, one cannot escape the fact that most computer-based approaches are aimed at modifying an existing image rather than creating a face from scratch. For the moment use of the computer in our own studio is confined to experiments in adding colour to the skin, hair and eyes of scanned photographs of conventional reconstructions in order to add realism and thus help towards identification.

But this is looking ahead. In the 1970s computers were still the province of a few specialists, and the very technique of facial reconstruction was little known outside North America. Yet our story so far will have made it clear that it needed only the coming together of a few researchers with a common interest to set if off in new directions. Such a moment came in the University of Manchester in the 1970s when one of us – Richard Neave – was caught up in an exciting research project which was being developed at the University's museum, and which led to the first of the many reconstructions carried out at Manchester. That story is best told as it happened.

CHAPTER 3

Richard Neave's Egyptian Encounter

The skull of Nekht-Ankh vanished silently from view, along with the confidence that I been feeling for the previous few days, as the layer of alginate rose slowly inside the glass tank (fig. 1). Looking back at those uncertain moments in the summer of 1973, I find it difficult to believe that the project would have had such far-reaching effects upon my life and career, or upon that of my colleague and co-author John Prag. Let me explain more fully what was going on, and more importantly why it was going on.

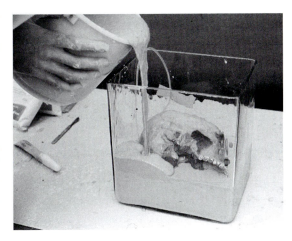

1. The skull of Nekht-Ankh being cast: the lower part of the skull is already surrounded by alginate, which will form the lower half of the mould.

The Manchester Museum possesses a very fine collection of ancient Egyptian material. In 1970 the museum's new Egyptologist, Dr Rosalie David, had begun a detailed study of all the mummified remains, particularly the human mummies. Fortunately Manchester University also has a very large and prestigious Medical School with close links to several teaching hospitals. Naturally it was to her colleagues in the Faculty of Medicine that Dr David turned for expert advice and assistance in the examination of these remains. In due course a group of interested people drawn from a wide range of disciplines, predominantly from the medical fraternity, began to meet and plan on a regular basis.

The Manchester Mummy Team, as it became known, beavered away happily for several years, studying the anatomy, the pathology, the odontology, the entomology, indeed every sort of 'ology' that could usefully be brought to bear on those ancient remains. The enthusiasm, the sense of interdisciplinary camaraderie and mutual co-operation that was generated by this collective effort was exhilarating. Ideas seemed to form out of thin air. One of these ideas was that illustrations might be prepared of the various ancient Egyptians to give some idea of how such people may have looked when alive. The emphasis was to be upon the effect that certain physical peculiarities and abnormalities would have had on the outward appearance of these individuals.[1]

In my capacity as Medical Artist attached to the Faculty of Medicine in the

University, my background was reckoned to be best suited for this task. So it was that Dr David invited me to join the group. Initially the exercise appeared straightforward enough. Much of my working life had been spent creating images that clarified unclear situations within medical science. To understand and interpret facts or images that made sense only to the specialist or the initiated, illustrating one form of abnormality or another, interpreting the descriptions of various clinicians concerned with the examination, all this was very much in line with my routine work. Needless to say illustrations of abnormalities can only be prepared if there is some form of pathology to illustrate. In the event it turned out that no such pathology was to be found in the first mummies to be examined, and thus my role in this fascinating project seemed rapidly to be becoming redundant. And yet, as I have said, ideas seemed to come out of the air at that time. I recall another colleague, Dr John Prag, suggesting something about building faces, perhaps upon the skulls. The possibility of somehow trying to 'breathe a little life' into the mummified remains and thus allowing the museum visitor to identify more readily with those ancient people seemed to catch the imagination of the Mummy Team.

As a child and as a young student, skeletons, particularly those of the dinosaurs at the Natural History Museum, were a source of great fascination to me, and I would spend hours drawing the bony framework of some of the great reptiles. The sauropods, such as diplodocus, were too long to manage comfortably in my small sketchbook, but skulls and smaller skeletons were ideal to study. When I tired of drawing there were always the reconstructed models of the animals to ponder over, which illustrated how they may have appeared when they were alive. These reconstructions were based upon studies of the skeletal remains. To artists, particularly those who had the privilege of a classical training, such an attempt to recreate an animal from the skeleton makes perfect sense, for the skeleton provides the armature of the creature's body. Clearly if a skeleton is 20 m (say 65 ft) long then the animal has to be at least 20 m long; should a skull be massively formed with a vast lower jaw, as it is in many of those carnivorous reptiles, then such features will strongly influence the outward form and appearance of the head. Given a knowledge and understanding of anatomy it is possible to make a reasonably accurate and truthful reconstruction of a creature's appearance. Naturally colour, surface texture, hair (if any) and a number of other details must be more speculative, but in general terms one can be fairly certain about its morphological appearance – that is, the shape of the soft features which cover the bone underneath.

At the time when I became involved in the Egyptian project I had been unaware of any published work in this field until my colleague Dr (later Professor) Ian Isherwood drew my attention to an article that had appeared in 1966 in the *Journal of Egyptian Archaeology* by Professor R.G. Harrison, Professor of Anatomy at the University of Liverpool, entitled 'An Anatomical Examination of the Pharaonic Remains Purporting to be Akhenaten'.[2] As part of this examination Harrison had asked the medical artist at Liverpool University to prepare some diagrams and drawings of a face using photographs of the skull together with measurements of flesh thicknesses produced by the Swiss scientist Kollman working together with the sculptor Büchly. I had already proposed making casts of the skulls of some of the mummies and rebuilding the soft tissues of the faces on these casts: without knowing it, I had suggested exactly the same method as that used by Kollman and Büchly. The discovery of their soft-tissue tables was a great step forward. It seemed obvious right from the start that to work directly on the original skulls was out of the question, for the risk of damaging such valuable specimens was too great. The original intention was that we should make paintings and drawings using the modelled faces as a guide to the shape and proportions of the portrait, and develop the details of morphological features in the drawings from known facts and from contemporary figurative material.

Dr David suggested that the mummies of the 'Two Brothers', Khnum-Nakht and Nekht-Ankh, who lived during Dynasty XII around 1900 BC might be the perfect subjects upon which to try this approach. They were found in the rock tombs of Rifeh in Middle Egypt, about eight miles south of Assiut, during excavations conducted in 1907 by Flinders Petrie, who presented them to the Manchester Museum, where they have pride of place in the Egyptian collections. The tomb in which the two were found was itself rather unprepossessing, being nothing more than a small chamber cut in the rock in one corner of the courtyard of a much grander tomb, and it was almost passed by altogether. 'The interior of the tomb-chamber was so completely filled with tomb-furniture that it was impossible for any but a small boy to get inside.' The first thing to greet the excavators were the two rectangular outer coffins: inside each were decorated body coffins which in turn contained the embalmed bodies of the Two Brothers. Both pairs of coffins were painted with hieroglyphs from which we learn the names of the brothers and of their mother, Aa-Khnum. No paternal name is given, and since their remains exhibit markedly different ethnic characteristics, it is easy to conclude that they were half-brothers, the sons of different fathers. They were accompanied by the customary assemblage of funerary artefacts, including model boats complete with crew to ensure that the soul could travel safely to its new life, but rather oddly only Nekht-Ankh was buried with the canopic jars in which were stored the organs removed and dehydrated during the embalming process. Khnum-Nakht's mummy was altogether less well preserved.[3]

In 1908 Dr Margaret Murray, then curator of Egyptology, had arranged for these two mummies to be unwrapped before a large audience numbering some five hundred people. Dr Murray was assisted by a small team of medical and scientific specialists. It was the earliest modern 'scientific' examination of an ancient Egyptian mummy, preceded only by a study in Leeds in 1824 to which we shall return later. Before this time many mummies had been unwrapped or 'unrolled', to use the fashionable term, but nearly always as an entertainment and always in the anticipation of finding treasure. Any archaeological findings were generally of only marginal interest.

Although at the time of Dr Murray's investigation a considerable amount of preserved soft tissue was present, only the bony skeletons now remain (fig. 2). One brother, Nekht-Ankh, was thought to have eunuch-like features. The examination of the remains carried out in 1975 supports this view. The skull has a number of female characteristics: it is smaller, with less well-developed superciliary ridges above the eyes than might be expected in a male. The long bones in the skeleton are also rather smaller, more lightly formed and with less well-developed sites for muscle attachments than would normally be present in a male skeleton. He was about sixty years old when he died. Very little tissue was found attached to this mummy when it was

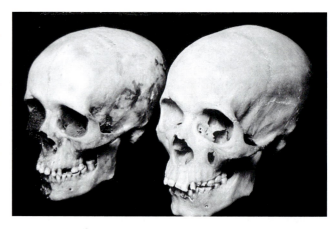

2. *The skulls of the Two Brothers.*

originally unwrapped in 1908, most of it falling away as the bandages were removed. This material was all stored in a glass jar and not touched for another seventy years, when a careful histological study revealed that during his life Nekht-Ankh suffered from pneumoconiosis, a condition affecting the lungs caused by the inhalation of fine grains of sand: many miners and quarrymen have suffered from similar conditions from working in dusty conditions ever since. He also had pleurisy and pericarditis as a result of an attack of pneumonia, leaving him with breathlessness and probably a harsh cough. However, the actual cause of his death remains a mystery.

His half-brother Khnum-Nakht was only about forty-five years old when he died. He suffered from osteoarthritis which had seriously affected his back, leaving him with a disfiguring and perhaps disabling stoop. One of the conclusions arrived at by Margaret Murray and her associates in 1908 was that Khnum-Nakht, the younger of the Two Brothers, suffered from talipes varus (club foot) of the left foot: however, the radiological studies made in 1975 showed this not to be the case. Examination of the teeth of Khnum-Nakht revealed an unusual developmental condition: the two upper central incisors were abnormally large, the left tooth being considerably larger than the right, with two roots. The immediate impression was that the two upper left incisors were fused into one, with a supernumerary tooth lying immediately behind. In all other respects the teeth and the skull bones of the Two Brothers were in good condition and quite normal: it was this that made them such good candidates for reconstruction. When Dr Murray opened Khnum-Nakht's mummy it had been completely dry and the soft tissues had collapsed into powder: no histological study was possible, and thus no conclusions could be drawn for his state of health and cause of death.

There was also an academic conundrum which one thought might be answered by this rather novel approach to their skulls. Amongst the items found with the remains were three carved wooden figurines, two of them small and one rather larger. Of the small figures, one was rather stylised and had been placed in the coffin of Khnum-Nakht; the other two figurines, both from the coffin of Nekht-Ankh, appeared more naturalistic. However, the names inscribed on them did not match those on the coffins: one of Nekht-Ankh's figurines was found in his own coffin, but the other two were the wrong way round. Did the figurines therefore represent the individuals in the coffins or were they placed in the wrong coffins by mistake during the funerary preparations, or – a third possibility – did they offer no indication at all of how the brothers may have looked? Whatever the answer to the question, the mere fact that such confusion was possible at the embalmers suggests that the two men died and were buried at the same time, although none of the investigations have found the cause of their deaths. Both skeletons were quite different in appearance: Khnum-Nakht, the son of a negro father, was taller with a long, dolichocephalic skull which showed marked prognathism of both upper and lower jaws, pushing his teeth forward and giving him a prominent mouth, and he was obviously male in every respect. Nekht-Ankh on the other hand was smaller and had a short, brachicephalic skull with numerous female characteristics, yet his body coffin had its face painted black and contained the negroid figurine. The two naturalistic figurines are beautifully carved and clearly depict two very different types of men (see fig. 5). Margaret Murray mentioned that during the unwrapping in 1908 it appeared that Nekht-Ankh had what looked like very short grey hair, although no trace of this survives. The smaller of the two figurines does have hair painted on his head in such way as to suggest that it is short and grey.

Appraised of all these facts, I took possession of the precious skulls and carried them back to my studio. The prospect of handling bones, skulls and specimens was perfectly normal to the studio staff: after all we did it all the time with new or fresh human material. It was the realisation that these particular skulls were nearly four thousand years old that filled us all with awe. To make a mistake and damage one or both of them was unthinkable. We had carried out trials on a modern skull which demonstrated that the technique we planned to use was sound. Nevertheless the tension on that Saturday morning was very real.

The preparation of the skulls of the Two Brothers differed very little from the techniques used today on strong or modern skulls, but the actual making of the moulds and casts was very ponderous when compared with the more modern methods described in the previous chapter. The cranium – the skull without the lower jaw – was placed on its side in a glass tank, raised from the bottom on three plasticine stands. We prepared a quantity of alginate and poured it into the tank until it reached the midline of the cranium. One half of the cranium was now totally invested in alginate (see fig. 1). When it had cured, a second batch was mixed and poured over the exposed half of the cranium, which vanished silently from view. When this second batch had cured came the tricky task of removing first the mould containing the cranium from the glass tank, and then the cranium from the mould. Having managed to extract the mould from the tank, rather like emptying a giant blancmange from its mould, we located the join between the two halves of the mould and gently prized them apart, once again revealing the cranium which appeared none the worse for its temporary re-entombment.

Replacing the mould in the glass tank took only a few moments. A square hole measuring 2.5 cm (1 in) was then cut in the top of the mould through which plaster of Paris was poured until the mould had been filled. A short wait while the plaster cured, and the mould was stripped away to reveal an accurate cast of the original cranium. The mandible was cast as a separate item, using the same split-mould technique as on the cranium. When the two pieces were relocated we found that they fitted perfectly.[4] Common sense and my training as an art student dictated that the plaster skull must be set on a substantial mount before the next stage could be carried out. It can be a very heavy item, and others have found that they ignore this precaution at their peril. Both skulls were therefore mounted on stout wooden poles, and these in turn were fitted into solid wooden boards to form stands which would allow us to work on the head with ease. Although the studio was well equipped to handle all the medical tasks which we were routinely called upon to undertake, at that time those tasks did not include casting skulls, and the equipment that we have today, and indeed which I had used at art school, was not available and so a good deal of improvisation was necessary. The absence of a turntable and a modelling stand were less of a problem than simply procuring and storing a reasonable quantity of clay and plaster, and carving suitable modelling tools. As usual in the academic world, there were never funds for acquiring special items of equipment which were not going to be used in our everyday duties, and the building of clay heads on the casts of ancient skulls certainly did not fall into this category. Hence the need for improvisation and ingenuity, which may give the unjustified impression that we were going about things in a somewhat unconventional and haphazard manner.

The building of the faces in clay was very simple by the standards of today which we describe in the next chapter, and relied upon the shape of the skull alone. Whilst a great deal of attention was paid to the areas of muscle insertion and their probable effect upon the face, we put little effort into developing the muscle groups themselves. Nonetheless two very distinct and distinctly different faces began to emerge. When they reached a fairly advanced stage, measurements of the thickness of the soft tissue were made at specific anatomical points according to tables produced by Kollman and Büchly in 1898 (see pp. 15–16). These measurements included the maximum and minimum thickness in both males and females. It was of course argued that these tables were only averages for one racial group and not universally applicable, but at that time no other measurements existed and there was no alternative if we were to be as objective and scientifically accurate as possible. Every attempt was made to ensure that these measurements were accurate. Right from the beginning I

3. Drawing of Khnum-Nakht.

46

had endeavoured to ensure that I was not relying merely upon intuition – what was always irritatingly referred to as 'artist's licence'.

When all the modelling had been finished and the measurements checked, we realised that these three-dimensional images had far more impact than any drawing might have: although I made one drawing of Khnum-Nakht (fig. 3), we dropped the original plan to use them as a basis for carefully finished drawings or paintings. In fact the faces of the Two Brothers seemed rather blank and expressionless, but my colleagues felt that to add any real expression or personality would be to indulge in pure speculation and that we should adhere strictly to the rules (fig. 4). Today we take a slightly different attitude in reconstructing archaeological subjects, and at an

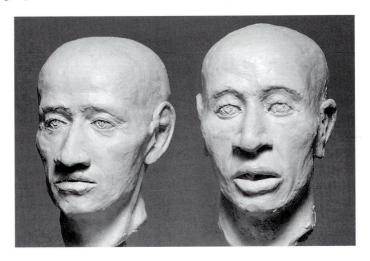

4. The finished reconstructions of the Two Brothers: Nekht-Ankh is on the left, Khnum-Nakht on the right.

early stage all the information available from other sources, both historical and medical, is called into play, resulting in a much more 'human' end product. However the same rigid code that was established right at the beginning is still applied to forensic specimens.

The time had now come when some comparisons could be made between the reconstructed heads of the Two Brothers and the small figurines found in the coffins. As the figures were only about 15 and 25 cm (6 and 10 in) high respectively, a certain amount of rescaling was called for in order to identify any striking differences or similarities. The results of this exercise seemed to confirm the suspicions held by a number of people that the figurines had indeed been placed in the wrong coffins at the time of the original burial. The reconstruction of Khnum-Nakht shows a broad, powerful head with full lips and a broad nose, and although this does not provide conclusive evidence, what we see on the reconstruction is consistent with what can be seen on the wooden figurine. In the case of Nekht-Ankh the resemblance is much more striking, both in the shape of the head and in the profile. In both front and side views the similarity is unmistakable (fig. 5).

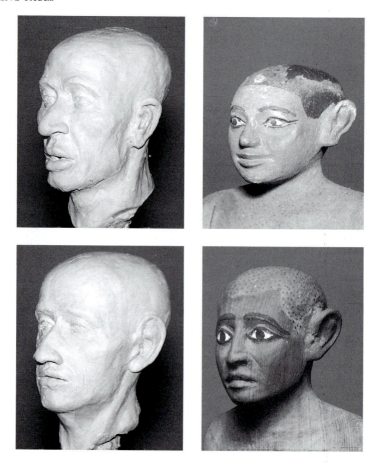

5. *The reconstructed heads of the Two Brothers compared with the figurines from the coffins: top, Khnum-Nakht; bottom, Nekht-Ankh.*

All things considered this had been a fascinating project which had produced the kind of result for which one had hoped, but we reckoned that it was over, and that it was time to return to routine medical drawing and model-making. This was not to be so. Already Dr David was planning her next move in her multidisciplinary campaign, this time actually to unwrap an ancient Egyptian mummy.

The details and circumstances of the techniques, research and results of this project are all carefully documented in the books *Mysteries of the Mummies* and later *Evidence Embalmed*, and therefore need only be touched on here.[5] Briefly, the advances in medical science had led to the view that were a 'post-mortem' to be carried out on a mummy, which is after all an elaborately preserved human body, it could provide valuable new insights into the living standards, health and medical problems of the ancient Egyptians. The unwrapping of such a specimen is a very rare event, for there is not an unlimited number upon which to work, and inevitably it attracted a great deal of attention from all quarters. There were obvious constraints upon which specimen in the Manchester collection could be selected. It would not have been good curatorial practice to use one with a full archaeological provenance, any more than one would wish to destroy a beautifully decorated or particularly well-preserved specimen. There was one mummy which seemed a possible candidate: it was identified only as 1770, its museum accession number, for it was not known who it was or for certain where it came from, and it was in a poor state of preservation. Correspondence between Sir Flinders Petrie and the Museum, and papers in the archives of University College London suggested that 1770 may have come from his excavations at Hawara in Egypt; it dated from the Greco-Roman period of Egyptian history. Radiological studies had revealed that it was the body of a girl of about thirteen and that her legs had been amputated, one above and the other below the knee, but whether this had occurred before or after death was not known.

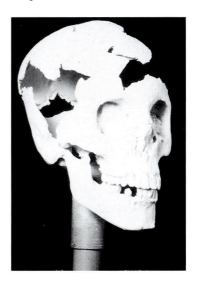

On 10 June 1975 the unwrapping began, and lasted for about five days. Contrary to the popular image of Egyptian mummies, 1770 was little more than a skeleton. Carbon-14 dating later demonstrated that the remains of this child had been rewrapped some 1700 years after her first embalming, raising many questions about her identity. At the time of the unwrapping all this was unknown, but what soon became very clear was that the skull was in a very fragmented state. The extent of the damage became apparent the moment the wrappings in the region of the neck were removed, for it lay in a jumbled heap of about thirty pieces inside the cartonnage mask, thickly encrusted with the remains of mud and bandage. At the time we had little experience of dealing with such material, and so I decided to cast each piece of bone separately before attempting to rebuild the skull. This approach

6. *The skull of mummy Manchester 1770 reconstructed from casts of the fragments.*

seemed to work very satisfactorily: each piece of bone was cast in methyl methacrylate (a form of cold-curing casting plastic). As it turned out the majority of the skull had survived, and by modelling in wax those areas that were missing we produced a complete skull suitable as the basis for facial reconstruction (fig.6).

We next made a cast of the rebuilt skull and mounted it in the same manner as we had done with the Two Brothers. When I came to reconstruct 1770's face I made what was to be the first of many changes to the technique. We had had some difficulty in locating the bony landmarks on the skulls of the Two Brothers when they were covered with clay, so I drilled holes at the appropriate anatomical sites and inserted small wooden pegs cut to precise lengths to indicate the tissue thickness. It then became possible to build the face up to the level of the pegs rather then having to cut back or add clay as one progressed in order to correct differences in tissue thickness when compared with Kollman and Büchly's tables of measurements. Work on the skull was very much easier with 1770 than it had been with the Two

Brothers, for the method had been refined and I had a gained experience. Features peculiar to the faces of the young were incorporated together with those traditionally associated with the ancient Egyptians as we know them from Egyptian art. In this respect the almond shape of the eyes and the rather large nose were particularly important.

The tremendous public interest in the whole project now led us to attempt a complete three-dimensional model of the head with hair, eyes and colour. Casting quite large specimens in wax was something that we were doing regularly as part of the routine medical work of the studio, and to produce a wax copy of the clay reconstruction of 1770's head was not a problem, although the acquisition and fitting of some prosthetic eyes was more challenging (most people who require glass eyes need only one so they do not come in pairs). The addition of colour was no problem either

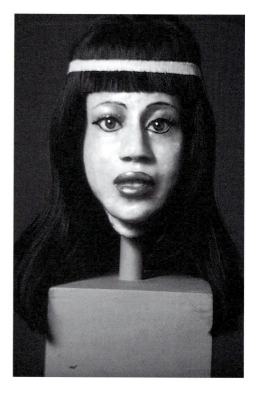

7. *The first reconstruction of mummy Manchester 1770.*

as that too fell within our everyday work, and the fitting of eyelashes and a cheap nylon wig completed the head. It was astonishing how eyes, colour and hair, no matter how simplistically applied, changed that reconstruction and brought it to life (fig. 7). Several years later another version of 1770 was made for a new display at the Manchester Museum: the head was given neck and shoulders, and she acquired an expensive new wig and more elaborate make-up with dramatic eye-shadow (pl. 11). But the face of this now rather glamorous young lady was still the same as it had always been. No changes were made to its structure or its morphology.

Had I been aware of the difficulties and challenges that lay ahead when I first ventured onto this path I might have been more cautious, but it really did look as though 1770 would be the last head that I would be asked to reconstruct in quite this way, and I wanted to put as much into, and get as much out of, the project as I could. As it turned out, 1770 was just the start, although it was another fifteen years before I was asked to build the head of another ancient Egyptian. During the intervening years, much as we had all hoped and indeed predicted, techniques had been developed which allowed a mummified body to be examined without the need for destructive unwrapping. The modern scanning and endoscopic techniques, developed primarily for use in medicine, have now virtually eliminated the need for direct access to the body in order to carry out an examination. During those years, in an attempt to develop a system whereby faces could be reconstructed without the need to make a cast of the actual skull, I started building skulls using the ever-increasingly sophisticated images being produced for diagnostic purposes as reference.[6] These models were made primarily for clinical use, but the technique proved invaluable during the reconstruction of the heads of other ancient bodies on which tissue remained, notably those found in bogs such as Lindow Man in 1985, followed by the girl from Yde in the Netherlands, described more fully in Chapter 8. By the time my fourth mummy, Natsef-Amun, came along technology had taken another step forward, making it unnecessary to create a replica of a skull by hand. This could now be done by a milling machine, controlled by the same statistical data that enables a scanned section of the body to be viewed on a television monitor. Again this facility is used for clinical purposes in medicine.[7]

Natsef-Amun was a temple priest and scribe at the temple of Karnak at Luxor in Upper Egypt. He lived and worked in the reign of Ramesses XI (1113–1085 BC) a little over three thousand years ago. The mummy had been taken from 'the catacombs of Gournor, the burial place of Thebes' across the Nile from Karnak in 1823 by one Giuseppe Passalacqua, 'a most successful spoliator of the tombs of the ancient Egyptians'. From his base in Trieste the mummy travelled to London where it was eventually bought by Mr William Bullock, showman and dealer in antiquities, from 'a gentleman who had brought it into England as a speculation'. In 1824 it was purchased on behalf of the Leeds Philosophical Society. The mummy duly arrived in Leeds and in September of the same year underwent a thorough examination by a multidisciplinary team. Along with the study of another mummy acquired by the Society shortly before, this was almost certainly the first scientifically conducted unwrapping ever carried out. The examination took several months to complete, and a report was published in 1828.[8] Natsef-Amun was described as being middle-aged and 1.67 m (5 ft 6 in) tall. He was totally clean-shaven, having no hair on his face or head, as was customary for a priest in ancient Egypt.

The interesting aspect of this reconstruction from our point of view was that it was the first time we had worked on a mechanically-made skull, and as such it represented another advance in the quest for non-destructive methods of examining wrapped mummies. Natsef-Amun's body was studied using X-ray computed tomography (CT-scans), which gives information on the varying densities of different materials within the body of the mummy. The examination showed a freedom from disease apart from degenerative arthritis of the neck and hip, which is not particularly unexpected in a man of his age. His teeth showed marked attrition, a common feature of ancient Egyptian life where sand was apparently added to wheat to help the grinding process. All this information is stored in digital form on magnetic tape. By careful manipulation of the data three-dimensional views of the mummy's skull can be displayed on the computer screen (fig.8).

The next stage was to use the information to produce a solid replica of the skull, achieved by using a computer-controlled milling machine which carved the replica from a block of styrene foam. This provides a dimensionally accurate model of the skull upon which one can then develop the face without disturbing the original specimen. Although the methods for making such replicas are becoming ever more sophisticated, the fine surface detail is always missing, but I do not believe this lack is likely to affect the outcome of a reconstruction significantly because the basic shape is correct, and any detail that is required can be picked up from the CT-scans or the radiographs. Although the material from which the skull is made is different, the method for modelling the muscles and other soft tissues in clay is basically the same as for any of other reconstruction.

Apart from his rather poor teeth Natsef-Amun had a fine skull. It was quite symmetrical with a broad nose, well-developed brow-ridges and high cheekbones. He had a strong well-developed mandible giving him what is often referred to as a wide 'square' jaw. Both the mandible and the maxilla were prognathic — in other words

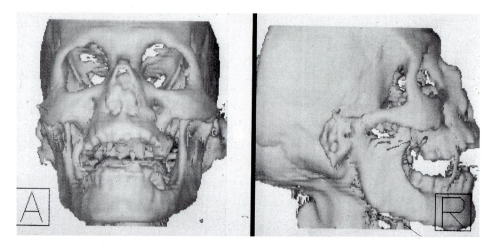

8. Computer image of the skull of Natsef-Amun, based on CT-scans.

both jaws were rather prominent — but not markedly so. This rather curious mixture of features suggested a broad flat nose and rather full lips but a face without the marked forward projection which one might expect from a negroid skull. Intriguingly, the face that finally emerged was not one that those who had been expecting a classic Egyptian physiognomy had anticipated. Yet it fitted with the provenance of the mummy, coming as it did from Upper Egypt where there was a strong Nubian influence on the population, still to be seen today. Strangely forceful, even handsome to modern eyes, Natsef-Amun had a well-proportioned head set on a powerful neck and displayed markedly male features (pl.iii). Clearly Nubian blood had once coursed through his veins as he went about his business under the pitiless Egyptian sun.

Four Egyptian faces from our studio: technically the reconstruction of Natsef-Amun belonged to a new generation from the first three rather tentative heads that we had created. In between lie almost a score of historical figures, supported by the cast of forensic faces which we have already described.

CHAPTER 4

'And a certain man drew a bow at a venture': King Philip II of Macedon

W hat happened next was pure serendipity. After those first cautious steps among the Egyptians, we took a great leap forward with the king of Macedon. Originally we had simply felt that at this stage a change of scene, both historical and racial, would be a good thing lest the reconstructions became locked into a kind of ethnic stereotype. Our first tentative enquiries in 1979 after Greek skulls to reconstruct, any Greek skulls, led us by a series of happy chances to the doyen of Greek archaeologists, Professor Manolis Andronicos, who had recently made spectacular discoveries in the village of Vergina in Macedonia, southwest of Thessaloniki. To our disbelief and delight he agreed to give us access to his most important skull, that found in Tomb II at Vergina in November 1977, though not before he had, tactfully and courteously, put us through the most searching and perceptive questioning.[1]

The reason why Andronicos was so ready to let us work on the skull from Vergina was closely linked to the forensic background of our work. Behind his excavations lay two related questions, at least one of which had been perplexing archaeologists for decades. First, where was the original capital of the Macedonians? And second, who was buried under the Great Tumulus in Vergina?

Around 400 BC King Archelaus had moved the Macedonian capital from Aigai or Aegeae, on the edge of the hills, down to Pella, lying on the plains to the north in the valley of the river Lydias, which was navigable from there to the sea. The site of Pella is well known, but where was Aigai to be located? Many suggestions had been made: recently Nicholas Hammond, Professor Emeritus of Greek at Bristol University and a man who knows not only the history but also the terrain of Macedon intimately, had argued strongly for the village of Vergina. Hammond's topographic and literary evidence was persuasive, but so far unproven. One crucial clue would be to find the tombs of the kings of Macedon, for even after the capital was moved to Pella, the Macedonians continued to bury their royal dead at Aigai.[2] Thus if Andronicos could find a tomb that could be proved to have contained the remains of a member of the royal family, he could also claim to have located their early capital.

The plain below Vergina is dotted with tombs dating back as far as 1000 BC, many of them containing objects of considerable wealth, but those that had been found unrobbed were clearly not the burials of royalty, while those of the fourth and third centuries BC, whose architecture and decoration were of a scale and quality to make them candidates for royal graves, had all been robbed of their contents in antiquity. Outside the village of Vergina lay an enormous Hellenistic palace, from which the neighbouring village of Palatitsia took its name, while in the centre of Vergina itself was the Great Tumulus, a mound now measuring *c.*110 m (360 ft) in diameter and still on average 12 m (40 ft) high. Earlier archaeologists had shied away from excavating it, deterred in part by its sheer size, but since 1951 Andronicos had made it the focus of his excavations of the 'Cemetery of the Tumuli' which lay to the east of the village. By the end of 1976 much of the Great Tumulus had been cleared, revealing an interesting and complex history. The mound had been built in at least two stages: the first was made principally of the same red earth as that found in the 'Cemetery of the Tumuli', but the fill of the second stage included a quantity of broken grave stelae. The latest belonged to the early third century BC: it seemed clear that somewhere before 250 BC a major clearing up and refurbishment had taken place. The obvious source for these gravestones, now regarded as good only for hardcore, was the cemetery below. There were various important pointers here. Plutarch, writing in the early second century AD, recorded that the Galatian mercenaries of King Pyrrhus of Epirus, stationed as a garrison at Aigai in 274/3 BC during his second war against the Macedonians, had 'set themselves to digging up the tombs of the kings who had been buried there; the treasure they plundered, the bones they insolently scattered'. The debris in the mound seemed to confirm Hammond's identification of Aigai with Vergina, for here were signs of the trail of destruction left by the Galatians. The stelae did not come from royal burials, but it seemed fair to assume that these lay nearby, some at least under the Great Tumulus itself. It did not, of course, bode well for any hopes of finding the royal tombs unplundered.[3]

Only in 1977 did Andronicos find the tombs that lay under the Great Tumulus. In the end there were three in all, each of them a dramatic discovery in a different way. The earliest and smallest had been thoroughly plundered, and only a few sherds and scattered remains of three individuals had been left, but the excavators' disappointment was outweighed by the fabulously beautiful fresco paintings of the Rape of Persephone that covered its walls. Nothing like this had been found in Greek art until now. The quality of the painting on some of the stelae had been a pointer, but here was a much stronger hint that the traditional view of the Macedonians as semi-civilised barbarians was less than true.

After this not-unexpected disappointment (and with Plutarch's warning in their minds) Andronicos and his colleagues were surprised and delighted when at the very end of the 1977 excavation season they found the second tomb not only unrobbed but filled with 'wonderful things' – Andronicos gives a vivid and well-illustrated account of the discovery and of the finds in his book *Vergina: The Royal Tombs* (fig. 1). This tomb also had a fresco painting, this time set above the door on the exterior and depicting a hunt scene. The tomb itself was in two parts, and while the antechamber was well finished, the main chamber showed signs of haste – for example it had never received its final coat of plaster. The painting and the finds – silverware, bronze vessels, armour, a parade shield of wood, glass, gold and ivory, the remains of a couch – matched the artistic level of the first tomb. There are many rich tombs from fourth-century Macedonia, but the finds from this one were outstanding in the craftsmanship and artistry and even the sheer weight of metal that went into their making. Towards the back of each chamber stood a marble

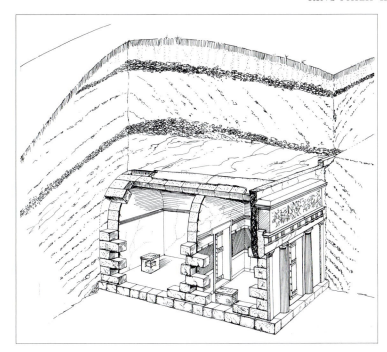

1. Cutaway drawing of Tomb II at Vergina, showing the different stages in the building of the Great Tumulus and the vaulted tomb with its two chambers.

2. The gold larnax from the main chamber: the lid is decorated with the Macedonian royal starburst (Thessaloniki, Archaeological Museum).

sarcophagus, containing a gold larnax or box decorated with the starburst that was the symbol of the royal house of Macedon (fig. 2). Inside each larnax were the cremated bones of the dead person wrapped in cloth woven of purple wool and gold thread. Macedonian burial practice followed the ritual accorded to the Greek heroes at Troy as Homer describes it in the *Iliad* and the *Odyssey*: the dead person was cremated, and after the fire had died down or been extinguished with wine the bones were collected, cleaned with wine and ointments, wrapped and placed in a golden container, which was then buried in a tomb which was in turn covered with a mound of stones and earth.[4]

The third tomb, the latest of the three, was a 'conventional' two-chamber tomb. It too was unrobbed, and as well as silver vases, armour and weapons and other goods it held a silver vase of the three-handled shape known as a hydria or water jar, crowned by a gold wreath, in which had been placed the cremated bones of a young man.

The problem at Vergina was that despite the wealth of finds there were no inscriptions to identify the occupants of the tombs, although a silver strainer was inscribed 'Machatas', an unusual name borne by one of King Philip II's brothers-in-law. The dating of the tombs thus became the first step in identifying the dead. It rapidly became a matter of furious dispute among archaeologists. No one doubted that Tomb II belonged in the second half of the fourth century BC, and it seemed likely that it contained members of the royal family, on the basis of its siting, its wealth, and above all because of the starburst on the two larnakes – although even this was not certain proof, since members of the nobility occasionally used this symbol to proclaim their loyalty to the royal house. The bones in the larnax in the main chamber were those of a man aged between thirty-five and fifty-five years at death. Among members of the royal house this produced two probable candidates, Philip II, father of Alexander the Great, murdered in 336 BC at the age of forty-six, and Philip III Arrhidaeus, his other surviving son, half-brother and successor to Alexander, murdered along with his wife Eurydice at the age of thirty-nine or forty in 317 BC. Alexander himself was not a candidate: he died at the age of thirty-three in Babylon and was buried in Egypt, almost certainly in Alexandria, and the other members of the family were all much younger at the time of their deaths. The tomb was built as a barrel-vault behind a classical façade, and according to received thinking at the time of the discovery, the Greeks did not learn to construct barrel-vaults until after Alexander the Great's campaigns in the east. Further, among the black-glazed pottery found in the tomb were three 'salt-cellars' of a shape that recently had been down-dated to the last fifteen or twenty years of the fourth century BC. On this basis the bones were most likely those of Arrhidaeus, but there were a few arguments against such an identification.[5]

After his charismatic, world-conquering son Alexander, Philip II was the most famous and most distinguished king of Macedon; indeed, some historians both ancient and modern would regard him the greater of the two men. When Philip acceded to the throne in 359 BC at the age of twenty-three as regent for his young nephew Amyntas IV, the very existence of Macedon as an independent kingdom hung in the balance (fig. 3). Philip's two older brothers had met violent deaths, and he himself had been a hostage first with the Illyrians and then for a further three years in Thebes. When he was himself assassinated twenty-three years later he had created a state which included all of northern Greece, much of Albania, the land that two millennia later is known as the Former Yugoslav Republic of Macedonia, part of Bulgaria and all of European Turkey; for the first time in their history he had united the rest of the Greeks after the battle of Chaironea in 338 BC, and when he was murdered in 336 he had already begun the attack on Persia which his son Alexander III – 'the Great' – was able to continue and extend to the furthest Hindu Kush. Philip was a man who aroused strong feelings. Demosthenes, his implacable enemy in Athens, saw him as a perfidious and half-civilised tyrant, who had succeeded only because of the weakness and corruptibility of the Greeks; other less prejudiced ancient writers such as Ephorus and Theopompus, both contemporaries of Philip, noted his leadership, his outstanding strategic skills, his military and political courage, and the brilliance of his personality. The best summary of his career is

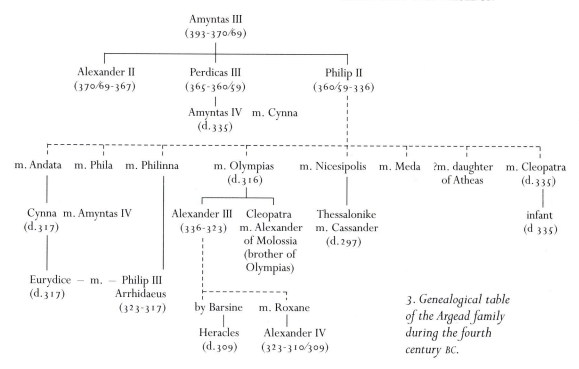

3. Genealogical table of the Argead family during the fourth century BC.

perhaps that put into the mouth of Alexander by his biographer Arrian, as he addresses his mutinous troops at Opis:

When Philip took over you were nomadic and poor, the majority of you clad in skins and grazing sparse herds on the mountains, putting up a poor fight for them against Illyrians, Triballians and the neighbouring Thracians. He gave you cloaks to wear in place of skins. He brought you down the mountains to the plains, making you a match in battle for the neighbouring barbarians, trusting for your salvation no longer in the natural strength of places so much as in your own courage. He made you dwellers in cities and graced your lives with good laws and customs. As to those very barbarians by whom previously you had been constantly plundered and pillaged, both your possessions and your persons, from being slaves and subjects he made you their leaders and he added most of Thrace to Macedon. Seizing the best-situated places on the seaboard he opened up the land to trade, and he made it possible to work the mines without fear. He made you rulers of the Thessalians – you were once scared to death of them – and by humbling the Phocian people he made the way into Greece for you broad and easy instead of narrow and difficult. The Athenians and Thebans, who used constantly to look for any chance against Macedon, he humbled to such an extent (and by now he had me to share in his efforts) – to such an extent, I say, that, instead of us paying the tribute to the Athenians and being at the beck and call of the Thebans, they have to depend on us for their security. He went into the Peloponnese and set things in order there, and was appointed Leader with full authority against the Persians. By this he brought as great glory on the Macedonian state as on himself.

Although written some five centuries after Philip's death, this ghosted speech, 'reported' by a historian noted for his sober narrative and careful use of sources, conveys much of the achievement and personality of Philip, even if (like most Macedonian kings) his personal habits were not always above reproach by his southern Greek neighbours or by modern historians.[6]

In accordance with Macedonian custom, Philip II was polygamous: he had seven, possibly eight wives, most of whom he married for political reasons. Of these by far the most formidable and ambitious was the fourth, the Molossian princess Olympias who became the mother of Alexander the Great. However, Philip already had a son Arrhidaeus by his previous wife Philinna. Arrhidaeus is a rather pathetic figure, who suffered much at the hands of his stepmother Olympias: Plutarch wrote that he 'was deficient in intellect owing to bodily disease. This, however, did not come upon him in the course of nature or of its own accord, indeed, it is said that as a boy he displayed an exceedingly gifted and noble disposition, but afterwards Olympias gave him drugs which disabled him and ruined his mind.' Olympias achieved her aim: Philip nominated her son Alexander as his successor, and Arrhidaeus merely became his partner in matters where the king had a religious role to play. When Alexander died prematurely in 323, Arrhidaeus was elected joint successor as Philip III together with Alexander's posthumous son Alexander IV, but he was never more than a figurehead, and his name and authority were used by four of Alexander's generals in turn as they jockeyed for power. Plutarch likened him 'a mute guardsman on the stage, who was the mere name and figure of a king, exposed to the wanton insults of those who chanced to have the real power'.[7] In 317 he was captured and put to death by Olympias so that her grandson Alexander IV should have the full succession. It is difficult to see how so insignificant a figure should have been given such a splendid tomb, particularly at a time when Olympias was seeking to downgrade his position by every means possible. There are more practical arguments too, to which we shall come later.

The murder of Philip II occurred during the wedding of Cleopatra, Philip's daughter by Olympias, to Alexander, king of the Molossians in northeastern Greece and brother of Olympias – a marriage that Philip had arranged in order to heal the rift that had developed between himself and Olympias (with their son Alexander taking his mother's side). The wedding was planned to take place in the theatre at Aigai during the great Macedonian festival in October 336, on the eve of the projected campaign into Asia and against Persia. The climax of the procession was to be his own entry into the theatre, immediately preceded by his Corps of Bodyguards and flanked by his son and heir Alexander and the other Alexander who was about to become his son-in-law. At the last moment Philip seems to have changed his mind, sending the others ahead and following them into the theatre alone. As he stood in the theatre acknowledging the applause, one of the seven Bodyguards named Pausanias attacked and stabbed him. Three of the others ran to the dying king, the remaining three pursued Pausanias who was running to the gate where horses were waiting, but he tripped on a root and was overwhelmed and despatched.

There are several ancient versions of the motives for the murder, some of them as sensational and as selective in their presentation of the evidence as any modern tabloid newspaper account, ranging from homosexual infatuation and rape on the part of Pausanias to political intrigue by the Macedonian nobility and the dynastic, matrimonial jealousy of Olympias.[8]

What is clear, however, is that Alexander reacted very quickly and efficiently to the death of his father, first in establishing his own powerbase by a convenient series of purges of those who might have been involved or who might have formed an opposition, and then by following through his father's plans for an eastward campaign, reaping the glory for himself. The Macedonian succession was not entirely automatic: although he had been named by Philip as his successor and had been accepted as such by the Macedonian court and army, in the turbulence following the assassination Alexander needed to confirm that succession and to forestall any rival factions. He had a very busy time between Aigai-Vergina, where his father had to be buried and where he was acclaimed king, and the capital Pella where political decisions were taken. During one of his absences in Pella Olympias seized the opportunity of murdering Cleopatra, her latest rival in Philip's bed (not to be confused with her own and Philip's daughter), along with her baby son, whom she saw as a rival for her own son. Alexander was apparently furious when he returned and discovered what she had done, as well he might be. Philip's marriage to Cleopatra had been a political move intended to cement an alliance with a powerful Macedonian family that had seemingly been showing some unrest, and whom he could certainly not afford to upset at this crucial and confused step in his climb to power. Philip had lately been buried in the magnificent barrel-vaulted tomb, hastily constructed and not yet complete when his remains were interred – the fact that the main chamber never received its final coat of plaster is but one of the signs of haste. Perhaps this provided Alexander with a solution to the Cleopatra problem – it was undoubtedly politically convenient to have her out of the way, but to give her royal burial in the antechamber to her late husband's tomb, now completed and decorated, provided a place and an opportunity to appease her family and its supporters. Tomb II at Vergina is unique among Macedonian tombs in having a second burial in its antechamber; normally multiple burials were placed together in the main chamber, as in Tomb I. Later we became convinced that the remains in the antechamber supported this scenario, but that is a story that belongs outside this book.

As well as the cremated bones in their wrapping, the gold larnax from the main chamber of Tomb II contained a golden oak wreath of great beauty. When restored it proved to have been slightly damaged by the heat of the pyre, and a few acorns and leaves had been melted off at the top. Among the sun-dried bricks and the sweepings from the pyre found on top of the vault of the tomb, where they had been brought after the cremation, the excavators discovered a few of the missing acorns. The scenario which this suggested to Andronicos was of the dead man laid out on the pyre in all his finery; as the pyre was lit the choicest items were hastily removed, to be placed in the tomb later, but not always quite quickly enough: although the wreath showed other marks of having been wrenched roughly away from the body, the flames had already damaged it, perhaps in the first blaze as the pyre caught light (Homer says that Achilles' body was covered in unguents and honey when it was burned, which would certainly have made the fire flare up as it was lit). The acorns fell away, to be swept up and collected afterwards with the other remains, and to be rediscovered over two thousand years later. This implies that the dead man had been cremated immediately before final burial in the tomb, as happened to Philip II, whereas Arrhidaeus' remains had to wait six months before they were finally given royal burial by Cassander in 316 BC. Practical experiments in cremation, described below, served to confirm that these bones had been burnt with flesh on them, not 'macerated' after a period of burial in the ground.[9]

Thus the probability lay in favour of the remains in the main chamber being those of Philip II, but there was still no proof, and it must be said that it seemed too good to be true. The implications were such that extra caution was needed, but it also explains why Andronicos was interested in a new approach which tackled the problem from a completely different angle – quite apart from the exciting opportunity it gave him of seeing what the man whose remains he had discovered looked like, at a time when this was almost unique in the ancient world.

Because the body had been cremated, some of the bones of the skull, notably those from the top and the back of the head, appeared too fragile or too badly damaged to make them of any value for a reconstruction. One of the results of subjecting a head to great heat is that the back of the skull becomes distorted and can bend or curl almost at right angles to the adjoining bone. Such was the case in this instance. Further action of the fire had produced cracks in the frontal bone, in the region of the forehead. The maxilla had separated from the upper part of the cranium. The mandible was intact but the bones forming the side of the cranium had been so badly damaged by fire and by the passage of time that they were of no use in reconstructing the form of the skull. In essence there existed enough bone to provide information about the length and breadth of the face, together with the relative positions of the eyes, nose and mouth. The shape of the rest of the head would have to be developed on the basis of the experience and knowledge born of handling numerous skulls. Casting such fragile bones in the field away from the security of the studio, however, was something of which we still had very little experience: with the help of one of the technicians at the museum in Thessaloniki, where all the finds from Vergina were kept, we made simple moulds from dental alginate supported by a substantial and solid plaster casing. One long morning saw the creation first of the moulds and then of accurate casts of the three important surviving (if damaged) pieces of the skull: frontal bone, maxilla and mandible.

Back in England interesting points began to emerge as soon as the casts were unpacked. As one studied them and tried to fit them together it became clear that this was not going to be straightforward. These bones had, after all, been cremated, but the effects of an ancient cremation on bone are not the same as those of a modern one. A modern cremation oven operates at a much higher temperature than did an ancient pyre, and further, the bones are passed through a mill after being burnt, with the result that no recognisable fragments remain. Most ancient cremations reduce the bones to small pieces, but the remains from Tomb II at Vergina as they were laid out in the museum at Thessaloniki looked at first sight to be surprisingly complete – even from photographs one could readily make out whole ribs and near-intact long bones (fig. 4). It was striking too how much of the skeleton had survived – whoever had gone through the remains when the cremation was over had

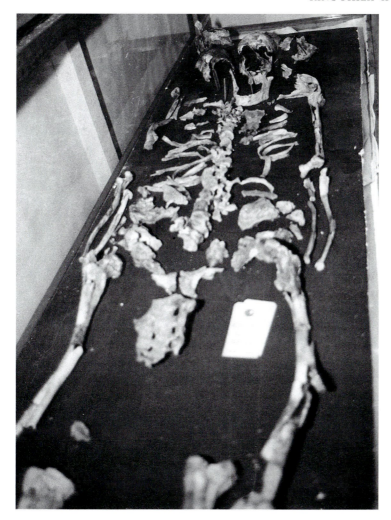

4. The cremated skeleton, as it was first laid out for study in Thessaloniki Museum.

managed to gather up almost every bone in his body. Possibly the Macedonians had followed some special procedure for this individual, for the remains from other cremations at Vergina and elsewhere were nothing like as complete as this one: suggestions range from his having been laid out on a platform of bricks around which was piled the wood for the pyre, so that it did not collapse around him and precipitate him into the midst of the flames in what might seem an undignified manner (and thereby smash the bones, rendered brittle by the heat), to the notion that rather than having been placed on a pyre in the conventional manner, his body was placed inside an oven. This would also explain why so few bones had been missed. We have taken a sample of bone on which to carry out electron spin resonance spectroscopy: this should give the temperature profile at which the remains were incinerated, and thus show whether they were burnt on or in the heat source; we still await the results. Although perhaps the simplest answer would be that a pyre built of wood does not always reach a sufficiently high temperature to have much effect on the bones, let alone consume them, the condition of the skull seems to argue against this.

However, it was only later that we became concerned with these nicer points of cremation. What occupied our minds as we looked at the casts of these seemingly warped and cracked bones was how to proceed with the reconstruction, indeed whether the whole notion of an accurate reconstruction was still feasible. Whatever cremation procedure had been followed, it seemed plausible that the bones would have shrunk and twisted under the heat of the fire. It was not something any of our colleagues in Manchester could solve for us, but until we knew the answer we were unsure how (and if) to proceed with the reconstruction. We therefore consulted Dr Jonathan Musgrave, an erstwhile classicist turned anthropologist who now taught anatomy at the University of Bristol, and who had made his speciality the study of human remains from excavations in Greece, above all in northern Greece. He accepted the invitation to join our team with enthusiasm, and in the course of the following winter he put five damaged skulls through a glass-annealing oven in the Medical Faculty Glass Workshop in Bristol for five hours at c.900°C (1650°F). His observations of these skulls, and of modern techniques in action in a Bristol crematorium, demonstrated that although bone does shrink by around ten per cent or a little more during cremation, only in exceptional circumstances does it warp or twist, and that any asymmetry noted on a cremated skull, though perhaps slightly increased by the effects of the fire, will have been there before the individual was cremated.

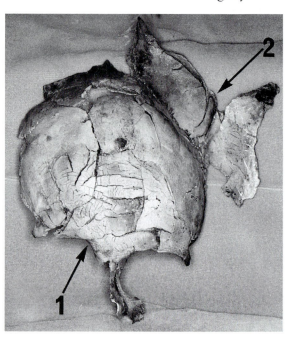

5. *The frontal bone (forehead) of the skeleton. The back of the skull has been blown out or twisted by the effects of the cremation (arrow 2), and there are shrinkage cracks across the forehead and at the orbits. The nick at the top inner corner of the right orbit (arrow 1) was not caused by burning, but is the mark of an old injury.*

This was very important for interpreting the remains of the skull from Vergina. The back of the head was present but blown out during the cremation: all that remained of it were parts of the left parietal and temporal bones, still attached to the frontal bone but warped through 90° along a suture (fig. 5). This implies that the cremation fire reached a high temperature, and the result is a rather flexible join that needs care in handling, which adds force to the argument that the cremation was carried out in the protected environment of an oven. However, it was the front of the skull that concerned us more if we were to re-create his appearance. The mandible, though complete, was striking in its asymmetry: the ends were uneven – the condyle, incisura and coronoid process on the right were much higher than those on the left, the left side showed considerable thickening, and if one counted the teeth the midline was a long way round to the individual's right (fig.6). Looking more closely, one saw that the hollow which we all have in the middle of our chins was also off-centre to the proper right, and a new one was forming in the true centre. This imbalance on the lower jaw was matched by an asymmetry on the maxilla, most noticeable where the lateral walls curve up towards the zygomaxillare – that is, between the upper back teeth and the cheekbone. The experiments in Bristol had shown that mandibles shrank with remarkable symmetry under cremation conditions, so this imbalance was real. Therefore we sought advice from John Lendrum and Eddie Curphey, two colleagues at the Facio-Maxillary Unit and the

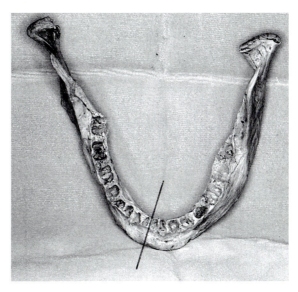

6. The mandible (lower jaw) of the skeleton. The unevenness of the condyles (ends) and the thickening on the proper left side are immediately noticeable; the line marks the midline of the jaw.

Plastic Surgery Unit respectively of Withington Hospital (the University Hospital of South Manchester) who as facial surgeons were regularly involved in treating patients whose faces were congenitally deformed or who had suffered injuries to the face. When shown the casts of the mandible and of the maxilla they immediately identified this as belonging to a man the left side of whose face was underdeveloped, with the right side overdeveloped to compensate. Although they were at first reluctant to say whether this was a congenital malformation or the result of an injury, it seems clear that he had lived with it so long that his body had remodelled the central hollow in the chin, while the thickening of the bone on the left gave extra anchorage to the muscles on that side of the face which had to work harder in compensation – so he was not restricted to a diet of soups and gruels for he obviously had no real problems in chewing meat off the bone. With so much natural remodelling it seems highly probable that he had suffered this minor physical imbalance from birth; we were assured that physically it would hardly have been noticeable (a factor to which we had to return later), and that it would certainly not have affected his mental abilities.

Interesting though this was, it caused us some embarrassment, for Andronicos had already asked two of his own colleagues to study the skeleton, and their official report had noted that 'fresh or healed damage to the bones or changes due to illness could not be established'.[10] How were we to explain that we could come to such startlingly different conclusions? The answer must lie in the fact that while their experience lay in the fields of general medicine and anthropology, we had the good fortune to be able to call on specialists who had particular expertise and particular interests in fields as diverse and as relevant as the finer points of cremation and facio-maxillary surgery.

There was more to follow. Perhaps it is worth stressing first that there were two completely separate problems in approaching this skull: for Andronicos there was the large question of the identification of the dead person and its potential implications, while for us at that moment, preoccupied with trying to fit the seemingly misshapen fragments of bone together to make a 'usable' skull on which to build the reconstruction, there was simply the practical problem of identifying and explaining the irregularities in the bone. It was crucial that we approached the task with completely open minds, although of course in order to produce a valid and complete reconstruction it was also essential that we gathered as much medical and archaeological information about our 'patient' as possible. So having explained the basic imbalance of the skull in terms of its medical history, the surgeons began looking for traces of injury.

A layman looking at the broken and incomplete pieces of the skull sees only the cracks formed as the skull shrank in the heat of the fire, cracks that run across and down the forehead, one of them reaching as far as the left eye-socket (see fig. 5). Striking though they are, these cracks have no pathological significance. What was significant to the surgeons' eyes was a small nick at the inner top corner of the right orbit, matched by a healed fracture of the cheek at the point where the two bones met (the malar-maxillary suture between the maxilla and zygomaxillare); there was even a small piece of bone missing at the suture. To the surgeons this showed that at some time well before his death this man had suffered a blow to the face that had left him blind in the right eye but had not affected him in any other way. Suddenly even before the reconstruction proper had begun we had the answer that Andronicos had hoped for: Philip II's battle injuries are well known, for although the ancient authors tell us nothing about his physical appearance, there are many passages describing the wounds he received – so many and often so conflicting that a recent study has attempted to separate the basic facts from the rhetorical and dramatic embellishments.[11]

The basic list is that given by the fourth-century Athenian politician and orator Demosthenes, Philip's sworn enemy and calumniator. In a chapter where he is contrasting the way in which the Athenians have declined from a glorious past into spinelessness with their dynamic Macedonian opponent from obscure Pella, he catalogues the parts of the body that Philip was prepared to let fortune take away – to have an eye cut out, a collar bone broken, hand and leg maimed – all so that with the rest he might live in honour and glory.[12] Demosthenes does not specify how he lost the eye, nor which eye, but for the moment that was sufficient: the surgeons were satisfied that a battle injury, such as might have been caused by an opponent's blow with a spear or sword, was compatible with what they had detected on the skull. We were happy too.

Yet two days later we received a telephone call. The surgeons were not happy with the notion of a blow from an opponent; the marks on the skull implied an injury caused by an angled blow coming from above, not from in front – in the Accident and Emergency Department of a hospital it was the kind of injury they would expect to meet on a patient such as a building worker who had left off his safety helmet and had then been hit by a piece of falling scaffolding or a roof tile. During those two days further research among the Greek texts had given us more information on the historical background too. Demosthenes mentions the Macedonian king's readiness to submit his body to hardship and injury again in one of his speeches attacking Philip: this time he does not give any details at all, but one of the ancient scholars does, an Alexandrian academic of the first century BC called Didymus, who was so prolific that he later came to be known as Didymus Chalcenterus or Didymus Copperguts. He wrote a commentary on Demosthenes using earlier sources in which he says that Philip had his right eye cut out by an arrow during an inspection of the siege-engines and the protective sheds used by his troops while filling in the defensive ditches at the siege of Methone on the Thermaic Gulf. The Greek word used by both Demosthenes and Didymus is actually 'cut out', used to describe both felling trees and surgery, though it can also be used for breaking down or bursting open a door. This was in 354 BC, eighteen years before his death. Other ancient authors confirm that the wound was caused by an arrow, and Didymus actually cites the eyewitness evidence of Philip's fellow campaigners to reject the elaboration of the historian Duris, who wrote that a man called Aster claimed to have done it with a spear. The account of the geographer Strabo, in which the eye is taken out by a bolt from a catapult, must arise from a confusion with the circumstances in which the wound occurred – Philip was inspecting his own catapults at the time; besides, as Hammond has pointed out, even Philip would hardly have survived the blow from such a missile, which would have caused far greater damage to his face.[13]

In view of the doubts that have sometimes been expressed over the disinterestedness of this exciting and conclusive part of the work, it is important to stress that neither party in Manchester knew of the other's doubts and further research during those two days: on the one hand the expert medical witnesses had identified this skull, discovered in a later fourth-century Macedonian 'royal' tomb, as that of a man who had been blinded in the right eye by a missile that struck him from above; on the other the ancient historian had found the account of a particular Macedonian king, assassinated in 336 BC, who some eighteen years before his death had had his right eye shot out from the walls above while on a tour of inspection of his troops and equipment below a besieged city. It was one of those moments about which researchers dream.

It was time at last to reconstruct the face that covered this battered skull, for after all from the standpoint of the medical artist the primary aim of all this research was not yet to identify the individual but to gather together as much information on his physical history as possible in order to provide a solid basis in every sense for the reconstruction. Identification comes afterwards. There was a very interesting demonstration of this point in the case of Philip, for despite the fact that we had of course kept Andronicos informed of our findings on the nature of the injuries, to which he had reacted with the enthusiasm that one might have expected, he did not actually let himself believe in them, and the identification which they proved, until he had seen them expressed graphically in a photograph of the reconstruction.

Even fitting the casts of the usable parts of the skull into their correct alignment is a form of reconstruction: achieving a balance between the distorted and

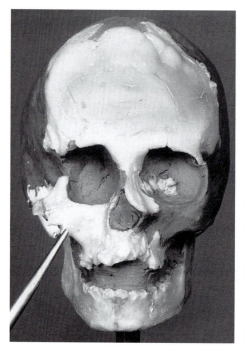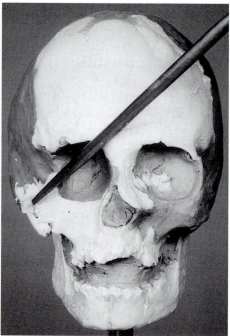

7. *Wax casts of the three significant fragments of the skull (frontal bone, maxilla and zygomatic bones) 'floated' into place on a grey clay matrix. The pointer indicates the healed fracture at the point where the two bones in the cheek meet (the malar-maxillary suture); a small piece of bone was knocked away in the incident.*

8. *The reconstructed skull with a 'missile' demonstrating how the injury occurred.*

fragmented remains of the skull in such a way that one created an acceptable whole took time and patience. As no two pieces of the skull aligned exactly, the separate fragments were 'floated' onto a clay armature. In this way their relationship one with the other could be seen, understood, and where necessary adjusted in three dimensions, even though there were large areas where the bone was missing altogether. The facial surgeons had been able to see the skull at this stage and move the fragments as necessary, ensuring the most consistent and balanced relationship between each piece. The missing areas of bone were modelled in between the casts, bridging various gaps and indeed replacing the whole of the posterior section of the skull (figs 7 and 8). Subsequent studies have demonstrated that very acceptable reconstructions can be undertaken even when quite extensive parts of a skull are missing.

The more delicate bones of a skull are of course always subject to damage and loss; the nasal bone seldom escapes, and this one was no exception. While the missing bones or parts of bones can either be remodelled as mirror images of the other side of the skull or be developed with reasonable accuracy from the existing material to form large but relatively uncomplicated shapes, bones of the facial region are less straightforward. The absence of such a bone cannot be ignored, and has to be replaced by a form of 'splint'. Some will claim that from merely looking at a bare skull they can tell how the face would have looked in life. Experience has taught us that such preconceived ideas will always be shattered when the reality, carefully and painstakingly built up, starts to appear. Even more disconcerting is to try to predict how the face may have looked from a very early stage in the reconstruction process, when tissue has been re-created in one area but not yet in another, temporarily distorting the balance and harmony of the face as a whole. An observation made during the reconstruction process in the case of the Vergina skull hinted at a long face, not unlike the only sculpture tentatively identified as a portrait of Philip III Arrhidaeus (see fig. 14), rather than the square face associated with portraits of Philip II. This is a question to which we shall return later, but as it turned out the hint proved incorrect. It is the recognition of the balance and harmony of a face that makes it possible to develop features that are reasonably accurate even in the absence of certain clues. In the case of the Vergina skull the width of the nasal aperture could be established from the remains of the maxilla and the nasal bone, although the latter was too damaged to give an accurate profile of the nose. Given that the rest of the face had 'grown from the skull' in the normal way, after a false start the nose acquired its final shape, one that harmonised with the rest of the face: it was based in part on the fact that by now we felt reasonably confident from the archaeological evidence that whoever this was, he had to be a member of the Argead royal house, among whom a rather prominent nose seems to have been a family feature.[14]

At this stage the wound did not appear too difficult to understand or to reproduce. The soft tissue was cut to the bone, which in turn was traumatised; the eyeball must have been lacerated and have collapsed and atrophied. On the straightforward presumption that relatively little skilled surgical attention was available, one could assume that scar tissue would form over the open wound, and the whole area would sink into what was now virtually a hollow eye-socket.

The completed head with its great scar was very stark, uncompromising, almost ugly when first cast in plaster; but that is often the case, for the artist making a reconstruction takes a very different approach from the conventional sculptor (fig. 9). There can be no compromises.

The case for Philip II had been proved by the discovery of the injury, and the white, hairless plaster head amply fulfilled its function as a three-dimensional report on the research that had been carried out. However, the experience of the Egyptian mummies had shown how much more effective a waxwork could be in conveying that information: hence the decision to do the same for Philip. This was not to be the king of Macedon at his daughter's wedding-feast, the day he died, but a little earlier, perhaps after a day's hunting. To give him a suitable Mediterranean complexion was easy enough, but hair and beard needed to be based on contemporary evidence. The only thing the ancient authors tell us about Philip's appearance is that, as was customary in Macedon at the time, he wore a beard (and we know that only because Alexander made a point of shaving his off).[15] For details like this, which have no bearing on the identification, one need have no qualms in turning to the ancient portraits.

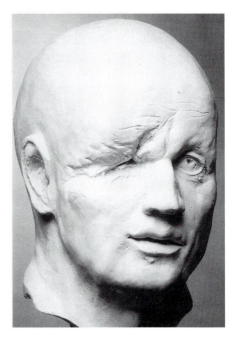

9. *Plaster reconstruction of the head of Philip II without hair, showing the untreated eye wound.*

There are some half-dozen images from antiquity that have been identified at various times as portraits of Philip II, to which we shall return later in the chapter. For the beard, by far the most useful piece was the tiny ivory portrait head, made to be set into the couch which was later buried in the tomb at Vergina. It showed Philip with a short, neatly trimmed beard and moustache, but because the hair had been made separately and is now lost it gave no clue to his hairstyle (fig. 13). The portrait that seems to come next in order of authenticity, a marble head now in Copenhagen, has the hair rendered in a very distinctive style, parted over each temple with the side locks swept back over the ears, but this portrait was almost certainly done posthumously, for this manner of dressing the hair became fashionable only in the early third century BC (see fig. 12). Middle-aged men in fourth-century Greece generally wore their hair fairly short, trimmed clear of the ears and at the nape of the neck, without any clear parting: this is how Philip is shown both on the contemporary coin attributed to Kapsa (see fig. 11) and on the much later Roman gold medallion from Tarsus, and this was the style which it seemed right to follow.

Once covered in the beard, there was very little trace of the twist to the face, apart from a slight list of the mouth to the figure's left, the side where the mandible was shorter and thicker. In fact very few faces are exactly symmetrical: a mirror placed down the centre of the face reveals not the viewer's own familiar face twice over, but two different people. A person's face must be very badly deformed before it becomes noticeable, so that it is not at all surprising that no ancient description refers to Philip's misshapen face – in a world where deformity of all kinds was much more common than it is now such a minor irregularity would not have been worthy of comment. All the same one sometimes wonders whether Alexander might not have laid such emphasis on shaving off his own beard counter to the Macedonian tradition, compelling his soldiers to do the same, in order to make the point that, unlike his father, his face was perfectly balanced.[16]

The eye wound was another matter. It is rare that even television make-up calls for the face of a man who has had his eye shot out by an arrow and who in all likelihood received little proper treatment. Our colleague at Granada Television doing the make-up on the waxwork did the best she could, and then went to the canteen for a break. There, unbelievably, she met a colleague who had with him a friend who was a Canadian lumberjack. Sixteen years previously (Philip lived eighteen years after losing his eye) this man had been felling a tree in northern Canada when his colleague up in the tree dropped his axe. As it fell it caught his head, missing the eye but cutting open the side of his face. They were in far too remote an area for him to get more than first aid, and by the time he could get proper treatment two or three weeks later the wound had effectively healed, leaving a gaping scar with dried blood healed into the scar tissue and with a shiny, wet appearance. The lumberjack was invited to the make-up studio; the make-up was wiped off the face of Philip of Macedon, and replaced with something close to the Canadian's face (pl.IV).

Serendipity took us further yet. Two of the ancient historians at Manchester University were specialists in ancient armour, and one of them was also an amateur archer. With their advice one could reconstruct the scenario in which Philip lost the eye. For an archer the most vulnerable place on the body of a fully armed opponent is the eye – one recalls the tradition of Harold's fatal injury at Hastings. It is easy to imagine a sniping archer with his bow at the ready, waiting his moment on the walls of Methone while Philip was somewhere below making his tour of inspection, and loosing off an arrow at the instant when Philip raised his head and looked around or even through the protective siege-shed below as he checked its positioning. Philip, a seasoned campaigner and a great survivor, perhaps glimpsed the archer's movement or heard the twang of the bowstring, or else one of his companions shouted a warning, and he ducked, so that what would have been a fatal shot became instead a glancing blow that blinded and disfigured him for life. One can argue at length whether he was wearing a helmet

10. *Drawing of the iron helmet from Tomb II. Even if Philip wore a helmet of this pattern at the siege of Methone, it would not necessarily have protected his eyes.*

at the time or not: in the tomb was an iron helmet with gold decoration; of course there is no reason why he should have been wearing this particular magnificent piece of armour on campaign eighteen years before, but it is a good example of the type of helmet worn by the Macedonians in the second half of the fourth century BC (fig. 10). Unlike the all-concealing classical 'Corinthian' helmet of the previous century it left the face exposed and thus allowed the wearer to see and hear what was happening around him, but by the same token it offered less protection from frontal attack. Through the kindness of colleagues at the British Museum we were able to experiment in fitting contemporary helmets onto our reconstruction, which showed quite clearly that one of fourth-century type would not have offered Philip full protection against the arrow that came from in front or above, particularly if he had tilted it back because of the heat. Greek vases and sculptures show many warriors with their helmets pushed right back onto the top of the head, and one of us is old enough to have been through National Service and recalls the reluctance of soldiers today to wear their steel helmets in hot weather. With or without his helmet, Philip was vulnerable.

Having identified the wound to the eye to such dramatic effect, we turned our attention to the other injuries which Philip is reputed to have suffered: a broken collar bone, at least one wound to the leg, another to the hand, and of course the stab-wound that killed him. Although our original brief only covered the skull, by now there were many other questions we wanted to answer which followed on from the discovery of the eye wound, and which we believed the combined exper-tise of our colleagues might be able to answer.

In 1984 we returned to Thessaloniki. Some questions were simpler to answer than others. First of all, we felt that we should respond to sceptical comments made by archaeologists who did not fully appreciate the niceties of specialist bone analy-sis in contrast to traditional pottery dating and architectural history, and check the conclusions that we had drawn from the casts of the skull on the actual bone: there was no doubt – the evidence for malformation and trauma were there for those who had the eyes and the knowledge to see, although this has not prevented others from setting the hare running again since.[17]

Second, it was often suggested that if Philip's death came from a stab wound, then there must be traces on the ribs. We found none, but this is not surprising: one of the functions of the ribcage is to protect the organs within it, and it needs a well-directed blow with a slender blade to penetrate it. Pausanias, Philip's assassin, was a trained soldier and would have known this well. The effective deadly thrust came from in front and below, under the ribs, and might easily leave the bones unmarked.

As for the injured collar bone, we could extract no further information from the bones – unlike the skull, here we found ourselves in full agreement with our Greek colleagues' conclusion, that one could not draw from them any evidence of fresh or healed damage. The leg bones offered a greater challenge.

In the outer chamber of Tomb II were buried the remains of a young woman aged between twenty and thirty. In addition to goldwork that matched the quality of the finds in the outer chamber, she was buried with a pair of gilded bronze greaves which together with a brilliantly decorated gold quiver and remains of the arrows it once held, and some alabaster and pottery vases, were found propped against the door of the inner tomb.[18] Although the finds included other gear that went with the fields of hunting and battle, there was a suggestion that at least the greaves actually belonged to the man buried in the main chamber: that they had been forgotten in the haste of his funeral and had been left against the door afterwards. It deserved serious consideration because although clearly a pair, they were of different sizes: the one for the left leg was 3.5 cm (1¼ in) shorter than that for the right and slightly more slender. The immediate reaction of many scholars, long before the evidence for the eye wound became apparent, was that this was proof that Philip II was buried in the main chamber: Philip was known to have been lame from his war wounds, and such lameness must have been apparent in the armour which he wore, since it would have been made to measure to fit him. As with the eye wound, Demosthenes is not specific about which leg was lamed, and the later texts seem to confuse rather than clarify the question: Didymus specifies the right leg in one, possibly two passages, but a century or two later Plutarch was treating the question 'In which leg was Philip lame?' as one of those problems that were unanswerable for lack of evidence. Whether or not he is right about which leg, Didymus does give the detail that he suffered a thigh wound when a Triballian's spear went right through it and killed the horse under him.

There is a problem in connecting these injuries with the unequal greaves, let alone in drawing any identification from them. First, in the main chamber were three much plainer sets of greaves, each of which made a perfect pair (two pairs were almost the same length as the longer of the two from the door, but the third was shorter); second, the king of Macedon fought on horseback, when greaves would have been a positive hindrance, particularly before the invention of the stirrup, so that any greaves buried with him were probably pieces he had acquired as honorific gifts rather than for practical use – it is a rather odd collection of armour that was buried with him anyway. And finally, the only wound of which we know for sure is one to the thigh, though there may have been another to the calf depending on how one reads a passage in Didymus' description; either way although a spear wound might cause serious damage to the muscles it would not actually shorten the leg. And of course it may even have been the other leg.[19]

However, the greaves had raised so much excitement that we felt we should not only check the measurements for ourselves, but more to the point examine the bones themselves for any trace of injury or disease. Once again, none could be found, but that this lack is not the result of the ordeal that the bones went through during the cremation but a representation of the true state of affairs in life is clear from the fact that both tibiae were the same length and, to the specialist's naked eye at least, undamaged.

Of all the wounds Philip received it must have been the blinding of his eye that troubled him most; there was even an ancient anecdote that he was so sensitive about it that he became very angry if anyone mentioned the word 'eye' in his presence, let alone the one-eyed giant Cyclops, which perhaps suggests that this had become his nickname.[20] In fact Philip was lucky to have survived the blow he received to the eye: we know of only one case from the Greek world of the skeleton of a person with such a wound who survived to tell the tale, from the excavations of the sixth-century BC site at Assos near Troy, while ancient medical and historical literature describes only three cases where an arrow was extracted from the eye by human hands, one of them Philip himself (we shall return to a couple of men whose sight was restored by divine intervention after receiving similar injuries, but even they are only a couple).[21] The obvious implication is that in every other case the injury was fatal. We envisaged a scenario where Philip received the arrow in the eye from above – further study of the injury by our surgeon colleagues led them to think that the blow was perhaps at a slightly shallower angle than that shown in fig. 8, but that it still caught the supraorbital margin, then probably but not necessarily cut the eyeball, and finally struck the cheekbone at the join between the maxilla and the zygomaxillare with such force that it caused the suture to open and the two bones to move out of alignment, sending splinters up into the eyeball which would have pierced and blinded it even if the arrow itself had not already done so. Then, we reckoned, it probably fell out or was pulled out, leaving Philip in great pain but with only the most basic of first-aid treatment to treat the wound.

In one respect at least we found we were mistaken: our attention was drawn to book VII, chapter 124 of Pliny's *Natural History*: 'Kritoboulos achieved great renown for having extracted the arrow from the eye of King Philip, and for having treated the loss of the eyeball without causing disfigurement to the face.' Thomas Leland writing in the eighteenth century described it more elegantly: 'Philip…committed himself to the care of Kritoboulos, a chirurgeon, whose skill, in so important a cure, history has thought worthy to be recorded: and who, though he could not save his eye, yet contrived, by his dexterity, to take away all the blemish which might have been expected from such an accident.'[22]

The medical and surgical story that emerged as one absorbed the implications of this passage has been fully described in the *American Journal of Archaeology* for 1990, and much of the account that follows is taken from that article.[23] Our primary sources were the ancient medical literature, in particular the *Corpus* of writings attributed to the most famous of all Greek physicians, Hippocrates of Cos. The surgical part of the Hippocratic collection is particularly confused, and certainly not by Hippocrates himself, but it is generally accepted that the section *On Wounds in the Head* was first compiled around 400 BC by a skilled medical practitioner, and is based on long practical experience. If Kritoboulos had the standing attributed to him by Pliny – and he appears again later in the story of the Macedonian royal family, extracting a massive Indian arrow from the chest of Alexander the Great when all other doctors had refused to operate – then we can be sure that he was familiar with many of the techniques described in the treatise. It contains no exact description of how to treat Philip's particular case, but section 11 discusses wounds caused by different weapons and section 13 begins a detailed description of wounds to the head, including a solitary reference to wounds to the eye and eyebrow, saying only that these are the only head wounds that may be bandaged. However, by looking at a number of the treatments for different injuries suggested here and elsewhere in the Hippocratic *Corpus*, one could attempt to reconstruct the kind of treatment that Kritoboulos might have used on King Philip.

The first problem was the removal of the arrow: from Pliny's account it is clear that Philip arrived at the dressing station with the arrow still in the wound. Our description of the likely treatment in the *American Journal of Archaeology* suggested that Kritoboulos might have extracted the arrow using a newly invented piece of surgical equipment called the 'Spoon of Diokles'. According to the ancient literature, this was shaped like an elongated ladle with an open-sided bowl, and was inserted into the wound around the arrowhead so that it could then be drawn out without the barbs tearing the flesh. Unfortunately what appeared to be the only surviving example of the instrument, for long apparently lost, has now been proved by its rediscoverer, Dr Ernst Künzl, to be a forgery. Furthermore, considering the problem from a medical point of view, it seemed increasingly improbable that so skilled a surgeon as Kritoboulos would have introduced a large metal spoon into an already cracked and shattered bony cavity. The Roman writer Celsus in his book *On Medicine* recommends its use only in extracting broad weapons that have become embedded. It may have been very difficult to get the arrow out, since if it took the course suggested across the eye the point at least would have been embedded in the maxillary antrum, far from the surface, and simply widening the wound with a knife of some kind was much less likely to cause scarring at this spot on the body: we know Kritoboulos followed this course later when operating on Alexander's chest wound, and it is thus that the Celsus advises the surgeon to act when dealing with arrow wounds, suggesting that the barbs should be nipped off when they are located in the wound, or else covered by split reed pens before the arrow is drawn out.[24]

We can only speculate how he would have dealt with the collapsed eyeball, but we may assume from Hippocratic practice in other cases that having removed any dead matter Kritoboulos began by washing the wound in white wine, and patted it dry and clean with a sponge and with pieces of clean, dry linen. If he detected traces of bruising and potential infection he would have helped the wound produce pus, for the Hippocratic *Corpus* taught that pus made bruised flesh 'melt away'. To modern notions this seems a horrendous instruction, for pus is itself a sign of infection. The point has been much discussed by students of Greek medicine: ancient injuries almost inevitably became infected – indeed, the Greek word *helkos* used in the title of the Hippocratic treatise *Peri Helkon* can be translated either as straightforward 'wound' or as infected 'ulcer'. Pus followed as a result of infection: different bacteria produce different discharges or pus. Greek doctors in a slight oversimplification distinguished two kinds: the dark, smelly variety, a bad omen and an indication of what a modern surgeon would see as severe infection caused by bacteria such as *streptococci* or *Clostridium Welchii* leading to septicaemia and gangrene respectively; and the 'pure and white' kind, a sign of benign infection by *Staphylococcus albus*, where as modern medicine knows the damaged area creates a wall around itself, and which the Greek surgeons and their successors right down to Lister in the nineteenth century AD took as the course of events to be hoped for and encouraged. Since the two are mutually exclusive, it was obviously better to have 'white pus': it is also true that the white blood cells which comprise the pus, and which enter an infected wound to destroy the bacteria by suppuration, will in so doing remove the dead and bruised tissue – make it 'melt away', in fact – and leave the wound more

case.[25] The wound was washed with wine, and because it was a head wound and required stitching it was gently purged; drying the wound properly was very important — wounds that bled badly were held to benefit from the application of sponges, wrapped with leaves and then bound in place. Different types of wound required particular poultices or dressings: the writer's prescriptions incorporate seventeen different substances, all of them intended as a form of desiccant. As with any doctor, precisely which combination Kritoboulos used will have depended both on his diagnosis of the state of the wound as well as on his personal preferences – 'the drug that seems appropriate' are the words of the writer of *On Wounds*. If the injury needed further cleansing, he advised a poultice such as one made from the boiled leaves of a variety of mullein, yellow stonecrop, felty germander, and the raw leaves of *triphyllon* which is possibly 'strawberry clover'. If the wound itself was clean, but the surrounding area had become inflamed, then a poultice of lentils boiled in wine, finely pounded and mixed with oil, was recommended. This dressing was changed every other day, and because it protected an injury to the eye it was covered by an elaborate bandage – Greek doctors prided themselves on their bandaging technique, so much so that the ancient handbooks have to urge restraint, but as we have seen in the case of head wounds the Hippocratic *Corpus* only allowed those to the eye or eyebrow to be bandaged: elsewhere it was necessary to make sure that the blood, pus and humours that might have leaked into the cranial cavity could escape.

All this was normally followed by a course of purgatives. There can be no doubt that Philip had to be tough to survive this treatment. When we discussed it with a modern successor to Kritoboulos, he made the wry comment that 'Philip survived, as do most patients, in spite of and not because of treatment. The result is *extremely* unlikely.' Yet the treatment had evidently achieved the desired result, and survive he did. One does, however, begin to appreciate why Hammond might be right in suggesting that having endured such a course of treatment, Philip allowed the inhabitants of Methone to go free after the final capture of their city, wearing the clothes in which they stood. This was a very lenient treatment for the time: though he had achieved his objective, Philip was in great pain and simply wanted to return to Pella for the winter to nurse his wound as soon as he possibly could.

It is perhaps worth adding that this course of treatment which we have pieced together from roughly contemporary medical texts was exceptional in terms of how a highly skilled physician and surgeon would employ the accepted procedures of his time. One can set the comment of Pliny against a couple of inscriptions set up at the shrine of the healing god Asclepius in Epidaurus by two men who could not call on the skills of a doctor like Kritoboulos, and who followed what was presumably the more usual course in such extreme cases, that of praying for divine help: first Timon, who 'wounded by a spear under his eye, saw in a dream while sleeping in the temple that the god rubbed down a herb and poured it in his eye, and he became well'; and then Antikrates of Knidos, who 'in a battle had been hit by a spear in the eye and had become blind, and the spearpoint he carried with him sticking in his face. While sleeping he saw a vision: it seemed to him that the god pulled out the missile and then fitted into his eyelids again the so-called pupils.

When the day came he walked out sound'.[26] Antikrates must have been suffering horribly until the god intervened. Considering that he called on mere human aid, Philip was very fortunate indeed.

This new medico-historical evidence did much to help us understand the pain and the risks that someone like Philip had to be prepared to undergo, and gave new meaning to Demosthenes' description and grudging respect for the man. Of course the added detail did nothing to further the identification, but it had never been intended to do so since we reckoned that this had effectively been proved by the actual discovery of the eye wound. It remained to express the new evidence in three-dimensional form. Even if correct in other respects the reconstruction we had made in 1983 was now inaccurate as far as the visible effects of the eye injury were concerned, since it showed a face that was badly disfigured and hardly the advertisement for Kritoboulos' skills that Pliny had heard it to be.

Here two new factors entered. Obviously a waxwork was the most vivid way of expressing Kritoboulos' dramatically successful treatment, and as a record to be photographed (and to be filmed if the need arose) it was ideal – this had been the intention behind the original waxwork – but from the nature of the materials it will not survive indefinitely, particularly under display conditions. When the original waxwork had been put on show at the Manchester Museum soon after its creation, in a position where it caught the public eye but was also exposed to sunlight, it had provided rather lurid proof of this, and Philip began to look as if he suffered from a rather nasty skin complaint. A new waxwork was made, with glass eye, wig and make-up, and after being recorded on film it went to Professor Andronicos in Thessaloniki. Yet somehow it did not convey the excitement and fire of the first version: it was not only that the well-healed wound made the face look less striking and eye-catching; perhaps this 'repeat performance' had simply lost some of the original fire. We were already looking at other ways of communicating our results in more permanent form: the outcome was a version in bronzed resin with sculpted hair and beard that appears at first sight more like a conventional portrait sculpture, yet also conveys all the information in a way that distances the spectator a little, so that he or she does not feel the slight discomfort of being brought into too close contact with a stranger that a too-realistic waxwork can bring (see frontispiece).

In the end we did make another waxwork. The initiative came from a producer at Scottish Television, who wanted to make a programme on reconstructing heads in the children's series 'How to...' As usual, Philip was the obvious choice as a television star, for his was the best story of all those on whose heads we had worked, even in 1993, ten years after the original reconstruction. However, to make the necessary impact a new waxwork was needed, for the previous model was now in Thessaloniki. The new version was made with the help of a make-up artist whose training was in waxworks rather than television make-up and who had worked for Madame Tussaud's in London. Technically this was a great bonus, for after its television appearance this version was destined to have a permanent place in the recently opened Mediterranean Gallery at the Manchester Museum as part of a display on ancient warfare. Even in his 'improved' form King Philip II was still a powerful illustration of the injuries that an archer could inflict, and at the same time demonstrated how the careful study of the minutiae of the evidence by a team of specialists could solve a mystery, and in so doing re-create the face of one of the great figures from the past.

None of the faces of Philip of Macedon that we had produced could be classified as a portrait: all were based purely on the physical evidence of the skull as it was understood at a particular moment, and the relatively minor changes to nose and eye would in no way have altered the fact that Amyntas III, Olympias and Alexander the Great would immediately have recognised this face as that of their son, husband and father respectively. A true portrait includes in some form of physical likeness not only the artist's reaction to his sitter but also those elements of his character and lifestyle that need leave no trace on his physical remains. 'A portrait should show the motions of the mind' was how Leonardo da Vinci put it. For some elements, such as the crows' feet and the laughter lines around the eyes, there can be no testimony at all. Others one can infer from circumstantial or historical evidence: we know that Philip wore a beard, and we can infer that a man living a strenuous life in Greece will probably screw his eyes up constantly against the sun. Some inferences may seem to go beyond the evidence. We were bitterly attacked for altering the shape of the nose apparently in order to suit the face shown by the ancient portraits of Philip, but this attack was based on a double misunderstanding. First, by the time the change was made we were sure that we were dealing with a member of the royal family of Macedon, among whom a rather larger nose with a prominent bridge was a common feature. We could have used portraits of *any* member of the Argead family to make the point: it is found, for example, on many of the less idealising portraits of Alexander the Great, and on that identified as his half-brother Philip III Arrhidaeus (see fig. 14). Second, large or small, the shape of the nose itself had nothing to do with the identification, which was based on the injuries, and what is important for recognition is not the detail of individual features but the overall proportions of the face: the case of Sabir Kassim Kilu, described in Chapter 2, illustrates this most clearly.

We have glanced at the surviving ancient portraits of Philip II only insofar as they could help us supplement minor details in the reconstruction, but of course once the reconstruction was complete it was interesting to make comparisons between the face of Philip as we had built it up from the physical evidence and the same face as it was seen by his contemporaries, or at least by the Greco-Roman world. In antiquity there were many portraits of Philip: the ancient authors give us a long list including a famous set made in gold and ivory by Leochares for the sanctuary at Olympia, but to try to link any of these with the surviving images has been a fruitless pastime. Only one of the 'portraits' that has come down to us is inscribed with the name of Philip, and that is a mosaic of the fourth century AD from Baalbek which shows him as a young and nervous father sitting by during the nativity of his son Alexander. Quite apart from its late date, we can discount it on the grounds that it omits the one feature of Philip's face of which we have independent evidence, namely his beard.[27]

The coins struck by Philip are of little use: though inscribed with his name, they do not show his head, but many of his issues carry instead the figure of a bearded rider wearing a cloak and the large Macedonian hat or kausia, round which is tied the ribbon often identified as the royal diadem. The rider is generally identified as Philip himself: the scale is far too small for the face to be recognisable, but it may be significant that in contrast to the normal Macedonian numismatic tradition, this rider is shown moving to the left and therefore showing us his left side – what would in the case of Philip have been his 'good' side after 354 BC. A striking contrast is provided by a very small silver coin probably minted by the town of Kapsa on the opposite side of the Thermaic gulf to Pella and Vergina, probably between 348 and 336 BC: only one example is known (fig. 11), discovered

11. Silver coin of Kapsa, probably minted 348-336 BC. It shows the head of Philip II wearing a flat Macedonian hat; across the right eye runs a crescent-shaped gash (private collection).

by the late Dr Martin Price, at that time Deputy Keeper of Coins and Medals at the British Museum and a specialist in the coinage of Macedonia. He first published it at that same conference in Athens in 1983 where we brought our reconstruction into the public eye. It shows the head of a bearded man again wearing the Macedonian flat hat, with a square head, deep-set eyes and rather fleshy features, prominent but straight nose, small chin, and short but thick hair, beard and moustache. It shares many features with the other known portraits of Philip and incidentally with our reconstructions, but what is striking about this coin is that the head faces right, and running across the right eye between the upper and lower lids is a great crescent-shaped gash. Hellenistic coins often illustrate minor deformities and injuries very clearly. Even the famously attractive Cleopatra VII of Egypt is shown with a flabby neck that suggests a goitre. Dr Price assured us that to him it did not look a flaw in the die, appeared to be a deliberate attempt on the part of the engraver to indicate Philip's injury: 'If this is a portrait of Philip II, this is the first known portrait in coins in a Greek milieu,' he wrote, 'the first in a long line of royal portrait coins which led in turn to the custom of using portraiture on the coins of the Roman emperors and of medieval and modern Europe.'[28]

Looking to the left again is the head on a gold medallion of the reign of the Roman emperor Caracalla (AD 211–17) found in Tarsus: this shows a well-shaped, rather square head and face set on a thick neck, again somewhat fleshy but now rather careworn; the nose has a marked bridge, the chin is strong, the beard and hair are thick and curly, and the latter is held in place by a cloth band which is the original Macedonian diadem, the symbol of royalty. One should not place too much confidence in the accuracy of this 'portrait' (indeed, some have doubted its authenticity), for although presumably based on a contemporary or near-contemporary original, it is one of a series struck by Caracalla to boost his own image. Although it is the image of uncompromising authority that Caracalla wished to foster, it has enough in common with the other pieces for one to believe that at the least it derives from a portrait of Philip, whether idealised or not we cannot say. Remembering Philip's alleged touchiness over his eye wound, there may after all be some significance in the fact that all these portraits show his 'good' side: one recalls the memorably battered profile of Federigo di Montefeltro, Duke of Urbino, painted by Piero della Francesca in the fifteenth century, which now hangs in the Uffizi in Florence: having lost his right eye and the bridge of his nose during a tournament when in his twenties, he too would only allow his 'good' side to be shown. The fres-

co above the entrance to Tomb II at Vergina shows a hunting scene: here too is a bearded rider – Philip II – turned awkwardly to aim at his quarry with his left eye and thus to present the viewer with his left profile.[29]

When we come to large-scale sculpture, we find two traditions of portraits of Philip, the one that portrays him as the idealised philosopher-king, which may tell us something about the history of portraiture and about ancient attitudes to Philip (and perhaps about Philip's notion of his own image), but which helps us less in finding out what the man actually looked like than does the more realistic tradition represented by the marble head now in Copenhagen (fig. 1 2).[30] Although this is a Roman copy from the time of the emperor Trajan, the original on which it is based is reckoned on stylistic

12. Marble portrait of Philip II: Roman copy based on a late fourth-century BC original (Copenhagen, Ny Carlsberg Glyptotek 2466).

grounds to have been carved in the later fourth century BC, therefore either during Philip's lifetime or a few years after his death. It has much in common with the gold medallion from Tarsus, but this time we have the frontal view as well as the profile. In addition to the square, firm shape of the head, and the short, thick hair and beard concealing a jutting chin, one notices the high, wide cheekbones and widely set eyes. Only when one stands in front of the sculpture in Copenhagen is it really apparent that the mouth is a little askew and the whole face slightly off-centre, illustrating, as we now know, Philip's real physical deformity. The nose is broken away, but two other features are noticeable even in the photograph: the altered hairstyle to which we have already referred, again held in place by the cloth diadem; and the idiosyncratic lift to the left eye, which adds a touch of humour – perhaps rather cynical and brutal humour – to a face whose other features convey the impression of a powerful and strong-willed personality, tough and battle-scarred in mind and body. The right eyebrow lacks that lift, and has instead a distinct nick in its upper right corner.

That nick is found again on the right eyebrow of the little ivory head from the tomb itself (fig. 13). This is one of a set of fourteen which were once fixed to a wooden couch; all are clearly intended as portraits, and although as with much else concerning the naming of individuals in these tombs there has been fierce debate over the identification of some of the other heads, there can really be little doubt that this one represents Philip II, and that whether it is he whose remains are buried in the tomb or not this is a contemporary portrait of him. It is little over 3 cm (1¼ in) high – the same size or even a little smaller than

13. Miniature ivory portrait of Philip II originally attached to a couch in Tomb II. The nick above the right eye is deliberate (Thessaloniki, Archaeological Museum).

the top joint of most people's thumbs – yet it is a masterpiece that conveys a wealth of detail and character. Here is the face of a mature man with much experience of life behind him. Although less fleshy than most of the other heads in the set, his features are rather heavy, like those on the gold medallion, an aspect that is perhaps emphasised on the ivory by the rather prominent nose: though not as large as some Argead noses it is still a striking feature of his face, thickened and very slightly hooked at the bridge, more markedly so than on the medallion. It could be said that the lips recall the 'strong sensual mouth' which some have noted on the Copenhagen head, while the little wrinkles around the nose and eyes again give the man a touch of humour. The cheekbones are less prominent than on the Copenhagen marble, so that the face as a whole is less square, but the chin juts out obstinately again under its short beard. It is in the treatment of the eyes that the skill of this artist becomes fully apparent, although one really needs to hold the piece in one's hand in order to comprehend it fully. The eyes are set beneath rather prominent brow-ridges which add to the strength of the face. They are slightly more angled than on the Copenhagen head, which again reduces the squareness of the face as a whole and gives it a greater feeling of individuality. The left eye is set slightly lower than the right, and the left cheek is slightly flatter; one might attribute this simply to the fact that the ivory was made to be fixed to the side of a piece of fur-niture, were it not for the information we had gleaned from the bones themselves. It must reflect what was really there on the face itself. The right eye appears to be open wider – sightlessly? – and through the centre of the right eyebrow runs a diag-onal nick that is not the result of accidental damage but was cut there by the artist himself.

Classical Greek sculptors set out to portray the sitter's personality and ethos rather than his or her physical peculiarities: their art was rooted in an idealising tra-dition that did not allow excessive realism, and conveyed character by gesture and stance rather than 'true-to-life' detail. While the artists working on a small scale in the so-called 'minor arts', such as terracotta or bronze figurines or these ivories, were less bound by such conventions, nonetheless like its fellows this ivory is almost unflattering in its realism and its attention to detail. Here we have the work of an artist who on the one hand was trained in the older tradition, which was beginning to break down in the later fourth century, and on the other caught up in the new realism. He could not yet show the eye wound in its full horror (one might ques-tion whether any artist would ever want to do so, or whether any sitter would ever want to be seen thus, particularly if Philip was as sensitive about the wound as the stories tell); nor was it strictly part of Philip's character, which is what he was aim-ing to portray. Yet it has been suggested that the eye wound was also a way of flaunt-ing his toughness, in the same way as the eye patch became the trade mark of General Moshe Dayan.[31] Recalling Demosthenes' catalogue of the bodily marks of Philip's physical endurance, such a notion seems plausible. It is interesting too how the Copenhagen marble head, probably conceived a generation or so later when large-scale sculpture too had moved towards greater realism, picks up this idea, although it retains enough of the idealising tradition to explain some of its more conventional features: the result is, to modern eyes at least, a blander piece.

There are two factors of primary importance in making any comparison between the various representations of Philip II, be they large or small, in three dimensions or two. First, the faces which are being compared one with another have been cre-ated by the hands and eyes of artists. As such they are not exact photographic records but interpretations of how the individual was perceived by the artist. The second point concerns the extent to which the conventions and restraints within which the artist was working may have played a part in the final appearance of the face. Although such restraints are likely to have modified the handling of the eye wound they are unlikely to have affected the way in which internal proportion was used – and here one is talking not of the canon of proportions between different parts of the body, a theoretical question which preoccupied Greek artists through-out the fifth and fourth centuries, but only of the proportions of different parts of the head and face to each other, not to the rest of the body. As proportion is impor-tant in any figurative work it is there that comparisons should start, for while a similarity of proportion may not in itself positively demonstrate that two heads rep-resent the same person, clear differences will argue against their being the same. Comparison of the reconstruction of Philip II with the marble head of Philip III Arrhidaeus in Naples (Museo Nazionale 187 [138]) demonstrates this quite clearly (fig. 14). Seen in profile the nose of Philip III preserves the rather prominent bridge that we have suggested is an Argead family feature. However, the distance from the nasion to the nasolabial junction (or the vertical length of the nose) of Philip III is much greater in proportion to the rest of the face than it is on the reconstruction: as far as we know this is not a feature that will have been affected by the Greek sculptors' canon of proportions, and this alone indicates that two separate people are represented.

Much scholarly discussion has been devoted to all the known images of Philip II, but one must not lose sight of the fact that the most impressive of them all is the tiny ivory from Vergina. The proportions of all of them are broadly consistent with those of the reconstruction, although it has to be said that the coins cannot be realistically included in this exercise. The faces are square and robust with a noticeably convex dorsal ridge to the nose. Seen

14. Marble portrait of Philip III Arrhidaeus (?). The nose has the prominent bridge typical of the Argead family (Naples, Museo Nazionale 187 (138)).

from the anatomist's rather than an art historian's viewpoint, and so without an awareness of the traditions of classical art, there is little evidence of a scar on any part of the face of any of the ancient images, apart from some slight marking on the lateral border of the supraorbital margin of the right eye, discernible on the marble head from Copenhagen and the ivory head from Vergina. Both position and direction of these marks appear to be in conflict with the evidence adduced from the skull, for they run in the opposite direction, and without a knowledge of the traditions of classical sculpture one might be tempted to view them realistically and attribute them to less ferocious injuries – an interpretation that has on occasion been brought forward by those who would argue that the Vergina skull is not that of Philip II, or that our reconstruction is based on false anatomical premises.

To attempt to compare the finer detail is very tempting and can become most compelling, but if one were to follow it to its logical conclusion a comparison of the eyes of the marble head with those of the little ivory would demonstrate that their shape and angle are very different. While the ivory is likely to be physically the most accurate as well as the only portrait in the round that is contemporary with the man himself, these are not details that would have concerned the ancient artist, as we have tried to show. More important, this inconsistency gives the lie to those who suggest that our approach is circular, that our reconstruction resembles the portraits (themselves not identified with complete certainty), and that having adjusted the detail to match the portraits more closely, we then use the ensuing similarity as an argument for identifying our reconstruction with the subject of those portraits. Given the variety of detail between the different portraits, this would be a frustrating and fruitless pastime.[32]

The starting point for our research had been the skull from the main chamber in Tomb II; Andronicos' reason for encouraging us to 'come over into Macedonia and help' had been that he wanted assistance in identifying the man buried there: forensic science hand-in-hand with archaeology. The identity of the man in Tomb II should in turn provide the basis for naming the occupants of the other tombs under the Great Tumulus at Vergina. The historical arguments have been debated many times elsewhere, with the same passion that has coloured much of this investigation. No skulls survived, but the expertise we could bring to the question was above all the anthropological and anatomical skills of Jonathan Musgrave, and he returned on more than one occasion to Thessaloniki to study and to reconsider the remains. However, this book is about the conclusions one can draw from skulls and faces rather than from what anatomists call the post-cranial bones alone, so we refer the reader who would pursue this sequel to our work to Dr Musgrave's articles in the *Annual of the British School at Athens*.[33]

Although we are certain that the work that went into making this reconstruction has elicited the evidence that identifies the dead man in Tomb II as King Philip II, there are of course still those who are not convinced. The debate continues, and books and articles continue to appear. On the one side stands Andronicos, who died in March 1992 after a long illness: he had always tended to the belief that this was Philip II, and once he got over his initial caution he accepted the evidence of the bones as one piece in a complicated jigsaw of identifications. His final position is stated in general terms in *Vergina: The Royal Tombs and the Ancient City*, published eight years before his death, which involves not only each individual tomb but their relationship with each other and the topography of the site as a whole. Detailed final reports are promised from his erstwhile colleagues. The arguments against the identification as Philip II are summarised by Eugene N. Borza in *In the Shadow of Olympus: The Emergence of Macedon*, who gives a balanced account with good references for those who wish to pursue the matter further – even if, as we believe, he comes down on the wrong side.[34]

A point that is perhaps worth reiterating is that the dating of pottery and of architecture is founded on stylistic comparisons, except in those very rare cases where a clearly datable object such as a freshly minted coin is found together with a vase in pristine condition or in the foundation-deposit of a building. In any other context one has to allow for the fact that in any period of history some people are more conservative in their tastes than others, some artists and architects more progressive than others. The human mind is a far less predictable thing than the human body. While it is possible to identify the form and origin of a piece of pottery with considerable confidence, nearly all pottery dating is relative, and hangs on other external evidence – and these words are written by an archaeologist who has in his time published reports on pottery of precisely the type which has caused the problems at Vergina. The 'royal' salt-cellars in the tomb at Vergina were made in Athens and have been dated to the last quarter of the fourth century BC on the basis of identical examples found in a well in Athens that went out of use around 295 BC; in fact that well contains other pottery which could easily have been made as early as 340 BC, and so long as one is prepared to accept that Philip of Macedon was no semicivilised northern barbarian but a man of taste who wanted to have the latest and the best in his household, then those salt-cellars found in his tomb in pristine condition need be little older than the time it took a merchantman to sail from Athens soon after they first went into production.[35] One thing that the finds from Tomb II demonstrate beyond all shadow of doubt is that the person buried there was just such a man of taste.

Similar arguments have been put forward for updating the introduction of the barrel-vault into Greece: rather than look to the southern 'civilised' parts of Greece, one should acknowledge that the Macedonian engineers had a problem in preventing their traditional tombs built under great mounds from collapsing under the weight of the earth above so long as they had to continue using the traditional flat roof; and that there was no reason why with the contact with the east that came as Philip turned Macedonian eyes eastward long before Alexander's campaigns they should not have found a solution for themselves in the barrel-vault, where the curved roof transferred the load to either side – a point which Professor Richard Tomlinson has made very clearly in a study of Macedonian tombs, in the process turning himself from a sceptic to a supporter of the notion that here lay Philip II and none other. The argument was clinched when, in 1987, among burnt remains associated with what must be the earliest Macedonian barrel-vaulted tomb, that of Philip's mother Eurydice, Andronicos found a fragment of a Panathenaic prize amphora: it is firmly dated to 344/3 BC from the name of the Athenian magistrate stamped upon it.[36]

The human body, by contrast, can be interpreted with much greater certainty by those who have the training to see: therefore the evidence from the bones, which depends on no outside imponderables, can provide one of those rocks on which archaeological dating is founded. This chapter may appear to have wandered along a somewhat circuitous and lengthy route from its intended starting point, a simple and straightforward reconstruction of our first Greek skull, to its conclusion, a recognisable and identifiable face. The reconstruction proved to be neither simple nor straightforward, either as a technical exercise or as the unravelling of a vital clue in an extremely complicated historical puzzle. If it has taken us a long time to explain it, that is because the reconstruction cannot stand on its own if it is to have any real intellectual value. With the skull from Tomb II at Vergina and the face of Philip of Macedon facial reconstruction as an academic technique came of age.

CHAPTER 5

King Midas has Ass's Ears?

W e had launched ourselves into the reconstruction of the skull from Tomb II at Vergina largely because we felt that after the three Egyptians in the Manchester Museum it would be interesting to tackle some ancient Greek skulls. We had never imagined that our first Greek candidate might be the remains of someone discovered in the most exciting circumstances, amid the most spectacular finds, the remains of someone who was possibly a famous historical figure, remains whose identification were not merely in doubt but a matter for deep academic and indeed political debate. The fact that almost as a matter of routine we could call upon such a range of medical, historical and technical skills added a completely new dimension to the work; and the consequence, that what had until now been a topic for searching and often bitter dispute among historians and archaeologists was suddenly open to forensic proof in the most dramatic way, and could be treated in the same dispassionate manner as the unidentified remains brought in by the police, had effects more exciting and far-reaching than we could ever have imagined. Undoubtedly the timing of the first publication of the original reconstruction helped: a major international congress in Athens on which much national pride (and much media interest) was centred and of which the Vergina excavations were a major focus; undoubtedly too the horrendously vivid rendition of Philip II's eye wound had its effect, as it stared out at one from every news-stand in Greece the next morning.

It seemed a propitious if bewildering start, even if controversy continued to grumble on, and sometimes to rage. Understandably, archaeologists and historians, particularly those brought up in the traditional milieu of the classical world, sometimes find it difficult to accept the findings and the implications of disciplines with which they are completely unfamiliar. It is surely true that if the man who was buried in Tomb II at Vergina was Philip II of Macedon, who died in 336 BC, then the dating of Greek black-glazed pottery in the later fourth century would have to be revised yet again, and the history of Macedonian tomb-building and thus the introduction of the barrel-vault and the arch into European architecture would have to be reassessed; it is also true that some archaeological problems, such as the apparent presence of a Hellenistic Cypriot vase in the tomb, will need serious thought. Nonetheless this should not excuse those who still hold that they cannot see and so cannot comprehend the medical evidence, and that therefore they would prefer to ignore it in favour of the argument provided by the traditional archaeological data which they can understand. Such problems are the stuff with which historians work, and fixed points such as the date to which this tomb can now be assigned are rare but vital anchorages in the shifting world of the archaeological chronology, which *faute de mieux* often has to tie itself to fluid stylistic comparisons.

After the publication of the first reconstruction of the man who we were now certain was Philip II of Macedon, there was more work to be done with the skull, above all to correct the scarring to the eye, as we have described in the previous chapter. While this work was going ahead during the winter of 1985–6, Dr Veli Sevin of Istanbul University paid a visit to Manchester. Unlike many people he was less concerned with the finished product than with understanding how the reconstructions were made, and he appeared particularly concerned with the problems associated with the soft parts of the face. We explained to him the rules for the nose, for the width of the mouth, and the lack of evidence to guide one towards the shape and size of the ears, the feature which seemed to preoccupy him particularly. In the end Dr Sevin came clean: 'You see,' he said, 'in Ankara we have the skull of Midas.' Would we come to Turkey and reconstruct the skull of Midas?[1]

The story of Midas is an intriguing and fascinating one, woven from several strands, and to appreciate why we might rise to this challenge, and why this skull might prove interesting from both the archaeological and the medical standpoints, it is necessary to recount it briefly. What kind of a man would we have before us, both literally and figuratively, when his skull reached the studio bench?

Midas belongs in Phrygia, a kingdom or a coalition of kingdoms that flourished in what is now central Turkey from the later second millennium until at least the sixth century BC. The Phrygians seem to have come to the Anatolian plateau as a loose tribal federation from eastern Europe: the Greek historian Herodotus places their homeland on Mount Vermion or Bermium in Macedonia.[2] Greek tradition set this invasion before the Trojan War (c.1200 BC), for Homer lists the Phrygians among the Trojan allies.[3] They are normally identified with the Mushki of the Assyrian annals, where they are first mentioned around 1160 BC, by which time they seem to have occupied the whole of the Anatolian plateau. Only the coast was barred to them, first by the native rulers, later by Greek settlers.

However, there was apparently more than one figure named Midas, and it is sometimes difficult to distinguish them, for stories about one Midas seem to transfer to another. In part this reflects the changing perceptions of this oriental people by the Greeks: since the Phrygian language has not yet been properly deciphered, effectively all our information comes from outside, from the Assyrian records or from Greek and Roman writers – an important point when one tries to disentangle fact from folktale.

The 'first' Midas is the legendary ancestor and founder of the Phrygian royal house, about whom the Greeks knew various tales: the best-known tell of how he captured Silenos and returned him to his master, the wine-god Dionysus, whereupon the god in gratitude allowed him to choose whatever he wished. Midas asked that all he touched should turn to gold, but the wish misfired when his food and drink were transformed too, and he feared he might starve (the version where even his little daughter became a golden statue as he embraced her is a modern addition to the story). When he thereupon begged for remission, Dionysus advised him to bathe in the river Pactolus, which ever after ran with gold that could be retrieved by panning. Later Midas became involved in judging a musical contest between the lyre-playing Apollo, god of music, and the goat-god Pan with his pipes. When he found in favour of Pan, Apollo declared that he must have the ears of an ass. The Roman poet Ovid gives the fullest account of the story, and of what happened next:

Now the king himself, ashamed of his disfigurement, was anxious to conceal it, and tried to do so by wrapping his head in a purple turban. But the barber who used to trim his long hair saw what had happened. Eager though he was to tell what he had seen, he did not dare to reveal the shameful secret, and yet he could not keep quiet about it. So he went off, and dug a hole in the ground: then he whispered softly to the earth he had dug out what kind of ears he had seen on his master's head. Throwing the earth back again, he buried the information he had given and, after filling in the trench, went quietly away. But a thick carpet of trembling reeds began to push up on the spot and, at the end of the year, when they were full grown, the reeds betrayed their gardener: for when stirred by the gentle south wind they uttered the words that had been buried, and revealed the truth about his master's ears.

In other versions the second musician was the satyr Marsyas, who himself later came to a bad end at the hands of Apollo, but for Midas the punishment was the same.[4]

Traditionally the first 'real' Midas was the son of Gordios or Gordias, and was reckoned to be the founder of the Phrygian kingdom around 900 BC, either alone or jointly with his father: they arrived in a wagon at the Phrygian capital of Gordion during a riot, and Midas (or Gordios) was made king, in fulfilment of an oracle that had advised the Phrygians to choose as their ruler the man who should come among them in this manner. The kings of Phrygia were thenceforth called Gordios and Midas alternately, and the wagon in which the new king had arrived was dedicated in the temple, its traces tied in the Gordian knot that appeared impossible to unravel: according to an oracle he who succeeded in loosing it would win the mastery of Asia, and when Alexander the Great passed this way in 333 BC he, typically, took the short cut through the knot.[5]

However, there is no hard historical evidence for the existence of this first Midas, nor any other king of the name save the famous one. Like the legendary Midas, he appears as ancestor of the royal house and founder of numerous Phrygian cities, while the shadowy Gordios is perhaps merely a creation of the Greek passion for having named heroes as the founders of cities. There was almost certainly only one real Midas, the late eighth-century king, whom the Greek and Roman authors came to see as a quasi-mythological figure, to whom all the curious stories and characteristics which they believed typical of Phrygia came to be attached.[6] Perhaps the parallel lies somewhere between King Arthur, a shadowy historical figure about whom legends grew up, and Napoleon Bonaparte, a very real character who also became a bogeyman in the popular lore of nineteenth-century England.

This historical Midas succeeded his father Gordios in 738 BC, and died when his capital city was sacked by the invading Cimmerians in 696/5 BC.[7] He was the most famous king of Phrygia, the only one to feature prominently in international politics, a thorn in the side of the Assyrians and often mentioned thus in the records of King Sargon II under the name of 'Mita of Mushki', until in 710/709 BC he sued for peace and became an ally if not a vassal. Midas-Mita was clearly an ambitious and energetic leader, perhaps the first king to have built up an important state in central Anatolia since the collapse of the Hittite empire around 1200 BC.

Midas' ambitions on the world stage also led him to look in other directions, and so to make contact with the Greeks in the west. Herodotus says that he was the first foreigner to make offerings in the sanctuary of Apollo at Delphi: 'Midas dedicated the royal throne from which he used to give judgement: it... is well worth seeing.' He is said to have married a Greek princess, the daughter of the ruler of the Greek colony of Kyme in Aeolis on the west coast of Asia Minor.[8] Such a marriage implies close political contact: it was valuable to Midas because it gave him a route to the western ports and thence to Greece. The new trade went in both directions: Phrygian goods have been found at Greek sanctuaries in Ionia and on the Greek mainland, and sherds from Greek vases were discovered at Gordion. The Greeks, ever intellectually curious, were interested in the new ideas they might learn from this oriental people with whom they were now making contact; the Phrygians seem to have responded, if with rather less enthusiasm. The stream of Greek artefacts into Phrygia never became much more than a trickle, but that trickle began in the late eighth century, the time when Midas reigned, and is reflected in the way in which the Phrygians adapted Greek motifs and types in their pottery and their jewellery. Professor Keith DeVries, who directed the excavations at Gordion from 1974 to 1988, summed up the relations between Greeks and Phrygians in the Early Iron Age as follows: 'What does emerge from the excavations...is that at the time when the [Homeric] epics were coalescing along the Ionian Greek fringe of Anatolia, [Greek] society in some of its most striking aspects had a living counterpart in lands not far to the east.'[9]

Conversely, the new contact will have given the Greeks their first view of this oriental king, even if, as we shall see, the picture was afterwards coloured by later events. The most thought-provoking argument for intellectual contact between the Phrygians and the Greeks in the later eighth century BC comes from the fact that at this time, when alphabetic scripts were developing, their alphabets have much in common. Whether the Phrygians took the alphabet over from the Greeks, who had learned it from the Phoenicians, or got it themselves by a more direct route from Phoenicia, the fact remains that 'Phrygian letters most closely resemble the earliest Greek examples yet known.' Phrygians and Greeks felt they belonged to the same intellectual milieu; when they needed to communicate they both chose this alphabet, and not the more traditional but cumbersome Assyrian cuneiform nor any form of hieroglyphic script.[10]

To the dispassionate observer the picture that emerges of King Midas, then, is of an energetic and dynamic ruler of a people that had so far played no great part in world affairs, who immersed himself in international politics during a period of upheaval and change, and who opened his country to new ideas from his neighbours to east and west and established contact with the Greek city-states just at the time when their great economic revival was gathering momentum after the slump of the Dark Ages; a man both ambitious and wily, but canny enough to seek alliance with his powerful neighbour when he judged it inevitable. In fact, he was a figure who would certainly have felt at home in the later twentieth century AD. Very possibly King Sargon of Assyria met his death in battle against the Cimmerians in 705 BC in response to an appeal for help from his new ally: had Midas perhaps seen the greater threat coming when he made his peace with Sargon a few years earlier? At any rate he and his own people were saved for almost a decade longer, until the Cimmerians, the Gomer of the Bible, continued their destructive passage from the Caucasus westward through Phrygia before finally coming to rest in the Crimea. In 696/5 Gordion was burnt, and after a reign of forty-two years Midas died in the sack: Strabo says that he committed suicide by drinking bull's blood. This seems a strange way of killing oneself, for fresh, uncontaminated bull's blood is not poisonous – there are peoples in Africa who drink it as part of their daily diet, while in many European countries it is safely cooked and eaten as sausage, and the Romans already had their black puddings. Nevertheless in ancient Greece, Rome and even Egypt numerous characters both legendary and historical were recorded as achieving death by drinking it, among them Jason, Psammenitus of Egypt, Themistocles, even Hannibal, and it was clearly regarded as a poison in antiquity. None of the ancient authors who describe these suicides suggest that anything was added to the blood to give it this lethal effect, and the simple answer must be that if it is allowed to stand and become contaminated with botulism-producing bacilli – which could happen relatively quickly in a hot climate – it will indeed become very toxic, inducing death within a matter of hours.[11] The list of men who died in this way seems to be made up chiefly of leaders who suffered disillusionment as much as disgrace: unhappy Midas falls readily into this group. Although little is known about his kingdom in the following period, Phrygia survived as an independent country for nearly a hundred years, until it was conquered by the Lydians in the late seventh century.

Midas' capital city of Gordion lies in the wide valley of the river Sakarya, the ancient Sangraios, an important natural route across the Anatolian plateau to the Aegean coast that is still busy today (the main railway line from Europe and Istanbul to Ankara and the east runs this way); in antiquity it was the Royal Road of the Persian Empire, and Alexander the Great wintered here in 333 BC on his way to attack the Persian king. The plain is dotted with more than eighty mounds: most conceal burials, but the two largest, on either side of the ancient bed of the river, cover the acropolis and the southeastern suburb of the Phrygian capital. In 1900 the German Koerte brothers carried out a season of excavations; since 1950 the American Gordion project, based at the University of Pennsylvania Museum in Philadelphia, has been excavating here.[12]

The largest of these burial mounds, the Great Tumulus, is also traditionally known as the Midas Mound (fig. 1). It overshadows the modern village of Yassihüyük, and still rises to a height of around 53 m (175 ft). When it was erected

1. The Midas Mound at dusk: the length of the shadow cast by the mound and the first houses of the village of Yassihüyük demonstrate its size. Other smaller tumuli stretch to the left.

89

it probably stood 70 to 80 m (230–60 ft) high: erosion has reduced its height but increased its girth from the original 250 m (820 ft) to 300 m (980 ft). As with all the tumuli at Gordion, in order to prevent the tomb being robbed the builders had made no entrance-way, nor left any indication of where the burial was located inside the mound: in the smaller mounds it was generally placed off-centre, but in the larger ones they obviously reckoned that the sheer bulk of the mound would act as a deterrent, and the tomb could be left in the centre. The Great Tumulus was a monument in its own right, so to dig it away in order to find the burial was out of the question; besides, as the builders had foreseen, the quantity of spoil that would have had to be moved made this an impractical course. Therefore in 1956 the director of the excavations, Professor Rodney Young, decided to locate the tomb chamber by drilling into the mound from above along a grid-pattern until he discovered the stone casing that protected it. In the following year an entrance-way was cut into the tumulus, and the burial chamber excavated.

The tomb was itself an impressive structure: inside the stone casing of rubble heaped within a roughly dressed wall was a double wooden chamber, comprising an outer layer of round cedar or juniper logs which took the pressure of the stone, and inside this a room built of neatly squared timbers of yew, cedar and pine, measuring 6.2 x 5.15 m (20 ft 4 in x 16 ft 11 in), with a pitched roof (fig. 2). From its design it was obviously impossible that such a monument could have been

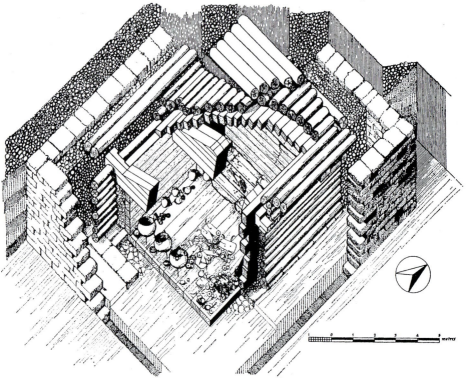

2. Cutaway drawing of the tomb inside the Midas Mound.

completed ahead of the death of its intended occupant, but it would have been surprising if some preparations had not been made for the construction of so massive an edifice. The excavator suggested that the tomb chamber had been built in advance as far as the roof level, and the outside piled with rubble: this was necessary to secure the round logs as they were put in place, for these were not fastened together in any way. The tumulus itself was also built up to the same level if not higher.

The contents of the tomb were as impressive as its construction, and because the chamber had been sealed for almost 2,700 years, until the drill had penetrated it the previous year, most were in excellent state of preservation when found. Scattered around the tomb were over 350 bronze objects: cauldrons, bowls, jugs, cups, ornaments and fibulae (some of these found in the remains of a cloth bag), nearly all so well preserved that with relatively little cleaning many still gleam like gold. Some had a high zinc content, and should be identified as brass rather than bronze.[13] The absence of any items actually made of gold or silver may seem surprising in view of at least one Phrygian king's reputation for wealth, but it was not the Phrygian custom to put objects of precious metal into graves, however high the status of the dead person. The use of brass may here be significant as a substitute, for when it is new brass glitters like gold, much more brightly than bronze. No arms or armour were buried with the dead man, but that also was normal Phrygian practice. The tomb did, however, contain eighteen pottery vessels that had once held food, packed inside three bronze cauldrons resting on iron stands and some wooden furniture: two inlaid serving stands, eight plain three-legged tables, and a fantastic inlaid 'pagoda' table – seeing them restored in the Ankara Museum one can understand why Midas was so proud of his Phrygian woodworkers that he dedicated his royal throne to Apollo in faraway Delphi, and why nearly three hundred years later Herodotus still thought it worth seeing. At one end of the tomb, lying on a thick blanket in a coffin made from a hewn-out log of yew, was the skeleton of a rather small elderly man, 1.59 m (5 ft 2½ in) tall, originally clothed in trousers or a skirt of leather and textile, an upper garment, and leather buskins.[14]

Although there were inscribed wax strips attached to some of the bronzes and graffiti on some of the pots, they all appeared to record different names, and gave no guide to the identity of the occupant. From the quality of the tomb, both of its construction and its contents, it was clear that he must be a king. However, Young, and others with him, doubted whether after the disaster of the Cimmerian sack the Phrygians could have afforded so rich a burial even for King Midas, and he noted that although some of the goods in the tomb showed signs of damage from use, none evinced any trace of the burning which he believed they would inevitably have suffered had they been placed there after the sack of Gordion. Therefore he concluded that the mound must have been erected by Midas for his father Gordios, perhaps in the years 725–720 BC rather than immediately after his death in 738, and he found confirmation for this in the style of some of the objects found in the tomb.[15]

Nonetheless there were problems with this attribution too. After Young's death in a road accident in 1974 Professor Keith DeVries took over as director of the Gordion project. He and his colleagues argued that what is by far the largest of the eighty-plus tumuli at Gordion was much more likely to be that of her most famous king, the only one really to have made an impression on the international political and cultural scene. They wrote, 'It is the tomb with the most explicit Near Eastern associations in its display of large cauldrons with siren and demon attachments and situlae of oriental manufacture, and in its style of petaled omphalos bowls. Yet, the man buried here was surrounded by authentic Phrygian equipment, wooden furniture, textiles, and personal paraphernalia that characterise him as a typical representative of the Phrygian West' – a summary that matches exactly the picture of Midas that we have built up from the historical accounts.[16] The Cimmerians did not after all conquer Phrygia, but merely passed through, albeit destructively: many Phrygian cities survived unscathed, while even Gordion itself was not totally burnt, and Phrygia continued independent and prosperous at least until the Lydian conquest nearly a century later. It was obviously important to us to know that there was a good chance that the man in the mound was King Midas, and many letters passed between us and both Professor DeVries and Professor Kenneth Sams, the current director of the Gordion project. In the course of this correspondence they also suggested that the style of the finds as well as of the burial ritual – for example the very small amount of pottery found in the tomb – fall much better into the early seventh century than into the years 740–720 BC.[17] Further, as Young himself noted, much of the preparatory work for the burial mound could be done in advance, including the preparation of the stonework and the timbers. The timbers themselves ought to provide help in dating, since the logs in the outer layer were excellent material for a dendrochronological study, where the growth rings of the trees from which they were cut, which vary according to weather and climate conditions, can be matched across a worldwide sequence. Work by Professor Peter Kuniholm at Cornell University showed that some of the timbers had been felled up to eight centuries before they were used in constructing the tomb chamber; until 1995 the closest date that he could achieve for the most recently cut timbers was 757 BC ±37, which although it is no bar to the tomb having been built for Midas, would still be compatible with it being that of Gordios. However, Kuniholm's latest research, only published in 1996, could pinpoint the cutting of the last timbers in the Midas Mound quite precisely to 718 BC. This really rules out Gordios as a candidate, and leaves Midas as the most likely contender for the occupancy of the tomb.[18]

The skeleton buried inside the tomb was that of a man of sixty to sixty-five years old, a considerable age in Iron Age terms, so he had plenty of time to prepare his burial arrangements. DeVries has pointed out that Midas ruled for forty-two years: his likely age at death and that of the skeleton in the Midas Mound match nicely. Besides, the fact that it was found necessary to use damaged bronze vessels in the burial of the king is itself an argument for sudden, perhaps temporary, poverty. There was no reason why everything in the city should have been burnt in the sack, but good cause why there might be a shortage of large cauldrons fit for a king.

But despite all these rather complex arguments, endlessly discussed on both sides of the Atlantic, there was no firm proof here, either way. It was in the hope that, as in the case of Philip of Macedon, the Manchester team might be able to find some medical evidence to identify the dead man that Dr Sevin proposed the reconstruction of the skull from the Midas Mound. At the time of course none of us knew that the tree-ring dating might be narrowed down so precisely. Even so it would still be good to seek confirmation from the human remains.

After its discovery in 1957 the skeleton had been lifted by Professor Muzafer Şenyürek and taken to the Palaeoanthropology Division in the University of Ankara for study, but aside from noting its sex, age and height, Şenyürek only commented that the skull and face were long and narrow, with a very heavy jaw. He did not note any medical or pathological peculiarities.[19]

On all the evidence brought forward so far (before Kuniholm's new date) it seemed fair to assume that the Midas Mound was a royal tomb dating from somewhere between 750 and 690 BC, and the debate had produced two royal candidates for its occupancy, Gordios or Midas. About the physical appearance and age at death of the shadowy Gordios nothing is known. About Midas there was at least the assumption that after a reign of forty-two years he was likely to be over sixty when he died; and there was the Greek story of the Phrygian king's ass's ears. What could one make of this seemingly fanciful tale? If history and archaeology could only give pointers but no definite answers, did the ass's ears hide any useful clues?

The story of the king with ass's ears (or horse's ears or goat's ears) is not restricted to ancient Greece or to ancient Phrygia seen through Greek eyes. It is found in modern Greek folklore, in Serbia, in Celtic lore in Ireland and Brittany, in India, even Mongolia, and no doubt elsewhere. In the Irish version the king is endowed with horse's ears, which like Midas he can keep hidden from all save the man who cuts his hair. To ensure that the secret spreads no further, all who are given this task must die once they have performed it. One day the king shows pity on a young man to whom the lot had fallen, and spares him on condition he keeps eternal silence. But the youth falls ill under the weight of the secret, and a Druid in whom he confides recommends he entrust it to a tree. The young man follows this advice and quickly recovers, but when a harper has an instrument made from the wood of the tree, the harp plays of its own accord, 'our king has the ears of a horse'.[20]

It is difficult to find a logical interpretation for the story. There are some significant differences in the way it is told. Often no reason is given why the king should have the strange ears. In the ancient Greek version there is never any threat of death to the barber, while in the Breton/Cornish one it is the dwarf Frocin or Meriadoc who is privy to King Mark's secret, and when he lets it out deliberately to some courtiers (by the ruse of digging a hole under a whitethorn tree, through which it is then revealed) the king slices off his head.[21] However, all other accounts seem to share the importance of concealment, and therefore to stress the role of the haircutter. Perhaps then the most consistent explanation is still that put forward sixty years ago by Sir James Frazer in *The Golden Bough*, seemingly overlooked by all archaeologists and historians, which runs as follows.[22] In primitive societies the head is considered the seat of the soul, and is sometimes even regarded as sacred. Thus the cutting of the hair becomes a dangerous operation, for two reasons: first, there is the simple risk of injury, spiritual or physical (exacerbated, in practical terms, before the invention of scissors by the nature of the implements used as well as the fact that the subject is particularly vulnerable to attack while the operation is being carried out); and second, it was held that a sympathetic link existed between a person and any part of his body, even when the actual physical connection had been severed, and thus possession of the shorn locks could give power over the person from whom they had been cut if they fell into the wrong hands. While the risk was there for any man or woman, it was obviously particularly great for a ruler. The simplest way of avoiding it was not to have one's hair cut at all: Frazer quotes the Frankish kings, who from childhood were forbidden to cut their hair, so that to crop it became a symbol of the abdication of royal power. To keep long flowing locks out of harm's way the obvious solution is some kind of restraining headgear, such as the Sikhs still wear today. As we have seen, this is precisely what Ovid tells us that Midas did in order to hide his newly sprouted ears. Because the Phrygians traditionally wore a curious kind of stocking-cap with ear-flaps, some scholars have argued that the Greeks misunderstood it, and that from this misunderstanding grew the story of the Phrygian king with ass's ears.[23] But as their vases show, the Greeks understood Phrygian caps perfectly, for they after all had the opportunity to see them in use, unlike modern archaeologists, and what Midas wears on the Greek vases is in any case not a Phrygian cap, but the kind of turban worn by Greek women (and very occasionally by Greek men) to cover their hair and to keep it in place.

The Greeks already knew Midas a mere fifty years after his death as a proverbial figure whose great wealth did not bring him happiness: in a poem written around 650 BC the Spartan poet Tyrtaeus included him in a rather odd list of virtuous men whose apparent good fortune took an unlucky twist, and two hundred years later Herodotus tells the story of Midas' capture and questioning of Silenos, the follower of Dionysus, in a search for the meaning of life.[24] From Silenos he gets a very pessimistic answer: better for a man never to have been born at all, but once in the world, it is best for him to die as soon as possible; Midas' reward for returning Silenos to his master Dionysus is the golden touch. In Ovid's account Midas then abandons his palace and his wealth and lives in the woods, worshipping Pan, 'but he remained a foolish person, and his own stupidity was to injure its owner again, as it had done before'. As he follows Pan, Midas has to meddle in his musical contest with Apollo: the result is ass's ears.

The first Greek pictures of any part of the Midas story show the capture of Silenos and date from the middle of the sixth century, a hundred years before the time Herodotus was writing, so the story was already widely known by then, but it was only in the third quarter of the fifth century that the king appears with ass's ears. Three Athenian red-figure vases survive depicting the incident, the best of them a stamnos (wine jar) in the British Museum: Midas is shown with neatly trimmed beard and hair; his cloak comes up to cover his neck and the back of his head in an unusual fashion, and on his head he wears a neat round turban, from the front of which protrude two long ears that point like those of an alert donkey towards the guard and Silenos, who is here depicted as a typical satyr, with bushy tail and little goat's ears (fig. 3).[25] One can only speculate as to why the king should suddenly appear in this manner, but the way Midas is shown and the iconography of the scene strongly recall Persian illustrations of the kings Xerxes and Darius giving audience. Bearing in mind what else is known about the Greeks' attitude to

3. King Midas sits in judgement on Silenos: his ass's ears protrude from under his turban (Athenian red-figure stamnos [wine jar]), c.450–425 BC; British Museum E447).

Orientals after the Persian Wars, and to the Phrygians and to Midas in particular at this time, we suggest that the story has taken on political overtones, and that Midas here stands for a caricature of the Athenian statesman Pericles. Such an interpretation would be quite in keeping with the way in which the Greeks used such stories. Although they were very reluctant to put real characters, living or dead, onto the serious stage or to represent them in art, the ancient Greeks loved a good story, and they often used mythological figures as a vehicle for comment on contemporary events. Other instances of such political cross-referencing in Greek art, for example the identification of the Athenian tyrant Peisistratos with the hero Herakles, do not entail any reference to the 'victim's' possible physical peculiarities, and one should not go out of one's way to seek them in this instance: however, while none of the ancient authors says anything about Pericles having had funny ears both they and the sculptors who carved his portrait made much of the fact that his head was disproportionately long. Besides, fragments of the lost comedy *Dionysalexandros* by Cratinus, published in 430 BC the year before Pericles' death, mock him as 'king of the satyrs'. Satyrs and Sileni were often confused by the classical authors, and in the fifth century both these semi-human creatures could still be shown with either horse's or goat's ears. Here, perhaps, we have both versions. One has to remember that the ancient Greek vase-painter is much closer to the modern cartoonist than to the Royal Academician.[26]

For at the same time there was a change in the Greeks' perception of the Phrygians – no longer were they seen as the great warriors whom Homer describes as allies of the Trojans (and who incidentally were treated with respect by the Assyrians too).[27] By the fifth century BC Phrygia had come down in the world: it was now a source not of wealth but of slaves – the Phrygian slave was a stock character on the Athenian comic stage, and 'Midas' had even become a common name for slaves.

Nevertheless, although this line of argument might provide a context for the new image that the Greeks gave to King Midas, it did not take us much further forward in accounting for the origin of the ass's ears themselves. The ancients already found the ears difficult to explain. The story of the musical contest was only one answer of several; the Greek mythographer Conon, writing at the turn of the Christian era, thought that they reflected the fact that Midas surrounded himself with spies; Athenaeus, around AD 200, tells a story of a nobleman pulling Midas' ears out of shape to show how stupid he was; others said he had exceptional hearing, or that they came as a punishment from Dionysus.[28] All this goes to show that they found it as curious a tale as we do, and while the implications of the cutting of hair, suggested by Frazer half a century ago, may give the correct answer from the anthropologist's point of view it would not have satisfied an ancient Greek, and it did not entirely satisfy us. Other great rulers have been turned into figures of fun – for example Alfred the Great and the burnt cakes – or like Napoleon have been made into bogeymen. Yet it is Pinocchio who gets the extending nose and Punch who has the hunchback – characters who have no historical basis at all. The mere fact that the story could appear in such similar form in such different places made us ask if there might not be a medical explanation for Midas' problem.

Our medical colleagues suggested a number of conditions that might give rise to the seemingly worldwide story of the king with ass's ears. Only one of them, a neurofibroma, might perhaps have left traces on the bone in the form of knobs. Solitary neurofibromas can occasionally be associated with hairiness, but more commonly show as brown spots on the skin. True, in very severe cases of a condition that goes by the resounding name of Von Recklinghausen's neurofibromatosis there might be hundreds if not thousands of neurofibromas leading to widespread and severe bone deformity, whose outward appearance could be very disturbing – it is traditionally held that the 'Elephant Man' in the nineteenth century suffered in this way, but no ancient author suggested that Midas' appearance was anything like as grotesque. Other possibilities included Darwin's tubercle, a genetic trait which can affect the outer cartilage of the ear; or sebaceous horns or cysts, horny growths which can occur on different parts of the body, sometimes dropping off and regrowing: one heard of cases that included a Scotsman who had such a growth at the base of his spine which stayed with him; and of an unfortunate girl in Cheshire in the seventeenth century, who was afflicted with a pair of very painful sebaceous horns on her forehead, which regularly fell off and then regrew. However, none of these seemed an adequate diagnosis of the case of our patient. Much more attractive was the answer proposed by Dr Roger Wood, the Reader in Genetics at Manchester University, who suggested a hereditary condition known as 'hairy pinnae', sometimes found associated with Darwin's tubercle. It is one of the very few genes on the Y-chromosome – in other words it is passed through the male line only – and it

PLATE I

The final version of the head of King Midas in bronzed resin. (Chapter 5)

PLATE II

The final reconstruction of mummy Manchester 1770. (Chapter 3)

PLATE III

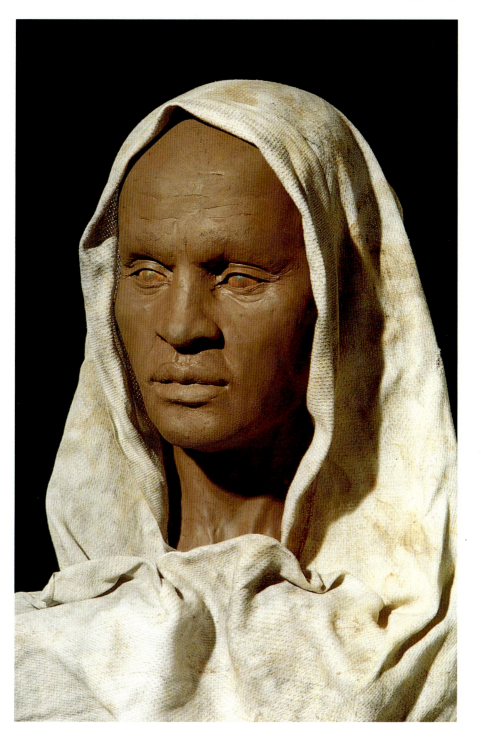

The reconstructed face of Natsef-Amun. (Chapter 3)

PLATE IV

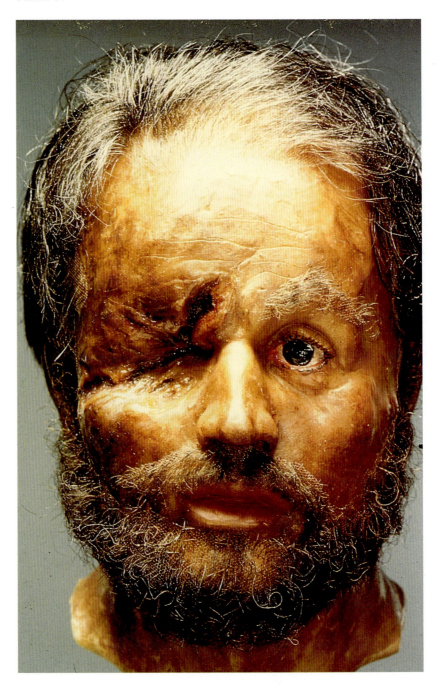

The first waxwork reconstruction of the head of Philip II. The eye wound is rendered as it would have healed without treatment. Even with the beard and moustache the slightly lopsided mouth betrays the malformed face in this frontal view - but only if one looks hard. (Chapter 4)

PLATE V

The final waxwork version of the reconstructed head of Philip II. (Chapter 4)

PLATE VI

The painting of the 'mummy' from Grave Circle A (Grave V) at Mycenae, made for Schliemann at the time of its discovery in 1876. (Chapter 6)

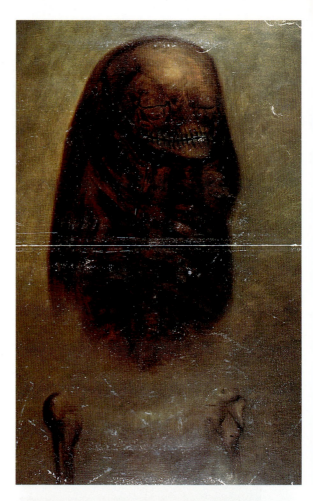

The electrum mask from Grave Gamma in Grave Circle B at Mycenae. (Chapter 6)

PLATE VII

The five gold masks from Grave Circle A at Mycenae. (Chapter 6)

PLATE VIII

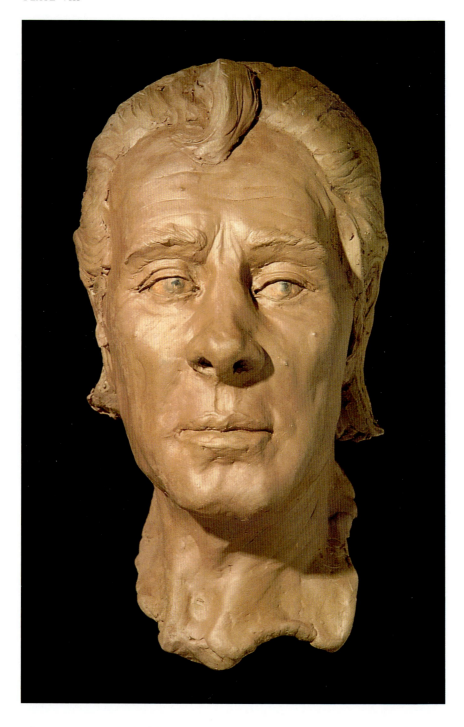

The reconstructed head of the priest from Anemospilia, showing the quiff of hair on his forehead. (Chapter 7)

PLATE IX

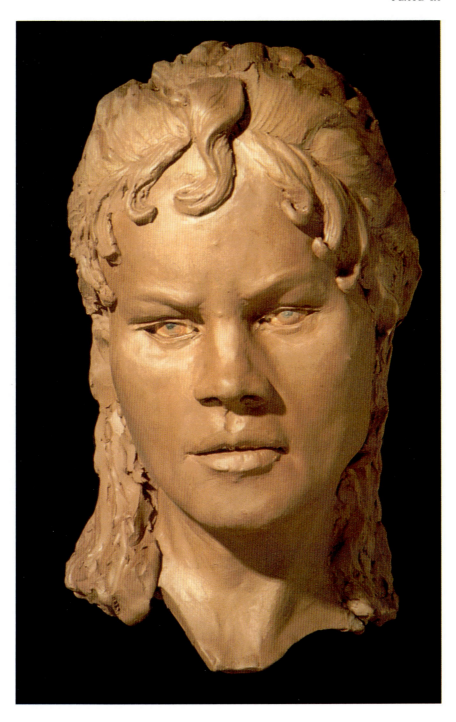

The reconstructed head of the priestess from Anemospilia, showing the locks arranged over her forehead and framing her face. (Chapter 7)

PLATE X

The body of Lindow Man as found. (Chapter 8)

PLATE XI

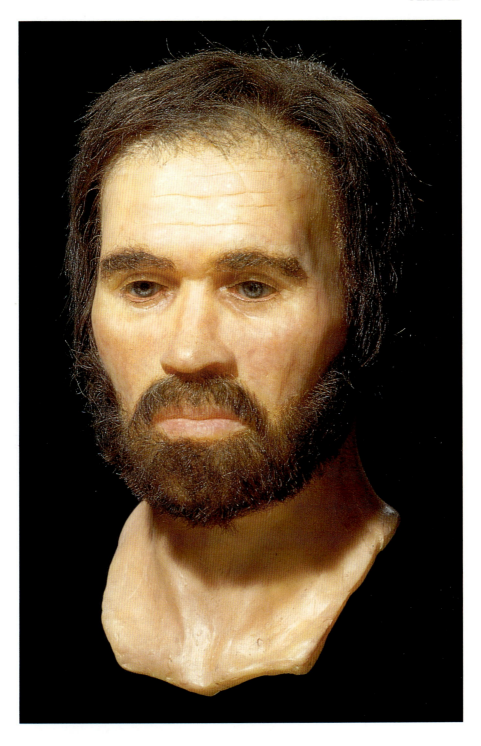

A 'studio' photograph of the waxwork reconstruction of Lindow Man. (Chapter 8)

PLATE XII

The Yde Girl shortly after discovery. (Chapter 8)

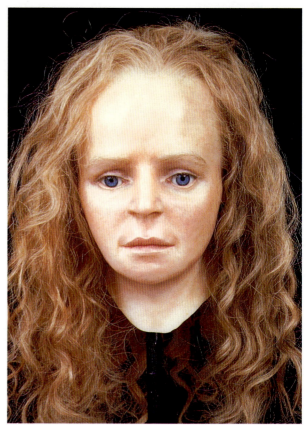

Waxwork reconstruction of the head of the Yde Girl. (Chapter 8)

PLATE XIII

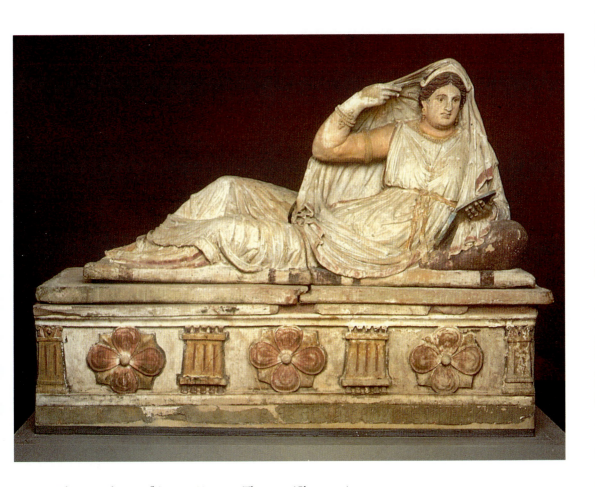

The sarcophagus of Seianti Hanunia Tlesnasa. (Chapter 9)

PLATE XIV

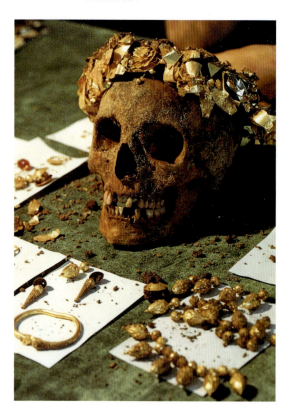

The skull of the 'Carian Princess' immediately after discovery, with some of her gold jewellery. (Chapter 10)

Profile view of the reconstruction of the head of Ada I, the 'Carian Princess', in bronzed resin. Details of the hairstyle and the hairnet are clearly visible. (Chapter 10)

PLATE XV

Front view of the reconstructed head of Ada I, the 'Carian Princess', in bronzed resin. (Chapter 10)

PLATE XVI

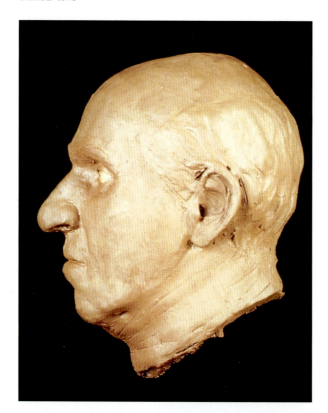

The reconstructed head of the 'unknown Dutchman'. (Codicil)

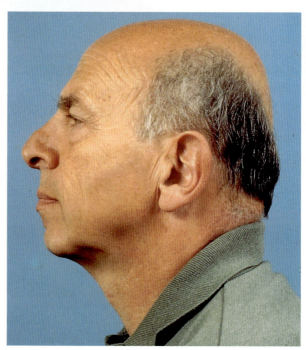

Professor Peter Egyedi. (Codicil)

causes hair to sprout on the outer or upper edges of the ear (or both), and usually first shows itself in the third decade of life. In extreme forms it can take on a distinctly animal-like appearance, 'recalling the ears of monkeys' according to an Italian doctor describing a case in 1901. E. Thurston described a case among the Todas tribe in southern India, where a man 'showed a dense growth of long, straight hairs diverted outwards on the helix of both ears', and commented that this bore a striking resemblance to the development of hairs on the ears of the 'Madras macaque' or 'bonnet' monkey. It is precisely the condition of which only one's barber would be aware. The condition is apparently now most common in the Indian subcontinent, but it is also found in modern Italy, and less frequently in Iran, Malta and Great Britain.[29] How prevalent it is in modern Turkey and in northern Greece, the traditional homeland of the Phrygians, is obviously something that would merit further research. There is, for instance, the case of St Hilarion, whose story is painted on the walls of the church in the monastery of Sumela, in the mountains above Trabzon in northern Turkey: such were his good looks that he was continually pestered by the girls, and so he prayed for something to put a stop to this; when he thereupon sprouted ass's ears the young ladies soon found him less attractive, and he was left to meditate and pray in peace. If Dr Wood's theory is tenable it would prove interesting to investigate whether there is any correlation between the places where hairy pinnae occur, and where the tale of the king (or the saint) with ass's ears is found.

Armed with this knowledge, we set off for Ankara in September 1988. Midas' remains were now at the Palaeoanthropology Division of the University of Ankara in the care of Professor Berna Alpagut, who for the next week allowed our team to turn her office into a makeshift conservation laboratory and casting studio, and with magnificent lack of concern for the mess we were creating offered us every form of assistance for which we could wish, practical, administrative and academic. The moment when she brought in the skull was exciting for everyone, herself included: whether it proved to be Midas or not, even the sceptics agreed that this had been a great king. It looked as if the skull was still in the same cardboard box in which it had been brought from Gordion long before. As far as we knew, little if any work had been done on it since then, and few people had even seen it. Professor Alpagut had certainly never had the chance to study it before: later she compiled the first proper anthropological report on the skull for us. There was no skeleton with it, and searches revealed nothing further. This was a disappointment, but not a surprise, for the other bones had not been discussed since they were brought to Ankara thirty-one years previously. The explanation probably lay in the circumstances of their excavation in 1957.

When the skull was discovered it was evidently complete save for a hole in the top of the cranium; there is no suggestion in the excavation notebooks or in the final report that it was in poor condition, in contrast to the very fragmentary human remains found in the neighbouring tumuli P and W at Gordion.[30] However, after nearly 2,700 years the airtight and environmentally stable conditions of the tomb were suddenly and drastically changed when the drilling process unexpectedly allowed quantities of the water used for cooling the drills to enter. Some was still

standing in the chamber when it was opened the following year. In complete contrast with the mint condition of the other metalwork from the tomb, the bronze
fibulae which had been in a bag by the body were very badly corroded, some of
them so much so that they were not considered worth publishing. The floor beam
at the foot of the skeleton had been badly rotted by water although the other timbers are as a rule perfectly preserved, and in contrast with the other furniture, parts
of the coffin in which the body lay were so badly decayed that for long it was not
properly recognised, and was wrongly identified as a bed. Having discussed the
problem with Professors DeVries and Sams, it seems to us most likely that the
water from the drilling lay just in the area of the body, so that after being in a near-
perfect stable environment for so long, the sudden and prolonged immersion was
too much for the bones, and without prompt expert conservation and controlled
storage the rest of the skeleton has since decayed. One has to recall that the sound
that had greeted Young when he first entered the freshly opened tomb had been the
gentle crackle of disintegrating wooden furniture.[31] Fortunately the skull excited
special interest from the outset, and as a result it has survived almost intact, though
now in need of attention.

The skull is noticeably light and all the exposed edges are extremely brittle, particularly in places that have already been damaged, such as the top of the cranium
or the sockets of the teeth on both jaws, and in areas where the cancellous inner
bone was exposed. When it was excavated a piece of the vault towards the back of
the head was already missing; since then this hole has apparently been enlarged, and
the skull has been damaged further around the right eye-socket and cheekbone (the
supraorbital margin and the zygomatic arch) and on the right side of the nose where
the bone has become porous, possibly the effect of immersion in water: the nasal
bone is by its nature a thin and vulnerable area, and often suffers on ancient skulls.
Some areas have a loose encrustation of what appears to be calcium carbonate, others are covered with an unidentified soft whitish deposit. The lower jaw is in two
pieces, with part of the right side and some other small pieces missing. All the teeth
that remained to him at death have since fallen out, with the exception of three
roots that are still in place in the lower jaw, but we found several teeth which belong
to this skull loose in the box, as well as a few that belonged to the occupant of one
of the other tumuli.

It was obviously essential that this very fragile skull was made fit to handle before
any serious work could begin, and with this risk in mind we had invited Danaë
Thimme, Objects Conservator at the Indiana University Art Museum, to join our
team: as on any archaeological project, conservation is always a relatively unpre-
dictable factor. The delicate, friable surface with its loose deposits was quite unsuit-
able for taking a mould in its present condition. Some consolidation of the surface
had been undertaken earlier, presumably by Professor Şenyürek when he took
charge of the skull at the time of its discovery in 1957, and this had undoubtedly
prevented it from deteriorating in the way that the rest of the skeleton had done,
but his treatment made some parts such as the mandible appear deceptively sound.
It also caused other problems, not merely because it had darkened the bone and,
being slightly sticky, had attracted dirt, but also because it had (deliberately)

rendered much of the surface impermeable, so that it was very difficult to make the new consolidant penetrate the bone at all: because the old and new consolidants were incompatible, the new material had to be injected carefully into the exposed edges until we felt that the skull was strong enough to withstand the rigours of casting, however gentle. Some of the cracks were reinforced with fibreglass, and one or two pieces that had become detached in the box were glued back in place. Then at last the skull could be handled safely, and was ready for the next stage.[32]

It was photographed both before and after conservation, so that we should have as accurate a record as possible. Because none of our medical colleagues had been able to come to Turkey, we next set the skull on a stand and rotated it slowly in front of the videocamera to a running commentary on its condition and any visible pathology: thus we created a 'guided tour of the skull for anatomists' on which they would be able to comment later. This tape proved to be an extremely valuable *aide-mémoire* and visual notebook for others as well.

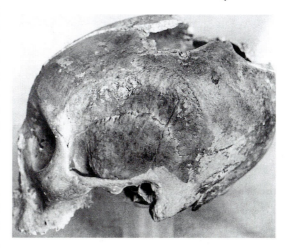

4. *Profile view of the skull of Midas after conservation: the elongation of the cranium, caused by bandaging in infancy, is clearly visible.*

One of the most noticeable things about the skull as one held it in one's hands was its unusual shape (fig.4). The posterior part in the region of the occipital, temporal and parietal bones was strongly flattened on each side of the skull: that is, the sides were noticeably flattened and the top pushed up almost into a ridge. The frontal bone (forehead) also sloped backwards. According to Professor Alpagut's anthropological measurements the skull was low and long-headed (dolichocephalic), long-faced (at least in the upper face), with medium nose and high eye-sockets. She suggested that the unusual flattening was the result of cosmetic bandaging in infancy, when bands of cloth were wrapped tightly around the baby's head to make it grow into what was regarded as an attractive elongated shape. Such treatment would have had no effect on the brain inside, and was not uncommonly found on Anatolian skulls of this period.[33]

While the skull was being treated the casting of the two pieces of the mandible could already begin. Small two-part moulds were made from dental alginate. This normally straightforward procedure produced the only serious problem of the whole exercise, for when the moulds were removed we found the bone to be less robust than it appeared: the consolidant with which it had been treated on excavation had in fact hardly penetrated the bone at all, but had formed a thin layer on the surface, so brittle that a stiff alginate mixture might have torn it apart. Happily the mandible had not been seriously damaged, but it was a salutary reminder of what

can happen, however careful one may be. Thereupon the bone was further strength-
ened with cellulose nitrate adhesive and strips of fibreglass to forestall any further
damage in handling.

The preparation of the skull followed a now-familiar pattern. The foramen magnum in the base of the skull was gently blocked with a soft plasticine-like material
called 'Plasterlini' mixed with talcum powder, which was squeezed into and around
holes and indentations without the risk of adhering to the surface. Then the cranium was packed with polyester waste, which we had by now found to be a better
substitute for cotton wool, for it does not catch and tear on protrusions, and the
missing area of the vault filled with a thin layer of 'Plasterlini'. Next the eye-
sockets and the nasal cavity were packed and covered in the same way. All those
areas that would create 'undercuts' and thus put strain on the skull when it was
removed from the mould were filled, and the fragile, damaged edges masked with
'Plasterlini'. The final stage was to cover the whole of the skull with a layer of very
thin aluminium foil, burnished into place. This
procedure takes some time, but it does guarantee
(as far as possible) that specimens will not be
damaged. By the end of the second day the
mandible had been cast, and the skull in its glittering silver sheath stood ready to be cast in its
turn.

The following day work began on making the
mould by fixing a 'collar' horizontally around the
middle of the skull. A layer of dental alginate was
then puddled over one side of the skull up to the
collar, and this in turn covered with a thin layer
of plaster to give it support. When this had set
the skull was turned over, the collar removed,
and the procedure repeated, thus creating the
two halves of the mould (fig. 5).

The opening of the mould under these circumstances can be a rather tense affair, and after
the trouble with the mandible it came as a great
relief when the skull came out of the mould in
perfect condition. The mould was ready to be
used for making the plaster cast, and the actual
skull could be returned to safe storage. First it
was further consolidated, and when thoroughly

5. The skull of Midas being cast:
the two halves of the mould
(dental alginate inside a plaster
casing) are checked.

dry it was packed with acid-free tissue and put into a new padded box. By the time
we had finished we reckoned that the mortal remains of Midas (if he it is) had again
been treated with at least some of the respect due to royalty.

However, even after making the cast of the skull we were not quite finished.
Before leaving England we had agreed that we should make a reconstruction of the
face, of a very preliminary nature, and leave it in Ankara as a token of thanks to our
Turkish colleagues. It would be the equivalent of an artist's sketch.

The actual reconstructing of the face is not necessarily a slow process. Indeed if everything is to hand it can be carried through very quickly, but of all the heads that first Midas was probably made with the greatest speed and in the most concentrated manner. The cast of the skull was mounted on a simple wooden stand, and the cast of the mandible fixed in position by 'floating' it into place on clay that had been packed around the base of the skull. The eye-sockets had to be hollowed out before the skull was mounted to allow eyeballs – prepared before we left home – to be put in place. Then on to drilling small holes at twenty-one prescribed points, and to cutting and inserting the wooden marker pegs to indicate the correct thickness of the soft tissue. Next the measurements for the nose and the building of the supports for that area. Preparation is all-important, for without it there would be so much guess-work that the technique would lose all credibility.

As the basic muscle groups were added the skull began to change into a head, not recognisable as an individual but no longer just bone. The layers grew, the different facial muscles were put in place – orbicularis oculi, temporalis, masseter, buccinator, orbicularis oris, zygomaticus major, and so on. A slightly protruding lower lip, a nose with convex dorsal ridge. That strangely shaped cranium. The old man's features grew slowly and in an orderly manner to the point at which one could do no more in the time available. One never knows in advance how a particular face will look: those who wait for the results with preconceived ideas are frequently taken aback at what they see. The face that stared back sadly into the room was unlike anyone we had ever known. However, because the cast of the skull that was our working tool was still inside that sombre face we could not leave it behind, and it was necessary to make a quick three-quarter cast of the face in a single-piece mould to leave with Berna Alpagut before removing all the clay and packing the cast of the skull ready for the journey back to Manchester.

Once safely home in the familiar surroundings of the studio one could settle down and rebuild the face all over again with more care and consideration, and finish the final version in much greater detail. The face grew again from the surface of the skull outwards. Again the same curiously shaped head became clear to see, the long face, lightly built in its upper half with fine features but more substantial below and having a well-developed lower jaw, the old man's slightly curving nose and the slightly protruding lower lip. There is of course no evidence for his hair, but since we knew the man was in his sixties it seemed uncontentious to give him receding hair and a bald spot.

We had to admit that so far we had found no evidence for the ass's ears either, no knobbly protrusions on the skull that might have indicated neurofibromas, but if Roger Wood's theory of the hairy pinnae was correct then we could not have expected to find any. Intellectually, the correct thing was to make this reconstruction 'straight', adding nothing for which there was no hard evidence. However, we had after all explored the possibilities behind the story of the ears fairly thoroughly before going to Turkey, and it would have been wrong not to use the opportunity which making a reconstruction provides to illustrate ears with hairy pinnae in three dimensions, not least because by now there was considerable Press interest in the whole venture.

At this point we had another of those strokes of good fortune that seem to come our way at just the right moment. During our earlier discussions on asinauricularity someone happened to notice Dr Ali Ahmed from the Department of Pathological Sciences passing by, with what looked like distinctly grubby ears. When one remarked on his obviously keeping his ear well to the ground he muttered something about having forgotten to shave them, and reappeared soon after with nice clean ears. After some gentle probing we learnt Dr Ahmed's secret: he too suffered from hairy pinnae. His family came from northern Pakistan, one of the areas where the condition is found. After some persuasion he agreed to 'grow' his ears for us, in the name of scientific research. But he is a man who cares about his appearance, so

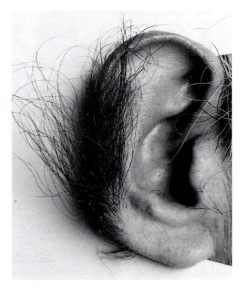

he also let his hair grow longer to cover them – at least the fashions of the later twentieth century AD allowed him this cover-up, though he admitted that as it grew the hair on his ears became so straggly that he had to use a gel to keep it neat. By the time Dr Ahmed took early retirement in 1991 (and was at last free to shave his ears again) the outer edges of his ears were covered in a fairly thick growth of hair: over some three years it had gradually thickened, but had never grown much longer than a few centimetres (fig. 6). Nonetheless it was easy to see how it could provoke suspicion and even alarm among people who could not understand its cause, and even after a year Dr Ahmed had already provided us with an excellent model for Midas. The result was a clay reconstruction sprouting a convincing growth of hair on the pinnae of its ears (fig. 7).

6. *The ear of a sufferer from 'hairy pinnae',*
after seventeen months' growth.

However, things were moving on already. Dr John Lilley, a Consultant and Senior Lecturer in Conservative Dentistry at the Turner Dental Hospital in Manchester University, studied the dentition of the skull from the casts and photographs. He commented particularly on a feature of the lower jaw which we had already noticed, namely the form of the alveolar margin, that part of the bone in which the front teeth are set. It was turned forward very markedly, suggesting that the lower teeth were set at a very shallow angle: even if they did not actually protrude themselves, they pushed the lower lip forward even further than our first reconstructions had indicated. He added that he had seen this condition on only two living patients, both teenage girls who had been thrown from their horses, and who had needed surgery to correct it. If Midas suffered such an accident, he evidently had to live with the consequences. The second full version of the reconstruction was thus slightly different in the region of the mouth – seen best in profile – but no other

8. *The final version of the head of King Midas in bronzed resin: profile view, showing the protruding lower lip caused by the angle of the lower front teeth.*

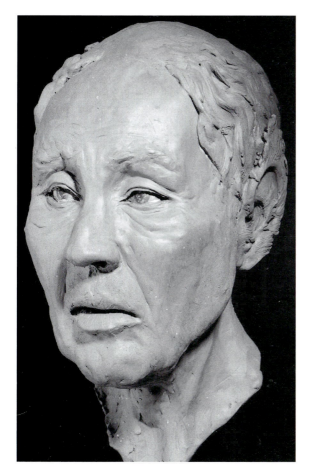

7. *Reconstruction of the head of King Midas in clay: the ass's ears are represented as hairy pinnae.*

significant physical changes have yet been suggested (fig. 8 and pl. 1). There is undoubtedly still more that the skull can tell us, using modern investigative techniques: however, this would mean bringing it to England, and although Professor Alpagut herself suggested this we have not yet been able to arrange it.

All the reconstructions are in effect three-dimensional reports on the work that has been done so far, and thus one can never call any version 'final' because further comment and research may call for changes – witness Philip II's eye injury. However, all try to be as objective and detached as possible, as any academic report should be: because there really is no hard evidence for the hairy pinnae, on the most recent reconstruction Midas' ears are now shown 'clean'. Without this crucial evidence which Veli Sevin had hoped that we might discover we could of course not bring forward any medical proof that he was actually Midas. None the less we found the archaeological arguments in favour of the identification convincing, and this, added to the impressions left by visiting the tomb itself with the director of the Gordion Museum, and seeing the magnificent finds in the museum in Ankara, inevitably influenced the artist into creating the face of a sensitive, careworn and balding old man, a figure who matches the stories that were told about Midas and who died, perhaps by his own hand, as the barbarians swept through his capital city. Because the rendering of the hair disturbed some scholars, we produced an adaptation of the last version that avoided the issue by covering his head with a 'turban' similar to that worn by a silver statuette of a priest found recently in a tomb at Elmalı in southwest Turkey and dated between 730 and 670 BC – contemporary with the tomb and reminiscent of the turban of the Midas stories: although actually in Lycia, the site (or at least the tombs at Elmalı) are thought by many scholars to be those of Phrygian settlers.[34] But Midas or Gordios, the finds from his tomb suggest that the man in the Midas Mound was a man of taste. Sometimes the archaeologist feels he has to keep the artist in check, but restrains himself as he realises how much of the excitement would be lost if he did.

We are often asked whether much of what we do could not be done more quickly by computer: as computer graphics develop they can certainly take over some of the groundwork, particularly when dealing with heads where tissue remains such as bog bodies and mummies, as we have shown in Chapters 3 and 8, but the final detailing and interpretation has to be performed by an artist who understands his subject. Without that element the result will be bland and unstimulating. We have not proved that the skull from the Midas Mound is the King Midas who ruled Phrygia from 738 to 696 BC, but we have reassessed the story of the ass's ears in a completely new manner. One may indeed question the assumption that the stories about the legendary Midas should really be attached to this historical figure. Many of them seem to hark back to folk memory, and to Greek travellers' tales. The Phrygians are already known in the Old Testament as traders in copper.[35] It is easy to see how the gleaming bronze and brass with which the man in the Midas Mound – King Midas – was surrounded in life as well as in death could inspire a traveller from a Greece that was still poor, still emerging from the economic depression of the Dark Age and entering into a period of fast-growing contact with the wealthy cultures of Western Asia, to return home with reports of the fabulous riches that he had seen in Gordion: the excavations have made it clear that Gordion was indeed a very wealthy city, and the 115 bronze or brass drinking cups from the Midas Mound must have been put there as a piece of ostentation.[36] A Greek traveller might well report, 'That king is so rich that everything he touches turns to gold.' Another such traveller's tale could readily turn the custom of the king's unshorn hair, or a sight of the hairy pinnae of medical fact, into the ass's ears of folklore.

One might add that hairy pinnae are only a mild form of superfluous facial hair: like the unhappy 'Elephant Man' disfigured by severe neurofibromatosis, those who suffer from more extreme conditions, where the whole of the face except the lips is covered with a thick growth of hair, have usually been regarded with fear and horror as wolf-men, and have at the very least been driven out of society. Perhaps Midas was treated more kindly after all.

CHAPTER 6

Have I gazed upon the face of Agamemnon?
Grave Circle B at Mycenae

Whose face did we actually want to reconstruct after completing the first version of Philip? His son Alexander the Great was the obvious choice, but Alexander's bones have not been excavated, indeed his tomb has not even been discovered.[1] So if not Alexander the Great, why not Agamemnon? It was an intriguing suggestion. As with Midas, we were once again on the borders of legend and history, though not this time with any prospect of using our team's resources to prove an identity, but rather to put a face behind a mask. As so often with our reconstructions, if others were to take what we were doing seriously, if we were truly setting out to answer important historical questions rather than merely providing display pieces to excite and intrigue, then we had to understand the background to the people whose remains we were studying.

The background to Agamemnon was a complex one. There was Agamemnon, king of Mycenae and leader of the Greeks against Troy in the poems of Homer; and there was a gold mask found at Mycenae known as 'the face of Agamemnon'. Here we came up against that other Homeric figure, about whom almost as many stories have grown up as about Agamemnon himself, the German businessman-turned-archaeologist Heinrich Schliemann. Unlike the academics who were his contemporaries, Schliemann approached the problem of the Trojan War with the overriding belief that real events and real people lay behind the ancient texts, whether they were the poems of Homer, probably composed in the eighth century BC, or the guide book which the traveller Pausanias wrote in the second century AD. To Schliemann it did not matter that the places which they named as great cities were now ruins or at best small villages. Homer described Agamemnon's capital at Mycenae as a 'well-built city', 'rich in gold', but even at the time he composed his poems in the eighth century BC this can no longer have been true. Destroyed in the Late Bronze Age, it never recovered its greatness. After a revival in the third century BC as a dependency of Argos, Mycenae faded away, and by the second century AD it was a deserted ruin, above which stood ruined walls so great that they were believed to be the work of the giant Cyclopes. Having already discovered and excavated the city of Troy on the hill of Hisarlik above the Dardanelles, Schliemann now came to Mycenae in order to find the graves of Agamemnon and his followers, which the local people had shown to Pausanias within the ruins some seventeen hundred years earlier.[2]

In November 1876, within weeks of starting work, he located the circle of shaft graves that we now know as Grave Circle A, and excavated them in the following weeks, often under extremely difficult conditions. He cleared five shaft graves; his

Greek colleague Stamatakis later discovered the sixth. Because of their position inside the walls, corresponding to Pausanias' albeit sketchy description, and because of their great wealth, Schliemann was convinced that he had found Agamemnon and his companions. In total he discovered the remains of nineteen bodies, probably eight men, nine women and two children. Five of them had gold masks (pl.vii) placed over their faces, while the bodies of the two children were covered with plain gold sheets. The excitement which he felt at these discoveries, and at the conviction that his faith in the ancient texts was again being proved right, comes through in his reports, in the telegrams and letters to *The Times* in which he announced his discoveries, in letters to his friends in Germany and England, notably to Professor Max Müller in Oxford, who frequently had to tone down some of his more dramatic accounts before sending them on to *The Times:* 'I am quite in despair today, my painter having left me…life is terrible here; there is no shade, all is dirty and the privations of all kinds are litterally [*sic*] overwhelming. One must have the holy fire for science to support all this…'; or, more cheerfully, 'The three bodies are literally overwhelmed with jewels' and 'There are in all 5 tombs, in the smallest of which I found yesterday the bones of a man and a woman covered by at least five kilograms of jewels of pure gold, with the most wonderful archaic, impressed ornaments…' Schliemann has often been accused of embellishing the accounts of his discoveries as he wrote them up later. The evidence for this is far from conclusive, but in trying to piece together what Schliemann actually thought and did on a particular day one often feels like a detective investigating a case where every witness is prejudiced. However, none of this takes away from the sheer thrill that Schliemann so clearly felt. On 1 December 1876 he wrote in his notebook a draft of the report which he intended to submit to *The Times,* which runs:

But of the 3ᵈ body…the round face, with all its flesh, had been wonderfully preserved under its ponderous golden mask; there was no vestige of hair, but both eyes were perfectly visible, also the mouth, which owing to the enormous weight that had pressed upon it, was wide open, and showed 32 beautiful teeth; by these, all the physicians who came to see the body were led to believe that the man must have been at the age of 35. The nose had entirely gone…In its squeezed and mutilated state the body measured only 2 ft 4½ inches [72.4 cm] from the top of the head to the beginning of the loins; the breadth of the shoulders did not exceed 1 ft 1¼ inch [33.7 cm] and the breadth of the stomach 1 ft 3 inch [38.1 cm]; and the pressure of the rubbish and stones and rubbish [*sic*] had been such that the body had been reduced to a thickness of 1-1½ inch [2.5–3.8 cm], but the 1 ft 8 inch long [50.8 cm] thighbones could leave no doubt regarding the real proportions of the body. The colour of the corps [*sic*] resembled that of an Egyptian mummy…The news that the tolerably well preserved body of a man of the mythic heroic age had been found, covered with golden ornaments, spread like a rolling fire through the Argolid, and people came by thousands from Argos and Nauplia to see the wonder, but nobody being able to give advise [*sic*] on how to conserve the body, I sent for a painter to get at least an oil painting made [see pl. vi], for I was afraid that the whole body would fall to pieces. [In the printed report he later added: 'Thus I am enabled to give a faithful likeness of the body, as it looked after all the golden ornaments had been removed.'] But to my great joy, it held out for two days, when a druggist from Argos, Spiridon Nikolaou by name, consolidated it by moistening it with spirit in which he had dissolved sandarac. Thus I have now strong hopes that it can be saved…

It was of the mask belonging to this body, 'with the round face', that Schliemann telegraphed to the minister in Athens, and to the Greek Press, that he was 'very like the picture which my imagination formed of wide-ruling Agamemnon long ago'.[3] The story has been dramatised further in archaeological folklore and Schliemann is supposed to have sent his telegram to the king of Greece himself, describing instead the finest and most beautiful of the masks, the one with the beard and moustache. This was the one of which our colleagues were thinking when they suggested, even if in jest, a reconstruction of Agamemnon. To avoid confusion, we shall refer to this one as 'the beautiful mask' (pl. VII, centre).

Later work has made it clear that none of the remains found by Schliemann could be those of the king who led the Greeks against Troy in the Late Bronze Age, around 1250 or 1190 BC (opinions differ). For the moment he remains a figure who hovers between legend and history like King Arthur, for the Shaft Graves are to be dated at least three hundred years earlier, to the sixteenth century BC, and span the transition from the Middle into the Late Bronze Ages. Yet with such wealth, the men and women whom Schliemann had discovered were still people of power and authority. Five of them had been buried with gold masks placed over their faces, and a sixth such mask was found later during the excavation of the second Grave Circle at Mycenae in 1952–4. These masks are unique in Bronze Age Greece. One may try to seek parallels in contemporary Egypt, and connections have been sought there for some of the other finds from the Shaft Graves, but only with very limited success. There is nothing of which we know that bursts upon the Mycenaean world in the same way. The whole period of the Shaft Graves covers perhaps five generations: in Bronze Age terms this is probably little over a century, from late Middle Helladic to the very beginning of Late Helladic IIA, which can be variously taken as the years between c. 1625 and 1500 BC or 1600 and 1480 BC.[4] The Mycenaeans who came after, in the fifteenth century and later, stated their social position in different ways.

Whoever their owners were, the gold masks stand as powerful testimony to the wealth and power of the people in the Shaft Graves, whether in life or in death. But whose were the faces behind the masks, if not those of Agamemnon and his family? The date when the Greeks first came to Greece is being steadily adjusted. Fifty years ago and less the Bronze Age Mycenaeans could still be thought of as non-Greek-speaking 'barbarians', but now it is generally held that the first Greek-speakers arrived in Greece around 1900 BC if not earlier. Against the background of Egyptian reunification and expansion in the Middle Kingdom and the upheavals of the Second Intermediate Period, of Hurrian and Hittite attacks and consolidation, of Assyrian commercial growth and of Mesopotamian influence in Anatolia, and above all of the prosperity that led to the building of the first palaces in Crete, there came the first flowering of the Mycenaean civilisation. During the hundred or so years when the Shaft Graves were in use, roughly the sixteenth century BC, many features that became typical of the Mycenaean civilisation took shape on the Greek mainland, from innovations in pottery and the introduction of new types of artefacts to new forms of tombs. It seems to have been a process of acculturation as different elements were adopted or developed at different times in different parts of the Peloponnese, to mingle with each other and with the earlier Middle Helladic traditions to form a relatively homogeneous culture by about 1500 BC (Late Helladic IIA). Behind this cultural upheaval lies historical and social turmoil as petty states were created under the leadership of a ruling class which showed its status through increasingly elaborate tombs, and with costly possessions, often imported from abroad or made in Greece by foreign craftsmen, especially from Middle Minoan Crete. The nature and extent of this Cretan influence is a fertile field for debate, and the most ardent proponents of the 'Minoanisation' theory would even suggest that among the new ruling families were actual Minoans, who had brought these objects and these practices with them from Crete: there are anthropologists who hold that it is possible to distinguish Mycenaean from Minoan skulls by their measurements.

A focus of these great changes lay on the plain of Argos, 'the powerhouse of the Late Bronze Age Greek world'. During the seventeenth and sixteenth centuries local petty chiefdoms seem to have grown into palace-based societies. Mycenae acquired great wealth in the process, and was probably already building the commercial links that later became vital to Mycenaean life and power. The Shaft Graves provide the best if not the only sequence to span this period of consolidation.

Short though this span is, the two Grave Circles provide a crucial and fascinating key to the change (fig. 1). Thus far we have dwelt on Grave Circle A, that found by Schliemann in 1876, but it must be treated together with the second circle, Grave Circle B, discovered nearly a century later. The differences are as important as the similarities. Grave Circle B lies a little further from the citadel of Mycenae than Circle A. It is some two generations older, and contained twenty-six graves of different types seemingly arranged in three or four groups within the circle and not laid out according to any regular orientation. Many had been disturbed by later graves – indeed, it was perfectly clear that no great shame was incurred in moving the occupant of an earlier grave roughly to one side and taking his or her grave goods away if a later burial intruded on it.[5] Most significantly, a completely unrelated built grave (Rho) was inserted into one of the burials in the mid-fifteenth century BC, and the east side of the circle had been cut into by the construction of the tholos-tomb known now as the 'Tomb of Clytemnestra', probably late in the fourteenth century. If Grave Circle B was still visible, it is likely that the builders of these tombs were deliberately claiming prestige, even a connection, with the earlier tombs; but if not – and the intrusive cutting of the 'Tomb of Clytemnestra' into the Grave Circle makes this more likely – then we must assume that within two or three hundred years at most and probably less than a century after the last burial the inhabitants of Mycenae no longer knew of or cared for its existence.

In sharp contrast, Circle A, Schliemann's circle, though it incorporated a number of earlier simple graves, contained only six shaft graves (all save one with multiple burials), closely grouped and generally laid out east to west. While the largest and richest graves in Circle B were closely paralleled by the poorer ones in Circle A, three of the graves in A (numbers IV and V, containing the gold masks, and number III, where the children were wrapped in gold sheets), were far richer than any of the others. In contrast to the neglect and slighting of Circle B, Circle A was left untouched, and in the thirteenth century it was tidied and given a new wall, and the citadel walls were extended in order to take it into the city itself. Pausanias described the tombs of Agamemnon and his followers as lying within the city walls, and it was this point that convinced Schliemann that he was on the right track – and convinced his opponents that he was *not*, for in historic times adults were virtually never buried inside a town wall. Evidently even in the Late Bronze Age the graves in Circle A were felt to be of such great importance that those who ruled Mycenae at this time wished them to be treated with special respect. In order to appreciate fully who they were, and what kind of people they were, we had also to appreciate what image of themselves they were intending to project, for before this amazing

1. Mycenae: the site from the air. Grave Circle A is in the centre of the picture, inside the curve of the 'new' wall; Grave Circle B lies below, across the road from the modern car park.

blaze of gold Mycenae in the Middle Helladic period had been a relatively unsophisticated and unpretentious place.

The Shaft Graves are noteworthy because they seem to have been planned as distinctive groups of burials, apparently used by family groups and often 'flagged' by grave markers in the form of ornately carved limestone stelae. Since it is very unlikely that these elaborate graves could have been dug in the time that could elapse between the death of the intended occupant and his or her burial, we must assume that they were prepared during the lifetime of the first occupant, and reopened when further bodies were to be interred. There may have been a two-stage burial process, but in practice it is clear that the earlier bodies were simply moved to one side, sometimes rather unceremoniously, and sometimes not so very long after their interment. Therefore the nature and situation of the tomb were probably intended to say more about the image the family wished to project in life than to indicate the respect in which they were held in death. Second, the graves are generally striking for the richness of the goods buried with their owners, an example of conspicuous consumption of 'consumer durables', with the added economic drawback that this wealth was being permanently withdrawn from the economy. At the end of the Middle Bronze Age the message that was being sent out can only have been one of status and of power.

In Grave Circle B we can see the development from simple pit graves cut in the rock to contain a single body to more elaborate multiple burials placed in lined and roofed shaft graves, but the variety of burial types and the fact that there seems to be no overriding preconceived grouping or orientation to the twenty-six graves suggests that these are still the tombs of discrete family groups, reopened when necessary to insert a further body as the custom changed from single burials to the repeated use of a family tomb. The graves in this circle overlap in time, covering three or perhaps four generations, so this is no single line of rulers. Their wealth is growing, and the fact that the whole assemblage was enclosed by a wall makes it clear that locally at least this was a class apart. But even so, perhaps as little as a century later these people were already ignored and forgotten at Mycenae.

The burials in Grave Circle A also overlap with these and with each other in time, but extend a generation or so later. These graves too were reopened from time to time so that further burials could be made – a very cumbersome practice. So perhaps not surprisingly these are the last Shaft Graves, for then the Mycenaeans adapted the custom that had been developing in Messenia in southwestern Greece, of burying the wealthier dead in chamber-tombs dug into the hillside with doors that could be reopened, with the variation that for those whom we must assume to be the nobility they built nine tholoi, beehive-shaped chamber-tombs lined with corbelled masonry. The first six of these tholoi overlap with the Shaft Graves in time and then form a sequence with them, and the way in which they are grouped on the slopes around Mycenae, particularly over the next fifty years (1490–1440 BC = Late Helladic IIA), may imply that they are the graves not of a line of kings, ruling alone, but of a group of leading families, 'warrior chieftains', who were possibly related to each other and who shared power between them in some way. It is difficult to explain otherwise why six such tholoi should have been built and used for repeated burials over half a century, and to have been treated with special respect for many generations afterwards. These tombs were clearly intended as statements of status by the people who had had them built, but because most were eventually robbed of their grave goods we can no longer be sure if here too their owners were indulging in the kind of display that was being made in the Grave Circles.

Then the pattern changes and for a hundred years or so authority at Mycenae seems to have been marked in different ways, until in the mid-thirteenth century the citadel wall is rebuilt and extended in such a way as to take in the newly refurbished Grave Circle A, now three hundred years old. There is no parallel for such an action, and as a piece of engineering it was a difficult task, for the new wall, which terminated at the new Lion Gate, had to be built up to overcome a sharp drop in the rock. The new ruler of Mycenae wished to make his statement of authority by creating or stressing his link with the former rulers who had so pointedly grouped their graves in the midst of the earlier cemetery. On the chronology suggested by Michael Wood in his book *In Search of the Trojan War*, this new builder might conceivably be the man who led the Greeks against Troy, but although these might be the graves attributed to him and to his followers in Pausanias' time, he was not himself buried in the Grave Circle, however much he wanted to underline his connection with it.[6] This change of dynasty – if such it is – might be reflected in the legends of the foundation of Mycenae. It was Perseus, son of Zeus and Danaë, who founded the city, as every Greek knew, according to Pausanias. He had four or five sons and one daughter; at least two sons and then his grandson Eurystheus ruled in succession over the city. When Eurystheus was killed in battle against the Athenians and the sons of Herakles, the people of Mycenae entrusted the command of their army to Atreus and his brother Thyestes, the sons of Pelops, who had taken refuge at Mycenae after incurring the anger of their father Pelops. When the war ended in victory for the Mycenaeans and their allies, they duly proclaimed Atreus king, as an oracle had commanded, and from thenceforward the Pelopid dynasty ruled over Mycenae. Are we to see the Perseids as the original builders of the grave circles, and Atreus or his son Agamemnon as the new ruler who extended the walls of the city and refurbished Grave Circle A?[7]

On any interpretation, such arguments suggest that the graves in Circle A were those of the first group of people who had organised themselves as rulers of Mycenae, and who displayed their personal authority through their monuments and their wealth. If they were not a single line – and the evidence from the tholoi that overlap and follow them in time suggests that they may not have been – there is still the possibility, even the likelihood, that they were branches of a single family. The six Shaft Graves in Circle A (reflected in the six tholoi later) may represent six separate families or six related branches. We may be able to think of them as the first real dynasts of Mycenae, the men and women who founded her greatness. Those buried in the earlier Circle B, with their poorer grave goods, were less highly regarded, if not of lower status. Perhaps they are the earlier rulers, from the time when the divisions of family or clan were still more marked. As one group established itself more firmly, it constructed for itself a new and more splendid burial circle on the model of the earlier one. Since the old one remained in use for at least a generation the change was not a sudden one.[8]

This long and seemingly complicated introduction to a problem that has occupied archaeologists at least since the time of Schliemann in the nineteenth century, if not Pausanias in the second, perhaps helps to show why from our point of view there were two reasons that could make it rewarding to reconstruct the faces of some of these people: first, the simple excitement of discovering what they looked like, of finding out if they bore any resemblance to the gold masks; second, and much more important from the scientific angle of the project as a whole, there was the possibility that if these were all members of one family, directly or indirectly related, their skulls would reveal some facial similarity.

Aside from the six masks there was very little to tell us what these people looked like: the graves in Circle A contained a silver rhyton (a conical cup) embossed with the scene of a siege, the famous dagger depicting the lion hunt and gold rings decorated with scenes of hunting and battle, but these, like the little cut-out plaques of a goddess and a worshipper and the plaque attached to the head of a pin, all found in Grave III, were on too small a scale to be useful as illustrations of specific physical types, even had the artist had this in mind; they might nonetheless be useful later in our work as an overall guide to hairstyles in Bronze Age Mycenae.[9] The graves in Circle B were poorer than those in Circle A, and contained no figured metalwork aside from the one electrum mask (pl.VI). Grave Gamma in Circle B did contain a fine amethyst gem carved with the striking profile of a bearded man, which we later used as evidence for the hairstyle of a Minoan priest (see Chapter 7, fig.4). It was once regarded as Mycenaean work, but is now believed to have been made on Crete, so one should not use it as a close guide to the appearance of the occupant of the grave in which it was found. The art of the Middle Minoan III and Late Minoan I periods, contemporary with the Shaft Graves, is much richer in figured scenes than that of the mainland Greeks, but one cannot use Cretan art as evidence for the appearance of the mainlanders at a time when their two cultures were still quite distinct.

The six gold and electrum masks formed a fascinating company of faces, whose personalities could not be ignored (pls VI and VII). Ever since their discovery they have aroused strong reactions. Schliemann's impassioned cry of recognition may have been uttered in the excitement of discovery, but he naturally felt that they were the faces of particular individuals, and on 25 November 1876 he wrote to *The Times* about the three masks from Shaft Grave V:

Each mask shows so widely different a physiognomy from the other, and so altogether different from the ideal statues of gods and heroes, that there cannot be the slightest doubt but every one of them faithfully represents the likeness of the deceased hero whose face it covered. Were it not so all the masks would show the very same ideal type. One of the masks shows a small mouth and a long nose, large eyes and a large head; another a very large mouth, nose and head, the third a small head, mouth and nose. The mask with the large mouth, nose and head is conserved with the greater part of the skull of the deceased.

Others were less enthusiastic. C.T. Newton, Keeper of Greek and Roman Antiquities at the British Museum, wrote:

If the criteria by which we are in the habit of judging the art of the Greeks and other ancient races are applied to these Mycenaean antiquities, we shall find that they rank very low in the scale. They present to us, it is true, considerable vigour and invention in the designing of mere patterns and ornaments, but in almost every case in which the representation of animal life is attempted we see a feebleness of execution, the result of barbarous ignorance; those qualities and proportions of visible nature, on the observation of which the representation of organic beings in art depends, are either not perceived at all, or are so rendered as to be unintelligible…After reading Dr Schliemann's glowing description of their discovery, we confess that it was not without a shudder that we first beheld the hideous libels on the 'human face divine'. As representations of life, we can hardly rate them much higher than the work of New Zealanders and other savages…Let us hope that no race so repulsive…ever dwelt in the fortress of the Atreidae.[10]

Other scholars since have dismissed them as works of art, not necessarily in such strong language, and it is easy to see why. Newton had been brought up in the traditions of classical Greek art, and found the masks impossible to interpret in that context (to which after all they do not belong). Nevertheless like Schliemann himself and many scholars since, he assumed that they were intended as portraits, if not of the actual individuals then at least of their general racial type. Since the masks in Grave Circle A were found laid on the faces of the dead person, possibly over a shroud, this was a reasonable assumption.[11]

The truth is that the masks do not fit into any easy classification. Part of their impact and excitement comes from the confidence with which they have been made: it suggests that their creators were not breaking completely new ground, but nothing else like them survives from the Mycenaean world. The most natural interpretation is that they were designed as death masks, although when viewed from the back none of the masks look as if they were shaped to fit over actual features, even allowing for the repairs since their discovery. The fact that most, but not all, have holes near the ears through which a cord can be passed as if for tying or suspending them does not really help us in defining their primary function. Yet although they may be unclassifiable, even at first glance the masks fall into two distinct groups, the 'flat' masks and the 'round' ones. Setting the bearded 'beautiful' mask on one side for the moment, the flat masks are generally more primitive – one triangular mask from Grave Gamma in Circle B, and two oval ones from Grave IV in Circle A. It is interesting to note in passing that these three come from slightly earlier burials than do the round masks; these two bodies from Grave IV were oriented north-south when everyone else in that grave and that circle was laid out east-west, suggesting that perhaps they had been moved thither from somewhere else, or had been interred before the east-west orientation became important (witness the apparently casual layout of the graves in Circle B, fig. 2). The three share the same triangular face and high forehead, the same treatment of the eyebrows (or rather single eyebrow, arching across both eyes), the same firm, long nose and small, full-lipped

mouth; the eyelashes look 'stitched', and scholars have argued as to whether they were intended to be shown closed, as on a death mask, or open as in life. The round masks, from Graves IV and V in Circle A, are quite differently conceived, and are clearly by a different artist. They appear to have a third dimension, although the features are in effect added to the front of a rounded sheet, with the ears set towards the back; the face

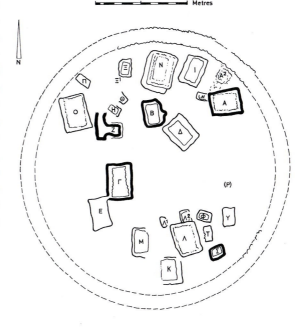

2. Plan of Grave Circle B, Mycenae: graves from which skulls were reconstructed are marked with a heavy outline.

113

is round, the eyebrows more fully modelled, the eyes appear open, the nose is shorter and wider, and the large mouth seems to smile. Mylonas has suggested that one of these two represents a woman, on the grounds that the grave goods buried with the body were more suited to a 'richly dowered princess' than to a warrior prince, but he was presumably led to think in this way because he believed that this body was a mummy with Egyptian connections. We believe this interpretation to be incorrect, and shall consider it shortly. Dr Oliver Dickinson looked at the grave goods again in his fundamental study of the world of the shaft graves, and found the 'female' argument unconvincing, not least because this would be the only female mask: certainly there is nothing feminine about this severe, large face.[12]

The 'beautiful' mask belongs with the 'flat' group, but technically and artistically it stands apart from all the others. The goldsmith who made this piece was far more skilful than his colleagues, and could indulge in a greater interest in the form and structure of the face, and in greater realism, something that is particularly noticeable in the rendering of the beard and moustache, which are not shown at all on any of the other masks.[13] For those who believe that the masks are an attempt at portraiture, this is without doubt the most promising specimen. 'He must have been in the prime of life when he sat for this likeness...a man of power and determination', was how the American archaeologist Carl Blegen described the mask. However, on this mask as on the others, while individual features are shown and characterised, the characterisation does not seem to be of the kind which reflects a particular, known individual, which is the fundamental requirement of a true portrait. Indeed, it is questionable whether the modern notion of making a physical likeness had any place in the Greek Bronze Age mind.

Dr Katie Demakopoulou, at the time curator of the prehistoric collections at the National Archaeological Museum in Athens, was enthusiastic at the idea that we should attempt a reconstruction of the skull that lay behind the 'beautiful' mask or indeed of any of the skulls from Grave Circle A. Of all the working trips that any of us have made to Greece, this one flowed most smoothly. Within a couple of hours of arriving in Athens we were being welcomed into Dr Demakopoulou's office at the museum, and then we went into the stores together to have a look at the skulls – a great disappointment. Although the human remains of these kings are now carefully kept in well-lined drawers, they had not always been so well cared for in the hundred-plus years since their excavation. Greek soil, with its high alkalinity, is not kind to bones: at the time of their discovery Schliemann wrote to *The Times* that 'unfortunately, the skulls of the five bodies [in Grave IV] were in such a state of decomposition that none of them could be saved...in one of these has remained a large part of the skull it covered'.[14] In the light of later photographs this is undoubtedly more pessimistic than what a modern archaeologist might have written, but it must illustrate the fact that like most archaeologists of his time he was generally less interested in the skeletons than in the artefacts buried with them. The end result was that, aside from the 'mummy' which, much to Schliemann's credit, the Argos chemist had treated on the spot, the fragile bones from several different skeletons, often already fragmentary when discovered, were now a confused jumble of small pieces, two or three individuals to a drawer. From the photographs taken by the

American anthropologist Dr J.L. Angel when he studied them in 1937 it looked as though it might be possible for us to attempt a reconstruction of one or two of the skulls. However, his description and numbering imply that when it came to identifying particular skulls with Schliemann's excavation records, he could only attribute the skulls to their respective graves, but not actually link them to specific burials within each grave.[15] When we came to look at them in the summer of 1985, we found the remains of different skulls in the same drawers, lovingly packed but too fragmentary and too confused for one to be able to distinguish individuals from among the jumble of cranial fragments. Two years later we returned to the museum to try to convince ourselves that we could do something with them after all, for the temptation was very great, but after a considered survey of the remains we decided reluctantly that with the state of our knowledge at the time all that we could have done was to reconstruct a 'composite' face, made up from the most important surviving pieces of skulls from the different graves: it would have been a very interesting technical exercise, particularly if one can assume that all these individuals were related to one another, but too much would have been based on speculation and too little on anatomical fact to satisfy either our own standards or those of the National Museum. It would have laid us open to all sorts of justifiable criticism, and it would have satisfied no one.

Reluctantly, we abandoned 'Agamemnon', for the time being.

Nonetheless we did not need to abandon the Mycenaeans altogether. First, there remained the 'mummy' from Grave V in Circle A (pl.vi). Schliemann's dramatic description of its discovery and preliminary conservation has already been quoted. After its treatment he announced that it would be sent to Athens along with the rest of the finds, but then it was lost from view. Nearly a century later it was rediscovered in the stores of the National Museum,[16] where there are now plans for a proper investigation. If the skull survives one may be able to use computer-assisted X-ray techniques (CT-scans) to re-create this royal Mycenaean's appearance without even needing to subject a potentially fragile skull to the rigours of casting.

This body has always been described as a 'mummy' since its first publication, and on this basis many scholars have tried to interpret it as evidence for Mycenaean contact with Egypt, seeing here either an Egyptian princess married to a Mycenaean chieftain, or a Mycenaean warrior who had died on foreign service and had been embalmed for his final journey home, rather like Alexander the Great or Admiral Lord Nelson; but such fancies all arise from a simple misunderstanding. As the passage we have already quoted makes clear, Schliemann merely said that he had found a 'well preserved body', whose colour 'resembled very much that of an Egyptian mummy'. His pressing problem was to preserve that body, which the chemist from Argos solved for him by crudely embalming it. Infuriatingly, Schliemann appears to have abandoned his excavation diary in the middle of clearing this particular grave, and we have to rely on his reports to *The Times*. The next one – which is undated in the manuscript but which we have to assume refers to the following day – begins, 'The now nearly mummified body...'. In other words, thanks to the chemist's actions it was *now* becoming mummified (in 1876 AD, not BC), and was almost ready to be moved.[17] At no point did Schliemann say it was an Egyptian mummy. In fact his description really precludes it, for he mentions only the gold ornaments and none of the cartonnage or wrappings that one would expect on a true Egyptian mummy. He even went so far as to say that 'there was no vestige of hair'. Having ourselves seen the body, we can vouch for the fact that it looks as one would expect it to do from Schliemann's description: a mass of hard earth in which can be distinguished fragments of bone, amber beads and other ornaments, quite unlike a true mummy embalmed after the Egyptian manner.

Even more exciting, this is of course the body over which had been placed the round-faced mask to which Schliemann *really* referred as 'Agamemnon' in his telegram. So, working together with colleagues at the National Museum in Athens, we may yet find ourselves reconstructing Schliemann's 'Agamemnon' after all. As with so many aspects of this project which develops as we go along, that is still for the future.

Our second reason for not giving up yet lay in the fact that in 1951 a second circle of shaft graves, Grave Circle B, had been discovered at Mycenae, on a low knoll a little to the west of the acropolis, very close to the modern entrance to the site (see fig. 1). It says much for the emphasis which the ruler of Mycenae who built the citadel walls and the Lion Gate succeeded in laying on Grave Circle A that most visitors to the site probably pass the old Circle B without noticing its existence. It was discovered by chance during restoration work on the later 'Tomb of Clytemnestra' that had cut into it, and was excavated between 1952 and 1954 by the Archaeological Society of Athens under the direction of Dr John Papadimitriou, Professor Spyridon Marinatos and Professor George Mylonas. To distinguish the graves from those in Circle A which had been given Roman numerals, those in Circle B were catalogued with letters of the Greek alphabet in the order in which they were excavated. The finds were divided between the National Museum in Athens and the local Archaeological Museum in Nauplia, which retained the skeletal material, for with modern excavation techniques the bones were more carefully lifted than Schliemann had been able or willing to do three-quarters of a century earlier.

The twenty-six graves were scattered around the circle (fig. 2). One can see a development in the types of graves, for they generally become larger, deeper and richer, but the fact that many were often reopened and reused makes it difficult to set out a precise chronological order. They can, however, be divided into phases. The plan of the circle shows that the graves are grouped in different sectors – northwest, northeast, southeast and central, and there are graves of different phases in most groups. Because there are enough burials here to represent several families (or several branches of one family) over three or four generations it would be tempting to suggest that these were family plots. Dr J.L. Angel from the Smithsonian Institution had examined and measured these bones in 1954, numbering the skeletons in the order in which he studied them, so that now each is identified by a Greek letter indicating its grave plus Angel's record number. His report was based on so many years of experience that, reading it, one felt that he had really come to know these people. He reckoned that he could distinguish relationships between skeletons that had come from widely separate burials.[18]

The excavators had found the remains of thirty-five skeletons, but because so many of the graves had been reused and the previous occupants merely brushed to one side, and because all were fragile and often broken as a result of the high alkalinity of the soil in which they had lain, by no means all of them were complete; some were only represented by a few teeth or broken pieces. In 1954 Angel had studied twenty-three of them, and his full and detailed report suggested that it would be well worth considering reconstructing at least a selection, bearing in mind their possible relationship to each other and to Grave Circle A. He himself later confirmed this when we wrote to him.

We began by sorting through all the boxes in the 'Circle B room' in the stores of the Nauplia Museum. Most of the skulls had been boxed separately. We located fourteen, and fragments of seven more from the relevant period.[19] After sorting and checking them, we compared them with Angel's descriptions, making additional comments and noting any discrepancies, both for what might now be missing and for medical aspects that he might have missed. Quite apart from the level of his knowledge and scholarship, Angel's descriptions and comments were invaluable because the conditions in which the skeletal material had been stored since excavation were less than ideal. The skeletons had been in a friable state when excavated some thirty years earlier. Most of the skulls had been consolidated and mended for Angel in 1954, but time and storage conditions had resulted in many of his repairs coming apart, and the bone itself had become even more fragile. In more than one case the skulls were now less complete than when Angel had studied them, and his descriptions enabled us to identify and reunite loose fragments. However, the greatest loss since Angel's visit was the disappearance of nearly all the lower jaws: the remains of only four could be found, and of those four only one went with a skull that was in the running for reconstruction. Despite going to considerable and sometimes mildly absurd lengths to try to locate them, in the end we had to admit defeat. Fortunately the notes and the photographs made by Angel were so detailed that we could use them to re-create the missing mandibles later.

Having considered and sorted the material, we selected four skulls for casting and reconstruction on the basis of their interest, condition and the time available: Gamma 51, Beta 52, Zeta 59 and Sigma 131. Gamma 51 is a man who died aged around twenty-eight, whose skull fractured and shows evidence of a trephining operation; Beta 52 was perhaps two years older than Gamma 51, another large man with a 'narrow, beaky and toothy face'; Zeta 59 was a powerful man of perhaps fifty with a long face and an arthritic shoulder, described by Angel as 'in his prime perhaps the most powerful of the champions'; and Sigma 131 was another fifty-year-old, massively built but suffering from gallstones as well as arthritis, perhaps the founding father of the whole dynasty, and now the proud possessor of the only lower jaw among them.

This was our first venture into the field as a team, for the work on Philip II had through circumstance been done in a piecemeal fashion and the session in Ankara described in the previous chapter actually came after these sessions in Nauplia. One would have thought that after eleven years or so of casting skulls and rebuilding faces all the major technical problems would have been ironed out, but the

Mycenaeans were to prove just how wrong that assumption was. At first all went smoothly, despite the fact that these skulls were both porous and fragile. At this stage we had neither wish nor intention to meddle with the conservation done thirty years earlier by Angel, who had had the skulls repaired where he could, often inserting wire struts to give strength to the damaged bone but never replacing missing portions with plaster. As a result numerous large holes and empty spaces were left which required filling and covering before the skulls could be cast, in the same manner as we had done for the skull of Midas. It was a method we had already worked out in Manchester for dealing with particularly delicate crania, and in the lab it had worked superbly well.

It worked well this first time in the field too. However, the problems came when we began making the actual casts. The method adopted for making earlier moulds involved constructing a simple box from cardboard or a similar material or using a large glass tank or box, in which the skull could be surrounded by a thick layer of alginate to produce a solid and substantial two-part mould supported by the box or tank (see Chapter 3, fig. 1). However, having cast the first skull in Nauplia, it became clear that despite all the careful calculations we had made before leaving England, to employ such a technique in the field was not practical, since it used far too much material which we were in no position to replace. Perforce we evolved the new technique, described earlier, whereby the skull was covered with a thick layer of alginate supported by an outer casing of plaster. Although much more complex and demanding it proved to be both more accurate and more economical in time as well as materials and also puts less strain on the skull itself – all important considerations for work in the field.

One is always under pressure to work quickly, for the expedition budget never allows unlimited time, so these gains were important. Making the cast itself is less stressful although rather more energetic, and so we generally planned the work so that moulding and casting were done in the early morning before the summer heat built up. When possible the second part of the working day was used to prepare the next skull with its silver sheath, ready for the following morning. The satisfaction (and relief) of making a good mould and subsequently an accurate cast was something that the whole team seemed to share.

So successful was this new method that we felt we could justify a return visit in 1987 to cast the other three skulls we had noted as 'having potential for the future, subject to conservation and on the basis of expertise gained so far': these three were Alpha 62, a young man in his early twenties, in whom Angel saw a massive physique and evidence of heavy exercise, as well as an interestingly shaped face; Gamma 55, a 'notably tall and strong man…of around 33' and the only skull with a death mask from Grave Circle B; and Gamma 58, sadly damaged, but the only woman of whose skull enough remained to make her a candidate for reconstruction. She was a potential sufferer from back trouble, and the final surviving skull from Grave Gamma. The disproportion of the sexes among the burials makes it clear that they represent only a selection of the elite among the population, but whatever the relationship of the different graves to each other it seems reasonable to assume that all the bodies buried in a single grave were members of the same family, though of course we do not know if this lady was wife or sister to the men with whom she shared her final resting-place.

There were some changes in our approach in 1987. The first was a small point. In 1986 we had found cotton wool rather unsatisfactory for packing the inside of the skulls during casting, for not only did it require great care to prevent stray fibres from catching on the broken edges of bone, but it had little natural 'spring'. We needed something that would not compact when compressed but would press outwards again. Waste polyester proved ideal for the task — the most convenient supply was sold as hamster bedding from a local petshop in suburban Manchester.

There were also other more important considerations to our return visit. In the reports on the 1986 season we had written, 'It is clear from Angel's comments and photographs that much potential information has been lost since the skulls were studied in 1954, particularly if one is to attempt a reconstruction; therefore it should be part of any project to do further work on the skulls to carry out as much conservation as possible, at least on the most important skulls.' The team in 1987 was smaller, but it included for the first time a conservator, Danaë Thimme from Indiana University Art Museum, who had long experience of working in the field in Greek museums, and who worked with us on the skull of Midas as well. Her principal attention was naturally focused on the seven skulls which we had selected for casting: for instance she was able to replace some of the damaged bones of Gamma 55, so that although he was not restored to the relative completeness in which Angel's technician had left him in 1954, at least there was now enough of the central face to make it worth attempting a cast and a reconstruction that would not be largely speculative (see fig. 19). Basically what she did was to carry out a very valuable, indeed essential, first-aid operation on our 'magnificent seven' and on a number of other skulls which were in particular need. Some of the old glue was removed, and some of the wire struts inserted in 1954 were replaced with perspex. Complete conservation would have taken months, not least because it would have been necessary to remove the old consolidant, which had not always been allowed to penetrate the bone properly, perhaps because Angel was working under even greater pressure than we were. We would also have needed to clean and take down his repairs before undertaking any new work ourselves. In 1987 we also came prepared with acid-free tissue and bubble-wrap. Thus with the help of the authorities in Nauplia we could complete our task by repacking all the skulls and some other skeletal material in specially made boxes. We hope that, along with the first-aid conservation that they have received, this will allow these Mycenaeans to rest more securely for a while.

So now we had casts of the skulls of seven people who were almost certainly all from among the rulers of Mycenae, though not necessarily from the same family. Their potential was very exciting: from a technical standpoint because the skulls vary so in their completeness, which not only made each one into a separate challenge but also raised questions about how one should treat the reconstruction of the whole group; and perhaps even more so from the point of view of the archaeologist and the anthropologist, because of what we might now learn of their appearance and their family relationships.

The first result of our work is that there now exist faithful replicas of these seven skulls, the ones which we considered the most important of the group. Two of the team spend our working lives in museums, and have to take a realistic attitude to the likely future storage environment of the skulls themselves, even despite our limited efforts at conservation and packing, so we believe that simply making such replicas is itself a valuable contribution, particularly as scholars become more interested in dry bones. This is in no way to impugn the Nauplia Museum, for it is a problem curators face everywhere from the day an object is brought into a museum. Yet just how valuable these casts might be has already been shown by the fact that Beta 52, one of the skulls which we had cast in 1986, had collapsed by the time we returned in 1987 despite our careful preliminary packing.

Second, for all but the skilled specialist the casts are often much easier to 'read' than are the skulls themselves. This is because the originals are very often fragmentary, or at least full of holes and breaks, whereas the casts, on which all this damage has been made good, give the appearance of being much more complete.

This, we thought, should lead to a third gain. Angel gave some very vivid descriptions of the faces that he felt lay over the skulls, and went on to suggest family relationships among the occupants of the graves on this basis. For all but the most skilled specialist, it is difficult to make these comparisons between different skulls when one is dealing with damaged and often fragmentary crania, and of course once away from Nauplia Museum one can only make checks from photographs and notes – unless one has a set of plaster casts. From these casts it ought to be relatively easy even for an inexperienced skull-watcher to notice broad similarities and differences between individuals. There are perhaps even certain advantages in comparing different individuals before the flesh has been put back on the skull, certainly before potentially distracting details such as facial hair have been added. But we also came to appreciate that to reconstruct a face required a careful and well-thought-out analysis not merely of the details of the face but of its entire structure. This in turn led us to understand and appreciate the head as a whole much more fully than Angel had been able to do from just the bare bones. On more than one occasion we came to suspect that he had been a little hasty in his deductions about the faces which overlay the skulls and thus the family relationships which he deduced among the occupants of the graves. It must be said that we found ourselves suggesting similarities and thus possible relationships on the basis of the casts which disappeared or changed later as we built up the complete face.

The next step was to flesh out the bones. The obvious first candidate was Sigma 131 (fig. 3). We chose him first because he is the only one to have come down to us complete with his mandible, but he is also a particularly appropriate man to stand at the head of the line of Mycenaean reconstructions. Angel had trailed the notion that he was perhaps the founder of the dynasty that built the Mycenae of the Grave Circles: not Agamemnon, we know he is too early for that; not even Schliemann's Agamemnon, for we have moved back a few generations from him; so he must be old Pelops himself, for in legend the line runs back from Agamemnon and his brother Menelaus to Atreus and then to their grandfather Pelops, after whom the whole Peloponnese was named. So, seriously or not, we gave him the name of Pelops.

His grave was one of the earliest to survive in the circle, a simple pit or cist with a shelf cut in the walls to take the roof. The floor was covered with dark earth and pebbles. He did not take any pottery or metal objects into the next world with him, neither sword nor jewellery, but he was a man of importance to those who buried him, for they honoured his grave by marking it with a heap of stones. Angel reckoned that he lived to be about fifty-five years old, judging from the exostoses on his shoulders and feet (small bony growths that appear with age and use), and although his dental age may be slightly younger he was still the oldest of all those buried in Circle B. Angel described him as massively built, big enough to cause comment in

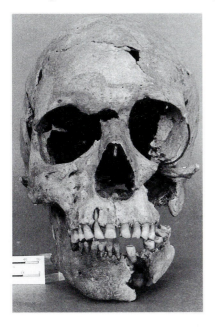

3. *The skull of Sigma 131.*

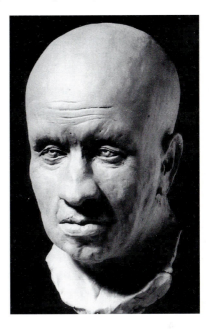

4. *Sigma 131: the first 'fleshy'*
reconstruction.

a crowd. Even from his skull we could see that he must have been a fine figure of a man, for the muscle attachments showed that he had had a powerful neck and jaw, while his square jaw and pronounced mastoid process are very male characteristics.

The notion that we should reconstruct skulls from Mycenae had originally come from our Manchester colleague Dr Elizabeth French, Mycenaean specialist and *inter alia* joint editor of the Helleno-British excavations at the site. Her moral and practical support so far had been invaluable, and it was perhaps ironic that the trigger to begin work on the reconstruction of 'Pelops' was her appointment to the directorship of the British School at Athens. To mark her departure from Manchester her students organised a conference, and when we were invited to take part there was no doubt that this man would be the subject of our contribution. The version that appeared on that day in May 1989 was of a round-headed, brachycephalic man with a relatively high, straight forehead, rather close-set eyes, a wide and rather large nose, and a prominent mouth that concealed his prognathous teeth (fig.4). While it was exciting to see our first Mycenaean, the immediate comment from our audience was that his face was perhaps too fleshy, that it was the face of a fifty-five-year-old from the later twentieth century AD, not the sixteenth century BC.

This was a very fair point when one looked at his health record. He had three diseased teeth, including a large abscess above the upper right lateral incisor (actually a very good record for a man of such advanced age at any period of history); Angel had noted slight arthritis of the spine, and had also found several gallstones resting between his lowest ribs and pelvis. Both Angel and our own colleague Dr Jonathan Musgrave had noticed thickening or pitting of the bone, which they associated with possible osteoporosis. If the traditional connection of this condition with anaemia is valid, then he would have felt some of the weakness that affects anaemia sufferers, but as we shall see in our discussion of the Minoan priestess (Chapter 7), this connection is no longer certain and it is safer to treat it simply as evidence that his health was less than perfect, for reasons that may have had a dietary or a hereditary backgound. Indeed, some of the received interpretations of bone thickening on archaeological skeletons are no longer always accepted – more of this later when we come to discuss Gamma 51. Associated with the bone thickening, the skull of 'Pelops' also showed evidence of cribra orbitalia, perforation of the bone around the eye-sockets: if this extended to the frontal sinuses then it could provide a route for infection. But whatever physical reaction he might have had to this bone condition, the arthritis, toothache and above all the gallstones most certainly gave him fairly continuous pain. The poor man was most unlikely to have shown such a serene face to the world, and he was duly remade with a more lean and pained expression, the effect of which was to make his whole face look rather narrower, and to draw more attention to his rather prominent nose (see fig. 11). This of course is only window-dressing, and his friends and relatives would have (recognised him perfectly well in either version – compare the two photographs of the Finnish girl in Chapter 2 (fig. 8). Either version would have satisfied a forensic case, but reconstruction of archaeological specimens aims at more than mere recognition, and involves reporting all the evidence in visual form.

Thereafter work on these skulls tended to proceed in fits and starts, interrupted by other candidates such as Midas, the two Minoans and even the Carian Princess, who all seemed to have deadlines to meet while our Mycenaeans stayed in the background, a friendly presence and still in many ways promising the most interesting archaeological rewards. The others all provided useful experience. The missing mandibles were re-created from Angel's notes and photographs. In 1991 what one might think of as drafts of three more (Gamma 51, Beta 52 and Zeta 59) were presented at a seminar at the British School at Athens arranged by Dr French in her new capacity as Director. These hairless 'drafts' already gave cause for some interesting speculation on the relationship of these three men. We had chosen them next because, apart from the lack of lower jaws, they were the most complete. Thanks to Angel's excellent notes and photographs, we had re-created the missing mandibles in wax, from which it was easy to make plaster casts which were reunited with the casts of the skulls of their owners. We could then proceed as if they had never been lost.

Zeta 59 could be regarded as another of the founding fathers, along with Sigma 131 ('Pelops'), though perhaps a slightly more junior founding father, for the group of graves in the northwest of the circle in which he was buried generally contained more and better vases and the first bronze implements, and so are a little later than those in the southeastern sector where 'Pelops' had been buried. He too had been interred in a crouched position in a simple cist grave (fig. 5), but it was longer than most, for he was a large man, and its perimeter had been picked out with a ring of stones. It lay in the northwest sector of the Grave Circle, and so it seems likely that he belonged to a different section of the hierarchy. Four holes in the floor of the grave showed that there had been posts to support the roof in addition to the shelf cut into the walls. Unlike 'Pelops' he had been given some grave goods: in front of him stood one of the earliest tall-stemmed goblets of yellow Minyan ware of the type which became popular in the years that followed, and some finely decorated cups and jugs. Of especial interest was a spouted jug which was very probably imported from the Cycladic islands. Although it is of rather coarse pottery, it was clearly a prized possession, a token of contact with other parts of the Aegean world. Between the pots lay a very long sword. Angel had described him as:

…in his prime perhaps the most powerful of the champions. He is tall and broad-shouldered, and thick-boned with large hands and feet. At the age of at least 49, probably older,…he has…marked arthritic changes in cervical, lumbar and lower thoracic vertebrae

involving fusion of thoracic vertebrae through ossification of the disk portions of the anterior longitudinal ligament, and slight arthritis of metacarpal bones. It is uncertain how far such arthritis might link with a large abscess-derived cyst at the site of the upper second molar tooth: this has penetrated the maxillary sinus…Since the left clavicle shows a pseudoarthrosis…possibly from over-use of the shoulder (supporting a heavy many-layered shield in battle?), it is possible that all the hypertrophic arthritic changes reflect simply hard usage…Strikingly

5. Grave Zeta in Circle B at Mycenae as excavated: the dead man's sword and the vases buried with him lie to the left, and the holes left by the posts which supported the roof of the grave are clearly visible in the corners.

large, long ovoid and high skull, with its marked muscle attachments, almost concave side-walls, and long rectangular horse-like face…Large mouth, deep chin, vertical face profile, and notably high and narrow nose fit this picture. Noticeable depressions in the skull vault 2 cm [¾in] above the left eye and behind the left parietal boss are apparently results of heavy blows or wounds inflicted by a right-handed opponent.

Angel had also noted a possible healed fracture to the spine, and had estimated his height at 1.75 m (5 ft 9 in). In brief, he was an imposing figure of a man, with more than a touch of arthritis in his lower back, hands and left shoulder, whose teeth were also giving him a spot of trouble, an old soldier with battle scars on his brow and on the top of his head, and undoubtedly elsewhere on his body too, although there the injuries had not reached the bone, at least not so as to be noticed by Angel. We had no brief to examine them, but on a flying visit in 1994 to collect samples for analysis we noticed evidence of arthritis on his sacrum (the large bone in the pelvis), at least two healed rib fractures, and new bone growth on his shoulder blades that suggested healing after his neck muscles had been wrenched away. The old soldier had really been in the wars. When one looked again at the figures on the lion-hunt dagger from Circle A with their massive shields (see n.9) one could readily understand Angel's suggestion that carrying such a weight into battle and onto the hunting field over many years might quite literally leave its mark. It gives a whole new perspective to the epithet 'carrying a shield like a tower' which Homer uses to describe the hero Ajax. No wonder Ajax felt that 'his left shoulder was weary, as steadfastly he held up his glittering shield' during his duel with Hector in book XVI of the *Iliad* (lines 106–7). Our hero would undoubtedly not have appreciated the soubriquet of 'Old Horse-Face' by which we came to know him, but the tall skull, widening towards the back from the narrow nose, close-set eyes and rather narrow, high fore-

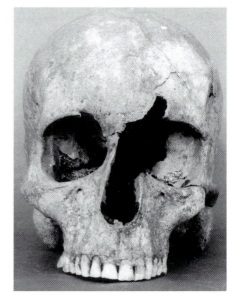

head and (once replaced) the powerful jaw made it irresistible (fig.6). The face that emerged from the skull of course reflected this: a rather idiosyncratic feature was the small mouth, which reflected the proportions of the upper part of his face rather than the deep chin.

Gamma 51 was a much younger man, both in terms of when he lived and of his age at death. The grave in which he was found was one of the largest and latest in the circle, for among the grave goods were a number of Late Helladic I vases (fig.7). It contained the remains of four or possibly five people, three men and a woman. The skeleton of one of the men, presumably the first occupant, had been swept to one side when the later burials were inserted. The woman had also been pushed to the side, evidently before her body had

6. *The skull of Zeta 59.*

7. *Grave Gamma as excavated: Gamma 55 lies on the left, with a sword and two daggers by his side, and more weapons and pottery behind his head (the electrum mask is still concealed near the projecting stone in the top left corner); pushed to the right is the woman Gamma 58, while next to her and rather confused with her remains are the disturbed bones and weapons of the first man to be buried in the grave (whose skull is lost); at the foot of the grave, with a few vases, rests Gamma 51.*

decomposed sufficiently for the bones to become disarticulated, so that her skeleton, like those of the other two men whose bones were undisturbed, was complete. It was clearly the burial place of important people, to judge not only from the electrum mask and gold cups found in it, but also from the fact that this was one of only four graves in this circle where the burials were marked by stelae. We shall return later to Gamma 55 and Gamma 58, the other two complete bodies, and concern ourselves first with Gamma 51. Despite the wealth with which his fellows were buried (they were probably his relatives, but we could not yet be sure), this young man had been given only a few vases, but neither gold nor even a sword. It is not that they have been swept to one side, for his was probably the last body to be put into the grave. Rather than being laid out along the length of the grave in what was by now the customary manner, he was placed across its southern end, where he only just fitted. It seems likely that he was buried at much the same time as his wealthy and well-armed neighbour Gamma 55, for there is little sign that he disturbed the latter's remains.

One can hardly argue that he was given this apparently shoddy burial was because of his youth: he was around twenty-eight when he died, and the average age of all the bodies in this circle was estimated by Angel at thirty-six years. Physically he was a fine specimen: 'a tall, particularly strong-boned, long-bodied, and large-footed man' was how Angel described him, estimating his height at 1.73 cm (5 ft 8¼ in). There was more to be learned from the skull (fig. 8). Angel had noticed that the bone in the outer table of the skull was a little thickened (tentatively confirmed on our visit), which he had identified as 'slight traces of healed osteoporosis'. If the osteoporotic thickening was a side-effect of anaemia, then our Mycenaean warrior would have felt the lassitude and general debility associated with that condition, but forty years on from Angel's diagnosis our medical colleagues doubted

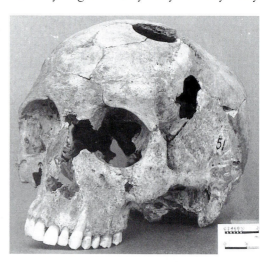

8. The skull of Gamma 51: the hole left by the trephination is visible on the top of the head.

whether the thickening of the bone in the skull was evidence for osteoporosis at all. This is not a part of the skeleton normally affected by the disease, which is more usually found in sites such as the long bones, where Angel does not mention it. They suggested a number of other possible complaints which might have given rise to the thickening, such as osteomalacia and Paget's Disease, but they were not prepared to commit themselves without a further examination. Unfortunately by this time we were back in England and the patient was still in his box in Nauplia Museum, so final diagnosis will have to await another occasion.

In the meantime there were other more striking and less contentious features of his skull to concern us. On the right frontal bone – that is, on top of the head above the right eye – was a shallow depression nearly 2.5 cm (1 in) long, most likely the result of a battle injury. Even more interesting was an oval hole in the top of his skull measuring 2.7 x 3.0 cm (1⅛ x 3¼ in) with a clean sloping cut made in such a way that the inner diameter is slightly greater than the outer. There is no sign of splintering that such as an injury would have produced. This has to be the result of a trephination, where a hole was cut deliberately into the skull. Horrendous though it may seem, this practice has a history going back to the Neolithic period. Over a thousand examples are known from the ancient world; the survival rate was surprisingly high, and around 400 BC the writer of the treatise *On Wounds in the Head* in the Hippocratic corpus gives details of the technique and recommends it in cases of injuries to the head. There are at least four other sure instances from the Bronze Age and the Archaic periods in Greece, including a near-contemporary but much more crudely executed instance from Lerna, a little to the south of Mycenae. The Mycenaean surgeon used a sharp chisel or gouge, and the results of his handiwork remain to be seen, for the two roughly semicircular pieces of bone that had been cut out were also discovered. The bone had been cut with great skill through the outer table only, and as it was cut it had sprung away from the head and split lengthwise into two, curling slightly in the process, probably because it was still attached to the scalp. Therefore one can deduce that the patient survived at least until the operation had been completed, in contrast to a case in Argos from the ninth century BC where the operation was abandoned before the bone had been cut right through, presumably because that young man died under the surgeon's knife. However, our man did not survive for long, for there is no trace of healing on the bone around the hole. We can only speculate as to why he underwent such drastic treatment. Some archaeologists have linked the trephination and the rather poor grave goods with which he was buried to suggest that perhaps he suffered from a mental illness (hence the meagre burial), but two fractures lead away from the trephination hole towards the front of the head. It is impossible to say if these breaks occurred post-mortem or were the effect of an injury which rendered him unconscious, but the latter seems more likely: if he did suffer from osteoporosis then his skull would have become more brittle and thus a little more susceptible to fracture. In this case the trephination was a desperate but unsuccessful measure intended to revive him.[20]

To cast his skull needed care, because of the many fractures (he had suffered others post-mortem) and the weakness caused by the trephination, and fully justified covering the skull with burnished foil to protect it. Angel had described him from the bare skull as having a 'full cerebellar region, strong brow-ridges, and a big rectangular face of longish intermediate proportions. The nose is big and high, chin deep, jowls strong, and teeth perfect.' When reconstructed, Gamma 51 proved to have the same long face, close-set eyes, small nose and large lower face and chin as Zeta 59. The nose was set high in both men's faces though on neither was it especially large or prominent. The nasal aperture appears much larger on Gamma 51's skull than it really is because part of it has been broken away, in particular the crucial nasal bone, and this may have misled Angel. The similarity between the two heads when seen from the front was quite uncanny, though it was a little less noticeable in profile (see fig. 10). It is very difficult to believe that there is not some family relationship between them, although these men must be at least two generations apart, one from the early period of use of the grave circle, the other from the very end, when it was already being overtaken by Grave Circle A. Grave Gamma lay a little to the south of Grave Zeta, in the centre of Circle B, an area where graves were only dug towards the end of its period of use.

The last of the trio was Beta 52, a different type of skull from the others and buried in a different part of the circle. We knew that he was going to look different, for his skull was of quite different shape – altogether a smaller head with a lower, sloping forehead, prominent brow-ridges, nose and teeth (fig.9). He had been buried alone in a grave cut in the northern part of the circle, close to Grave Zeta but probably belonging with the northeastern group. Like Grave Zeta, his grave had four posts to give additional support to the roof. He was buried with seven vases, including four of the yellow Minyan ware goblets with incised stems of which we saw the earliest example in Grave Zeta, and with a broad-bladed dagger which, along with the evidence from his skeleton, confirmed his sex; but he also wore a gold armlet on his left arm, and a plain strip of electrum found lying on his body probably decorated his clothing. These are the earliest such ornaments from the

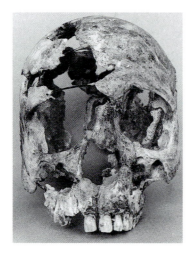

9. Beta 52: front and profile views of the skull.

Grave Circles, and elsewhere normally accompany the burials of women in the Middle Helladic period. He belongs early in the middle phase of the circle, and remains the only skull from this period which we have so far been able to reconstruct. We considered his near-contemporary Iota 68, but despite his potential anthropological and medical interest we had to abandon him because there was really no longer enough of the facial area surviving to make a reconstruction practical.

When his skull was given flesh, Beta 52 did indeed look quite different from the other two. 'A large man of about thirty…the skull has a narrow, beaky face with a long nose and rectangular facial outline', was how Angel had described him, estimating his height at 1.73 m (5 ft 8 in). 'A lot of face' had been our own reaction to his skull. Although the face was rectangular it was a much shorter, squarer rectangle than the other two for it did not have their lantern jaw, the eyes were set wider apart, and the nose appeared relatively larger. The entire proportions of the face were different when viewed from the front, and not a single one of the measurements used to match up faces in facial mapping seemed likely to correspond. When seen in profile the strong brow-ridges and the jutting lower lip caused by the prognathous jaws gave him a somewhat primitive appearance, and the contrast with the other two heads was increased by the sloping forehead, shared (though to a much lesser degree) by Zeta 59 (fig. 10).

Even this trio, then, were allowing us to make some interesting speculations about the social and political background of the people of the Grave Circles. Beta 52 with his beaky face from the northeastern group of burials stood apart, but we were beginning to see a link between Zeta 59 and Gamma 51 that stretched over two or three generations. However, their graves were in different groups, in the northwest and centre of the circle. Here the story becomes more complicated: Gamma 51 had been buried in one of a pair of multiple graves that had been dug late in the use of the circle in an area where previously there had been no burials. Other scholars had already suggested that this shift was the only visible evidence of a move by the two families, dynasties, ruling groups (we have as yet no means of

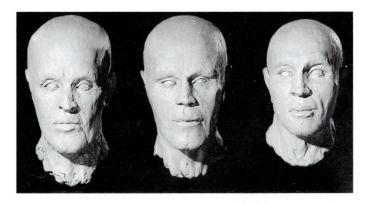

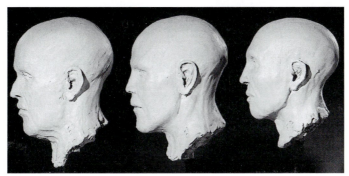

10. *Three reconstructed heads, shown hairless to draw attention to their physical similarities (and differences): from the left, Zeta 59, Gamma 51, Beta 52.*

defining them) who had until now had their burial plots in the northwestern and southeastern parts of the circle respectively, intended to form a political link – that this bridging of the gap between their burial plots represents the bridging of a dynastic gap. Sigma 131 – old 'Pelops' – was an early member of the southeastern group: at that stage we could only see that his facial structure set him apart from the other three men. It was going to be very interesting to see whether the other faces from Grave Gamma were going to throw up any resemblances to him, or whether they were going to shed any light on the notion of a dynastic connection created by the occupants of Grave Gamma. Could facial reconstruction give a firmer answer to a political question than the hints which more traditional archaeological methods had been able to provide?

The spur to complete the Mycenaeans was the imminent completion of the new Mediterranean Gallery at the Manchester Museum in December 1993, where the new displays were to include for the first time examples of each of the reconstructions from the northern side of the Mediterranean basin. As well as ageing 'Pelops' and completing the trio at whom we have just been looking (for they still remained in their hairless state), this meant at long last tackling the two much more damaged skulls from Grave Gamma, numbers 55 and 58, and also Alpha 62. These were the three individuals on whose behalf we had made the return visit to Nauplia in 1987.

It was also time for us to think seriously about the fashion in which these people cut their hair, and whether they wore beards. In their hairless state the reconstructions were extremely valuable as three-dimensional reports on the skulls, and for identifying the characteristics and features which might demonstrate a relationship, or lack of it. But relatively few people go about with their heads shaved, and a line-up of bald pates in a museum display would look distinctly odd, and not very convincing. Here we came up against the problem of working in a society where figurative, representational art was still in its infancy. Aside from the mask from Grave Gamma, there are no ancient illustrations contemporary with the burials in Grave Circle B that could guide us, for the carving on the only sculpted grave-stele from this circle is too sketchy to be of use. So for the hairdressing of the men, the first and most obvious place to turn was the suite of masks, taking the electrum mask from Circle B together with the slightly later golden examples from Grave Circle A. We have already seen that only the 'beautiful' mask from Grave V in Circle A is shown with beard and moustache, but save for the eyebrows on the other flat masks none of them are shown with any hair at all. It is possible to argue that the artists of the other gold masks did not give them beards and moustaches because they were learning from the artistic tradition of the Cycladic islands and of Middle Minoan Crete. Here full beards were rarely if ever shown and one may assume that men went clean-shaven, so that no convention existed for the depiction of facial hair other than eyebrows; therefore, it is argued, it needed an innovator like the artist of the 'beautiful' mask to create one, but such a suggestion raises a number of questions about what this artist or his audience actuallly expected from this or indeed any representation of the human face.[21] Nevertheless there are other illustrations of male faces which, if not exactly contemporary, are close enough to give us an idea of Mycenaean fashion at the end of the Middle Bronze Age (given the vagaries of human taste in these matters at the best of times). These suggest that there was no hard and fast rule: some men wore a full beard, others a beard and no moustache, while some shaved their faces completely and wore their hair short. It seems perfectly feasible that the gold masks illustrate these differences too. There is a theory that hair length reflects social status in the Bronze Age as it did later. This suggests that long hair was a sign of nobility, hair cut at the nape indicated an official, while the common people cut their hair short. Although this may be true of Minoan Crete, the evidence from the mainland does not really support it. For example, on the lion-hunt dagger from Shaft Grave IV (one of the latest burials, and so slightly later than our heads) the huntsmen are all clean-shaven and with short hair that sometimes covers the nape and is sometimes cut level with the ears; on the gold rings

11. Sigma 131: the final 'lean' version with hair and beard.

12. Zeta 59: the final version. The scar over the left eye is clearly visible.

from the same grave showing the 'battle in the glen' and a stag hunt, warriors and huntsmen are shown both bearded and clean-shaven, their hair long or short. The amethyst seal found in Grave Gamma shows a man wearing a beard combined with a clean upper lip. Even if this gem was made in Crete, it is at least contemporary with the warrior with whose burial it is associated (Gamma 55), and the fact that other evidence shows the hairstyle was found later on the mainland makes it at least possible that some of those buried in Grave Circle B were already wearing it (see Chapter 7, fig.4).[22]

In the end we opted to let our reconstructions reflect this variety of hairstyles, not least because in their finished form it still made comparison between the various facial types easier if they were not all

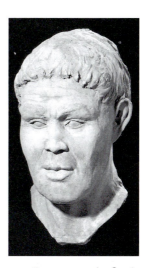

13. Gamma 51: the final version.

14. Beta 52: the final version.

covered by hair. 'Pelops' was given a style that reflected the 'beautiful' mask from Shaft Grave V as befitted his seniority: hair reaching to the nape, and a neatly trimmed full beard and moustache (fig.11). Zeta 59 should perhaps have had a beard too, in view of his age, but here we felt strongly that as much of his face as possible should be visible, so that the similarities with Gamma 51 would not be covered up. He is clean-shaven, with slightly receding hair that does not conceal his battle scars trimmed off at the nape (fig.12). Gamma 51 was left with the short trim – almost a pudding-basin cut – found on the lion-hunt dagger as befitted his relative youth (fig. 13). The effects of the trephining were not shown, since after all he never had to bear with that during life. We also gave Beta 52, the 'man with a lot of face', a short haircut and no beard, not because of his apparent youth, for his death at around thirty in a society where the average age at death was thirty-six only makes him seem youthful to modern eyes, but to allow his very individual features to speak for themselves (fig. 14).

So we turned to the three remaining skulls. Grave Alpha, a late phase grave in the northeast of the circle, had been the first grave to be discovered, and was excavated in the winter of 1951. It had cut into two small early graves, but was itself a large late grave that had been used at least twice, for apart from the principal skeleton – certainly male – the remains of another individual had been swept against the wall. It had been marked by a stele, crudely carved with a fight scene, and the grave goods were very rich: as well as a large number of fine weapons, there were metal vases, a faience cup, gold ornaments and two pins. Since these last seem more suited to a woman, it may be that the first occupant was female. When Angel saw the skull it was still in good condition, and from this and the other remains he described a broad-shouldered, strong-limbed and big-bodied man, 1.68 m tall (a little over 5 ft 6 in), perhaps twenty-three years old but whose spine already showed signs of heavy exercise and possibly also of a healed fracture. The muscle attachments on the lower part of his skull showed that like Sigma 131 and Zeta 59 he had had a powerful neck and jaw, and he too had the pronounced mastoid process that is characteristically male.

In 1987 the skull was extremely fragile: many of Angel's repairs were still intact but some of the lower parts such as the maxilla had become detached and broken. It needed very delicate conservation before it was stable enough for us to risk making a cast (fig. 15). Some loose pieces could be reattached, but the fragments of the orbit and maxilla that would give us the central and upper parts of the face were in such a fragile and delicate condition, and the areas where they joined the rest of the skull so badly damaged, that we reckoned that any attempt to attach them would do more harm than good, and would certainly not stand up to the strain of casting. We therefore decided to cast them separately. We did, after all, also have Angel's photographs and notes to help us out. This man had a high forehead and wide cheekbones tapering down to the chin; the features sat neatly within the face, with a fairly wide nose above a small, precise mouth (fig. 16). Angel had described it as a massive ovoid skull, 'extremely large, with wide forehead above a very wide-cheeked heart-shaped face with deep chin and wide nose'. Despite his relative youth it somehow seemed appropriate to give him the same beard and moustache and hair reaching to the nape, with which we had endowed 'Pelops' (fig. 17).

There remained Gamma 55 and Gamma 58, the other two surviving skulls from the grave in which had lain Gamma 51, the unfortunate young man who had died after the trephining operation.

Gamma 55 was an enticing candidate because he was the only person in this grave circle to have been buried with a mask, thus providing a link with graves IV and V in Circle A (pl.VI). It was of electrum rather than gold, the only mask of this metal, and belongs with the early 'flat' group of masks; it is probably the earliest of them all. Unlike the masks in Grave Circle A (pl.VII), however, this one was found not over the face of the dead man, but resting on its edge against a jug some way behind and to one side of the skull, where it had perhaps fallen from a box. It lay much too far from the skull ever to have rested upon it. This in itself calls into question the role of the masks as portraits in any sense of the word, at least in their original intention. Those in Grave Circle A certainly seem to have been intended to serve as death masks in some manner when they were placed over the face of the dead person, but the position of the mask in grave Gamma suggests that this may not have been their original function, indeed that this function had not yet been

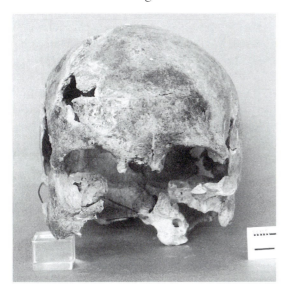

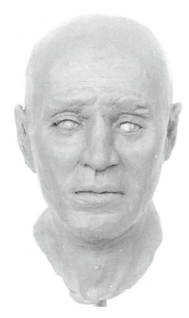

15. *Alpha 62: the skull after conservation in 1987.*

16. *Alpha 62 as reconstructed but still without hair.*

17. *Alpha 62: the final version with hair and beard.*

considered when this man was buried, with his mask beside him. It is conceivable that their primary role was as symbols of power and authority. For our own particular purpose of facial reconstruction we had thought at the outset that the electrum mask might give us a guide to this man's appearance, but the more we looked into its archaeological history, its function, and at the details of its appearance and method of manufacture, the clearer it became that the two could have no physical resemblance.

His skull was in a desperate state. Angel's technician had reattached numerous fragments, and as far as we could tell from his photographs

had left it reasonably complete save for some gaps in the vault (which would not have mattered to us) and in an area in the upper jaw (which would have made facial reconstruction a little tricky, but certainly not impossible). When we came to look in the box in the museum containing Gamma 55 we found a skull whose lower half had almost entirely gone: Angel's glue still held the nasal bone in place (just), but the wiring on which his technician had rebuilt the skull had all disintegrated, and so all those parts that would form the structure for the central part of the face had come away, and were lying loose in the box; and of course there was no mandible. While the search for the mandible continued – like the others, it was re-created in the studio in Manchester – the problems of consolidating the thin and friable fragments of bone taxed our conservator's skills even more than had the previous specimen: she succeeded in reattaching the nasal bone firmly along with both mastoid processes and the right orbit, so that now there was a reasonably solid foundation for a cast that extended down to the lower cheeks. Much of the maxillary dentition (the upper teeth) and some other portions survived, even if they could not be reattached to the rest of the skull and had be cast separately. Taking these together with Angel's notes and photographs, we reckoned that we had an adequate basis for a reconstruction. Nonetheless casting this man's skull was a delicate and tense affair despite all the practice his colleagues and relations (if relations they were) had given us. All went safely, and although to our relief none of the newly reattached pieces came away during the casting, it was good to have the first-aider standing by. Once again we realised how crucial it was to have a conservator with us as part of the field team (fig. 18).

Gamma 55 was another big man: Angel had calculated his height at 1.76 m (5 ft 9¼ in), and had put his age at around thirty-three on the basis of the pelvic development. He had commented on the strength and thickness of his bones, the likely strength of his neck muscles and on his nearly perfect teeth. When the skeleton was excavated the knees were spread wide, which led Angel to say that he had been buried in the position of a horserider, but it is more likely that he was laid out with his legs drawn back somewhat, perhaps to allow space for the body of Gamma 51 – the young man with the trephined skull – across the end of the grave, and that the bones fell outwards as the flesh decomposed. Angel evidently expected a rather massive face with a low brow: the reconstruction showed more delicate features, with a relatively high forehead, wide cheekbones and eyes set well apart, tapering towards the chin – much more the heart-shaped face that Angel had noted when comparing him with his female tomb-companion Gamma 58 (fig. 19).

When it came to comparing this reconstruction with the electrum mask (pl. VI) one could say that they both showed a face with small features, a face that was roughly triangular in outline and with a high forehead. But we have seen already that there were other reasons why the craftsman should have made the mask triangular that need have no connection with the physical appearance of the man for whom it was made, and when it comes to details the two do not match: like several of the masks this one has a long and rather narrow nose, and a small mouth; the reconstruction shows a relatively larger mouth, and a wider and much smaller nose with a deep hollow between the eyes. While we do not claim the reconstruction to be an accurate portrait, technically it must produce a face that is recognisable and identi-fiable; when one compares the two, it becomes clear that the mask cannot be a portrait in the sense of depicting this particular individual at all. At one stage we had wondered whether we should try to make a cast of the interior of the mask to match against the reconstruction, but now there seemed little justification in subjecting so precious an object to such an ordeal. It was clear that there was so little intended physical resemblance between the mask and its owner's face that it was not even worth our making a measured comparison between the two by the new technique

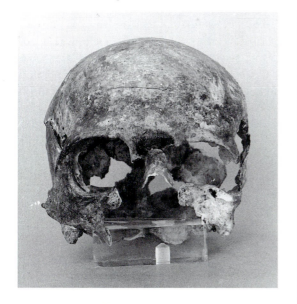

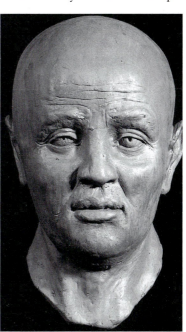

18. *Gamma 55: the skull after conservation in 1987.*

19. *Gamma 55 as reconstructed but before the addition of hair or beard.*

20. *Gamma 55: the final version with hair and beard.*

of photocomparison (facial mapping): on a flat mask the features must be too distorted and too remote from the original three-dimensional face for such a comparison to be either practi-cal or valid. The mask did not even give us an indication of hair or beard, but perhaps it was its markedly triangular shape that influenced us into giving this man a neatly trimmed beard, as clearly befitted his status, but leaving his upper lip clean-shaven, like the amethyst seal from his grave and the other later pieces to which we have referred (fig. 20).

The lady known as Gamma 58 was the last member of this burial family to be studied; whether they were a real family remained to be seen. There were several reasons why we should attempt to reconstruct one female skull, but women were under-represented in the grave circle and only four skeletons had been identified as female. Of these, two were lacking the skulls altogether; the skull of the third had been badly distorted by the pressure of the earth upon it, and even in 1954 the frag-ments, though restorable, were 'rotten-woodlike in their fragility': by 1986 not only the repairs but many of the actual fragments had disintegrated – she was cer-tainly no candidate for reconstruction. This left us with Gamma 58, who had the advantage that we might expect some kind of relationship with the men buried in the same grave, but the great disadvantage that so much of her face was lost: Angel's photographs already showed the entire nasal bone and much of the maxilla to be missing, so that the region of the eyes and the centre of the face appeared as a gap-ing chasm. However, in this case the surviving bone was better preserved than in many of the other skulls and matters had not deteriorated significantly since the 1950s. Although much of the face was missing from her skull, especially the centre, the rest of the cranium was largely intact and the vertical and horizontal dimensions were secure (fig. 21). This meant that the position of essential features such as the mouth and eyes was certain, even if their exact shape was speculative. That this lack need not prevent one from reconstructing a recognisable face has been proved the the identifications of the 'headless body' from Wyre Street in Manchester and the Hampshire body, both described in Chapter 2. In the former case the head had been deliberately disfigured by the killers in the hope of avoiding recognition, in the latter violent contact with a ploughshare had achieved the same effect.

Like her tomb-mate Gamma 58 was a strongly built person, though probably quite slender, and tall (1.61 m, 5 ft 7 in). She was in only her mid-thirties when she died, but must already have suffered some pain in her lower back from the begin-nings of arthritis in the lumbar vertebrae, and the arthritis was affecting her hands too. At some stage in her life she had broken her right upper arm, for the humerus showed a fracture, but it had healed very well: perhaps her royal standing had ensured that she received better treatment than her humbler contemporaries, for most broken arms at the time healed crooked or shortened.[23] The skull is theoreti-cally large enough to be male; however, other details such as the sharpness of the upper edges of the eye-sockets and the lack of brow-ridges, coupled with the fact that Angel, who had the opportunity to study the whole skeleton, commented on her markedly female true pelvis and noted the birth canal, all led us to agree that this was indeed the skull of a woman. The bone of the skull was noticeably thick-ened and heavy – again, it would need more work even to attempt a proper medical diagnosis, but one cause for the thickening could be Paget's Disease, a con-dition which has precisely this effect on the bone although it causes no discomfort. Because her remains had been pushed to one side of the grave along with those of the first occupant when the bodies of the two men (Gamma 55 and 51) were interred later, it is not possible to be quite certain which of the objects found near her skeleton had originally been buried with her: an ivory comb for sure, but quite possibly also some of the beads normally associated with Gamma 55, the next person to have been placed in the grave, for beads are more usually found with the burials of women or children. For the same reason it could even be that the amethyst gem with the bearded 'portrait' carved on it to which we have referred several times (Chapter 7, fig.4) belonged to her and not to Gamma 55.[24]

Her face has the same heart-shaped outline as Gamma 55; like him too the eyes are relatively small and wide apart, but her mouth seems proportionately larger (fig.22). Seen in profile her forehead is prominent, and the line of her jaw strong (though under the circumstances one should perhaps not rest too much on this feature); it is quite unlike the profile of the prognathous Beta 52.

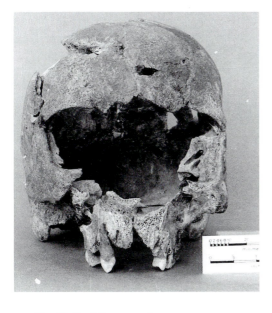

21. *The skull of Gamma 58.*

22. *Gamma 58: the head before the addition of hair.*

Her hairstyle was the subject of much discussion, and like any lady of fashion, she changed it more than once before we found a style that satisfied everyone. The four little gold plaques and a gold ornament on a pin (possibly Minoan work) found by Schliemann in Shaft Grave III and which can only have been a generation or two later, though small and crudely detailed, suggested a row of curls at the front and shoulder-length hair at the back which left the ears exposed.[25] We did not want to rely too heavily on the fresco paintings found at Mycenae and other sites on the mainland not only because of their Late Helladic III date – some three centuries younger – but also because there was a good chance that by then mainland fashions had been altered by Minoan influence. However, they too showed a row of curls across the brow and long hair hanging down the back of the head, with long curls in front of the ears, which were again left exposed (e.g. fig.24). We consulted several colleagues, and finally turned to Diana Wardle at the Mycenae Project in

Birmingham University, who was working on Mycenaean costume and hairstyles, and who had already been responsible for re-creating some dresses and wigs in the Late Mycenaean fashion. She produced for us a series of meticulous drawings of ladies of different ages wearing a variety of hairstyles, mostly based on the fresco paintings discovered in the building known as Xeste 3 on the island of Thera, which are much nearer in date to the Mycenaeans with whom we were concerned than any of the surviving frescoes from Mycenae itself (fig. 23). The actual lifestyle of the Therans in the Middle and Late Bronze Ages was perhaps closer to that of the Minoans of Crete than to that of the Mycenaeans, yet if we take the jewellery which the Theran

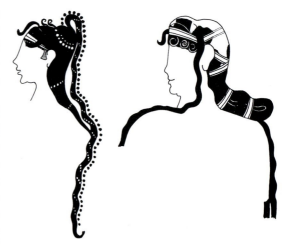

23. Hairstyle of the 'Mistress of the Animals' from Xeste 3 at Thera (c. 1550 BC). For clarity, details of jewellery and anatomy have been omitted.

24. Hairstyle of the 'Mycenaean Lady' from the fresco in the 'House of the High Priest' at Mycenae (c. 1200 BC).

ladies on the frescoes wore in their hair and on their heads as a guide, fashions in Mycenae at the time of the Shaft Graves had much in common with those at Thera. Although the jewellery has generally been omitted from our drawings to make the hairstyles easier to understand, the Mycenaean ladies in Grave Circle A were buried with similar earrings, hairpins and beads to those worn by their Theran counterparts, and so we felt that we could follow Theran hairstyles for our Mycenaean princess. The model became the figure of the 'Mistress of the Animals' from Xeste 3: like our Mycenaean, she too must have been a lady of riper years, for the painter endowed her with the beginnings of a double chin as well as generous and rather pendulous breasts. What was peculiarly Mycenaean, at any rate by the fourteenth century BC, was the fashion of pulling the hair up onto the crown and letting it fall down either in a single pony-tail or in three long locks: the highly idiosyncratic Late Helladic III 'idols' from the cult centres at Mycenae itself and at Phylakopi on Melos are shown thus. The fact that this penchant for pony-tails was found on Thera too seemed to justify our relying on evidence from that island for other aspects of the hairstyle.[26] So we gave our Gamma 58 a pony-tail and three long locks that hung down the back of her head and were held in place by a band wound round them, three little plaits on the top of her head that stood up in a rather spiky and modern fashion but copied exactly what the Theran paintings showed, and added a row of 'Mycenaean' curls over her forehead; these curls were not normally found on Thera but were very much a feature of Mycenaean taste (fig. 25). It was a fascinating and revealing exercise to try to translate both ancient and modern artists' interpretations of this ancient method of dressing the hair into three dimensions – one cannot do it unless one understands how the hair actually works, and every female member of the Unit's staff in Manchester was called upon to model and to give advice. The end-product still cannot be a definitive version of the hairstyle worn by the ladies of Mycenae around 1600 BC, but it should at least be seen as an addition to the lady's ensemble that helps to place our reconstruction in its historical setting. From a technical point of view it required us to make a reconstruction in the form of a bust rather than only a head, for without her shoulders the lady's long locks did not hang properly. Inevitably she became known to us as Clytemnestra, by far the most famous of the women in Agamemnon's family.

Now that at last we had all seven of reconstructions completed, our main concern was to consider whether they told us anything about their family relationships. We had already noted some shared features and some differences, and of course Angel had noticed a complex series of similarities between many of these skulls as well as those from Grave Circle A, which apparently cut across any suggested family groupings of the graves.

When one tried to make comparisons on a purely visual basis some similarities and some misfits became apparent, which one might interpret as reflecting possible relationships and outsiders. It involved looking at characteristics such as the overall shape of the skull – whether the forehead is high or low and whether it slopes or not, and correspondingly whether the back of the skull slopes or is rounded – and then at details such as the orbits and the cheekbones – are they close together or wide apart (the

25. Gamma 58: the final reconstruction with contemporary hairstyle.

answer does not always seem to be the same for both) – and at whether the chins are shallow or deep. First, there is the striking similarity between Zeta 59 and Gamma 51 that we had already noticed (see fig. 10): their long faces share a high and slightly sloping forehead and rounded skull, narrow cheekbones and closely set eyes, and a deep chin. The chief difference showed in profile: Gamma 51 was somewhat prognathic but Zeta 59 not at all, which meant that the old warrior had a much more prominent chin than the man we might assume to be his young descendant, in whose side-view the mouth becomes a much more striking feature. Seen in profile, Gamma 51 also has a straighter forehead and much less of a hollow at the top of the nose. Curiously, it was just in their profiles that Angel had noticed a resemblance. Sigma 131 ('Pelops') seemed to share most of these features, but his forehead did not slope, and did not have the hollowed sides that gave the other two their horse-like appearance; he was markedly more prognathic, and his skull was altogether shorter and more rounded, so that in profile one is struck by his eyebrows, nose and mouth. The shape of the nose and the straightforward form of the vault of the skull with a very marked occipital region at the back were like those of Gamma 55. We could see further similarities in the proportions of the front of the skull, most strikingly those between the chin and the bridge of the nose, and between the bridge of the nose and the top of the head. Both skulls showed faces with rather weak chins, but it is hardly fair to use this feature to judge their qualities as leaders of men.

Beta 52, the beaky young man 'with a lot of face', remained physically a loner. Although he

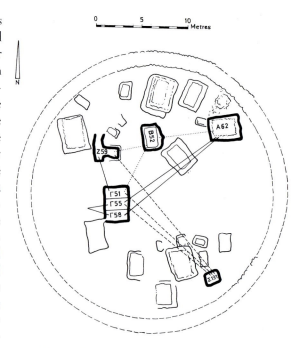

26. *Plan of Grave Circle B showing kinship connections between graves based on the facial reconstructions: solid lines indicate probable links, broken lines possible links, and dotted lines tentative links.*

shares the narrow cheekbones and close orbits of Zeta 59 and Gamma 51, his forehead is low and slopes sharply, as does the back of his skull; his chin is shallow, and with his prominent brow-ridges and long mastoid process – indeed a skull that is surprisingly long in relation to its other proportions – he seems at first to be quite unrelated to the other six. His skull looks surprisingly tall in relation to its internal proportions when seen from the front, because of his sloping forehead. Seen from the side he shares some features such as the sloping forehead and perhaps therefore also the overall shape of the top of the head, the brow-ridges and the dorsal ridge of the nose with Alpha 62, although his face is generally narrower but yet has a chin that is proportionately wider. However, there comes a point where the 'similarities' that one detects need be no more than those that can occur between any members of the same tribal or racial group, and one must not press them too far: family traits and likenesses do not always carry through down the generations, and it is easily possible for them to become diluted or be overidden by new intrusive elements (fig.26). Angel had suggested a link in vault form with skull 61 from grave Delta and skull 66a from Grave Nu, graves on either side of Beta where a connection is certainly possible on archaeological grounds. Unfortunately both these skulls were much too damaged to be considered for reconstruction. In fact the extent to which they survived even when excavated leads one to treat some of the links proposed by Angel with a little caution (of Delta 61 there remained only the frontal bone [forehead] and lower jaw, and Nu 66a was little better). On paper at least Beta 52 does share some features with the venerable Sigma 131 whose grave was on the other side of the circle, such as the closely set orbits and narrow cheekbones, the prognathic jaw and shallow chin.

It was very interesting that the faces on the other two skulls from Grave Gamma, 55 (he of the electrum mask) and 58 (the woman) were very similar to each other – wide orbits and cheekbones, rounded skull, high straight forehead, heart-shaped face – but were unlike Gamma 51 in almost every respect; they shared only the rounded back to the skull and fairly high forehead – Angel had noted a similarity in the shape of the vault between 58 and 51, and of unspecified facial detail between 51 and 55. We have already noticed that Alpha 62 has much more in common with them: his features are not as delicate as theirs, and his mouth is wider in proportion to the rest of the face, but they all three have the same profile, and many of the features that link Gamma 55 and Gamma 58 can be found on Alpha 62 as well, such as the wide-set eyes and cheekbones and the angle between the cheeks and the chin. This is already interesting because grave Alpha was in another part of the circle, far to the northeast. Sigma 131, who was buried in the southeast of the circle, also shares some features with this threesome – a neat, compact face with small brow-ridges; his jaws are not prognathic, and the lower jaw is not heavy. The outline of his face is round rather than having the heart shape of Gamma 55 and 58. Perhaps, as with Beta 52, it is better not to press the similarities too hard.

The relationships suggested by the facial similarities based on the reconstructions thus leave Sigma 131, the only representative of the southeastern grave group, rather on his own. Angel thought he was a key genetic figure in the creation and pro-creation of one of the Mycenaean dynasties. If so, then the evidence we have brought together so far suggests that his dynasty was not very successful, though perhaps he should take consolation from the 'dilution factor' we have just noted – and from the fact that our evidence is still far from complete, and so such a nega-tive view is probably unjustifed. He has rather tenuous links with Beta 52 in the northeastern group, who otherwise also stands alone at present: while one would like to see a link between Beta 52 and Alpha 62 in the same grave group, the only real similarity seems to be in the slope to the back of the skull, hardly sufficient to identify them as members of the same family, although in fairness one has to allow for the fact that the lower part of the skull of Alpha 62 was badly damaged. It is in the northwestern and central groups that matters become more intriguing. Gamma 51 must be descended from Zeta 59, champion of champions and potential ances-tor of many, but so far we have detected no others of the line, and the other two occupants of this late grave cut into the centre of the circle show clear signs of rela-tionship to each other but not, apparently, to the unfortunate young man who, dead from head injury or from the results of his trephining operation, was put last into their grave. Rather, they show physical links with Alpha 62 from the northeast corner. Are we to see in the occupants of this grave as well as in its position in the circle evidence of some kind of reconciliation or linking up between the different groups, who had until now ruled as separate families or separate units, and had buried their dead accordingly? This grave, late in the life of Grave Circle B, belongs to the period when some people – one single family? – were already burying their dead in the new Grave Circle A.

There is one other conclusion to be drawn from the relationships within Grave Gamma. As we saw, remarkably few women were buried in Grave Circle B – out of a total of thirty-five skeletons only four could certainly be identified as female as against fifteen, possibly sixteen identifiable males (the remainder are too fragmentary to be sexed). Were they wives or blood members of the family? The similarity of Gamma 58, the lady we know as 'Clytemnestra', to her tomb-companion Gamma 55, seems to argue irrefutably that they were closely related, if not brother and sister then at least cousins; certainly not husband and wife, while they are too close in age to have been mother and son. Given the imbalance of the sexes in the graves, perhaps the few women chosen for burial within the circles held some position of authority by right of birth rather than marriage.

Our original purpose in undertaking reconstructions of skulls from Grave Circle B had been twofold. The first was the simple fascination of looking at the faces of this group of people whom one could fairly say were among the first rulers of Mycenae as it set out on the road that led to a major role in the ancient world. In this we like to think we were wholly successful. Schliemann said that he felt that by his discoveries at Mycenae he had brought Agamemnon to life; perhaps we have gone a step or two further. As he was excavating Grave Circle B, Professor Mylonas found himself recalling one of the satirical *Dialogues of the Dead* which Lucian wrote around AD 160: Menippus, who has just arrived in Hades, asks the god Hermes to show him round:

Hermes: I am busy, Menippus. But look over there to your right, and you will see
    Hyacinthus, Narcissus, Nireus, Achilles, Tyro, Helen, Leda, all the beauties of old.
Menippus: I can see only bones, and bare skulls; most of them are exactly alike.
Hermes: Those bones, of which you seem to think so lightly, have been the theme of
    admiring poets.
Menippus: Well, but show me Helen; I shall never be able to make her out myself.
Hermes: This skull is Helen.
Menippus: And for this a thousand ships carried warriors from every part of Greece;
    Greeks and barbarians slain, and cities made desolate.
Hermes: Ah, Menippus, you never saw the living Helen; or you would have said with Homer:

            Well might they suffer years of toil
            Who strove for such a prize.

    We look at withered flowers, whose dye is gone from them, and what can we call
    them but unlovely things? Yet in the hour of their bloom these unlovely things
    were things of beauty.
Menippus: Strange, that the Greeks could not realise what it was for which they
    laboured; how short-lived, how soon to fade.
Hermes: I have no time for moralising. Choose your spot, where you will, and lie
    down. I must go and fetch new dead.

Reading that passage, we rather felt that Hermes, Messenger God and Guide of the Dead, would make a good member of our team: he could recognise the skulls for the individuals they had once been, and he was impatient to go and fetch more.[27]

One can rarely predict how a face will look from the skull alone, and there were arguable advantages in not making all the reconstructions together, in coming 'fresh' to each head, the most potent being that there was less chance for preconceived similarities to be built into the whole group. The actual reconstructions of these Mycenaeans were tackled in three groups, if not completely separately. The faces that have grown upon these skulls are all individuals. Of course one could argue that this is simply the medical artist allowing himself to be influenced by the world of Mycenae, both ancient and modern, and this is undoubtedly true to the extent that during our two expeditions to Greece to cast the skulls he was surrounded by ancient Mycenaean artefacts and by modern Mycenaean people (though how far these are related to the earlier inhabitants is a moot point). But that is only a very small part of the whole story, for as we have tried to emphasise, the fundamental technique is purely objective and it is only the superficial detail that can be subjectively influenced. These seven skulls have produced seven faces that certainly reflect not the features but the individualism and force of character conveyed by the gold and electrum masks, which persisted throughout Mycenaean art.[28] This rather than physical accuracy or idealism is perhaps one of the underlying elements of the representation of the human figure in Mycenaean art. Even the 'Mycenaean Lady' from the House of the High Priest at Mycenae, with her massive arms, double chin, and narrow eyes, is a personality rather than an idealised physical beauty (see fig. 24).

Our second aim was to discover whether, having re-created their faces, we might be able to judge whether they were in any way related to each other, or whether they came from a number of different families. In this period of late prehistory one has until now had to rely on the evidence of more traditional archaeology, or on occasional references in the annals of other already literate countries such as Egypt. Could we by this new approach learn something new not just about the people themselves but also about the social and political history of the time? Here we can claim modified success as fig. 26 shows: skulls from graves in different parts of the circle, tentatively identified as belonging to different groups, generally do not look alike, and so do not seem to be related to each other, but with certain notable exceptions, such as Zeta 59 and Gamma 51. Skulls from burials in the same graves sometimes show distinct family likenesses, even when of different sexes, and thus are very probably related. Of course the fact that two people's faces look alike may be pure chance, and not everyone who shares features with somebody else need be related to them, but lookalikes come from the same family far more often than not, in Bronze Age Mycenae just as anywhere else.

The fact that Zeta 59 and Gamma 51 share so many features raises an interesting point. Those who buried Zeta 59 laid in his grave with him some fine pottery and a long sword, a substantial offering for a grave in this early phase of the Grave Circle when burial goods are normally sparse; by contrast, fifty years or so later Gamma 51 was given only a few vases and no metalwork at all to take into the next world at a time when burials were generally much richer. One would expect the quality of the goods interred with the dead to reflect their social standing, and to some extent this has to be true of the burials in the Grave Circles, although the story is complicated by the fact that (as often in history) burials also tend to get richer as time progessed and the society in which they lived became richer, even within the relatively short time span of the Grave Circles.[29] However, the burials in Grave Gamma, certainly the last three (Gamma 58 – 'Clytemnestra', Gamma 55 – the man with the electrum mask, and Gamma 51 – the man who was trephined) were made within a very short time: Gamma 55 and Gamma 51 must have been buried within days of each other, if not actually at the same time, with Gamma 51 laid rather oddly across the feet of the other two. The contrast between Gamma 55, the last wealthy burial in the grave, and Gamma 51 with his few pots must on this argument be a sign of their different social standing: he is not however unique in being buried with only pots and no metalwork – the forty-five-year-old man interred in Grave Kappa at much the same time went into the next world with the same type of grave goods, and no one has sought a special reason for his relative poverty. There were only about five years in age between the two men in Grave Gamma, too little to suggest a knight-and-squire relationship of the kind found in medieval Europe, and at twenty-eight Gamma 51 was no longer a youth by Bronze Age standards. We have seen that Grave Gamma, a very large grave used four or five times, was one of a pair dug late in the life of Grave Circle B in between the northwestern group (of which grave Zeta happens to be the most southerly) and the southeastern burials (where the only late grave, Mu, was dug on the western edge of the group, closest to these two central graves) and have suggested that this was part of a political manoeuvre linking the two groups of people whose dead were buried there; this notion gains strength if we can see Gamma 51 as a scion of the old northwestern house, playing some kind of junior role in a rising branch of the new ruling group. We noted earlier too that Sigma 131 ('Pelops'), buried two or three generations earlier in the southeastern group, shared some facial features with the other two from Grave Gamma, such as the neat compact face and small brow-ridges. Of course by now Grave Circle A, Schliemann's grave circle, was already in use, and the real power lay with another branch, those who were interring their dead in this new burial ground a short distance up the hill, close to the citadel itself.

Bearing in mind that only seven skulls seemed suitable for the method we proposed, this seems a satisfactory result. Besides, perhaps we can now take the whole story another chapter further. When our project was conceived in 1985 biological or bioanthropological techniques for determining the relationships between human remains found in archaeological contexts were generally still in their infancy, and the challenge that this group of Mycenaeans presented was that we had a new approach that might provide some of the answers. However, in the intervening years other methods have taken great strides forward, and are being increasingly applied. Far from believing that these supersede the scientific value of what we set out to do at Mycenae, we see their development as a marvellous opportunity for collaboration, since none of our approaches tackles the problem in quite the same way, nor looks at exactly the same aspects. Two of these concern us particularly in the context of the Mycenaeans: biological distance study and DNA analysis.

Biological distance study in itself is not new, but it has not been applied to relatively detailed social and economic questions before. It involves the examination of small genetically heritable variations in the form and structure of the skull and of the teeth. Lisa Little, formerly J.L. Angel Fellow at the Wiener Laboratory of the American School of Classical Studies at Athens, has been carrying out a programme of research using this approach to identify the genetic traits which distinguish the Aegean populations of the Bronze Age as distinct biological units, looking particularly at the extent to which the populations intermarried and became mixed towards the end of the period. By one of those chance meetings from which collaborative academic research grows, one of us attended a seminar she was giving in Athens early in 1994: it seemed to both parties that we might have some interests in common, even though there are those who view her approach with a certain caution. At this stage we are still making plans as to exactly how our two methods will come together, but doing so in the belief that if we don't try we shan't know.

The extraction and regeneration of desoxyribonucleic acid – DNA – from archaeological bones is more familiar and perhaps less controversial: this too appeared to be a possible means of identifying genetical relationships between individuals, which, if it worked, would provide incontrovertible evidence of kinship.[30] The question was, would it work in this case? There appeared to be two major potential problems: the first was that after lying in the soil of Greece for three and a half thousand years the bones had become very mineralised, and there was considerable doubt as to whether enough organic material remained in them to yield any recognisable or reproducible DNA; and second, since alien DNA can be transmitted simply by physical contact, even if one did find traces, would it be the DNA of the ancient Mycenaeans themselves or of their contemporaries who buried them, or even of their modern heirs who excavated them, who studied them, or who packed them up in the museum; or even the DNA of the insects that sometimes crawl across the bones in order to feed upon the labels in the boxes? With the support of the Greek authorities and in collaboration with Keri Brown and Terry Brown in the Department of Medical Biochemistry and Molecular Biology at the University of Manchester Institute of Science and Technology, we took samples from six of our seven Mycenaeans to test them for DNA, taking them from parts of the bone where we felt contamination was least likely (the seventh, Sigma 131, we omitted only because his skull was in such good condition that we could not remove a sample without damaging it, and the rest of the skeleton was not readily accessible in the museum store: at this test stage we felt that he could wait). This is ongoing work, but as we write we already know that the first problem has been overcome, and there is a good chance that the second has as well: to our delight and excitement there is DNA there, in at least four if not all six samples; it is human DNA, and as far as one can reasonably tell at this stage it is ancient DNA. The next step is to confirm its age, to establish the sex of the individuals from which it comes, and to see whether from the evidence it provides they are genetically related. This will take two or three years, and we intend that it should form part of a larger project, in which we shall look at the DNA of a sample population from the Greek Bronze Age – all the occupants of the Grave Circles, for instance. The Mycenaeans' story is not over yet.

Disaster Victims from Minoan Crete: The Priest and Priestess from Archanes-Anemospilia

Our visit to Greece in 1987 had been concerned not only with the house of Pelops and Agamemnon in Mycenae, but also with a couple who had died a century or so earlier in altogether more macabre circumstances in the Crete of King Minos. The story of their discovery was dramatic and often controversial.[1]

During the 1970s Drs Yannis and Efi Sakellarakis had been excavating a Minoan palace in the small town of Archanes on the foothills of Mount Juktas in central Crete, some six miles inland from the famous palace site of Knossos. In the 1960s they had discovered nearby the cemetery of Phourni, perhaps the most important in Crete, and in searching for associated sites in the surrounding hills, they had found at a spot close to Archanes romantically called Anemospilia, 'the caves of the wind', what appeared to be a Minoan temple. There is much that we still do not know about Minoan religious practice, but as a temple it was unusual, for most Minoan shrines lay either in the confines of a palace or on the peak of a mountain, and this did neither, but had been built on a spur of Mount Juktas looking down onto the valleys that run towards Knossos and onto the coastal plain. The Minoan road from Knossos to the sanctuary on the peak of Juktas passed close by. Moreover, the design of the building did not resemble normal Minoan temples. It was laid out with three naves roughly on a north-south alignment which opened, not quite symmetrically, onto a corridor that ran the width of the building and formed the entrance lobby, very similar to the narthex at the west end of a modern Greek Orthodox church. We do not yet know if there were any other buildings nearby.

The building had been destroyed by earthquake, and then swept by a fire, probably caused by the oil lamps used in the temple. The excavation has not been fully published yet, but the excavators suggest that it was never cleared or rebuilt again, and the pottery, of Middle Minoan II/IIIA style, dated the destruction to c.1700–1650 BC, so the earthquake was probably the same as that which destroyed the first palaces in Crete.

Excavation began in the entrance hall, where around 150 vases were found, of varieties suggesting this area was used in the preparation of offerings and of rituals. Sprawled face down before the entrance to the central nave, the inner sanctuary, was a human skeleton, so badly damaged by the building blocks that had crushed it as disaster overwhelmed the building that it was even impossible to be sure of its sex. Nonetheless this was an important find, for despite the extensive destruction at Knossos and at the other palace sites in Crete, no body had yet been positively identified as an earthquake victim, though many had been discovered peacefully buried in their graves. This was the first. Scattered around were the remains of a spouted pottery bucket decorated in relief with rosettes on the rim and a bull on the side, and painted with crocuses, branches and spirals, in the exuberant and ornate 'Kamares' style of Middle Minoan Crete. It is an unusual shape, and probably formed part of the cult equipment: a similar vase is depicted on the sarcophagus from Agia Triada, where it is being used to catch the blood from a bull that has just been sacrificed. It had been smashed into more than a hundred fragments: such ruination of a solid piece of pottery in itself suggests that something worse befell it than simply being dropped.

Fallen from the platform at the north end of the central nave the excavators discovered a pair of clay feet in the middle of a thick layer of ash and fragments of burnt wood, all that remained of the statue of the deity to whom it had been sacred. The floor in front of it was covered with vases that had contained the offerings of the Minoans, including further buckets like that found smashed in the entrance hall. In the nave to the left were the remains of a stepped altar; on it and along the sides of

the room stood vases that the excavators interpreted as containing fruits and cereals, perhaps liquids such as honey and wine, and other bloodless offerings.

However, the greatest excitement came from the excavation of the asymmetrical eastern nave, whose architecture recalled elements of the 'pillar crypts' of other Minoan shrines where the blood of sacrifices was collected, and which contained other features which suggested to the excavators that this was the section of the tripartite temple where one might expect the blood-sacrifices to have taken place. The area was empty save for three human skeletons. In the furthest corner a young woman 1.54 m (5 ft ½ in) tall lay sprawled face down. A well-built man, 1.78 m (5 ft 10 in) tall, aged between thirty and forty, lay on his back near the west wall

1. The skeleton of the priest and priestess as they were discovered at Anemospilia: the priest lies on his back in the foreground — note his shattered left leg and skull — while the priestess has run for shelter into the corner of the shrine.

with his arms across his chest (fig. 1). His legs had been broken by fallen debris; the right leg was stretched out, the left drawn up. On the little finger of his left hand he had a ring with a large oval bezel, made of silver coated with iron; and on his wrist he wore a beautiful agate seal engraved with the figure of a man poling a high-stemmed boat. Such jewels did not belong to ordinary folk in Minoan Crete: similar rings have been found in later contexts in Crete, but only in royal tombs.

On an altar-like structure near him was the sacrificial victim. The excavators naturally expected it to be an animal, but as the work of clearing proceeded it became clear that this was the skeleton of a young man about eighteen years old, lying in a position that suggested that he had been tied up with his arms behind his back. Lying on his body was a magnificent bronze blade, 40 cm (15¾ in) long and incised on each side with a stylised animal head, part fox, part boar, part fantasy. At the time of the discovery there was no other sure evidence for human sacrifice from Minoan Crete, although there are references to the practice in both legend and history. On Crete itself legend recorded that the Minotaur demanded an annual sacrifice of fourteen youths and maidens from Athens, while Homer has Achilles sacrifice twelve young Trojans at the funeral of Patroclus; the sacrifice of Iphigeneia was a key element in the story of the Trojan War and of the house of Atreus and Agamemnon, and the sacrifice of Polyxena over the tomb of Achilles forms a pendant at the end of the war, but it is very clear that in the classical period the Greeks themselves felt uneasy about their implications. Yet even in the fifth century BC the Athenian politician Themistocles is said by Plutarch to have ordered three men to be sacrificed before the battle of Salamis in 480 BC, though some doubt the veracity of this account.[2]

Nonetheless the setting at Anemospilia appeared to be that of a human sacrifice. Although soon afterwards evidence of other even more savage rituals, seemingly involving cannibalism, was uncovered at Knossos itself,[3] at the time of this discovery the interpretation proposed for Anemospilia was received with considerable unease, if not dismay. The excavators suggested that at a time of great fear, as earthquakes threatened Crete, the Minoans had been moved to take desperate measures in order to try to appease the gods, and had turned to human sacrifice, but that these measures had failed and their prayers had gone unheard: the victim had died, his throat cut with the great bronze blade, but immediately the temple had been shaken by a further tremor which had brought the roof down, killing the priest who had carried out the sacrifice: he fell backwards, instinctively bringing his hands up to protect his face. His colleague, a priestess, had turned to run to the corner for safety, but there she too had been trapped and killed (see fig. 1). The third member of the group, holding the container with the victim's blood in his hands, had been overwhelmed in the entrance hall, perhaps trying to escape from the collapsing building after attempting to deposit the offering before the statue of the deity. A dramatic interpretation perhaps, but no other has yet been suggested in print.

In fact on any interpretation these were important and striking individuals, marked out by their physique and by their possessions: the bronze blade, be it knife or dagger, is exceptional by any standards, and although to modern eyes the iron-covered ring appears undistinguished and unexciting, one must remember that in the Middle Bronze Age this was a rare and new metal, difficult to work and attractive to look at. It was an exciting discovery, but one whose interpretation created much scepticism in the archaeological world at the time, although since then excavations elsewhere have produced other scenarios that have been interpreted as human sacrifice.[4] The excavation of the temple was part of a much larger research programme in the area of Archanes and Mount Juktas, which the Sakellarakises saw to be a region of great if as yet unappreciated importance in the history of Minoan Crete. Seeing what had been achieved at Vergina under somewhat similar circumstances, they proposed that we undertake a reconstruction of as many of the skulls from Anemospilia as might be practical, naturally not in the expectation that thereby the people might be identified, nor even necessarily that in the course of the study further light might be thrown on what really happened that day at Anemospilia – although there was always the hope that further eyes trained in different disciplines might see something that had been overlooked. Yannis Sakellarakis' basic request was couched in terms that these were important people, fine physical specimens, that we did not know what the Minoans really looked like although there were of course plenty of representations in their art of how they wished to be seen: this was an exciting occasion to remedy such a lack.

We spread out the three skulls: priest, priestess and victim. The fourth, who had been trapped in the entrance hall, and who for want of more information one might describe as the acolyte, was so badly crushed in the destruction of the building that we had rejected him at the outset. It rapidly became clear that the other three were not going to be easy to deal with either. We had accepted them in part because they would provide an interesting pendant to the near-contemporary Mycenaeans from Grave Circle B on the mainland with their possible Minoan connections; but also because of the technical challenge they might provide. These were real disaster victims, who had been caught in a collapsing building as well as a fire. Looked at clinically, they could give us a marvellous opportunity to develop skills that might prove useful later, when there might be less time to experiment. Almost on cue, a year later we were indeed asked by the British Transport Police to reconstruct the face of the last unidentified body from the fire at King's Cross station, described in Chapter 2.

For the Anemospilia victims we adopted what one might call the 'air crash' approach. Just as after an air disaster the crash investigators collect together all the pieces which they can find and lay out those that they can recognise, leaving the unidentifiable on one side in the hope that later they will be able to find further recognisable fragments among them, so we put the obvious pieces of each skull in its appropriate place, with a heap of teeth and other small pieces on one side (fig. 2): gradually the fragments of cranium and mandible were joined by portions of the upper face such as the maxilla and the mastoid process, until we began to get something that might provide the basis for a facial reconstruction. It was a slow and rather tedious process, but not insuperable. After all, Philip of Macedon had presented a not dissimilar problem. We found that it helped if we treated them like a particularly difficult jigsaw puzzle. Each of the victims was laid out on a separate table, and after the initial burst of sorting and piecing together he or she was left

2. The fragments of the skull of the priest spread out in 'air crash' style: the teeth, and all the small pieces laid out below them, had to be ignored in making the cast for the reconstruction.

alone, and members of the team – along with research students and other academics staying at the British School – would pause in the course of their other work and see if they could not make another piece fit. At least these fragments were not as fragile as the skulls from Mycenae, for after the initial savage destruction they were buried in kindlier conditions, and we could handle them safely in order to study them in detail.

Despite these combined efforts, we decided that the head of the young sacrificial victim was too badly smashed and too badly damaged by the fire for us to be able to bring him back to life with the techniques available. We found joins between some of the fragments which we were able to glue together, but then he was, reluctantly and carefully, repacked in his box.

With the priest we were a little more hopeful. As with all three skeletons it would have been useful to examine his post-cranial bones as well as the skull, but these did not fall within our brief. However, we reckoned that enough of his skull survived to form a justifiable basis for reconstruction, although some gaps remained in the centre of his face so that this area is to some extent still hypothetical. His body had been crushed in the collapse of the shrine during the earthquake and his remains were then further distorted by the heat of the fire that followed, for unlike the case of Philip of Macedon this was no orderly, planned cremation. Therefore the final reconstruction must show a slightly distorted skull. In reality his face was probably more evenly balanced, but because there is no hard evidence it cannot be shown thus: the reconstruction has to show what is actually there, not what might have been. Nonetheless this does not render the whole exercise valueless, as three of the forensic cases in which we were later called to help demonstrate (Chapter 2). The skull of the middle-aged Indian Sabir Kassim Kilu was reconstructed as a young Southeast Asian on the basis of mistaken informa-tion, but all the same he was still quickly recog-nised by his family. The chief difficulty in the case of the Minoan priest was to reconcile the distor-tion that the smashed bones of his skull had suffered in the fire with the gap in the middle of the face. Here too we had a forensic parallel: the face of 'the headless body' from Wyre Street in Manchester had been deliberately mutilated to prevent identification, much as the collapsing, burning building had accidentally done for our priest, yet his face too was identified by an acquaintance from a reconstruction, just as hap-pened with the plough-damaged body found in a Hampshire field in 1996. The end-product is inevitably something of a compromise, but, we believe, a compromise that his family would have recognised, just as in they did in the three foren-sic cases (fig. 3). None of the reconstructions are ever claimed to be portraits in the strict sense; in this case the parameters are simply a little looser.

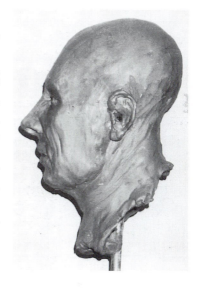

3. *Profile view of the head of the priest, before he was given hair. Despite the damage at the front, the shape of the back of the head is certain.*

In some of the reconstructions it has been pos-sible to compare the end-product with known portraits of the individual *after* the reconstruction has been completed (for instance the Vergina skull could be set beside portraits of Philip II). We could have no means of establishing the identity of this Cretan, and in any case from its nature Minoan archaeology is still prehistory, and so can hardly give us identifiable portraits: although a case can be made that a mere four or five Minoan seals or sealings out of the many thousands that survive show faces which are so idiosyncratic that they were intended to depict particular individuals, they cannot be individuals whom we can now identify.[5] In any case their very rarity should make us hesitate in calling them 'portraits', for there is little else in their art which suggests that the Minoans comprehended the notion of a portrait as we would understand it today. One does, however, have the possibility of using Minoan art to help with some of the information that the bones cannot provide, most notably the arrangement of the hair. The bulk of the evidence, including two of the possible 'portrait' seals, the Late Minoan I steatite seal of the so-called 'Chanting Priest' from Knossos and the amethyst gem (fig.4) from Grave Gamma at Mycenae (now generally reckoned to be of Cretan workmanship of the Middle Minoan IIIB or Late Minoan IA periods), suggests that most mature Cretan men at the turn of the Middle and Late Minoan periods wore beards. However, these are seemingly all laymen, and perhaps the only figure who can certainly be identified as a priest is the man leading the procession on the Late Minoan I 'Harvester Vase' from Agia Triada: he has long hair but no beard (fig.5). So the Anemospilia 'priest' was left clean-shaven and the hair over his forehead was brushed back, but he was given a long quiff in the centre of his forehead, hanging down to one side, again like the amethyst from Mycenae; as with the two gems, the priest on the Harvester Vase, and numerous Minoan clay idols, the hair at the back of his head was allowed to fall down his neck (fig.6 and pl.VIII). It has been

4. Amethyst gem carved with the 'portrait' of a bearded man: found in Grave Circle B at Mycenae (Grave Gamma), but probably Cretan work (Middle Minoan IIIB – Late Minoan IA: c.1600–1550 BC) (Athens, National Museum).

suggested that while long hair was a sign of noble birth in Minoan Crete and the common people had their hair cut short, officials wore a style like this that reached the nape.

The result is an impressive figure: a middle-aged man of powerful build with fine proportions to his face. He had a strong jaw and wide sloping forehead, the latter not surprisingly most noticeable before any hair was added to the head (see fig.3). Whilst the distortion to the skull is naturally echoed in the finished reconstruction it is not immediately obvious, for two reasons. First, the distortion is in the vertical plane, so that the face is not at right angles to the line which should run vertically from the centre of

5. The priest leading the procession on the 'Harvester Vase' from Agia Triada, Crete (Late Minoan I: c.1600–1500 BC) (Heraklion, Archaeological Museum).

the forehead through the nasal bone to the centre of the chin (the mid-sagittal plane). The second is that, as we noted with Philip II, a face has to show quite marked asymmetry before it becomes immediately noticeable to an observer.

The skull of his colleague was much better preserved and showed no signs of burning. She was in her early or middle twenties when she was killed. From her skull we could infer two or three interesting aspects of her medical history. First and most obvious to anyone who met her when she was alive, even if it was the least serious for her general health, she suffered from bad breath. Although her teeth were on the whole healthy and she did not suffer from caries – indeed at the time of her death she had only lost one tooth – the build-up of calculus or tartar on her teeth, particularly her lower front teeth, demonstrated all too clearly that she

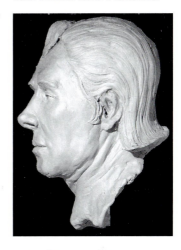

6. *Profile view of the reconstructed head of the priest from Anemospilia.*

had made no attempt to keep them clean, and that her dental hygiene was poor.

Second, the vault of her cranium was abnormally thickened, and the parietal bones – those that form the two sides of the skull – apparently showed marked osteoporosis. It was apparent on some of the Mycenaeans – we have discussed the problems of identifying it on skeletal remains in the previous chapter: in the case of the Minoan priestess we cautiously ascribed it to 'an undiagnosable haemoglobinopathy'. Among the Minoans osteoporosis appeared surprisingly frequently when compared to their low mean life expectancy: it is generally more common in post-menopausal women than in men, and leads to the bones becoming brittle, but is in fact a secondary symptom of a whole series of other diseases, mainly associated with the menopause. Recent medical research suggests that dietary, hormonal, genetic and even racial factors are involved. The explanation may lie in conditions such as prolonged breastfeeding and in premature ageing in the Bronze Age when contrasted with modern patterns.[6] The implications for the health of our priestess were not very encouraging, especially when taken together with what came next.

For third, the thickening of the skull also led one to suggest that she suffered from anaemia. Evidence for this blood disease can be traced to the bone because blood is formed in the bone marrow. Certain types of anaemic disease leave traces on the bone because they stimulate the marrow to attempt to make good the blood deficiency: this 'reactive hyperplasia' is particularly noticeable in the thickening of the bones forming the vault of the skull. Anaemia itself can be either acquired or inherited; it is not possible to distinguish the two kinds from the traces they leave on the skull, and we did not have the opportunity to examine and above all to X-ray the rest of the skeleton, which should have provided the necessary information. Acquired anaemia should give some indication of the standards of hygiene and nutrition under which the afflicted person lived: new research suggests that the acquired anaemias, in particular iron-deficiency anaemia, may in the end be responsible for more of the changes detectable in the bone than the inherited, congenital form. However, until recently it was assumed that because Greece was known to be a malarial area in antiquity, congenital anaemia was likely to be the more prevalent. This is because the congenital anaemias can provide some protection against the worst ravages of malaria, since the plasmodial parasite that causes the disease cannot thrive in the already damaged red blood cells of those suffering from mild congenital anaemia. There are two forms of congenital anaemia, sickle-cell anaemia and thalassaemia. If our priestess suffered from a congenital anaemia, it is more likely to have been the latter, since sickle-cell anaemia is chiefly found among black African populations, whereas thalassaemia has been so prevalent in

7. The usable fragments of the skull of the priestess, together with the casts from which the reconstruction was made. At the back is the occiput, still covered in the protective layer of aluminium foil.

8. Profile view of the reconstructed head of the priestess from Anemospilia.

parts of the eastern Mediterranean that its alternative name is Mediterranean anaemia. In the light of recent research, however, we believe it safer to propose acquired anaemia as the cause of the signs visible on her cranium. Though it is less painful and debilitating than for instance sickle-cell anaemia, she would nevertheless have suffered from loss of energy, and – had she survived the earthquake – the disease would probably have shortened her life.[7]

After reaching this rather gloomy diagnosis from our study of the skull, we took the precaution of covering each fragment with burnished foil before allowing it to come into contact with the alginate from which the moulds were made (fig. 7). The casts were safely made in Athens, and then the rest of the work was again done in the less pressured setting of the studio in Manchester. The casts of the pieces of skull were floated into place on a clay matrix (the priest had been given identical treatment), and then the face was built up in the now customary manner.

We cannot of course speak for Minoan taste or convention, but to modern eyes she appeared strikingly attractive, with wide forehead and cheekbones (fig. 8 and pl. ix). Her facial proportions were classically those of a female, the orbits large in proportion to the rest of the face and the width-to-height ratios of the reassembled skull very different from those of the male. Again, her hairstyle could be added on the basis of Minoan art, such as the frescoes of the so-called 'Parisienne' and of the dancer from the Queen's Megaron from Knossos (fig. 9), and other wall-paintings

9. *Fresco of the dancer from the Queen's Megaron at Knossos (Late Minoan IIIA: c. 1450 BC). The locks of hair framing her face are clearly visible.*

from the same site: long locks hanging over the shoulders, with a series of small curls framing the face, and a single curl in the centre of the forehead.[8] Again, we were having to rely on Late Minoan IIIA paintings that are up to two centuries later, because nothing suitable survives from the Middle Minoan, but on the whole it seemed a safe assumption.

Minoan art occasionally conveys a certain prettiness about its characters, but there is nothing 'soft' about either of these two. The reconstruction aims to be objective, and not to be influenced by any subjective or external factors. Aside from the hair, which is after all a purely superficial feature, we made no reference to any human representations in Minoan art until the reconstructions were finished, though of course one could hardly avoid having looked at the art of the period before and during the work. It is perhaps worth adding that in theory a computer-based reconstruction, programmed simply on the anatomical evidence and without reference to Minoan art, would have produced a much blander and probably less informative result. The medical artist is able to incorporate subtle but essential references to the Middle Minoan lifestyle that take into account the other available evidence from the circumstances of discovery, the associated finds, and the manner of death, which the computer is most unlikely to have been programmed to handle. As far as simply producing an identifiable image of the dead person goes either method would be equally valid, but the second, using the additional circumstantial evidence, is likely to give a much more rounded and informative picture.

The results can therefore stand as a first yardstick for the real physical appearance of the Minoans, as opposed to their own conception of their appearance as it is depicted in their art. That Minoan art was not necessarily idealising is clear from such idiosyncratic representations as the 'portrait' gems we have already mentioned: these pieces may represent 'special' people, but this unlikely to be true of the merry crowd on the 'Harvester Vase' from Agia Triada: the singer rattling a sistrum in particular has a very distinctive face.[9] We had after all been asked to reconstruct the two Anemospilia skulls for the specific reason that they too were 'special people', although in fact there is far too little evidence about the social background of Minoan religion for us to know how priests or priestesses were selected: although it is unlikely, there is nothing to tell us that one or both of them was not of humble origin, led into the priesthood by inspiraton rather than social standing. However, some time after the work was completed one of us was in Crete again, and spurred on by a suggestion thrown out after a lecture, visited Heraklion Museum to look at the two famous Middle Minoan III faience figurines of the 'Snake Goddess' from Knossos: they are fifty to a hundred years younger than the priestess, but they too have her wide forehead and cheekbones.[10] The face is perhaps more heart-shaped or triangular than that of the priestess with its firm jaw, but we saw that the overall shape of the face recurred many times in Cretan art, not only during the Minoan period to which the priestess belonged, but also in the 'Daedalic' art of the following Archaic period. Perhaps we should conclude that it was indeed a typical feature of the female Cretan face both before and after the upheavals of the later Bronze Age.

The next step should be a series of further reconstructions which will give us a more truly representative range of the Minoan people. Dr Yannis Sakkelarakis has suggested some further candidates (funds permitting), in particular a group of at least nineteen individuals from what has been called 'the most significant cemetery in Crete', which he has excavated at Phourni across the valley from Anemospilia.[11] They are from the same community as the priest and priestess, and are likely to be their near contemporaries: perhaps nine or ten of their skulls are complete enough to merit reconstruction. While such an undertaking may not answer the criticism, sometimes made, that few peasants receive the honour of having their faces reconstructed, it will take us some way along the road to presenting a larger selection of the Minoan people. This is not something that we have attempted anywhere else yet, and it forms an exciting prospect for the years ahead.

CHAPTER 8

Bodies from the Bog

Surely there can be nothing that reminds us more graphically of our own mortality than the sight of a corpse, a husk that for a brief span still retains the shape of its former living self before succumbing to the inevitable disintegration that is the ultimate destiny of all living things. Such a destiny may be reached in a few years, a few thousand years or a few million years, but reached it will be no matter how long it may take. There are, however, occasions when we find ourselves looking at a corpse that should not be there, one where the normal course of events has been interrupted by natural forces and where, despite the superficial changes wrought by the forces of decay, the husk still retains its shape. The recovery of a body that has been immersed in the chemical soup of a bog for hundreds or thousands of years presents just such an occasion. It moved Pitiscus of Oldenburg, writing at the end of the eighteenth century, to suggest that selected bodies should be specially preserved in peat so that future generations should be able to see how they looked.[1] One finds oneself gazing at a body which may have died centuries before, yet all the folds, creases and wrinkles, the scars and the hair are still to be seen, features which must have been so familiar to the dead person's contemporaries. Just such an occasion occurred in 1984 when the body of a man was found in Lindow Moss, a peat bog in Cheshire some ten miles south of Manchester (pl.x).[2]

The finding of a body under such circumstances is not unique: over one hundred cases of preserved human remains have been reported from the bogs of England and Wales alone, another thirty-odd in Scotland and perhaps ninety in Ireland, although in many cases only a few fragments of the body or some associated artefacts survived; indeed some are only 'paper bog bodies', known from old reports and stories, of which no actual remains survive.[3] The nature of preservation depends in part on the type of peat in which the body has been buried. In general, fen peat preserves the skeleton but not the soft tissues, whereas in bog peat the soft tissue survives well, the skeleton less so. Unlike so many of the bodies that have come to light over the years, 'Lindow Man' was studied so thoroughly that even the manner in which his hair had been cut was recorded by Scotland Yard.

Lindow Man was not, however, the first puzzle to have been found in that mysterious bog. On 13 May 1983 two men working for a commercial firm that excavates peat from the edge of Lindow Moss found what they thought at first was a burst football. When it had been hosed clean of peat, it proved to be the remains of a human skull, and the site manager at once took it to the police. A Home Office forensic pathologist reported that it was of a European female, probably between thirty and fifty years old at death. The cheek bones and both upper and lower jaws were missing. Some twenty years earlier a man named Peter Reyn-Bardt, in prison for another crime, had claimed to his cell-mate that he had killed his wife Malika,

dismembered the body and burned it, and then buried the remains in his back garden which bordered the Moss. When this story finally emerged as a result of a
totally different inquiry Reyn-Bardt was questioned in January 1983, but he denied
the accusation. A thorough search of the suspect's garden and of a lorry-load of peat
which had left the Moss for Somerset on the morning the skull was found had all
revealed nothing, except for an iron pin which the police discovered in the lorry.

The skull, with tissue and hair still adhering to it and even with part of the left
eye surviving, had been found in peat originally excavated only 330 m (300 yards)
from the garden. Presented with these facts, Reyn-Bardt confessed to the truth of
his earlier claim. However, although a further search of the area by the police at the
time yielded no further remains of the woman, they still felt some uncertainty
about the skull and sought archaeological advice. The Research Laboratory for
Archaeology at the University of Oxford provided a radiocarbon date for the skull
of 1740 ± 80 BP (AD 140–400), confirming the suspicions of the police that the
skull, by now christened 'Lindow Woman', was not that of the murdered woman.
Peter Reyn-Bardt was tried in November 1983 and convicted of his wife's murder
although no trace of her body has ever been found.

Formerly a vast marshy area of lowland raised peat bog covering some 600
hectares (1500 acres), Lindow Moss has become progressively smaller over the
centuries, largely as the result of agricultural pressures: by the mid-1800s it was
reduced to 300 hectares (750 acres), and today has shrunk to around 60 hectares
(150 acres). In the past peat was dug by hand, but now it is removed commercially
from trenches or 'rooms', 7 m (23 ft) wide and up to 200 m (650 ft) long, using
a large Hy-Mac excavator. The cut peat is stacked alongside the room from which
it has been taken and left to dry for six months to a year. Then it is loaded onto
a narrow-gauge railway and taken to a depot at the edge of the Moss. Here it is
lifted on a conveyor belt into a shredder, after which it may go to any part of the
country.

As the peat passes up the conveyor it is checked for foreign bodies such as stones,
tree roots and branches. The head of Lindow Woman had been spotted on this conveyor, and on 1 August 1984 Andy Mould, one of the men who had found the skull
of Lindow Woman the previous year, noticed a well-preserved human foot, with a
portion of skin from the leg still attached, moving up the conveyor. Again the police
were called, and later the Cheshire county archaeologist Rick Turner was asked to
comment upon the discovery. Visiting the site on the following day he noticed skin
tissue protruding from the edge of the trench from which the peat containing the
foot had been taken. After discussion with the police it was agreed that whatever
was attached to the protruding piece of skin should be excavated with great care.
Rather than try to extricate the body from its surrounding peat on site, they decided to cut free the block in which the remains were encased in order to allow a more
thorough and appropriate excavation of the body itself later. By the end of the day
the block of peat was lodged safely in the mortuary of Macclesfield District General
Hospital.

The body was now in the jurisdiction of the coroner: after the events of the previous year he had to be absolutely certain that this was indeed an ancient body

before he could release it for archaeological study. Despite all the more obvious indications, such as the depth at which the body had been found, the decalcified state of the bone and the lack of any amalgam or other evidence of dental treatment, it was not until final confirmation by Dr R.L. Otlet of the Atomic Energy Research Establishment at Harwell that the body was at least a thousand years old that he was prepared to make the final decision. The remains were now of no concern to him or to the police. The responsibility for this remarkable find was transferred to the British Museum, and the remains were quickly taken south and subjected to the most rigorous, numerous and intense examinations yet inflicted on any British bog body. Many specialists lent their expertise, led and coordinated by Dr Ian Stead, Deputy Keeper of the Department of Prehistoric and Romano-British Antiquities at the British Museum.

As the examination progressed it became clear that, apart from the portion of the lower right leg found on the conveyor belt, all that remained was the upper half of a male body, naked save for an armband of fox fur. The lower part had been sliced off at the waist during the cutting of the peat. Remarkably, in June 1988 part of the buttocks and left leg of an adult male appeared on the conveyor at Lindow Moss from a stack that originated close to the spot where Lindow Man had been found, and two months later the driver working near the same place noticed part of the right thigh in the bucket of his mechanical digger. Since these were body parts that 'Lindow Man' lacked, there can be little doubt that they formed part of the same person, and he is now effectively complete save for his left foot. In the previous year Rick Turner had followed up yet another discovery on the conveyor with a laborious and meticulous examination of both the peat still on the conveyor and the contents of the railway trucks in the yard, and had recovered over seventy pieces of human remains. It seems very likely that these come from the same individual as the skull known as Lindow Woman: they are, however, indisputably the remains of a male. Fragmentary skulls are not easy to sex with certainty, but one has to conclude that not only is Lindow Woman not Mrs Reyn-Bardt, she is not a woman at all.[4]

But this is looking ahead. The results of the tests and examinations carried out in 1984 revealed a story which is disturbing to modern notions. They have told us a great deal about Lindow Man's health and appearance, and about how he died, but we still do not truly know why he died. The evidence points to a ritual sacrifice which took place around the time of the Roman invasion of Britain in the first century AD; the manner of his death and the way his body was 'interred' in the bog are sinister and unsettling.[5]

The remains are those of a very strong and well-built male in his mid-twenties. He stood between 1.68 m and 1.73 m (5 ft 6 in and 5 ft 8 in) tall and weighed approximately 65.5 kg (10 stone). All the indications are that he was a perfectly normal healthy fellow with excellent teeth, although he suffered from mild arthritis in the lower spine and from an infestation of worms, as no doubt did many of his contemporaries. Because so much of the soft tissue was preserved one could distinguish some of his features, even if they had been somewhat altered by the pressure of the peat and the softening of the bone within (fig. 1). His head was reasonably large with deep-set eyes below a broad, slightly furrowed forehead and well-defined brows; he had flared nostrils and very small ears. As a Celt it is probable that he had blue eyes and dark hair, a combination that is still common today. His hair was straight; examination under a scanning electron microscope showed that, like his beard and moustache, it had been roughly trimmed shortly before his death with a form of shears rather than a razor. Scissors were introduced into Britain only after the Roman period, and in the Late Iron Age world to which Lindow Man belonged even shears were not common items of personal equipment. Since it was not uncommon for the hair of victims consigned to the bog to be cut or even shaved shortly before death, we cannot be certain that the shears were his own. His fingernails, too, were remarkably undamaged, suggesting that his lifestyle did not involve manual labour. We

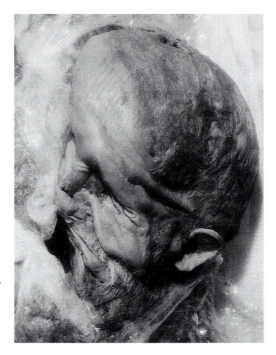

1. The face of Lindow Man after conservation.

begin to get a picture of a man with some kind of privileged position in society.[6]

Normally the stomach and intestines are among the first parts of a corpse to decay, but because of the circumstances of his burial in the peat bog, Lindow Man's gut and its contents were remarkably well preserved and it was possible to reconstruct his last meal, eaten shortly before he died. It was only a light repast, composed of cereals: emmer and spelt (both primitive forms of wheat) and barley, as well as a number of common weeds of cultivation, included accidentally along with other contaminants such as a minute quantity of animal hairs and sand. The pollen remains included a small quantity of mistletoe. Emmer, spelt and barley have a poor rising quality, and because it has been shown by electron spin resonance that the wheat chaff in the meal had been heated to a high temperature ($200-250°C = 400-480°$ F) for a relatively short time, it is probable that they were eaten in the form of unleavened bread – a griddle cake like a bannock. Small fragments of burnt food and charcoal found in the stomach seem to support this theory. It may even be that part of the bannock was burnt deliberately, and that it was broken in fragments and distributed by lot: he who drew the burnt piece was the selected victim. Mistletoe was used medicinally in antiquity, but Pliny wrote that it also had a religious significance for the Druids. It must, however, be said that Lindow Man had chewed his food very thoroughly, and the burnt fragments are so small – a mere 2–3 mm (perhaps ⅛ in) across – that they could equally well be the burnt remains of previous meals scraped off the cooking utensils.[7]

Soon afterwards he appears to have been taken to the Moss and struck twice upon the head with a relatively blunt implement sufficiently hard for the skull to have been fractured by each blow. A garotte made from twisted animal sinew was then put round his neck and twisted tighter and tighter with a stick until he was asphyxiated and finally his neck broke. The ritual, for that is what it seems to have been, was then completed by slitting his throat with a short, deep cut on the side of the neck. This cut was above the garotte, and as it severed the jugular vein the blood from the head and brain would have flooded out into a receptacle or onto the ground. It is possible that the final neck-breaking twists to the garotte were administered only after the throat had been cut. He also suffered a broken rib, possibly caused by the knee of one of his killers as he applied the garotte. Most Iron Age bog bodies have been found naked or partly clothed. Lindow Man was no exception, for he was naked apart from a band of fox fur on his left arm. There was not even any trace of the body-paint – woad or some other dye – so often associated with Iron Age Britain. Although such lower parts of his body as have been recovered were found in scattered fragments, no trace of any clothing has been reported. We do not know whether he was stripped before he was killed or afterwards, but at some stage before the body was placed face down in the water any clothes he might have been wearing had been removed.

The pollen evidence showed that Lindow Man's body had been put into the bog at a time of major change in the vegetation which corresponded with the beginnings of the forest clearance that mark increasing agricultural activity. Unfortunately both the pollens and the seeds found in his food are from plants which can easily have been stored before being used, so they do not guide us towards the season of his death; but the relatively small extent of putrefaction suggests that the incident occurred during cold weather, and that within a few hours of death the body had been immersed in the cold water where it was deprived of exposure to any warmth or air. Lindow Moss is a 'raised' peat bog, which means that it extends above the water table and relies on rain to maintain its existence. Such bogs are especially good for preserving organic remains: they are very wet, acid and anaerobic (that is, they lack free oxygen), conditions which inhibit the process of decomposition and thus encourage a build-up of vegetable remains. Pools of open water can form in such a bog, especially after the rains of winter. Lindow Man's body had begun to decompose slightly – for instance his lower left arm had decayed and several of his fingernails had become detached. This, together with the evidence of the plant debris, suggests that his body had been thrown into a shallow pool but that fairly rapidly it had been covered by sphagnum moss and other plants as it drifted towards the bottom and as the peat built up. Thus it had been protected from further microbial attack and decay.[8] While preserving the soft tissues very effectively, the chemical combination of such an environment leaches out the inorganic substances in the bone and leaves them soft and subject to distortion. In effect what one is left with two thousand years later is a human body that has been tanned: in chemical terms, the collagen in the skin has been 'fixed' by acid tannins and phenolic derivatives in the peat water. The effect upon the appearance of the remains is to render them almost unrecognisable as a human cadaver. The skin becomes a dark, tanned colour, and a combination of the pressure from the weight of the peat layers above with the softening of the bone results in a flattened, dark and wrinkled object which at first glance might be mistaken for an old, very wet and battered leather jacket. The body was in just this condition when we had the opportunity to see it for the first time.

Considerable interest was being taken in the find by academics and laymen alike, and yet it was going to be very difficult for those who were not familiar with corpses and cadavers to interpret the remains as those of a living, breathing, pale-skinned, dark-haired, blue-eyed fit young man. Despite all the scientific facts and details that were available, the appearance of the actual body, particularly after it had been freeze-dried to preserve it, did little to help in understanding how he would have appeared to those who knew him. This was the principal reason for undertaking a reconstruction.

The inaccessibility of the skull and the delicate nature of the remains obviously rendered making a cast of the skull impossible, and it was necessary to use indirect techniques in the form of radiographs and photographs to achieve our goal. The method we adopted – that of producing an exact replica of the skull based on information from a series of radiographs – was one that had already been developed for clinical use.[9] Once the simulated skull has been produced it becomes possible to carry out the soft-tissue reconstruction in the normal manner.

Radiological images were made for us at the Royal Marsden Hospital. Although not of the type normally used for this kind of work, they were as comprehensive and clear as was possible from such material, and the antero-posterior (front to back) and lateral views provided all the basic information from which the replica was constructed. These radiographs immediately made it clear that a considerable amount of distortion had taken place, and when viewed laterally the upper half of the skull appeared to have been pushed forward and the lower half backwards. Viewed antero-posteriorly, the skull was somewhat flattened, with the right-hand side totally obscured. A careful outline tracing was made of its lateral view, and then modified to remove the distortion. As there is no way of knowing how violent the distortion may have been, such modification has to be speculative and was kept to a

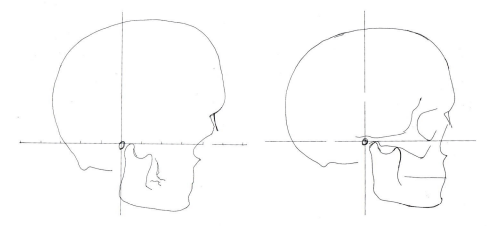

2. Lateral outline of Lindow Man's skull: unmodified and modified versions.

minimum, until we reached the point where the shape appeared to be 'normal' (fig. 2). Then we followed the same procedure in making an outline of the visible half of the antero-posterior aspect of the skull, which was then reversed to create a mirror-image of the right half. The two halves were then modified to a more normal shape, one that was compatible with the lateral aspect. Fixed anatomical points were visible on the radiographs at the temporo-mandibular joint and at the nasion, so these were marked on the tracings. Finally the modified outlines were transferred onto fibreboard from which templates were cut to form an armature upon which a replica of the skull could be constructed in clay.

Under ideal circumstances one can achieve a high degree of accuracy using this technique. Although it has now been superseded by digital computer technology, in its day it was used to assist in the planning of complex facial surgery, where bone grafts had to be shaped and where the potential alteration of existing bone structure needed to be assessed. The immobility of this 'patient' meant that the radiographs of Lindow Man could not be as comprehensive as those taken of living patients. This limited the amount of information available, and therefore the replica could be no more than a reasonable approximation of the original skull. The amount of diagnostic information that could be gleaned from the radiographs was considerable, but details of many of the individual parts of the skull were very indistinct. The maxilla was poorly displayed, with details of the orbits and the zygomatic bone obscured by unidentifiable shadows. Unusually, the nasal bone appeared clearly and undamaged. The mandible was not as robust as might have been expected in a skull of this size (it had been broken, though whether before or after death is not clear). Such facts play an important role in determining the individuality of a face as it is rebuilt. Much of the mid-portion of the skull had to be developed intuitively from the knowledge we had built up of the structure (and the variety) of the human face, using the relatively few available landmarks as guides. When the reconstructed clay skull was as accurate as seemed possible under the circumstances, a plaster cast was prepared from it to provide the foundation upon which the soft tissues could be developed.

The discovery of Lindow Man had been hailed by British archaeologists as the discovery of the century, and so the high-profile nature of this reconstruction demanded that particular attention be paid to the finish of the final model, for it had been conceived as an 'exhibition piece'. Specially prepared blank eyes were fitted into the skull in the normal way: on the advice of Dr J.M. Storey of the Manchester Royal Eye Hospital they were given a rather greater anterior diameter than is usual. This replicates one of the characteristics noted in people of Celtic descent in Southern Ireland. Very detailed eyes of the correct colour and shape were reserved for the final wax version of the finished head.

We have remarked before that surface details of the skin such as creases, folds, small scars, pockmarks and the like cannot be ascertained from the skull alone. Other features, such as hair, eyes and ears, are also likely to be unknown. However in the case of Lindow Man the finer details of the face that began to emerge were less of a problem, as one could refer to the photographs and original notes made of the preserved body. Although overall the details of the body were grossly distorted by the effects of the peat, by scrutinising the remains very closely it was possible to see many of them and to understand what their *in vivo* appearance would have been like. The ears were small with adherent lobes. The forehead had pronounced horizontal creases for a man of his age; the nose had a straight dorsal ridge, slightly raised towards the tip, and somewhat flared nostrils. It was not so easy to see the eyes and mouth, so these were rendered in a manner compatible with the other more accessible parts of the face. Every attempt was made to incorporate all these features into the final model as accurately as possible.

The results of this type of reconstruction are seldom predictable. Lindow Man was no exception, and it is very interesting to compare and contrast the bald clay

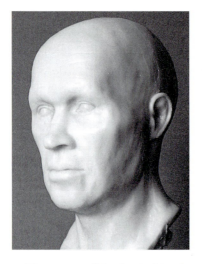

3. Wax version of the finished head of Lindow Man.

4. Reconstruction of Lindow Man in bronzed resin, with sculpted hair and beard.

reconstruction of the head (fig. 3), before any facial hair or colour has been added, with the version cast in bronzed resin having sculpted hair and beard (fig. 4), and with a photograph of the final waxwork (pl. XI). While it seems slightly bland at first sight, the hairless version conveys most clearly and most powerfully the fundamental information provided by the physical remains. The bronzed version is in many ways the most attractive: by interposing a material that makes no claim to represent the flesh and the features realistically, one is also distancing the viewer from the person whose face has been reconstructed, and thereby creating a psychological space between the two. Because the bronzed head looks like the work of an artist and not an apparently realistic recreation, consciously or not the viewer sees it as a work of art as well as a reconstruction. What one might think of as the 'studio' version, with more careful and more sympathetic lighting, sets out to show how Lindow Man would have appeared in life to those who lived and worked around him (pl.xi).

The face was broad and strong with a flattish nose, but with a rather smaller lower jaw than might have been expected. The eyes were deep-set under heavy brows. There had been the romantic idea in some people's minds that Lindow Man was a mysterious, handsome and rather magical individual: sadly for the dreamers, when all the hair and skin colour were added his appearance put paid to any such notions. With his shaggy dark brown but not untidy hair, short beard, moustache and sideburns, pale skin and blue eyes, Lindow Man comes to life. Once again there is a sense of reaching back in time and facing our own past. This time there was the added interest that this was the first time we had come face to face with an 'Ancient Briton': all the other faces until now had come from various parts of the Mediterranean. Who he was and why he was selected for sacrifice remain unanswered questions, and ones which are unlikely to be answered, for this is prehistory, or at best protohistory (that period when a people has not yet begun to write about itself, but when we can already rely on the accounts of others nearby). His hair, his fingernails, his fine physique, all suggest someone of importance. Anything further remains speculation. However, after initial problems with the radiocarbon dating of the body, probably caused in part by the fact that the body had sunk into earlier layers of peat on the bottom of the pool, it is now at least feasible that Lindow Man died around the first century AD. If nothing else, it lends plausibility to the notion put forward by Dr Anne Ross that he was sacrificed – willingly or not we do not know – as a desperate appeal to the Celtic gods to turn back the Roman invaders as they marched northwards. His triple death – blows to the head, garotting and throat-cutting – has many parallels in the Celtic world and beyond, as does the use of water as a vehicle for making an offering to the gods.[10] One of the most dramatic illustrations of the powerful tradition of making sacrifices through the medium of water is to be seen in the displays of the Danish National Museum in Copenhagen, where in a long history that begins in the Neolithic period (c.2800–1800 BC) and lasts into the fifth century AD the offerings range from bronze trumpets and ornaments of gold and other materials to weapons, tools and even boats. At some periods the offerings are clearly the possessions of the people who made them, at others they are the spoils of war. In Denmark at least the practice of making actual human sacrifices as part of this ritual had a relatively short vogue during the early part of our era in this centuries-long tradition.

Bog bodies are of course not confined to the British Isles, but are to be found in several other countries in northern Europe, above all Denmark, northern Germany and the Netherlands. The number of finds runs into four figures. The monumental – but quite undiscriminating – surveys by Alfred Dieck listed 1850 examples by the time the last supplement was published in 1986. Although Dieck included many bodies that were not ancient and many whose existence was based on no more than fanciful tales, the true figure must run into several hundreds. The latest study, by Dr Wijnand van der Sanden, reviews the evidence in a much more critical manner.[11]

The problem of concentrating in such a focused manner on a single specimen such as Lindow Man is that one risks falling into the trap of thinking that all bog bodies will be broadly speaking similar, particularly if they are of roughly the same period. Nothing could be further from the truth. This was demonstrated quite dramatically when we were asked to reconstruct the appearance of a Dutch bog body. Not only were the technical problems more complex, but as a person she could hardly have been more different from her British contemporary.

The 'Yde Girl' had been discovered in on 12 May 1897 by two men cutting peat at the small village of Yde in the municipality of Vries, a few kilometres from the northern Dutch town of Assen.[12] They were so terrified at their discovery that they ran away, believing her body to be the work of the devil. Later in the day they returned, but only to hide the corpse under some turves. There she was found by the mayor of Vries nine days later. He noticed that the right side of her head was damaged and that while the hair on the left side of her scalp was reddish (presumably the effect of the peat), the right half was 'shaven'. He had more remains taken up from the muddy pool where the body had lain, including the feet, one of the hands, and part of the pelvis. He was clearly an observant and conscientious man, for he also noticed that the skin had been badly damaged by the peat-cutters' tools, and that pieces of woollen clothing survived, including a band around her neck, later shown to have been woven by the 'sprang' technique.

He sent all this information to a member of the Drents Museum committee, J.G.C. Joosting, who thereupon accompanied him on a visit to the site. Unhappily in the meantime the villagers had pulled away the hair from the left side of her head leaving her almost bald. They had also removed most of her teeth and probably some of her skeleton. Joosting collected such pieces as remained, cleaned them and presented them to the museum shortly afterwards. In the end Drents Museum had the head, neck and upper body with part of her left arm (pl.xii); both feet and the right hand; the hair (which was returned by the villagers) and an assortment of bones including much of the pelvic girdle.

Inspired by the discoveries at Lindow Moss, Dr Wijnand van der Sanden, Keeper of Archaeology at the Drents Museum, had initiated in the years 1987–9 a programme of study of the bog bodies in his own museum, some thirteen in total. This had included commissioning a radiocarbon date for the Yde Girl from the Oxford Research Laboratory for Archaeology which placed her most probably in the first centuries BC/AD, as well as an anthropological study and the first CT-scans at Groningen University, which confirmed her sex as female and her age at around sixteen

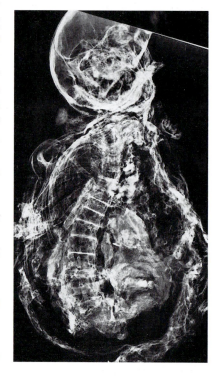

5. X-ray of the Yde Girl showing her curved spine.

years (all her teeth had erupted save her wisdom teeth, whose crowns were already complete). Even allowing for shrinkage she was a small person – only about 1.40 m (4 ft 7 in) tall. Her smallness must have been emphasised when she was alive by a slightly misshapen spine: the poor girl had suffered from scoliosis, which had twisted her spine into an S-shape, so that her body would always have been twisted a little to the left (fig. 5). Her hair, dyed red by the peat, was probably originally blonde. The woollen band which the mayor had spotted had probably been the means of her death, for it had been wound three times round her neck and fastened with a slip knot.

Inspired by the work that had been done in England as a result of the discovery of Lindow Man, by 1992 van der Sanden had extended his study to include the bog bodies in every museum in the Netherlands, and to incorporate the new techniques which had been developed over the previous five years. Thus he approached us with the suggestion that we might carry out a reconstruction of the Yde Girl.

There were many things that the Yde Girl had in common with Lindow Man. The big difference, however, lay in the fact that Lindow Man was fresh out of the ground when we were asked to work on him and had had the benefit of the most up-to-date conservation available. The Yde Girl by contrast, found almost a hundred years before, had only had Joosting's fairly rudimentary cleaning, and had been allowed to dry out. As a result her body had shrunk to about half its original size. It was very difficult to imagine how this shrunken and crushed face might have looked in life (fig. 6). As a follow-up to Lindow Man she was clearly going to present us with a technical challenge of the kind we had come to expect, and to relish. Perhaps if we had realised the extent of that challenge at the outset we might have been a shade less enthusiastic, and a shade less welcoming to Wijnand van der Sanden when he stepped off the Amsterdam plane with the young lady tucked up in her carrying box.

The first step was to call in the pathologist – not out of any disrespect or lack of confidence towards the work which had already been done in the Netherlands; rather, because Dr Bob Stoddart of the Department of Pathological Sciences in the university was now an essential

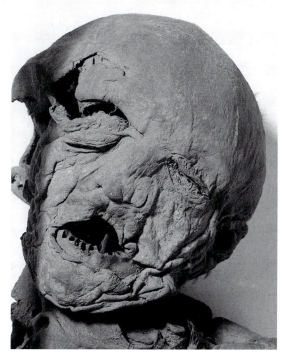

6. *The head of the Yde Girl.*

member of our team. Having collaborated with us on Seianti and Ada, described in the next chapters, he knew how we worked and what we needed to know; we had great confidence in his ability to discover important and interesting facts from almost any portion of the human anatomy placed before him, no matter what its condition might be. His overall assessment of the physical remains of the Yde Girl confirmed the Dutch diagnoses but with some nice additions. For example, a small and rather faint circular mark with a central dot on the sole of her right foot he suspected to be the marks of a verruca which had healed some weeks or months before her death.

However, Dr Stoddart's attention had first been drawn to a massive wound running across the back of the head as far as the right ear, 'caused by the edge of some sharp, heavy implement, which has struck the body, most probably from above, while it lay obliquely on its face…' Nonetheless he concluded that 'if the body was damp when the damage occurred, it is entirely possible that the injury took place long after her death, probably at about the time the body was unearthed'. All this matches with the fact that the mayor of Vries had other parts of her body fished out of a pool, and that he had observed that the right side of her head was damaged when discovered. So no firm evidence of foul play here.

Her neck told a different story. 'A deep ligature mark runs around the neck…about 6–8 mm (¼ in) wide, but broadens and deepens beneath the left ear…This suggests that the ligature was knotted and so tightened that the knot dug into the flesh at this point. The ligature, of itself, could have been the cause of death.' Because of later damage to the vertebral column, Dr Stoddart could not be certain that the ligature had not also broken her neck, but he reckoned it unlikely. 'Death probably followed from the obstruction of the airways as a result of garotting, with tightening occurring at the position of the knot on the left side.' One could hear the final sentence of this paragraph in his report sounding like a damning death-knell in a court of law.

But there was more. Below the ligature mark there was a cut about 4.5 cm (just under 2 in) long, and at least 2 cm (nearly 1 in) deep, extending from the middle to the left of her throat. It was quite different from other holes that had developed in the body after death. It seemed very likely that this stab into the base of her throat accompanied the garotting, just as Lindow Man's throat had been cut when he was garotted. Yet there was some comfort to be found in the fact that, despite this violent death, and the distortion that her body had undergone while in the bog along with the mistreatment it had suffered at the hands of her finders, the pathologist could still comment that 'her face had a calm appearance, with closed eyes and (at death) an almost closed mouth. The remaining right hand shows no sign of having been used defensively. She may have been killed while unconscious and was possibly a willing victim.'

The problem of the distortion of the skull is one to which we shall need to return for it caused great problems with the facial reconstruction. On the rest of the skeleton (or what remained of it) one had to distinguish between deformation caused by the pressure of the peat on the softened and demineralised bones, and changes that were the result of the girl's pathology. Thus a slight asymmetry in the bones of her pelvis was probably significant, and was matched by a slight malformation of her right foot, whose big toe was a little distorted, with callouses on the second toe, whereas all the other toes (and those of the left foot) were normal. This implies that she had a slightly uneven gait, turning her right foot inward so that the weight bore upon the two inner toes. (Dr Stoddart also noted that, like her toenails, the soles of both feet were well cared for and showed no signs of hard use: she wore good shoes.) Her legs have not been found, but there is further evidence of the effect of the misshapen pelvis in her spine which, as the Dutch specialist had noted, was slightly twisted to the left. Much of this is the result of the centuries spent under the peat, but not all of it, for some of the vertebrae are slightly wedge-shaped 'suggesting a mild scoliosis': in layman's language, the Yde Girl, like Seianti in the following chapter, carried her back a little to one side to compensate for her uneven pelvis, although unlike Seianti, she had borne this for all of her short life, and not as the result of an accident.

Despite the attentions of the villagers in the nineteenth century, her dental health was good, and the development of her teeth and bones and of her one sur-viving small breast imply that she was sixteen years old when she died, perhaps a little younger. Although evidently well looked after in life the Yde Girl was, as we have seen, strikingly small, even allowing for all the effects of her long immersion in the acid waters of the bog and subsequent drying out. The reason for this cannot now be determined: one might suggest a defect in her pituitary gland, or a problem in absorbing her food, but her remains show no signs of illness or poor nourish-ment. Her body was well proportioned for all its small size, and she had reached sexual maturity perhaps two years before her death, although there is no evidence that she bore any children.

When it came to giving the girl back her face we came up against very severe problems as a result of the distortion and damage that her skull had suffered. It was obviously impossible to make a cast of the skull, both because of the tissue that still covered it and because of its damaged and fragile state. Fortunately since the discovery of Lindow Man the advances in the art of image-scanning and in manipu-lating the data had eliminated the need to model the skull by hand in such cases. CT-scans had already been made at Groningen University Hospital. These radiographs made longitudinally approximately every half-centimetre through her skull and upper body, had proved extremely valuable in determining her age and in the first diagnosis of her scoliosis, but they did not provide enough information to reconstruct the skull, so badly was it damaged. Therefore a new set of scans was made at the Department of Diagnostic Radiology in Manchester University, once again thanks to the willing support of Professor Ian Isherwood. This time the inter-val was set at less than 1.5 mm ($^1/_{16}$ in), and the resulting tomographs, taken horizontally, were sent to Dr Robin Richards at the Department of Medical Physics and Bio-Engineering at University College Hospital in London, where a program had been devised which allowed one to move the broken pieces around on a computer screen until the skull was again 'complete'.

The first images that appear on the computer screen are in effect the same as the original body, and it is not until the necessary adjustments have been made to the data that the soft tissue can be eliminated from the picture to reveal the skull beneath. In the case of the Yde Girl the soft tissue had become so hard in some places that it was impossible to distinguish it from the bone. This was particularly true in the orbits, and even on the final image the eyelids remain tightly closed over the eyes for ever. The age of the body together with the circumstances of its preservation and discovery had conspired to create considerable damage to the skull: the bones of the cranium had been broken in numerous places, its posterior portion had been severely disrupted and the left maxillary bone had been reduced to small fragments. To rectify matters the posterior portion was manipulated into a more acceptable position, and a mirror-image of the surviving right maxillary bone was substituted for the missing left half part of the face.

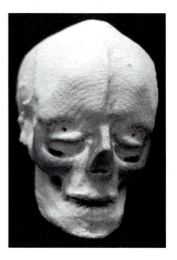

When we were satisfied that we had achieved as complete a skull as was possible, we left it to Dr Richards and his computer to mill out a three-dimensional replica of the skull in polystyrene.

Some days later a parcel arrived at the studio from London. Much to our consternation the skull appeared unrealistically tiny. After some discussion we realised that no allowance had been made for the shrinkage that the body had suffered and, rather chastened, we rang Dr Richards in London and explained the situation. The next parcel to arrive in Manchester contained a skull some 15 per cent larger, still small but perfectly acceptable: after all the medical reports had commented on the girl's small stature (fig. 7).

7. The skull of the Yde Girl milled from polystyrene.

As with so many of these ancient specimens the nasal bone had been broken and lost, and as the technology that is used can only create half of the skull at a time there was a certain amount of work to do before the reconstruction proper could be started. First the two sections were cemented together and then the nasal bone modelled onto the skull in wax. We could not of course be certain exactly what shape it had been, but we formed one that fitted the natural contours of the maxilla and frontal bones. Measuring pegs were pushed into the styrene skull to indicate the soft-tissue thickness for a normal female, and then the whole thing was mounted on a stand in the routine manner. It did look very small in comparison with those on which we had worked before, but this was no reason to change the method. Accordingly the basic muscle structures were built up in the same way as on all other reconstructions (fig. 8).

When the final layers had been put in place we found ourselves looking at a rather unusual face, with small features, wide-set eyes and a very high, straight forehead. This singular feature was to become very much more obvious later when the hair was added. As with the nasal bone, one can argue that the hairline could have been different. However if one looks at the face in profile one sees that had it been placed any lower it would encroach onto the vertical area of the forehead, which would be very unlikely. We have no alternative but to accept the ruling of the skull. Although it is not common, this characteristic is by no means unique and can be seen on people today, just as one sees the features of the lower part of her face reflected in numerous modern Dutch faces. As if to prove the point, our colleague Bob Stoddart looked up as someone sat down opposite him on a train crossing Denmark some time later, and found himself gazing at the spitting image of the Yde Girl.

The metamorphosis that a reconstruction undergoes never ceases to amaze, and even those of us who have seen the process before still find it slightly bewildering to see one of these heads looking so incredibly lifelike. The Yde Girl was no

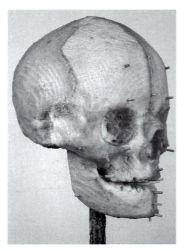 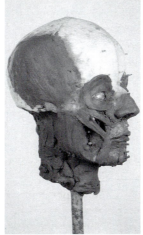 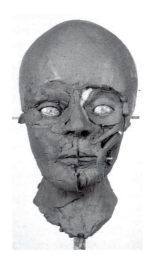

8. The muscle structures are built up on the milled skull of the Yde Girl.

exception. This reconstruction was intended both to illustrate the final report on the study, and to serve as the centrepiece of a new display in the museum at Drents. There had never been any doubt in Dr van der Sanden's mind that the final version should be a waxwork, for he felt that no other material would have as powerful an impact (pl.xii). In this he was surely correct, for this small, slightly peaky face with its blue eyes set well apart and wide mouth, with long blonde tresses falling down on either side of a remarkably high forehead, creates a powerful impression as soon as one meets her. The proportions of her skull have given her a face that one may not call beautiful, but it is certainly striking.

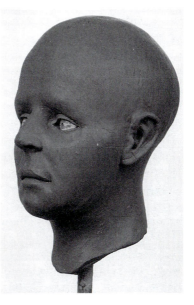

CHAPTER 9

Mirror, Mirror, on the Wall…:
Seianti Hanunia Tlesnasa

'What makes an Etruscan? Faced with the wonderment that these strange people's customs inspired in the ancients and indeed the moderns, we must first of all ask ourselves if, like Montesquieu's Persian, there was not "in his physiognomy something admirable". Was there an Etruscan type which allowed one to recognise at first sight among the Mediterranean crowds the pirate from Caere, the augur from Tarquinii, the courtesan from Pyrgi? It is not unimportant that we should know with whom we are dealing in the pages to come and so we must find out if the people whom we wish to surprise had their own unmistakable look.'

These are the opening lines of chapter 1 of Jacques Heurgon's *Daily Life of the Etruscans*, first published in 1961. Over the intervening thirty-odd years the question of the Etruscan look has continued to fascinate and to perplex, and has still not been properly answered. In 1989 the question was being discussed in the British Museum. On the one hand Professor Marshall Becker from West Chester University of Pennsylvania and Dr Birgitte Ginge from the Pennsylvania University Museum of Archaeology and Anthropology in Philadelphia were studying Etruscan skeletal remains and their containers in museums in Britain as part of a wider programme to coordinate data from physical anthropological studies with archaeological information on the Etruscans in collections all over the world and in Etruria itself. Surprisingly few intact Etruscan skeletons are known to the archaeological world, due no doubt in part to the fact that at many places and at various periods in their history the Etruscans practised cremation rather than inhumation. On the other hand, the British Museum was planning a completely new display on the Etruscans in a gallery to be called 'Italy before the Roman Empire'. Central to both projects were the coffin and the remains of an Etruscan lady by the name of Seianti Hanunia Tlesnasa, who died around the middle of the second century BC. On the coffin lid was the reclining figure of the dead woman, presumably her portrait. 'It would be very interesting to know how well her features matched with her portrait on the sarcophagus lid,' wrote Dr Judith Swaddling, the curator responsible for the British Museum's Etruscan collections and for the new gallery. Her invitation led to a collaborative investigation that involved not only the two Americans along with Dr Jonathan Musgrave (who had already got to know Seianti some fifteen years earlier during a study into the affinity of local Mediterranean populations) and ourselves, but also once again Dr Bob Stoddart to look at the pathology, Dr David Whittaker to age her teeth, and additional advice on the dental history from Dr John Lilley of the University Dental School. As a collaboration it was to produce some interesting and stimulating differences of opinion which led us to reconsider very carefully some aspects of the lady's history.

It had long seemed that in the technique of facial reconstruction might lie a means of testing the vexed question of realism in ancient portraiture, but the problem was to find an instance where both skull and portrait survived together. There are many statues from the classical world that portray individuals, both famous people whose images are familiar to ancient historians, such as Pericles, Themistocles and the Roman emperors, and also many less distinguished folk whose grave markers and portraits now line the walls of museum galleries throughout the world; but apart from the special case of Romano-Egyptian mummies it is rare indeed that their remains have survived along with their portraits. Here perhaps was the opportunity for which we had been waiting.[1]

However, Etruscan art is not Greek or Roman art: although it owed much to the Greeks, and passed on much to the Romans, its conventions were not necessarily the same as those of the Greeks or the Romans. The heartland of Etruria was roughly equivalent to modern Tuscany, stretching as far south as the valley of the Tiber. There were, however, Villanovan, or more correctly proto-Etruscan settlements, both here in the Po Valley in northern Italy and in Campania in the southwest dating from the Early Iron Age (900–700 BC). The heyday of the Etruscans was in the seventh and sixth centuries BC, but in the later sixth and early fifth centuries they suffered a series of defeats at the hands of the Greeks and the Romans and later the Celts from which they never really recovered. Nonetheless their culture continued to flourish for another three of four centuries. Because so much of their art has come to us from tombs; because their language is only slowly being deciphered, and not least because most ancient descriptions of the Etruscans were written by their old enemies in Greece and Rome, they have acquired a popular reputation as a mysterious people having an obsession with death and the afterlife. In fact one of the most striking features of Etruscan art is its zest for life and its exuberance: highly skilled craftsmen and artists – particularly in jewellery and metalwork – worked in a world of bright colours and ostentation where the enjoyment of fine things and of wealth carried no stigma. More than many other ancient races, the Etruscans seem to have been interested in people as individuals, and it was important to the question before us that in terms of what they have left behind them they demonstrated this interest most clearly in their funerary art.

The remains of Seianti were discovered by a local excavator in 1886, still in her terracotta sarcophagus in an undisturbed and undecorated chamber tomb at Poggio Cantarello, some 2½ miles west of Chiusi in northern Etruria, together with a number of silver objects which had been hung on the wall of the tomb. The whole ensemble was acquired by the British Museum in the following year.[2] The silver objects disappeared after 1939, presumably during the wartime evacuation of the British Museum collections, but it is clear from the Museum registers that they included many of the items which formed the normal toilet set of an Etruscan lady, such as a scent-vase, a toilet box and a mirror. Perhaps rather unexpectedly there was also a strigil. However, while such body-scrapers are generally associated with athletes they are not unknown in the female toilette and we need have no qualms about identifying the sex of the person with whom they were buried, or that there was any tampering with the find. That they were of silver shows that she came from a well-to-do family, although Helbig, who acted as the Museum's agent in the purchase, noted that the silver was very thin, which suggests that they were made specially for the tomb and were not intended for daily use.

The sarcophagus, which has been many times illustrated in books on the Etruscans, was made up of three elements: the coffin itself, made as a single piece measuring 1.805 m (5 ft 11 in) long by 70 cm (2 ft 3½ in) wide by 42 cm (1 ft 4½ in) high; a cover slab 6 cm (2⅜ in) thick made in two pieces measuring a total of 1.835 m (6 ft ¼ in) and 75 cm (2 ft 5½ in) wide, on which rested the lid. This was also made in two pieces (a common Etruscan practice) and comprises a figure of the dead woman in all her finery some 81.5 cm (2 ft 8 in) high, reclining on a thin mattress with her left elbow propped on a thick cushion. The front of the coffin itself has an architectural decoration of three metopes comprising large red rosettes in relief separated by yellow triglyphs. On its lower edge the names of the dead woman had been carefully cut in the clay while it was still wet, running from right to left in the Etruscan alphabet: Seianti Hanunia Tlesnasa (pl.XIII).

Although she has always been known as Seianti by modern archaeologists, it is an irony that despite the liberated position of women in Etruscan society when compared with, say, the Greeks and Romans, and despite her apparently rich dowry of names, they are all family names of various kinds, and we do not know what the lady was called by her contemporaries. Roman men of the upper classes had a standard set of three names, *praenomen, nomen* and *cognomen* – first name, family or clan name, and surname, to which later an *agnomen*, an epithet or nickname, might be added; Roman women of whatever class only had one name, followed if necessary by the name of the man on whom they depended – father, husband, or in the case of a slave, master. Etruscan names were slightly more complex. On the coffin of a man the inscription regularly included his first name, by which he was presumably normally addressed, but for women this was optional (although we can surely assume that in life an Etruscan woman was addressed by her own individual first name). By the time Seianti died (*c.* 150 BC) the rest of the formula normally included at least a selection from the father's family name, a given name, and the father's and/or the mother's name. A woman's coffin also bore her husband's family name. 'Seianti' and 'Tlesnasa' are both forms of family names: the Seiante and Tlesna clans are well known from other inscriptions from around Chiusi, and seem to have been prominent in local society for many generations. The name Seiante (for men) or Seianti (for women) and its variants is one of those Etruscan family names that derive from the name of a place. It seems likely that the family originally came from the town of Sentinum in the Apennines, north of Perugia and strictly speaking in Umbria rather than Etruria, and perhaps moved south to Chiusi after the Roman conquest in 295 BC.

Seianti, then is her own family name; Tlesnasa is her husband's family name Tlesna, in the possessive form as the funerary formula requires. We do not know his other names, nor indeed anything else about him. Her middle name Hanunia is the feminine form of Hanu, a given name often found in the Seiante family.

There are other elements in her story in addition to the quality of her burial and the family history suggested by her names which show that Seianti came from a good background, probably aristocratic and surely wealthy. One is the existence of other coffins belonging to members of the family, most notably the sarcophagus and grave goods of a lady inscribed with the name Larthia Seianti; the other is the appearance of Seianti herself as she is portrayed on her sarcophagus.

The burial of Larthia Seianti provides an interesting parallel to that of Seianti Hanunia. It was found in 1877 at La Martinella, 1¼ miles to the north of Chiusi. Whereas Seianti Hanunia had been given the honour of a single chamber tomb to herself (albeit a simple one), Larthia had been buried in a family tomb complex comprising a corridor with niches, leading to a main chamber with small side

1. *The sarcophagus of Larthia Seianti (Florence, Museo Archeologico).*

chambers. Her sarcophagus (now in Florence) is slightly smaller than Seianti Hanunia's although the different proportions and more relaxed pose make it appear larger. There are some technical differences between the two, and the decoration is more elaborate and more finely done even if the rendering is rather dry (fig. 1). The dead woman is portrayed on the lid in the same fashion as Seianti Hanunia. Her jewellery, her dress and her pillow are all slightly more elaborate and she herself is less plump than her cousin, but we have the same feeling that we are looking at a real person. The grave goods buried with her were more elaborate too, and included jewellery and toilet equipment of bronze and silver, alabaster and glass.[3]

However, the circumstances of her burial, surrounded by her relations, tell us much more about her family than we could learn from Seianti Hanunia's solitary grave. Two names survive from the inscription on the upper edge of her sarcophagus: Larthia was her first name, a common one in Etruria, and Seianti was her family name, showing she was of the same clan as Seianti Hanunia. The inscription seems to have run on to two further names, which have been read as Sinunia Svenias. The first of these must have been a given name like Hanunia, while Svenias is interpreted as the matronymic, her mother's name.[4] Although none of these names refers to her husband, it is clear from the fact that she was buried in this family tomb complex that she was related to the other occupants, presumably through marriage. We know the names of three of them (one possibly her husband). All belonged to the Larcna clan, another of the well-established families of Chiusi like the Seiante. We cannot of course tell what her relationship was to Seianti Hanunia – one tends to refer to them loosely as cousins. Stylistically their two coffins are very similar, though clearly from different workshops, and must have been made within a few years of each other in the second century BC.

It is difficult to date them more closely on grounds of style or burial practice. By the Hellenistic period the most common form of burial among the better-off Etruscans was in family tomb complexes such as that in which Larthia Seianti was found. Individual chamber tombs like Seianti Hanunia's were less common, and may indicate a higher social standing. The material from which the coffins were made – alabaster, volcanic tufo, or terracotta – varied according to availability, local custom and perhaps also status. The most important item of dating is provided by a Roman coin found with the other offerings in Larthia's grave, an *as* of a type with the head of Janus on the obverse and a ship's prow on the reverse. Though a common type with a long life, its weight standard changes through time, and this specimen can be dated by its weight (27 g, 1 oz) to the period 189–158 BC.[5] This, taken together with the style and similarity of their coffins, suggests that the two 'cousins' were both buried some time in the second quarter of the second century BC, perhaps even as late as 150–140 BC.

Like her cousin, Seianti Hanunia is depicted on her sarcophagus as a woman of substance. Her couch is a comfortable one, with its striped mattress and thick red cushion, and she is dressed to the nines. She wears a white linen sleeveless peronatris, the Hellenistic version of the classical chiton, with a dark red border, held in below the breasts by a long yellow or golden belt, and over it a cloak – also with a red border – which comes up over her head and which she holds to one side in a gesture which is always described as that of a bride unveiling herself to her husband. She is wearing a great deal of jewellery: over her luxuriant red-brown hair is a triangular diadem, in her ears elaborate earrings; round her neck hangs a heavy gold strap necklace with conical pendants – probably flower-buds; her left arm is covered by her cloak, but on her right she has a thick gold armlet, and a snake-headed bracelet twisted from particularly thick gold bands. In her left hand she holds a folding mirror open before her. Perhaps she is after all holding her cloak away from her face in order the better to consider her reflection in the mirror. In a later age such ostentation might suggest that there was something of the *nouveau riche* about Seianti, but both the pedigree that one can trace for her and the delight shown by all Etruscans in the good things of life render such thoughts unworthy. She looks to be in early middle age. Certainly the plumpness of her face, neck and arms are striking – there is more than a hint of a double chin – and forms a contrast to the more normal physique of Larthia Seianti.[6]

If the circumstances of the burial matched the opulence of her appearance (for this is surely what the silver grave goods together with her resplendent coffin are intended to convey), at first sight the dead woman's physical remains told a different story from the well-fed and well-preserved young matron presented on the lid. Even the two accounts of its first discovery differed in their interpretation of the age of the skeleton and thus of the intention of the artist: Helbig argued from the state of her teeth that she was very old, and that the maker of her coffin had rejuvenated her, while Milani thought her middle-aged, on the basis of the image on the coffin.[7]

The skeleton has been extensively demineralised since it was buried, and as a result most of the bones, especially the smaller ones, are very light. Many have discoloured to a dark brown. Because the skeleton was well protected inside its coffin there has been no distortion under pressure, and aside from a little differential shrinkage most of the bones retain their original shape. There can be little doubt that the remains inside the sarcophagus are those of the person for whom it was made, for the skeleton is almost intact. There is a little post-mortem damage, a few teeth have been lost post mortem, and some of the small bones of hands and feet appear to have gone astray between discovery and display in London, but there is nothing here that suggests reburial or reuse of the coffin. The pelvis leaves no room for doubt that these are the bones of a woman, while its general shape and articulation suggest that she had undergone at least one pregnancy.

On first inspection by Marshall Becker the pubic symphyses of the pelvis appeared to show quite exceptional erosion – normally the mark of ageing – suggesting that she was a very old lady, perhaps as much as eighty or ninety years old. This thesis seemed to be supported by other features of the skeleton, such as the extent of closure of some of the sutures on the skull. Her teeth too (or such as remained of them at death) appeared to be those of a very elderly person. This was not in itself as surprising as one might expect, for preliminary results in a study of longevity among Etruscans being carried out by Professor Becker was showing that individuals who survived into adulthood often then lived to a considerable age. Yet even this initial examination of Seianti's skeleton showed that her vertebrae had undergone none of the surface changes that one would associate with geriatric deterioration of the spinal column, and there was no evidence of osteoporosis, a scourge of older women. Indeed some of the bones, such as the shoulder blades, were remarkably dense and robust and, with exceptions that will be discussed shortly, in general her skeleton appeared healthy and consonant with that of a person in later middle age. Sutural closure on the skull is a less reliable indicator of age than was once thought, for there is much variation between different races and even different families. This is not to say that she did not suffer both from dental problems and from arthritis, but that need not be the result of ageing.

Fortunately, with such apparently conflicting evidence, and with a fundamental disagreement between the anthropologist and the anatomist in the team about Seianti's probable age at death, there was another technique on which we could now call. Dr David Whittaker at the Dental School of the University of Wales College of Medicine in Cardiff had developed a very accurate technique for ageing teeth by measuring the ratios of the two types of dentine (sclerotic apical dentine to nonsclerotic coronal dentine), by which it is possible to determine the age of a skeleton to within a very few years. Because of the differing interpretations of the skeletal evidence he tested two teeth, the first and second upper left premolars. The first of these gave a mean estimate of fifty-five years of age at death; the second only forty-five, a difference that could in part be explained by the greater wear on the 'older' tooth. A reasonable figure for her age at death seemed therefore to be around fifty. The tooth that gave the higher age was heavily worn, in contrast to the minimal wear on the other, and therefore Dr Whittaker added the rider that because attrition has a tendency to bias age estimates upwards, Seianti was unlikely to have been older than fifty-five when she died.

Not surprisingly, this apparent confirmation of the low age estimate created dismay, if not disbelief, among those of our team who considered that she had lived into her eighties, particularly as at the time when the tests were carried out, in the autumn of 1991, the technique was not yet widely known among archaeologists and anthropologists, and the results from the Spitalfields cemetery, where it was possible to compare such estimates with parish records, had not yet been published. Therefore we asked for a second opinion, and the two samples were sent to Dr Whittaker's colleague Dr G.J. Thomas. He too had considerable experience in this rather specialised field, and had developed his own database on teeth of known age using a modification of the method. So as to avoid any suggestion of prejudice, he was given no information about their origin or about any previous work. Indeed, he was under the impression that the two samples came from a single tooth rather than from two teeth from the same individual. Looking at both the length of the translucent zone in the root of the tooth on its own, and also at its length in relation to the total length of the root, and comparing these with his data from teeth of all kinds, Dr Thomas concluded that Seianti's age was between forty-six and fifty-four, with an average of fifty and a half. When compared with statistics based on vital premolars only, in other words based on similar teeth, her age could be narrowed to the middle of this range.[8]

Unless one was going to reject the whole technique of ageing by root translucency, these two sets of results did seem fairly conclusive. Some of the evidence which suggested old age has already been considered in the preceding paragraphs; there remained the problems of the eroded pubic symphysis, and of the osteophytes.

It must be said that in general the changes in the pelvic area of the skeleton, linked to osteoporosis as part of the ageing process, particularly in females, decrease the chances of survival in archaeological specimens, so that ancient comparanda are hard to find. Furthermore, although changes to the pubic symphysis have long been used in estimating age at death, they are not easy to 'read'. In the face of all the other evidence in favour of an age of around fifty for Seianti, one has to conclude that she may have suffered an otherwise unexplained abnormality in her pelvic bones which showed itself in this thinness of the pubic symphysis. It may well be connected with some of her other physical problems, but it is worth bearing in mind that although unusually thin, it still lies within the normal range of appearances for the pelvis, even if near one extreme.

A careful study of the remains with a pathologist's eye provided Dr Stoddart with evidence for an interesting if painful medical history. Although all traces of soft tissue, such as cartilage, ligaments and tendons were lost, enough evidence survived on the bones to indicate their condition and degree of development and above all their 'susceptibility to mechanical stress in life'.

Her skeleton is that of a mature adult and X-ray photographs of her long bones show that their cortices are thick and dense, implying that at death she was no more than a few years post-menopause: at most she might have been fifty-five years old. Though a few lines of arrested development could be detected, they were no more numerous or evident than in a modern western skeleton, suggesting that, although she had the usual childhood illnesses, she was generally healthy and well nourished until the end of her adolescent growth spurt at about fourteen to sixteen years of age. There were no traces of ante-mortem fracture, or of any mechanical injury suffered near the time of death; she was not afflicted by diseases affecting the skeleton, such as osteomyelitis, anaemia or tuberculosis, nor were her bones becoming soft or, as far as one can tell, brittle (osteomalacia and osteoporosis). She did not suffer from any bone tumours, nor was she at all hunchbacked (kyphotic), but she did have other problems which focused on an arthritic condition of her hip and lower jaw, which may have been associated with the abnormality in her pelvis which we have just discussed.

Continuing on the positive side for the moment, Seianti's thigh bones were remarkably robust with well-developed muscle-attachments; indeed, all the musculature of the upper legs, pelvis and lower back was well developed, in contrast to that of the lower legs. 'An individual who was athletic in her youth and acquired particularly powerful psoas magnus and iliacus muscles on each side: these are associated with flexion of the legs at the hips.' Her upper body, too, was robust and muscular, but less markedly so than the hips and thighs. Interestingly, the collar bones provided evidence of considerable strength in the muscles of the shoulders and upper thorax.

So far, a reasonably optimistic diagnosis, but like all good doctors our pathologist kept the bad news for last. It focused particularly on the right side of the pelvis and its articulation with the right leg and the spine. 'Seianti's skeleton shows numerous bony protuberances (osteophytes) around many joints and, in a few instances (such as the right acetabulum) actually on the articular surfaces. The distribution of these osteophytes is peculiar, in that they are most marked both in number and size in the pelvis and lower lumbar spine, particularly on her right side. The pathology of the articular surfaces is also most florid on her right side and in association with her pelvis.' Although there are no outward traces of any healed fractures, there is evidence of osteoarthrosis at the right hip, with a small area of 'polishing' (eburnation) on the head of the right thigh bone (femur). The position of this polished area is unusual and suggests that a very specific injury to the cartilage of the joint occurred at this site and eventually led the cartilage to fail, so that the bony surfaces could rub together and become polished. This would have caused severe pain and restriction of the movement of the joint. These signs and symptoms suggest that many years before her death Seianti had suffered an injury to the soft tissues on the right side of her pelvis, probably with a backward rotation of her right leg, which led to a tearing of the ligaments and probably of the tendons and muscles too, which in turn caused internal bleeding into the soft tissues and some joints. No bones were broken, but there was probably much clotted blood and severe bruising in the tissues over the sacrum and the right side of the pelvis, including those around the right hip. The residues of this bleeding eventually calcified, causing multiple osteophytes. These are small bony leaflets which form by the mineralisation of, for example, old blood and can then ossify or fuse with existing bone, or they may develop as outgrowths of the bone itself. Osteophytes are not unusual or in themselves harmful: they grew on the chin of Philip of Macedon as part of the natural remodelling of his malformed lower jaw, but he was never aware of them. In the wrong place, however, such as at a joint or in the path of a nerve, they can be the cause of great discomfort and pain. We can deduce where they caused pain in Seianti's joints by causing friction and restricting movement, but we cannot tell exactly which small nerves, if any, were trapped or irritated by them.

There were also changes at the back of the pelvis, with profuse new bone growth stretching from the lumbar region of the lower spine to the right hip, which distorted the sacrum, the part of the spine forming the central bone at the back of the pelvis. There was damage, probably with bleeding, at the sacro-iliac joint on the right side of the pelvis, and the surfaces of this joint were badly affected. All this was consistent with an accident in which the right leg was forced violently backwards and up until the top of the femur was rammed into the edge of its socket in the pelvis, damaging in a very specific and unusual way the cartilage which had protected and lubricated it. Eventually, perhaps years later, this produced the arthritis we have just described. If the accident occurred in childhood or early adolescence then it could easily have led to a shortening of one of the ligaments in the pelvic region (the right posterior sacro-iliac ligament), which would have had the effect of distorting the sacrum in this way. The absence of any radiological evidence for a growth arrest in later childhood suggests that Seianti's accident occurred no earlier than in her sixteenth year, so that her distorted sacrum might equally have arisen from a minor abnormality in her physical development.

The changes observed in Seianti's spine gave clues to two different activities or events in her life. Some are the long-term consequences of an activity earlier in her life, in adolescence or early adulthood, during which her spine was subjected to periodic vertical movement; others, in the lower spine, probably occurred in mid-adult life as her body compensated for the injuries around her right hip.

Painful though it may sound, this diagnosis only sketches an outline of Seianti's medical history in cold, clinical terms. Dr Stoddart's interpretation painted a far more vivid picture.

First, the powerful muscles in her thighs and lower back imply that she had been athletic in her younger days. The contrast between the very strong upper legs and the less powerful lower legs suggest that she had been a horsewoman from childhood, gripping the body of the horse with her legs. The Etruscans did not use saddle or stirrups (a medieval invention), and the changes on the bone around the insertions of the Achilles tendons may indicate the extra effort needed to control a horse when riding with only a saddlecloth. Her shoulder muscles testify to the strength required to control the reins. Her spine shows signs of the stresses caused by long hours on horseback. Had Seianti been a dancer her back would have suffered the same stress, but then one would expect the muscles in her lower legs to be more developed too, and perhaps also to see signs of arthritis appearing in her feet. Keen horsewoman she may have been, but in adolescence or soon after reaching adulthood – at any rate many years before her death – Seianti suffered an appalling accident while out on a horse which eventually ended her riding career. Perhaps her horse reared up in fright or anger; certainly it stumbled and fell onto its right side. Seianti was not thrown off; it might have been better if she had been. Instead she was trapped underneath the animal, and her right inner leg and pelvis were crushed and torn by the weight and the movement of the horse. Her leg was rammed into the hip bone, and the two bones which join at the back of the pelvis, the sacrum and the ilium, were similarly crushed and driven onto each other, damaging the cartilage and the soft tissue and causing extensive internal bleeding, which clotted and eventually calcified and led to the arthritis of the joint which we have described. As nature gradually repaired the tissues the ligament may well have become shortened, leading to a slight 'list' on that side of the body: her spine was slightly curved to the left (scoliosis) to compensate for this.

Two other features may be simply individual peculiarities, but under the circumstances are perhaps more likely linked to Seianti's fall. One is a small hollow in the top of the right femur, next to that where the ligament which held the femur in place in its socket (the ligamentum teres) joined the bone. This probably formed either to accommodate a portion of the ligamentum teres which had partially torn away, or because the synovial fluid which normally lubricates the joint had been forcibly driven into its deeper layers. The other peculiarity is the unusual shape and thinness of the pubic bones in her pelvis, which had sent such contradictory signals in the anthropologist's efforts to determine her age. A very pragmatic explanation put forward by the pathologist in the light of his report on other aspects of her health was that the physical shock of the fall was transmitted through the bones of her pelvis and damaged the pubic ligaments and the cartilage between the pubic bones, which suffered further (though normal) change during her subsequent pregnancy.

Before turning to the skull, Dr Stoddart concluded his report with the words: 'I suspect that Seianti continued to ride for some years after recovering from her injury, but had begun to experience pain and restricted movement in her right hip and lower back a considerable time before her death. As she became less mobile and could not exercise well, she would have put on weight, increasing the tendency to secondary changes in her lumbar spine.' The dry skeleton has become a person whom one might recognise, and with whose story one can readily sympathise. It is the sort of condition which today could be helped by a hip replacement, but for which Seianti would have been able to find little relief except through rest and restricted activity, which she must have found difficult to bear, at least at first. It is unlikely that she became bedridden or wholly inactive for any extended period, since her long bones show no evidence for a loss of bone mass, but she would have been disabled in walking and, possibly, in standing without support. Even lying in bed she will have suffered discomfort, and the difficulty and pain she must have experienced in moving her legs apart cannot but have affected other aspects of her life too. Of course this was not the end of the story. We have not even begun to consider her skull properly yet. Significantly, Dr Stoddart had added a postscript to this part of his report, 'It is also notable that she had long-established pathological change in the right side of her jaws, where teeth were lost early, and in her right temporo-mandibular joint', while her lower jaw had gone through considerable changes – 'remodelling'. This, he suggested, might well be the mark of another injury which she suffered in the same accident as the one that caused her such pain in her back and right hip.

The skull confirmed the evidence of the pelvis, that we were dealing with an adult woman. The small, gracile dental arch of the upper jaw, the rounded form of the front of the cranium and the very slight eyebrow ridges are all typical of a female skull, as are other features such as the shape of the mastoid processes. There was some post-mortem damage, but none of it severe enough to affect a proper diagnosis: perhaps the most serious was the loss of most of the upper teeth (fig. 2).

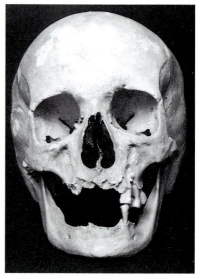

Overall the skull was very symmetrical, the only exceptions being in the face and the lower jaw: the right side of the face is shorter than the left, partly as the result of congenital asymmetry, but also perhaps exaggerated by the effects of injury to both jaws and the consequent tooth loss in the lower jaw. The imbalance appears worse today than it was in life

2. The skull of Seianti.

because more bone has been lost post-mortem around the sockets of the remaining teeth. The skull also provides evidence that Seianti died in middle age, say in her late forties or early fifties rather than when she was an old woman, for the sutures of the skull are still quite wide open at the sides and back, though on the top of the head they have closed to the point of being almost invisible. Except for the centre of the face, where the situation is a little confused because of post-mortem damage, there is little evidence on the skull for the thinning of the bone that is typical of old age. Particularly striking and significant is the absence of any of the changes in shape in the lower jaw found in old people (kindly known as 'senile remodelling' by the medical profession); such changes as there are can all be explained in terms of her pathology.

Seianti's skull had some other minor abnormalities: for instance the bones in her nose were distorted, but not so badly as to cause her any breathing difficulties. However, it was her mouth that was the source of particular interest to us. The fact that two of her premolars had bifurcate roots is an interesting feature, but not uncommon among both the Etruscans and the Romans and not in itself the cause of any problems. Other factors must, however, have been the cause of serious concern to the lady herself. For a start, her oral hygiene was poor, and she evidently suffered from dental caries, from plaque, and probably also from chronic gum disease. It is possible that she was reluctant to carry out any form of brushing or dental cleaning, so tender was her mouth. Some of her teeth have been lost after or possibly around the time of her death, but she was still very much alive when she lost all the lower molars on the right side of her face, for the bone has completely closed up over the sockets. Therefore the tooth loss took place at least five years before her death, and possibly when she was still an adolescent before the skull had quite

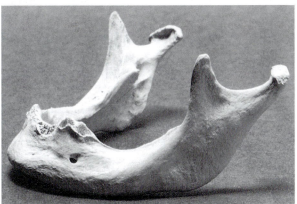

3. The left side of Seianti's mandible and the opposing maxillary dentition.

finished growing; in this case it would have added to the slight congenital distortion of the mandible and so to the slight asymmetry of her face. She lost other teeth at the front of her mouth later, perhaps within two years of her death, for there has been some regrowth of the bone.

It was the left side of her mouth that illustrated most vividly some of the misery that Seianti must have suffered. Here the situation was slightly complicated by some careless attention that she had received at the hands of archaeologists long after her death: radiographs confirmed that one of the premolars which belongs in the upper jaw had been wrongly replaced in the mandible, thereby upsetting its whole set in the face and pushing her chin down much further than was correct. Once this became clear, the offending tooth was removed (fig. 3). She probably still had these premolars in her lower jaw when she died, but she had lost all the molars here well before her death. Thus the opposing teeth had nothing on which to bite, and not surprisingly had built up a massive covering of tartar (again, it is confusing that the first upper molar has been cleaned of its tartar post-mortem; originally it must have been as well encrusted as its neighbour). There is a small abscess at the first molar, and evidence of caries on this tooth and the (missing) premolar next to it. The bone around both these teeth is badly eroded, and there are signs of severe periodontal disease. At the end of the row is a fully developed, but wholly impacted, wisdom tooth. Ironically, although it looks spectacular, this is the only aspect of Seianti's oral pathology that was not necessarily painful.

But this toothache was not all that Seianti suffered. The really dramatic evidence came from the bone of the lower jaw itself, especially from the temporo-mandibular joint on the patient's right side. This is the joint where the ends of the lower jaw – the condyles of the mandible – fit into the skull; it is the joint which normally works smoothly and painlessly each time we open our mouths to speak or to eat and drink. In Seianti's case the condyle had lost its cortical bony layer and was rough, with a distinct lip; the socket on the skull was also misshapen, probably as a long-term consequence of a blow or an injury, and it too had become rough, probably because of the changes in the bone and cartilage of a joint that regularly occur when osteoarthritis sets in. The bones in the joint had not actually fused, but movement was undoubtedly painful, and her jaw may have clicked and grated and even tended to lock as she spoke or tried to chew. The joint on the other side of the face is relatively normal, and her bite was probably noticeably off-centre. Chewing must have been difficult and she may have tried to ease the pain by grimacing or by grinding her (remaining) teeth. The muscles of her jaws were, if anything, oversized, giving her a rather wide, round face – the outward sign that betrayed all this misery. Although one cannot judge from her skull whether her face was actually plump, the rest of the evidence for her lifestyle in her later years makes this very likely.

A short but well-built lady, then: for all her youthful energy, Seianti was about 1.52 m (a little under 5 ft) tall. Our specialists disagreed in their figures for her precise height when she died, which is a calculation that depends partly on age, since it is reckoned that we lose 0.06 cm (0.023 in) every ten years after passing the age of thirty, but it is likely that she was around 1.47 m to 1.50 m (4 ft 10 in or 4 ft 11 in) tall. By the time we come to know her, Seianti has lost the vigour and athleticism of her youth; she suffers badly from arthritis in her right hip as a result of that dreadful riding accident in her late teens; her back is slightly bent to one side, and she probably walks with a limp. As well as having her right side crushed by her horse when it fell, she took a very severe blow to the side of her face, which, if it did not knock out a number of her teeth, loosened or damaged them so that she lost them afterwards, and also damaged the movement of her jaw, ultimately leading to arthritis here too. As if that was not enough, this in turn led to problems with her teeth and gums which must have caused her severe pain. Etruscan dentistry was without parallel in the ancient world, and unlike their Egyptian and Greek counterparts, Etruscan dentists were no strangers to false teeth. Examples of dental protheses using both human and animal teeth with gold bridge bands are known from Etruria, but Seianti's condition was such that false teeth would not have helped her, for the very act of moving her jaw caused her pain.[9] It is very likely that as her suffering became worse she came to prefer a liquid or near-liquid diet. The extent of the calcification of her bones shows that it included a lot of calcium, so she probably consumed a lot of milk or milk puddings. Exercise must have been out of the question for this once-vigorous woman, and the muscles built up in her youth gradually but inexorably turned to fat.

All the information which we had gathered so far – the skeleton, the pathology that could be gleaned from it, the unfortunate lady's dental history, the sculpture on her sarcophagus – all this, when taken together, built up the picture of a very real person. But was this only a word picture, to which our reconstruction would provide the flesh, or did the sculpture provide some real information on Seianti's appearance?

The Etruscan physiognomy has exercised an enduring fascination, first on the Etruscans themselves, and in more recent times on anthropologists and art historians, whether as a clue to their alleged oriental origin or as a stage in the development of portraiture. A symposium held in 1958 on 'Medical Biology and Etruscan Origins' reached only the most tentative of conclusions. A century and more of measuring Etruscan skulls produced few useful results, because it was of necessity based on very limited evidence: for long periods it was the Etruscan custom to cremate the dead, and almost inevitably the survey seems to have focused on the richer burials. A study of forty-four skulls from seven Etruscan towns found that thirty-four were dolicho- and meso-cephalic, and ten brachycephalic. From this it was deduced that the former were oriental invaders, the latter Italian natives. Yet since these proportions can be found in any group of skulls from the European side of the Mediterranean from the Neolithic period onward, such a conclusion is hardly valid. Anthropologists identified the 'typical' Etruscan skull as smooth in surface relief, lacking in brow ridges, the side walls of its vault converging to a narrow forehead, and with high orbits on either side of a narrow nose. This, it was noted, seemed to match closely Archaic Etruscan funerary sculpture, such as the two reclining couples from Cerveteri now in the Louvre and the Villa Giulia museums (fig.4). However, art historians traced the physical characteristics of the Cerveteri sarcophagi back to the East Greek art of Ionia with equal confidence, and as we shall discover later in this chapter, by the Classical and Hellenistic periods the heads and faces in Etruscan art were no different in racial type from those depicted in the art of their Italian neighbours or of Greece, so the anthropological conclusions appear somewhat flawed. Perhaps more than anything else this controversy illustrates the dangers of trying to identify a physical type or to infer the physical appearance of an individual or group of individuals from dry skulls, without going through the careful process of facial reconstruction. There is clearly an urgent need to reassess

*4. The reclining couple on the Etruscan sarcophagus from Cerveteri, c. 525–500 BC
(Paris, Musée du Louvre, Cp 5194).*

the skeletal and anthropological evidence on the basis of new data, as Professor
Becker and his Italian colleague Dr Elsa Pacciani are doing.[10]

Nevertheless the fact remains that the figures on these sarcophagi are immediately set apart from their Greek sources by the focus of interest on the heads, in
contrast to the cursory rendering of the bodies: the lower limbs in particular are
completely swathed and overwhelmed by the enveloping drapery, and seem to have
no forms of their own. Where the Greek artists were aiming at an idealised,
universal form, art in Etruscan society performed a less public and far more utili-
tarian role. The Etruscans had little interest in glorifying historical events or public
achievements: their art served a private and religious purpose, providing for the
needs of the afterlife, for they were a deeply religious people.

This leads to a number of idiosyncratic features in Etruscan art, which is in any
case full of local variations. First, one has to bear in mind that before the sixth
century the Etruscans practised two kinds of burial, apparently varied according to
local or family custom and social taste rather than any differences in religious belief.
Most common was cremation, which required only a small container to hold the
ashes, but the more ambitious method was to lay out the body of the dead on a
couch in all his or her finery, as if resting or reclining at a banquet, presumably the
eternal banquet that the Etruscans conceived as an essential feature of the afterlife.
Then around the middle of the sixth century, presumably under foreign stimulus,
the Etruscans at Cerveteri adopted the custom of burying the bodies of their dead
in sarcophagi. Artistically this was a crucial step, with profound and far-reaching
effects even into Roman and Christian art. The first decorated sarcophagi at

Cerveteri were terracotta gabled boxes which recall the rectangular cremation urns, but the last quarter of the sixth century has yielded the two sarcophagi which we have already mentioned. They each show a couple reclining on a couch that replicates the banqueting-couches or the couches on which the dead had been laid. Seen in the context of the eternal banquet of the afterlife, one begins to understand why the Etruscans placed their most important funerary sculpture not on top of the tomb as a marker for all to see after the Greek manner, but inside it, where it was of concern only to the dead and their families, and to the gods.

These first sarcophagi were of terracotta, the favoured medium at Cerveteri. The couples are shown as they would have been in life, reclining comfortably together at dinner in typically Etruscan fashion (no Greek would have permitted his wife to join him at table in this manner). Typically Etruscan too – aside from the cloaked and formless legs – are the interest in the superficial forms of the body rather than the underlying structure, and the focus on the heads of the two dead people. We have already referred to the way in which these reflect the earlier anthropologists' conception of the Etruscan physiognomy. Although without doubt the sculptures represent the dead persons whose tomb they honour, the notion that at this stage in the development of Etruscan art they might already be true portraits is given the lie by their very similarity. Scholars may argue whether they stem from the same hand or merely the same workshop, but the basis of such a debate rests on a physical as well as a stylistic affinity between the two portraits that is very unlikely to reflect real life, however Etruscan art may have developed in the following centuries.

The Etruscan preoccupation with the individual and its expression through the plastic arts had already shown itself early in the previous century in Chiusi with the first appearance of canopic urns – burial urns of terracotta to hold the cremated remains of the dead (so named after the superficially similar canopic jars of Egypt, although there the function of both the vase and its lid were different). The earliest such urns seem to have had masks of clay or bronze attached to their necks with wires, but by the end of the seventh century the mouth of the vase was covered with a head, modelled in the round and becoming increasingly realistic and less stylised. They have no parallel in the art of Italy, or of Greece, where concern with the individual first shows itself through myth and through poetry. Even if these early attempts can make no claim to be portraits in the true sense, they mark a very important psychological and artistic step from the general to the specific in the recognition and representation of individual human personalities rather than mere types.[11] After *c.* 600 BC the pace quickens, and their development continues down to the middle of the sixth century, when they are replaced by urns in the shape of a complete person. It is particularly fascinating to watch because this really is 'popular' art, in the best Etruscan tradition. The heads become rounded and the faces fully modelled. While one cannot claim that they are portraits in the sense that no real person actually looked like that, and even a fairly superficial analysis shows an underlying similarity of conception, nevertheless the fact remains that the artists were focusing on the physical differences that exist between different persons and not on any social distinctions, nor for that matter on any subtle characterisations. This is still a long way from portraiture as we know it, but the acknowledgement of, and interest in, the fact that faces are different because people are different is a major step along the road (fig. 5).

There are two other instances of the Etruscan predilection for the human face which we should consider before returning to the images of the whole person portrayed on the sarcophagi. The first is a series of red-figure kraters, mixing bowls for wine which in this case were intended to hold the ashes of the dead, made in Volterra between the late fourth and the middle of the third centuries BC. They are decorated with profile heads, singly or sometimes in pairs, done in a somewhat impressionistic manner that emphasises their rather quirky individuality. Although in using the head as the principal decorative motif these Etruscan painters were

5. *An archaic Etruscan canopic jar, and the lid from another, mid-sixth century BC (London, British Museum).*

following a tradition already popular among the red-figure vase-painters in the Greek colonies of Apulia and Campania and even in Athens itself (and one distinguished historian of Greek art made the shrewd comment that except in Rome 'in the last phase of any art, the human head is apt to receive more than its proper share of attention'), they stand apart from and above the Greek painters in the realism with which they endow their subjects.[12] Where the heads painted on the Greek vases, rooted in a long tradition of idealism, have descended to a fleshy vacuousness, these Etruscan faces give the appearance of being portraits of actual people. Given the technical and commercial background of the potters' workshops this is virtually impossible, although there is of course nothing to say that there were not particular Etruscans who looked like this, at least to the gently cynical artist who painted them.

Very much in the same tradition are the remarkably lifelike terracotta heads, roughly life-size, that are found in shrines in Etruria and further south in Latium and Campania.[13] They were intended as votive offerings: parts of the body were offered to the gods as a token or a thank-offering to accompany a prayer for a cure, but presumably the head stands for the whole person making the prayer. At first sight some of these heads are remarkably individualistic – a youth in the prime of life, the careworn, sick older man with the matted locks and stubbly beard that mark his poor health – yet closer examination shows that both come from the same mould, and that by making purely superficial changes the artist has given us a different personality, and in some cases has even changed the sex of his 'sitter'. These heads typify two essential features of Etruscan art on which we have touched already: an interest in people as individuals, focused on their heads and faces, matched by a concern with superficial features and the external aspects of personality rather than the underlying forms (here extended to the underlying character). The approach is in complete contrast to that of the Greeks, among whom 'there was the intention to be lifelike, but individual likeness was not important, the abiding essence of being human was'.[14] The result is a curious paradox. On the one hand the human face is recognised as the distinctive feature, indeed the distinctive property of one individual, an irrational work of nature in which age, experience and temperament are combined; yet on the other the notion is not fully worked out, and 'individual' features are simply added piecemeal to a ready-prepared model as appropriate, an approach which can never create more than a token representation. The question is whether this 'personalising' approach of a 'typical' product, which smacks strongly of late twentieth-century marketing, represents the true Etruscan attitude to individual portraiture, or was merely the result of technical convenience.

The definition of what precisely comprises a true portrait in art in the sense of a physical likeness has been many times discussed, but two requirements must be fundamental: first, that it aims to render a specific likeness, and second, that this likeness is of a named or at least nameable person (in the seventeenth century the *Vocabulario toscano dell'Arte del Disegno* of Filippo Balduccini defines it as 'cavata del naturale', 'wrested from the subject's nature').[15] There is thus a distinction between the representation of a live model in the role of a genre figure or a mythological character, and the portrait of the model as herself or himself. 'Princess Caroline as Venus' remains a portrait of the Prince Regent's wife because of its label, but the label taken together with the semi-nude and mildly scandalous depiction is also intended to tell us something of the sitter's character. On the other hand Rembrandt's painting of Bathsheba does not set out to portray the model, his adored Hendrijke, whatever his feelings towards her may have been, but simply uses her whole figure to convey a deeply emotional moment. Because Rembrandt could have no way of knowing what Bathsheba looked like, he could not render her appearance truthfully and could not (and undoubtedly would not) claim this as a portrait of King David's beloved. There is a difference of intention: the individual name and personality have been replaced by an identity that goes beyond personality into a wider social or historical context.

If the terracotta canopic urns and votive heads are thereby ruled out as portraits in the strict sense, what of the figures on the larger rectangular cinerary urns and the closely related sarcophagi? We have already rejected the Late Archaic 'bride and groom' sarcophagi from Cerveteri, on the grounds of a similarity that verges on identity. The tradition of the reclining banqueter is revived at Chiusi towards the end of the fifth century on cinerary urns made in limestone, alabaster and even bronze, on which the dead person is shown at roughly two-thirds life-size. They are interesting for a number of reasons, among them the fact that they introduce a feature that becomes common on Etruscan funerary monuments for the next three and a half centuries: some of the men have skinny bodies, many are flabby and even paunchy. Not for the Etruscans the perfect physique that was the ideal of the Greeks and later of the Romans. At first one regards the bellies and the fleshy breasts of the old men reclining on their coffins as yet another indication that this is the body of a particular individual – like Henry VIII of England, perhaps – but it soon becomes clear that Etruscan men of all ages can be shown thus, and the difference is merely one of degree. Etruscan artists were on the whole indifferent to the body in favour of the head and were obsessed with surfaces rather than internal structure. For this reason it is possible to explain the phenomenon of these heavy bodies as their translation of the monumentality of some of the contemporary Greek sculptures which were their models, so that bodies and garments are simply interpreted in terms of sheer physical mass and of surface detail and texture. This may be part of the truth, but that it is more than artistic convention is shown by the words of the poet Catullus some 350 years later, who refers to the 'obesus Etruscus' in a context that shows this was a regular if uncomplimentary epithet applied by the Romans to their northern neighbours.[16] It is often said that unlike, the Greeks and Romans, the Etruscans were not great athletes and preferred to amuse themselves with quieter games, although the physical remains of Seianti show that not all Etruscans disliked physical exercise. It is perhaps better to see the fleshiness depicted on the funerary sculptures as an indicator of status and wealth, matching the jewellery and fine dresses with which most of the women are decked: these men did not need to carry out hard physical work, and were proud to show it.

As anthropomorphic containers for the ashes of the dead these Chiusine products are something of a regional speciality, although they herald the appearance of full-size stone sarcophagi at Cerveteri, Tarquinia and soon Chiusi itself, in a tradition that then persists until around 50 BC. On the lids of these sarcophagi the figure of the dead person lies, either 'sleeping' (whether in this world or the next is not clear) or reclining. Men are often equipped for a banquet, but sometimes with a text that displays their achievements or announces their profession as priest or augur; women display their finery. The intention is clearly to represent the dead person. The quality is variable, and some clearly make no attempt at realism, either through incompetence or because they are following a more abstract, formal line. However, what makes these sarcophagi and the cinerary urns which parallel them important in the overall history of western art is that they are made of stone, which discourages the easy repetition which is possible in terracotta production. Some rise to considerable heights of artistic achievement and inventiveness in their rendering of both body and head, particularly among the products of Tarquinia in the south, carved in hard limestone and breccia. Although one would like to see them as 'total portraits', where all the parts of the body have been rendered to depict one particular individual, we have already seen that the apparently realistic and (to us) unflattering treatment of the male physique is now a commonplace in Etruscan art. However, the faces display great sensitivity and individuality, so that it is hard to escape the conclusion that they are intended to portray the specific likeness of a named individual – except that we do not know that individual, and until now we have not been able to check the veracity of the likeness.

It is worth quoting here two passages from Otto Brendel's masterly survey of Etruscan art, which underline the much wider significance of this moment in the story of the Etruscan sarcophagi.

There appears to be a serious possibility, not to be disregarded, that a turn from 'typical' to 'real' portraits indeed happened in Etruria about or shortly after 350. If the workshops of the sculptured sarcophagi led this change, they merely brought the old Etruscan insistence on facial differentiation as a mark of the human reality to its ultimate conclusion. Henceforward portraits in the modern sense, i.e. genuine likenesses of specific and nameable persons, may be expected in Etruria, though we will have to regard them as special and perhaps as exceptional.

What Brendel is in fact saying is that these sarcophagi should mark the start of true portraiture in western art, but one link in the argument is missing before it can be proven:

The crux of the matter is the unanswerable question of personal similitude. The subjects of this stony portrait gallery are beyond our reach: nothing can be known of their real countenances. In no circumstances can the portrait likeness of their image be taken for granted.[17]

The reason for this lengthy survey of Etruscan funerary art will now be becoming clear. However, before we put the question of the veracity of Seianti's 'portrait' to the test, we need to complete the overview in order to include the later Hellenistic period to which her sarcophagus belongs.

Although the great leap forward in 'the new and descriptive method' on the sarcophagi took place around 350 BC, and was paralleled by similar advances in free-standing portraiture, other conventions persisted (often under Greek influence) and of course mediocre artists continued to work in the old manner. Around 200 BC serial production of stone sarcophagi begins; in the terracotta workshops of places like Chiusi it was only to be expected. The result is a monotony of motifs and a neglect of detail in both the sarcophagi and the cinerary urns. For example, in the products of the Volterra workshops it is possible to identify a series of 'types', from which the customer might choose according to taste, wealth and social status – and given human nature and pretension, it is likely that some people chose above their proper station. In such a context the 'portrait' on the sarcophagus can be no more than a type assumed to match that of the dead person, with features and traits that fall within a coded social vocabulary. From the artist's point of view such a series and repertoire entail a prototype, and it is sometimes possible for the art historian not only to trace the development of the series but even to track it back to its artistic source, which at least by the Hellenistic period need not even have an Etruscan connection.[18]

The tradition at Volterra is perhaps an extreme example, where the human figure is effectively deformed in order to lay emphasis on the dead person's social position in this life and heroic dignity in the next. At its lowest end this yields a series of cinerary urns where the body is reduced to a short stumpy thing swathed in drapery and holding a purely conventional attribute such as a drinking cup or a fan, or sarcophagi on whose lid reclines a flat, formless and elongated body. Yet one cannot get away from the Etruscan preoccupation with the head. Only in the poorest workshops is the head reduced to a stylised cipher. Even on the most abbreviated ash urns the head remains large, and retains the appearance of having been given an individual character, for all that it stares into space without expression.

We have focused on Volterra because its products provide the strongest arguments *against* the notion of true realism and portraiture in Etruscan funerary

6. *Etruscan terracotta sarcophagus of an elderly couple from Volterra, late second century BC (Volterra, Museo Guarnacci inv. 613).*

sculpture. Yet even at Volterra there are clear indications of attempts to individualise particular coffins to particular requirements. For example, the figure of Aule Lecu, otherwise apparently completely within the conventions of second-century Volterra, is carved holding a sheep's liver in his left hand, thereby marking him out as a priest or augur.[19] It is true that this is but a small variation on the typical figure that holds a cup, but unless the workshop held a stock of 'priestly' funerary urns, this one must at least have been finished to order. The sculptures on Etruscan sarcophagi everywhere set out to commemorate people from different walks of life, unlike the socially more restricted funerary sculptures of the Greeks, and thus their approach to the physiognomical variety before them had to be an empirical one based upon actual observation: a specific individual was to be shown at a particular moment in his or her life. This is most vividly demonstrated on a second-century terracotta urn from Volterra, showing an elderly couple, usually interpreted as man and wife, 'the moving image of a couple with their sorrows etched on their faces' (fig.6). The difficult – and seemingly unanswerable – technical question is whether the mould from which this lid was cast was specially made, or whether the final product was merely superficially reworked to order from a standard model. Compelling and reasoned arguments have been put forward to show that even this pair of seemingly individual and idiosyncratic folk are no more than conventional artist's types.[20]

The elderly couple from Volterra typify some of the profound changes that pervaded the art of the Greek world during the Hellenistic period and which found a ready vehicle in Etruscan funerary monuments, for the new trends for the picturesque and for the expression of individual emotions were much to the Etruscans' taste and artistic traditions. There are many similarly powerful and apparently

7. *The sarcophagus of an unknown elderly Etruscan, probably from the area of Tarquinia, 200-150 BC (Copenhagen, Ny Carlsberg Glyptotek H.I.N. 429).*

'personal' monuments from the later Hellenistic period. As an example one may take the sarcophagus of Laris Pulena carved in Tarquinia in the early second century BC: the rather massive body we have come to expect, a thick bull neck, the heavy unfriendly face of a man with whom one would prefer not to do business; garlands on his head and shoulders, a ring on his fingers, and unrolled in his hands before him a scroll that lists his achievements. It is difficult to believe that anyone would have chosen so unflattering a memorial unless it truly portrayed the man whose remains were placed beneath the image. In a similar spirit is the nenfro sarcophagus of an older man in Copenhagen, of much the same date. His name is lost, but the rolls of fat below his chest and on his neck and his lined, crabby face leave one in no doubt that this is intended as the portrait of a particular individual (fig. 7).[21]

'Banqueter' urns and sarcophagi of the kind we have just described remain the most popular monuments in Etruria. Greek influence was now strong, and the bulk were made by craftsmen rather than artists, with no apparent pretensions at anything other than 'ethical' portraiture which illustrated the 'ethos' or moral as well as physical nature of the sitter. Yet the finest of them take this 'ethical' portraiture at least to the verge of actual likeness. The three pieces we have just described are still strongly Etruscan in feeling; others show Greek influence more clearly in the careful finish of the body and in the play between the folds and texture of the drapery and the smooth flesh. In the figures of men this may also show in the deep-set eyes and thickly clustered locks that recall some of the portraits of Hellenistic rulers in Asia Minor and elsewhere, while among the female sarcophagi that of Seianti has been taken as exemplifying this trend. The intense, staring eyes, the oddly extended torso whose proportions recall those of other Late Hellenistic figures such as the Aphrodite of Melos, the twist of her torso and the contrast between the folds and textures of her cloak, her tunic and her flesh would all be at home in the art of Greece.[22] Although Seianti's taste for flashy jewellery may be Etruscan, her dress is in the Greek style that was becoming popular in Italy in the second and first centuries BC.

This stylistic analysis did not augur well if Seianti was to be the test case for checking the veracity of the likeness of an Etruscan tomb sculpture, since it implied that even in a period when there appeared to be good evidence for growing truthfulness in the 'portraits' on sarcophagi and cinerary urns, hers belonged to a phase where realism was again being repudiated in favour of 'ethical' portraiture. A recent detailed study of the terracotta sarcophagi of the third and second centuries BC has argued for strong traditions of prototype and series within each workshop with variations of detail and finish very similar to those we have described on the votive heads, which override considerations of representational truthfulness, an impression which is confirmed by even the most casual survey of collections of such sarcophagi, be they of stone or terracotta.[23] Similarity of feature among members of a 'family group' may easily prove to be only the similarity one would expect from sculptures originating from the same workshop. And yet among the standard types there are always a few pieces that stand apart for their individuality.

First, there can be no doubt that Seianti's sarcophagus was made to order, for the letters of the inscription recording her name were cut into the clay while it was wet.

Second, it is important – and often not difficult – to distinguish second-rate products made by artisans from first-rate pieces made by artists. There is a very real difference in kind here. Simple designs, with the arms held against the body and the legs flat, can be and were readily repeated from the same mould almost in their entirety. For more complex 'façade' poses with much undercutting, intended to be viewed from more than one angle, it would have been difficult if not impossible to take the finished sarcophagus out of the mould without breaking it, and it is likely that these were made up from many smaller moulds with much individual modelling after moulding. There are real physical similarities among the effigies of people who were buried in the Tomb of the Treptie at Tuscania over about a century and who must be members of the same family. It might be debatable whether these similarities are the signs of kinship or the result of the re-use of a limited number of moulds, were it not for the repetition of many other details apart from the faces and the evidently inferior workmanship. By contrast Seianti Hanunia's sarcophagus shows a complexity of design that not even her cousin Larthia's can match.[24]

Third, when we compare features of Seianti's anatomy and in particular of her face as they are shown on the effigy on her sarcophagus and as they are reported from her skeleton by members of our team, it becomes at least possible that the artist was himself reporting what he knew of Seianti's appearance, either from personal acquaintance or from descriptions from those who knew her.

Her bones told us that she was a short, well-built lady. Bearing in mind the Etruscan artists' traditional lack of interest in the body, it is not surprising that in this Hellenising phase the proportions of the figure on the sarcophagus conform to those of the conventional Late Hellenistic ideal, however hard we may find it to equate Seianti's physique with that of her contemporary the Venus de Milo. Nor can we expect evidence for the arthritis in her hip or the slight twist in her spine to be apparent from her reclining posture, even had the artist wished to draw attention to them. On the other hand there is a hint at a more ample physique in the way her breasts press against the cloth of her dress, where Larthia Seianti is altogether more flat chested. Although most of her body is concealed by her clothes, where it is exposed, at the arms and of course the face, Seianti is noticeably plump, as the pathologist had predicted without reference to the sarcophagus. Despite the custom of showing men's bodies as well fleshed, Etruscan women were as a rule depicted as more slender – like Larthia Seianti, whose arms, though well rounded, are by no means as chubby and who certainly does not have the double chin with which the artist has endowed her cousin. The rather fleshy face recalls the comment that because the pain of the arthritis in the temporo-mandibular joint made chewing difficult she may have grimaced or ground her teeth when using her jaw, so that the muscles became slightly hypertrophied, 'giving her a rather wide, round face – the outward sign that betrayed all this misery'. Even though we believe that her slightly distorted nasal bones were unlikely to have caused her any difficulty in breathing, the problems of both arthritis and toothache render it likely that she kept her mouth open a little – as the artist has shown her. He has not shown the tiredness that constant pain brings; perhaps in a less Hellenising period he would have done so. However, there is no reason to believe that even at this time he would have disguised her age (for example the Treptie group includes at least one older woman). He has given us a rather plump lady of middle age, apparently with some oral problems, who took some care over her appearance to judge from her dress and jewellery as well as her carefully defined eyebrows. Within the conventions and traditions of Late Hellenistic Etruria it would surely be churlish to ask for more.

The next and final stage was to translate the medical findings into a reconstruction, and to compare this with the ancient artist's rendering. In theory the reconstruction should have been straightforward, aside from the familiar constraints of time and other work. The first version was prepared for two study days held at the British Museum in 1991, the second of which involved bringing together all the members of the team then involved with Seianti. Although at that time we did not have the benefit of Dr Stoddart's involvement, it proved a stimulating occasion as an interim report, not least because in true academic fashion we reached differing conclusions over a number of points, most of which have now been resolved. However, two factors were significant in producing a reconstruction which was erroneous as a strict interpretation of the evidence from Seianti's remains. The first was only a minor one, that the premolar, still incorrectly replaced in the lower jaw, altered the set of her jaw slightly. This was not crucial, for she would still have been easily recognisable to her family and friends, but it was irritating. The other was more significant: at that time there seemed little reason to doubt Marshal Becker's initial contention that Seianti had died a very old lady, at least eighty and perhaps ninety years old, and so this was how she was shown. Elderly ladies in ancient Etruria often did their hair up in a bun, so our Seianti had her hair dressed in this fashion. Especially when wrapped in a scarf, she resembled many an old lady whom one might meet in the streets of a town in Tuscany today (fig. 8).

It was an interesting face, but if this rendering of the head was correct then there was little chance that the figure on the sarcophagus was intended as a portrait. Although it was possible to find similarities in the proportions of the two faces, it raised many questions over the manufacture of the sarcophagi, and cast serious doubt on the notion that the figures on the lids were in any sense portraits from the life. At the very least it meant that the ancient artist must have been working from a portrait taken long before she died, or else that the model on which the lid was based, if not the lid itself, was made many years before her death. 'Milady finds science has a heart of stone – statue faked her beauty' was how a newspaper headline summed it up.

However, once it became clear that Seianti was only about fifty when she died the whole picture changed, quite literally. Seianti had the laugh on us – perhaps the statue had not faked her beauty after all. We had, of course, done something rather horrible to her, in showing her as she never lived to be, rather like computer projections of film stars' faces ten, twenty and fifty years on. Eventually, when time allowed and once we had satisfied ourselves beyond reasonable doubt that we were dealing with the remains of a middle-aged lady, a new version appeared.

8. Seianti reconstructed as an old woman.

The first reconstruction had been a particularly fascinating exercise because it provided an opportunity to build into the face all those features that make an old face so exciting to draw, to paint or indeed to sculpt. The more that the rigours of life have been etched into the fabric of a face, the greater is the story it has to tell. The owner of the face is unlikely to see it from quite the same perspective, for the loss of youth and the outward signs of the strains and stresses the body has undergone are seldom welcome. We were nevertheless rather sad when the incontrovertible evidence about Seianti's real age finally emerged, for the rather grand and somewhat imperious nature of her first appearance had given us great satisfaction.

To have to remove all those years was not in itself a problem, or would not have been a problem had it not been for the fact that the original clay reconstruction no longer existed. The fundamental proportions would not alter, for although there are changes that occur on the skull as a result of the ageing process, the new reconstruction was being built up on the same skull as the much older head. Apart from correcting the set of the lower jaw to account for the misplaced tooth, changes were confined to the soft tissue. The loss of elasticity evidenced by extensive creasing of the skin over most of the face had to go, together with the sagging flesh under the eyes and chin. The wrinkles radiating like crows' feet around the mouth and the eyes, the thinning of the lips, the lengthening and spreading of the nose and the increase in the size of the ears all had to be changed. There was one more very major modification that would have to be incorporated in the new head: she had to be quite fat! Dr Stoddart's studies had demonstrated that the size of the lady as depicted on the lid of her sarcophagus was quite in keeping with the size of the lady as she probably was in life. Seianti has in turn presented us with the opportunity to produce first the oldest (biologically) and then the fattest reconstruction for which we have ever been asked.

Helmer's measurements for 'Frauen – Maximum' were used in building up the new face, together with many rather more informal studies of large ladies as seen in the town – the latter not without its risks.[25] Of course the whole process had to be started again from the beginning, and the substantial changes to the soft tissue bulk mean that the younger version has a very different look. It is not just the wiping away of old age that is responsible for this: the new face seems to have smaller features, which in an odd way is true. The nose is smaller and the bulk of the face is greater, which makes the eyes and nose appear smaller, and thus although she has the same skull as before, the changes that occur in extreme old age have been eliminated. It seemed fair to adjust the hairstyle and include headgear to match loosely that worn by the figure on the sarcophagus, since no one could argue that it was not contemporary, whether this was a true portrait or not.

Then came the moment to compare our version with the ancient one (fig. 9). At first we simply made the comparison by eye, looking at the two side by side. It appeared to us then that the differences were greater than the similarities, especially when we looked at the two heads in profile. It was striking that where the sculpture showed a nose with an almost straight profile, the reconstruction has a very pronounced hollow at the nasion (the bridge of the nose). To give the two noses the same profile would have meant adding at least 5 mm (¼ in) of clay at the nasion, for which there was no evidence at all. However plump, no face has that much extra soft tissue at this point. As well as this more curved profile and consequently more prominent nose, the reconstruction has a shorter upper lip. Overall the upper portions of the reconstructed face, from the nasion to the nasio-labial junction (where nose and upper lip meet) are smaller in proportion to the lower face (from the nasio-labial junction to the point of the chin) than they are on the sculpture. This means that the 'portrait' renders the lower parts of her face smaller than they are on the reconstruction – in other words than they were in real life. This has given her a face that is more like that of a child, more feminine and attractive, or at any rate more traditionally 'female'.

Despite the fact that we had approached the question in a spirit of open-minded research, it could not be denied that this seemed a rather disappointing end to the undertaking. We had, however, always intended to go one step further, and to apply to this case the objective and measured superimposition techniques employed in some aspects of forensic photocomparison of the face. 'Face mapping' Seianti (to give it its other name) produced some fascinating answers. It could be demonstrated that there are some unreconcilable differences between the face of the terracotta figure and the reconstruction. However, from the front these differences are far less

9. *The final reconstruction of Seianti: front and profile views, compared to the same views of the figure on the sarcophagus.*

marked, and certainly not sufficient for one to conclude that the Etruscan artist had deliberately made no attempt to create some sort of likeness of the dead woman. In fact the overall shape and size of the face of the reconstruction prove to be consistent with that of the portrait. The spatial relationship between the morphological features of the two faces (especially the eyes, nose and mouth) is very similar, as is the space between the inner canthus of the eyes and the width across the wings of the nose. In other words the proportions of the two faces are very much the same, which is very important since it is these that give the face its basic identity – witness the case of Sabir Kassim Kilu, described in Chapter 2, where the face was still clearly recognisable despite having been reconstructed with the wrong age and racial features. The size of the eyes and the mouth on Seianti's portrait are, however, considerably larger, and so is the width of the nose in the region of the nasion. Under the circumstances such anomalies could be explained by the fact that the purpose and function of the two heads were altogether different, and that given the radically different methods and milieux of their creation the chances of their showing any greater similarity would be unlikely. This does not mean that one could not expect physical accuracy from the reconstruction, but that the portrait still harks back to the idealising traditions of the classical world, or rather that it belongs to a Hellenistic artistic milieu where idealisation is again coming into vogue. It is even possible that in making the eyes larger and the lips more voluptuous the sculptor was indulging in a little flattery. In making the reconstruction we enjoyed no such licence.

However, before considering the historical and the personal context of the sculpture further we must first look again at the profile views of the two heads, and look at them objectively. Here again we see a broad similarity in the general proportions, with of course the same enlargement of the mouth and eyes. The unreconcilable difference in anatomical terms lies in the shape of the nose and forehead, on which we have already commented. The upper two-thirds of the portrait's face projects forwards far more than does the same area of the reconstruction. The net result is that the eyes become much deeper set, the nose is longer, and most startling of all is the marked Hellenistic profile in which the indentation around the nasion has almost disappeared. It is the same 'Greek' profile that emerged in the reconstruction of Ada, described in the next chapter, but whereas in Ada's case it had surprised us when it appeared unexpectedly but undeniably from the evidence of the skull, here we have moved straight back into the classical artists' tradition of idealisation. Noses like this are still very common in Hellenistic sculpture (perhaps that is why Cleopatra's nose is such a famous exception) and however much it may seem to improve Seianti's profile, such a deviation from the original belongs to the Hellenistic 'portrait' of the ideal concept of woman as exemplified by one individual, not to the realistic traditions of Etruscan art nor even necessarily to simple artistic flattery. It bears little or no resemblance to reality as evidenced by the skull, and it would need very extensive remodelling of the bone before the reconstruction could bear comparison.

However, despite this undeniable element of Hellenistic idealisation in the 'portrait' of Seianti, there are very significant features about the sculpture which imply that the artist was intending to represent a real person. As far as it was going to be seen at all by human eyes, this sculpture was intended to be viewed from the front, and the profile was very much a secondary aspect. Not only is the similarity of the proportions between portrait and reconstruction much too great to be coincidental, but there was neither need nor convention for the artist to show her as such a plump lady if she was not really so.

Even in her rejuvenated aspect the reconstruction still looks some years older than the sculpture. We can offer two suggestions for this. First, that among those fashionable idealising touches the artist has also returned his sitter to the years of her prime. The second suggestion is really posed as a question: if this is truly a portrait, even a modified portrait, we still do not know how the artist took Seianti's likeness. Given the time normally available between death and burial, there was hardly scope to use a death mask, even when working in terracotta and certainly not for the sculptors who carved in stone. It remains irrefutably true that this sarcophagus was specially ordered for Seianti, for her name was cut into the clay while it was still wet. Large and cumbersome though these sarcophagi may be, perhaps we are forced to conclude that, like some Romans later, the Etruscans ordered their funeral sculptures ahead of time, and lived with them a while.

We noted at the outset that Seianti, living and dying at a time when Greek notions of ideal beauty were again taking hold in Etruria, might not be the ideal candidate for the test we were proposing. In the event she has served us well, lending strength to the argument that it was the Etruscans who brought true portraiture into western art and showing a road along which may lie many other interesting Etruscan faces. It is now surely necessary to reassess many of those other 'portrait' sarcophagi. We hope, too, that she will not feel that we have done her a disservice, and that she will forgive us that in our search for the true Seianti we have uncovered some of her inmost secrets. 'Do you think Greek art ever tells us what the Greek people were like?' asked Oscar Wilde. 'Do you believe that the Athenian women were like the stately dignified figures of the Parthenon frieze, or like those marvellous goddesses who sat in the triangular pediments of the same building: if you judge from the art, they certainly were so…The fact is that we look back on the ages entirely through the medium of art, and art, very fortunately, has never once told the truth.'[26] The truth is that Seianti was a much more interesting person than the artist would have us believe.

CHAPTER 10

The Case of the Carian Princess[1]

The port of Halicarnassus was one of the major cities of Caria: at some time in the fifteen years following his accession in 377 BC Mausolus, Caria's most ambitious and most famous ruler, moved his capital there from Mylasa, some thirty miles inland to the northeast, as part of a great political reorganisation. The tomb built for him by his sister-wife Artemisia was counted as one of the seven wonders of the ancient world. Little now remains above ground of this tomb, the Mausoleum, although in its ruined state it probably gave the town its modern name of Bodrum, the Turkish word for 'dungeon' or 'underground vault'. It provided a ready quarry for building materials for later inhabitants, above all for the Knights of St John when they arrived at the beginning of the fifteenth century and built the Castle of St Peter, which still dominates the town from its position by the harbour. Today the castle houses the Bodrum Museum of Underwater Archaeology, which comprises one of the finest – and one of the most excitingly displayed – collections of finds from ancient shipwrecks (and indeed of the remains of the ships themselves), dating from the Bronze Age to the medieval period.

In the later twentieth century the town of Bodrum in the region of Muğla has become a fast-growing holiday resort on the southwestern coast of Turkey, popular with both land-based visitors and with those who go down to the sea in yachts and other small ships. Inevitably the old and the new sometimes come into conflict as modern development encroaches upon ancient remains, and such building work is closely monitored by the Bodrum Museum.

In April 1989 an application came to the museum for the building (ironically) of a new office for a tourist company between the two ancient city walls, on the east side of the town at the point where the road from Milas (ancient Mylasa) divided, one fork going into the town itself, the other continuing to the tip of the headland at Turgutreis. Work on the foundations was closely supervised by a team from the museum under Aykut Özet, for the site lay in the area of the eastern cemetery of the ancient city. The excavations brought to light seven long stone blocks laid neatly side by side in an east-west orientation, apparently the cover of an ancient tomb. Dr Özet was not optimistic about finding much more, for most other tombs found in excavations carried out in this area since the nineteenth century had been looted in antiquity. However, when the blocks were lifted they revealed a tomb chamber of unmortared ashlar masonry measuring some 2.47 m long by 1.17 m wide (8 ft 1¼ in by 3 ft 10 in) and 1.35 m (4 ft 5 in) deep. Inside it was a plain but carefully made and – what was more important under the circumstances – well-preserved sarcophagus carved from a single block of stone, its lid shaped like a pitched roof, 2.20 m (7 ft 2½ in) long, 0.91 m (2 ft 11¾ in) wide and 1.13 m (3 ft 8½ in) deep. Both were of the local green limestone, also used in the construction of the

Mausoleum and later of the castle. The quality of the workmanship was such as to suggest that this might be the burial of an important person, and news of the discovery created great excitement in the town. A great crowd assembled to watch the opening of the sarcophagus, and had to be held back by the police. One can feel for Dr Özet at having to carry out a potentially tricky task in such a glare of public interest. To use his own words, 'After taking the necessary precautions, we lifted the lid of the sarcophagus. Inside, there was a well-preserved skeleton with arms crossed in the abdominal area and strikingly dressed with gold jewellery. This find was such as an archaeologist may experience only once in his lifetime.'[2] When lifted and cleaned, the 'gold jewellery' so baldly referred to by the excavator comprised a wreath of myrtle leaves, two bracelets with terminals in the shape of antelope heads, three rings, a necklace with twenty-one pendants in the shape of flower buds, two fibulae, and over six hundred pieces which had been attached to the dead woman's silk peplos or tunic, including two appliqué strings of beads, one of fifty pieces and the other of ninety-five. It scarcely seems worth mentioning the black-glazed pottery oinochoe (wine jug) found beside the sarcophagus after this torrent of gold, although it was important in fixing the date of the burial.

Who was this lady? From the richness of her burial it was clear that she was someone important. Locally she quickly acquired the soubriquet of 'the Carian Princess' and her fame became such that it was not long before she even had a luxury hotel named for her. But was she really a princess? Once again there were no inscriptions to provide the key, and the only clues lay in the circumstantial evidence of the remains themselves, both archaeological and anthropological. The preliminary examination of the skeleton by Professor Berna Alpagut from Ankara University, with whom we had collaborated on the skull of 'Midas', suggested that the skeleton was that of a woman 1.62 m (just under 5 ft 4 in) tall, who had died at the age of about forty, on the basis of the teeth, the condition of the sutures in the skull, and the pubic symphysis. The teeth were in extremely good condition and had all been present at the time of death, indicating a good diet, probably rich in calcium. Her limb bones were well developed, a fact that led Professor Alpagut to think that she was an experienced horserider. It was also suggested that she must have borne at least one child, because 'scars of parturition' could be discerned on her pelvis. These so-called scars – pubic pitting, scarring of the sacrum and the preauricular sulcus – have traditionally been taken as evidence for childbearing, but in studying the remains from the Spitalfields cemetery in London Dr Margaret Cox noted them on both male and female skeletons. They are much more common on the latter, but even here they are present on the skeletons of women known from the parish registers to have died childless as well as those recorded as having borne children. In short, the 'scars' have no connection with childbearing at all.[3]

The wealth of her grave goods and her apparent physical wellbeing at the time of her death both imply that this person belonged to the aristocracy of Halicarnassus. That she may perhaps have spent much time on horseback could be taken as further evidence for her high social status, while the fact that she died at around forty need be no reflection on her general health, for the average age at death of women in the late classical and Hellenistic periods was around thirty-six to thirty-eight years. The only positively identified 'noble' grave in Halicarnassus is that of Mausolus himself, but this was unique in its design as well as in its siting as the focus of the new city plan. The area where the other members of the Hecatomnid 'royal family' were buried is not known. One might expect their graves to have been near that of Mausolus, so that his splendid Mausoleum could form the centrepiece of a dynastic burial plot, but the other tombs found in the area and under the Mausoleum itself all belong to the archaic period, and date from the time before Mausolus enlarged the city: in other words, in accordance with traditional custom these graves had been dug outside the city walls as they then existed, while one of the distinctive features of Mausolus' tomb was that it lay within the new circuit of walls. The very uniqueness of the Mausoleum may be a further argument against its having been built close to any other tombs, whether belonging to his own family or not.

Excavations in ancient Halicarnassus are nowadays carried out jointly by the Turkish archaeological authorities and the Danish Halikarnassos Expedition, but it was not always so. In the grand style of the mid-nineteenth century an expedition was sent by the British Museum under Charles Newton, then Keeper of Greek and Roman Antiquities. Although 'the expedition…was sent out by Her Majesty's Government in the first instance with the special object of removing from the Castle of Budrum [sic], in Asia Minor, certain sculptures, which had formed part of the Tomb of Mausolus at Halicarnassus', it also carried out excavations at the sites of Halicarnassus and its neighbours Cnidus and Branchidae, and recorded their monuments. In 1855 Newton investigated the two cemeteries at Halicarnassus used in the period after Mausolus extended the walls, which lay outside the eastern and western gates on the roads leading to Myndus and Mylasa respectively. His descriptions of his findings are at best summary, after the manner of the time. In the western cemetery, on the road running out of the Mylasa gate, Newton discovered several vaulted chambers set on large square basements faced with ashlar masonry, but the only find he recorded was a single inscription, which not surprisingly did not refer to the Hecatomnids. In a neighbouring field he found pottery coffins, but he notes ruefully that the ground was so wet that 'the pottery had all rotted'. In the eastern cemetery, where the tomb of the 'Carian Princess' was found more than a century later, Newton discovered a number of different types of tombs extending as late as the Roman period. He recorded underground chambers, the largest of which contained two stone sarcophagi, and other vaulted chambers built above ground and perhaps originally faced with marble or dressed limestone – all of them looted in antiquity. He also found burials in pithoi, pottery coffins, and graves in the form of pits lined with freestone and covered with slabs of soft tufa or lined and covered with clay tiles. It seems that only in the pottery coffins did any grave goods survive: several contained one small silver coin of third-century type. The only exceptions were two stone sarcophagi, each with a lid cut from a single stone slab: in one of these was a black-glazed drinking cup of kantharos shape, in the other a silver coin minted on the island of Chios, probably in the early fifth century BC, and a red-figure amphora from the later fifth or early fourth century painted with a Dionysiac scene. These coffins sound very like that of the 'Princess' except that they were buried directly in the ground and not laid in a chamber; in this respect the

BC at the latest Caria had become a separate satrapy under 'the dynast Hecatomnus', son of Hyssaldomus. It may be that Hyssaldomus had governed Caria for a few years before his son, and indeed that the family held some hereditary right to power, but this cannot be proved. Hecatomnus had a sister named Aba, but she seems to have played no part in the history of Caria. What is clear, however, is that at Hecatomnus' death in 377 he was succeeded by his five children, singly or in pairs: first by the eldest son Mausolus, who married his sister Artemisia and governed jointly with her until he died in 353 BC, whereupon Artemisia became sole satrap until her own death in 351. Thereupon their younger brother Idrieus took over, marrying Ada, the younger of Hecatomnus' daughters: they seem to have governed as joint satraps until Idrieus' death in 344 BC, when Ada followed her sister's example and ruled alone. In 341, however, the youngest of the brood, Pixodaros, drove his sister out and became satrap in her place. There being no further sisters for him to marry, he took to wife a Cappadocian lady called Aphneïs. She did not become joint satrap, but instead at some point during or soon after 337 BC Pixodaros was joined – perhaps at his own request – by a Persian named Orontobates, who married the daughter of Pixodaros and Aphneïs, also called Ada. Pixodaros seems to have died in 336 BC; Orontobates continued as satrap, either alone or perhaps jointly with his wife Ada II, until Alexander the Great, sweeping down through Asia Minor on the first leg of his great campaign against Persia and on to the east, arrived in Caria in 334 BC.

Ada I, who at her younger brother's assault had retreated to the mountain fastness of Alinda, came out to greet Alexander: she not only offered him the keys to the city (which he graciously declined), but also proposed that she should adopt him as her son, a suggestion which he accepted, although the condition was that he should restore her to power in Halicarnassus. Since it was part of Alexander's plan to wrest control not merely of the Carian cities but of the whole of Asia Minor from the Persians, this proviso presented no real problem to him: having Ada as his ally meant that, having driven Orontobates out of the city itself, he could leave his new mother, now restored to control of the whole of Caria, to clear up outlying pockets of resistance while he moved on southward into Lycia, having first refounded her temporary capital under the name of Alexandria on Latmos. Its splendid remains above the modern town of Karpuzlu bear witness to the prosperity which it enjoyed in the years that followed. If we are to believe Plutarch, Ada took her new role seriously: 'When in the kindness of her heart she used to send him day by day many viands and sweetmeats, and finally offered him bakers and cooks reputed to be very skilful, he said he wanted none of them, for he had better cooks which had been given him by his tutor, Leonidas; for his breakfast, namely, a night march, and for his supper, a light breakfast. "And this same Leonidas", he said, "used to come and open my chests of bedding and clothing, to see that my mother did not hide there for me some luxury or superfluity."'[7]

Although archaeological research has shown that Arrian's statement that Alexander razed Halicarnassus to the ground is a dramatic exaggeration, there is no doubt that the city suffered badly from his siege, which Diodorus describes in some detail, and it never recovered the glory which Mausolus had desired and had very largely achieved for it. We do not know what happened to Ada after she was restored to power as satrap in Halicarnassus, except that she was replaced by one Philoxenos at some time before Alexander's death in 323 BC. Probably one need look no further for a reason for her replacement than that she had died, but we do not know: the only other thing we know about this Philoxenos is that he was described as 'obscure' by Arrian, Alexander's biographer. At any rate we hear no more of Ada after this.[8] Not long afterwards another Macedonian satrap, Asander, moved the capital back to Mylasa. The message was clear: the days of the Hecatomnids were over.

It is of course tempting to use the richness of the finds from her burial in order to identify the 'Carian Princess' with one of these Hecatomnid ladies: Aba, the sister of Hecatomnus, Artemisia herself, Ada I, or Aphneïs. Such a show of wealth was not uncommon on the fringes of the Greek world, and it does not prove 'royalty'. What makes this one stand out – just as in the case of the Vergina tomb – is the combination of quantity with the sheer quality of the material. This is not immediately obvious from photographs, nor even when one now sees the gold on display in the specially built gallery in Bodrum Museum, but it does become apparent when one handles it. This was not something that fell within our brief, but Professor Waywell noticed it when he studied the find soon after its discovery.

The two most important pieces for dating the tomb, and thus taking another step towards identifying its occupant, are the magnificent gold wreath and the humble black-glazed oinochoe. The latter was probably made in Athens: it is a more developed form of the type found in the Athenian Agora in the early fourth century, for the base has grown narrower and the spout more elongated, a fashion which became popular in the later fourth century.[9] The wreath is closely related to those from Tomb II at Vergina, in particular to the myrtle wreath found lying on the floor of the outer tomb, the antechamber to the tomb of Philip II, buried in 336 BC. Its details are matched on a number of pieces belonging to second half of the fourth century, from southern Italy, the eastern Mediterranean and even South Russia.[10] The dead woman was therefore buried in the second half of the fourth century, probably around 340–320 BC. If she was a Hecatomnid this really narrows the choice down to Ada or Aphneïs.

The excavator believed that the three rings from the grave provided further clues. The first, of gold, has a double palmette on the bezel and a twisted wire mount that is typical of the second half of the fourth century BC. The other two, also of gold, contain seals carved of semi-precious stone. The custom of engraving gems on the flat side of a semi-precious stone cut in shapes such as the scarab-beetle or its formalised derivative the scaraboid rather than on a pyramidal stamp was something which the Persians learned in the century after they overran the Lydian kingdom of Croesus in 546 BC and inherited the Lydians' control of the Greek cities on the west coast of Asia Minor. At first it is still possible to distinguish two streams in these 'Graeco-Persian' gems, the 'Court Style' of the Persian palaces, and the 'Greek Style' of Greek gem engravers working in their own tradition but using Achaemenid Persian shapes or subjects. However, by the second half of the fifth century and during the early fourth century BC there was a 'Mixed Style', where it is

difficult if not impossible to say whether the stone was cut by a Greek artist working in a Persian milieu for Persian customers, or a Persian carving under Greek
influence.

Not unexpectedly it is to this style that the two gems from the Bodrum tomb
belong. One is a chalcedony scaraboid (a shape and a stone particularly popular in
the Mixed Style), again with a twisted wire mount, carved with the figure of a
standing Persian warrior wearing sleeved tunic, trousers and pointed cap. It was
probably made soon after 350 BC. The other is an agate scarab carved with a female
head in profile, though the suggestion sometimes made that it is a portrait of the
dead woman is optimistic, and not supported by the other traditions of Graeco-
Persian gem-engraving (fig. 2).[11] It
displays some features that are
uncommon in the Graeco-Persian
workshops, such as the use of the
scarab rather than the scaraboid
shape and the rather ineptly cut
hatched border surrounding the
head. The rather heavy technique,
however, is Graeco-Persian, and
the unusual and slightly incompe-
tent features suggest that it was
made in the fourth century by a
provincial engraver working away
from the main centres.

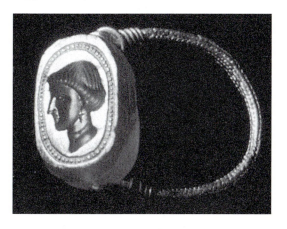

It has been suggested that the
presence of the Persian warrior
on the other gem is in keeping
with the eastward-looking, pro-

*2. Agate scarab carved with the head of a woman
set in a gold ring, from the tomb of the 'Carian
Princess' (c.400–350 BC) (Bodrum Museum).*

Persian tendency of Pixodaros, and that therefore this is evidence that the dead
woman must be his wife Aphneïs. Yet such an argument could equally be turned in
favour of Ada I, who during the first part of her satrapy was officially the representative of the Persian court, and may even have maintained the fiction of loyalty to
the Persian king after her reinstatement by Alexander the Great, in the confused
political climate that followed his eastward conquests when it must have been difficult to maintain a firm structure of government. In any case a Graeco-Persian ring
engraved with the fairly common motif of a Persian soldier is hardly the satrap's
official ring: if it existed at all, such a ring must either have carried a distinctive and
restricted design used only by the satrap or have been inscribed – and it would in
any case have passed to her successor Philoxenos.

The pose of the Persian soldier is interesting, one leg slightly ahead of the other,
one arm akimbo and the other lifted to rest on the spear which is planted firmly on
the ground before him. It is common on the Graeco-Persian gems, and so perhaps
in this context we should not make too much of it, but in the second half of the
fourth century BC and later it became popular in Greek art for statues of rulers:
known examples include the colossal bronze statue of a 'Hellenistic ruler' now in

Rome, perhaps Demetrius I of Syria, and – more relevant here – in a colossal statue from the Mausoleum itself which Waywell links with Idrieus.[12] In that case perhaps this ring really does (in a very generalised way) represent the satrap – in this instance Idrieus. If the agate ring shows an idealised Ada, then the two rings form a pair, 'his' and 'hers', although they were certanly not carved by the same artist, for the chalcedony is much more in the mainstream of Graeco-Persian gem-engraving than the slightly eccentric agate. That they were buried with the dead woman is a possible argument that she is Ada, once joint satrap and later (twice) sole satrap; Aphneïs was never more than Pixodaros' wife, and never held joint satrapal power with him.

Some of this argumentation is, it is true, based on slender evidence. Yet taken in the overall context of the find it suggests that we are indeed dealing with a member of the Hecatomnid family. The age of the dead woman may provide further clues.

Of Aphneïs' age at death we know nothing beyond the fact that her husband Pixodaros was born in/or before 377 BC (the year of his father Hecatomnus' death) and died in 336 BC. She certainly bore one child, Ada II, who was at one time destined to be married to Alexander the Great's half-brother Philip III Arrhidaeus of Macedon, but who eventually became the wife of Orontobates, Pixodaros' co-satrap, presumably before that worthy was driven from office by Alexander and the avenging Ada I in 334.

We know a little more about Ada I. Working back from the date of her father's death, she cannot have been born later than *c*.379 BC; she was still very much alive in 334 BC when Alexander restored her to satrapal power, but it is highly probable that she had died before Alexander's own death in 323 BC. Her minimum life-span was thus forty-six years, from 379 to 333 BC; perhaps fifty years would be more reasonable, from 380 to 330 BC. The age of the dead woman had been estimated at around forty by Professor Alpagut, on the basis of the skull, the pelvis and the wear of the teeth, but such palaeoanthropological calculations are necessarily imprecise in that they cannot always allow for unknown individual variations of lifestyle, diet and health, nor does the developmental evidence of the skeleton on which they are based allow of precise measurement. By contrast, the dental evidence can now be used to age a skeleton much more accurately, as we have seen in the previous chapter. Looking ahead a little in the story of the 'Princess', through the good offices and enthusiasm of Dr Oğuz Alpözen we were able to send two teeth to Dr David Whittaker in Cardiff to age, using the same method as the one he had applied to Seianti. The first two teeth selected were not suitable, because their apices had been damaged post mortem, so they were returned and two more were sent over. From the dentine ratios in one of these Dr Whittaker was able to estimate the age of the 'Princess' at death as forty-four years, with a range of thirty-eight or fifty years. Because this technique is still a young one, it is important to build up a reference collection of specimens: Dr Alpözen kindly allowed the lady's sectioned canine tooth to remain in Cardiff for the benefit of future researchers.[13]

On grounds of age, then, it is perfectly possible that the 'Carian Princess' is Ada I, youngest sister and eventual successor of Mausolus; or, to take a different approach, one can say that the age as proved by the tests carried out on the teeth does not rule out the identification as Ada I. As a member of the ruling Hecatomnid dynasty one could no doubt think of her as a princess, even though officially she was, like the rest of her family, appointed by the Great King of Persia to govern Caria on his behalf, and the dynasty did not outlive her generation: as far as we know Ada II, Pixodaros' daughter and Ada I's niece, did not hold the office.

There is no record that any of the family except Pixodaros had children. We know that Mausolus and Artemisia were not survived by any offspring, else their siblings would not have succeeded to the satrapy. Strabo writes that Mausolus died *ateknos*, childless, but this does not actually preclude his and his sister-wife Artemisia's having had children who died in infancy.[14] It is also perfectly possible that Idrieus and Ada suffered the same misfortune, but now that we must discount the 'scars of parturition' on the pelvis as evidence that the 'Princess' had borne children we cannot tell without further examination. The ancient written sources are silent, and the political upheavals during Alexander's conquests are likely to have upset any established pattern of succession, so the confused story of the succession to Ada in the satrapy of Caria does not help. Hornblower examined the effects that sister-marriage might have had on the childlessness or otherwise of both couples, and concluded that here too the evidence was inconclusive, though he perhaps errs on the side of over-cautiousness: some of the studies which he quotes suggest that the proportion of infant mortality or abnormality is indeed much higher from incestuous unions than from exogamous ones.[15]

So here again were the remains of an individual which *might* be identifiable as those of a person of historical significance, indeed where it looked likely that they were so identifiable, but where proof positive in any form was elusive. Our attention was drawn to the find by Professor Geoffrey Waywell of King's College London, who had worked on the sculptures from the Mausoleum and on other problems at the site, and who was a frequent visitor to Bodrum: he had prepared the ground for us and knew that there was much interest in the idea in Turkey. The extent of this interest became apparent when, early in 1992, we received a letter from Bodrum enclosing a dramatic photograph of the skull just after discovery, surrounded by gold jewellery and still wearing the gold wreath (pl.xiv). The letter asked about the possibility of having a reconstruction made. Of course we agreed, and over the next fifteen months we met a series of exuberant, welcoming and enthusiastic friends and colleagues, both Turkish and English, and were faced with questions that tested our abilities and with moments of *Grand Guignol* that it will be difficult to forget.

Occupying a position in the rest of the story only a little downstage from the 'Princess' herself is Dr Oğuz Alpözen, Director of the Bodrum Museum. He is a remarkable man, whose career began as a diver, whence he moved into the world of underwater archaeology under the tutelage of its doyen, Professor George Bass of the Institute of Nautical Archaeology (INA) in Texas. Alpözen has made the Bodrum Museum in the Castle of the Knights his particular love and preoccupation so that it is now one of the finest in Turkey, and INA now has a permanent base there. From one visit to the next one does not know what new display will have appeared, what building within the castle will have been reconstructed and put to some new purpose. As we got to know him better we began to appreciate what it was like being caught up in this whirlwind.

Because there were neither the funds nor the time for our team to go out to Turkey, Dr Alpözen himself brought the skull of the 'Princess' to Manchester in the autumn of 1992. This had the advantage that, as well as being able to discuss his requirements with us in detail, he could give a seminar on the circumstances of discovery and his plans for the new display to a group of interested colleagues in Manchester, while the skull of the 'Princess' sat on the table before him, facing her audience through hollow eye-sockets. The seminar proved a lively and valuable occasion, not least for our medical colleagues who were able to get replies from the Turkish archaeologists to questions that normally had to be answered at second hand. Then the skull was handed over to Dr Bob Stoddart in the Department of Pathological Sciences to produce a report on her medical history that might help towards identifying her and that would certainly provide useful information for the process of reconstruction.

Pathologists' reports make surprisingly entertaining reading. Behind the academic prose with its medical and scientific terms there is a person trying to get out, and the dry phrases conceal a real feeling for the life and the sufferings of the dead person that is very reassuring. 'The size of the skull, the shape of the mandible, the eruption of the teeth and the general degree of closure of the sutures of the skull are consistent with an age between thirty and fifty years and I would tend to place her in the upper half of that range. The shape of the dental arch clearly indicates a female, though the rather pronounced superciliary ridges and moderate frontal eminences, while quite consistent with the skull's being female, suggest strong and, possibly, slightly masculine features.'

So far so good: nothing that contradicted the anthropologist's notes, nothing that ruled out an identification, but nothing that specifically confirmed it either. Strong and slightly masculine features do not make a ruler.

'There is no marked pathology, but there are some features worthy of comment,' Dr Stoddart's report continued. 'The occipital region is slightly asymmetrical, with the right side bulging out a little more than the left. This was probably unnoticeable in life, but she might have held her head slightly tilted at rest, or a little turned to the right.' And on the sutures of the skull, 'it appears that those at the vertex have closed early and that those at the front, and to a lesser extent, at the rear of the skull have closed relatively late, leading to a rather "flat-topped" shape of skull, which is not of a pathological degree, but may be a local or familial peculiarity.'

Aykut Özet had noted the open sutures in the frontal bones as very characteristic of Anatolians. She evidently took good care of her teeth, which showed little wear and which with the exception of one that had fallen out post mortem were all in place, and she had a satisfactory diet: 'the dentition is in remarkably good condition, with a good closure, no significant attrition and no real evidence of decay, disease of the soft tissues or bone loss. She had a good, non-abrasive diet and an adequate intake of calcium and vitamin D.'

And now for the less attractive news: 'there is some deflection of the nasal septum to her right which may well have led to her experiencing obstruction on that side of the nose when suffering from infections of the upper respiratory tract. She may also have tended to nasal dripping and mucus production on that side rather than the other and, possibly, to a unilateral rhinitis.' Or, as Bob Stoddart put it in his covering note, 'she probably suffered from a very unqueenly runny nose'.[16]

Aside from the runny nose and the possible tilt of the head, there was nothing here to suggest that the reconstruction of the head would prove anything out of the ordinary. Although the skull was in good condition and no problems in casting were anticipated, one took the now customary precaution of covering it with metal foil before applying the alginate to make the mould. One interesting feature that did appear as the face grew on the skull was the shape of the nose, which rather surprisingly gave her the classic straight-nosed 'Greek' profile, often found in Greek art, particularly on the early statues of *kouroi* and *korai*, but very rare in real life (fig. 3).

Thus far the reconstruction had as usual been made 'from cold', with no reference to any possible portraits of members of the Hecatomnid family, so that there was effectively no risk that the basic form of the face which grew on the skull was influenced by anything seen earlier. Even the straight 'Greek' nose had been remade three times, and had emerged each time with the same straight line: there was thus no doubt that it reflected the structure of the skull and not the wishes of the artist. All that remained was to add the superficial details such as the hair and the shape of the mouth (not its size, which was determined by the skull). At this stage one began to notice a striking similarity with two over-life-sized marble heads found in the last century and now in the British Museum, one from the Mausoleum

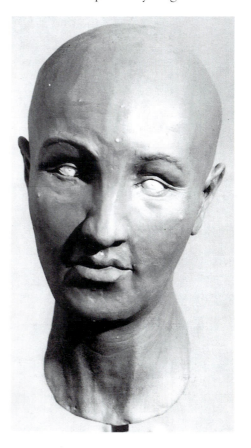

3. *The reconstructed head of the 'Carian Princess', without hair. The 'Greek' nose is apparent even in frontal view. The marker pegs indicating the thickness of the flesh are still visible: they are not covered until the final stages.*

itself, the other from the temple of Athena Polias at Priene, a Greek city to the north of Halicarnassus close to Caria's border with Ionia, which had benefited from the patronage of the Hecatomnid family (figs 4 and 5). Pytheos, the architect of the Athena temple (and possibly the planner of the city itself) was also involved in the building of the Mausoleum.[17] Both sculptures were apparently intended as portraits,

4. (Above) Head from a marble statue from the temple of Athena Polias at Priene, probably Ada I: traces of the paint indicating the hairnet survive behind her ear (c.334 BC) (British Museum 1151).

5. (Left) Head from a marble statue from the Mausoleum at Halicarnassus, thought to represent Ada I: the triple row of curls is probably an official hairstyle (c.350 BC) (British Museum 1051).

probably of the same person. Their similarity is undoubtedly emphasised by their identical headgear, and the differences between the two are no more than one might expect from the hands of two different sculptors or from the differing contexts for which they were made, although the Priene version has some more realistic and less idealising features that suggest it is closer to the actual appearance of the sitter: its overall shape is squarer and less 'pretty', because the distance between the brow and the base of the nose is proportionately greater, and the features are more powerful, so that it looks less chubby and more square-jawed, with a smaller mouth. Both have the rather heavy neck with 'Venus rings' of flesh that became fashionable in the Hellenistic period, but the Priene example has a more pronounced double chin. On the head from the Mausoleum the lower eyelid is more curved, and the hair rendered in a less formal manner, for individual strands are shown both at the front and side of the curls over the brow, and in the places where locks escape from the head-covering at the back.

We shall return to these differences later. Waywell had already seen a similarity between the Mausoleum head and the colossal female statue also from the Mausoleum that now holds pride of place in the Mausoleum Room of the British Museum known as Artemisia (certainly to be identified as a Hecatomnid, if not necessarily Artemisia herself), and had suggested that they represented members of the same family. In his study of the sculptures from the Athena temple in Priene, Carter made a very convincing case that this female head was from a statue of the dedicator of the temple, none other than Ada I herself. Later, in Roman Imperial times, the temple seems to have become an Imperial dynastic cult place, for it has yielded evidence for a whole series of royal portraits, including the emperors Augustus and Claudius. While Carter suggests that the identity of the female head had by now been forgotten, it seems much more likely that it was this statue of Ada I, last Hecatomnid dynast and adoptive mother of Alexander the Great, which gave the inspiration for setting up this royal 'portrait gallery'.[18] It cannot be accidental that the shape of the head and face of this sculpture and of the reconstruction appear so similar. One notices particularly the proportions and setting of the eyes and mouth, and above all the angle and relationship of the nose and forehead which are dictated by the nasal bone: on the skull it was these which produced the 'Greek' profile to which we have already referred, rare in real life but found nevertheless on the Priene head. The similarities were such that if this were a forensic reconstruction for the police it might have formed the basis for an identification, perhaps even an arrest.

But of course, matters were not quite so straightforward.

In theory, this was the stage when, as in the forensic reconstructions, one could begin to use external evidence to add or to emend the purely superficial details that have no bearing on the basic shape of the face and thus on the simple identification of the persons involved, but which add something to the personality of the individual. Therefore we decided to give the lady the slight double chin found on both the heads in the British Museum, and at the same time reduced the extent of the vermilion of the lips to correspond to the distinctively small 'Cupid's bow' of the Priene version. It is possible that this feature is an idiosyncrasy of the sculptor who carved the head rather than of the lady herself, for it is found on other sculptures from Priene such as the bust of a young girl, but this too has all the features of a portrait, so we may indeed be looking at a family characteristic.[19] Unfortunately the mouth of the Mausoleum head, which on the basis of its similarity to the Priene head presumably represents Ada too, is too badly damaged to allow a proper comparison.

If it was permissible to make these minor changes to the features on the basis of the sculptures without changing the fundamental and recognisable form of the face itself, then all the more could the hairstyle of the reconstructed 'Princess' be altered on such external evidence without affecting the basic validity of the whole exercise.

This was perhaps all the more important because of the nature of the reconstructions that we had been asked to make. Although the element of research and of extending the technique formed a crucial part of the exercise, as always, it would have been unlike Oğuz Alpözen to be satisfied with a straightforward reconstruction of the head and face of his 'Princess'. He certainly wanted this, and he certainly wanted as much information as we could provide, but he was planning what in Turkey would be a revolutionary method of displaying the find, namely to tell her story by rebuilding a tomb in his castle which would give visitors a chance to circulate and to see the finds properly.[20] Just how dramatic, in the literal sense, his intentions were only became apparent much later. For the moment our discussions focused on the reconstructions that he wanted us to make: in the end we settled for two heads in bronzed resin, and a lifelike reconstruction of the whole body.

These instructions naturally affected the manner in which we tackled the problems of detail in the reconstruction. As a first move we had shown her hair in a rather free fourth-century style; because the two sculptures showed it done up in a cloth, we had then wrapped it in a *sakkos*, a scarf wound around the head and knotted at the front, modelled on that worn by Deidameia on the west pediment of the temple of Zeus at Olympia. Closer study of the sculptures suggested some changes. While one might, for instance, have based the hairstyle on that shown on the agate gem from the tomb, there was a form of hairdressing that was particularly appropriate for this 'Princess'. The locks which appeared under the *sakkos* at the forehead were replaced by distinctive archaising tight pin curls, a style that seems to have been a mark of the satrapal family: it is found on both the carved 'Ada' heads, and also on the colossal statue of 'Artemisia' in the British Museum, as well as on other late fourth-century heads from Priene. Although it is not so easy to make out, the figure on the little relief from Tegea in the British Museum, who is actually identified as Ada by an inscription, is wearing her hair in this manner too.[21] On the 'Artemisia' the curls were left globular, without any indication of individual hairs; on the Priene head the front surface of the curls has not been finished to show strands of hair, but in uneven facets which still bear traces of a red substance like that used as a fixative for the gilding on three fragments of gilded hair of the first century AD, also in the British Museum: therefore Carter suggested that the frontal curls on the Priene head too were finished with gold leaf, in fact that she was represented as wearing a golden toupée of the kind known to the Greeks as a *tettix*. Such an extravaganza is perfectly possible in the opulent ambience in which the Mausoleum was conceived. However, we decided not to gild the reconstructions, partly because the arguments are not entirely convincing, but more important because no such *tettix* was discovered in the tomb, and thus to add one would have been to go beyond the evidence. Further, since the coloured reconstruction was to be used to display the brilliant gold dress ornaments that *were* found, any gilding that we might apply would have paled by comparison.[22]

Having used the two heads in the British Museum as models for what seemed to be the 'official' coiffure of the satraps of Caria, we were still faced with the question of her hair-covering. The knotted *sakkos* was only a provisional rendering to help us understand the problem. On the Priene head there are still clear traces of a painted pattern of hollow lozenges filled with smaller lozenges, while the band that forms the edge of the sakkos is decorated with a row of polka dots.[23] To try to represent in paint such a coloured piece of cloth as this appeared to be was both impractical and unrealistic, the more so as it would not be apparent on the bronzed versions. Indeed, when we discussed the question with our colleague Dr J.P. Wild, a specialist in ancient textiles, he suggested that what the sculptor was actually trying to show was not a printed, woven or embroidered cloth, but a hairnet made of the fabric known as 'sprang', a flexible, net-like material made without a weft by stretching the vertical warp-threads between two horizontal rods or cords and twisting them together. Although the technique was only rediscovered in the last century, both the fabric and its production are represented in Greek art from the sixth century BC on, and actual examples survive from Coptic Egypt.

The perfect solution to the problem of representing the hair-covering of the 'Carian Princess' was provided by a Roman bronze head of Hadrianic date in the Princeton Art Museum, where an actual sprang hairnet had been used on the wax model from which the bronze had been cast (fig. 6).[24] The same method was used in making the mould for our reconstructions: a net was put over the clay matrix and then the silicone rubber was applied to make the mould from which the reconstructions were to be cast. It must be admitted that we did not go to the lengths of making an authentic sprang net, but found a modern substitute that served the purpose equally well. On the 'lifelike' version the net and its edging band were picked out in paint, on the assumption that they would have been of a thread that contrasted with the hair; on the bronzes no further touching up was necessary (pls XIV and XV).

6. Roman bronze portrait head of a woman wearing a sprang hairnet (c. AD 120–140) (Art Museum, Princeton University, 1980-10).

Intriguing and technically challenging though this evidence might be, none of it is conclusive on its own. One can argue that Carter's identification of the head from the Priene temple as a portrait of Ada I is circumstantial, and that even if correct (and generally accepted) it shares numerous features with other sculptures from the same artistic and cultural milieu. Yet the fact remains that the reconstruction, which was based purely on the objective evidence of the skull and which in its crucial early stages was made without reference to this or any other 'portrait', produced a face whose structure appears in all essentials to be so similar to the marble head.

Rather than rely on mere visual impressions, we decided to carry out a more detailed comparison between the reconstruction and the Priene 'portrait', using the technique of photocomparison. This procedure, also known as facial mapping, is being increasingly employed in identifying suspects in cases where a crime has been recorded on film or videotape: careful measurements of the proportions of the face recorded by the videocamera are compared with similar measurements taken from photographs of the suspect. Even if the face of the person carrying out the crime is concealed under a mask, and however much he or she may have distorted it through emotion, the underlying proportions dictated by the skull remain the same, and will match those from a 'clean' image if the person behind the face is the same.

When this technique was applied to the reconstruction of the Bodrum skull and to the Priene marble, the horizontal proportions appeared similar, and the upper part of the two faces gave a possible match, but the vertical dimensions of the two lower halves did not correspond: the distances between nose and mouth, and nose and chin, of the reconstructed face and therefore of the skull, were markedly greater than those on the Priene head. In a British court of law, therefore, the evidence of facial mapping alone would not have been sufficient to prove the identification.

Yet the impression that the two are the same person remains, and is too strong to be ignored. The differences lie in the context and purpose for which the two heads were created rather than in actual fact. While the facial reconstruction has been carried out according to strict scientific rules and measurements, the fourth-century sculptor who made the Priene head (and his colleague at the Mausoleum) were working to different rules. If Carter's interpretation is correct, he was carving an official portrait, to be placed on a public building; and he was still working in the aftermath of the idealising classical tradition with its rules of proportion. In this context it is surely relevant that when they are set side by side the 'Ada' from the Mausoleum has a softer, more evenly proportioned and more feminine appearance than her counterpart from Priene: the Mausoleum in the centre of the newly expanded city of Halicarnassus was a focal point for the Hecatomnid family in a way that the temple of Athena at the outlying town of Priene could never be, and so it was at the Mausoleum that Ada must be shown in her most idealised form. In his account of the Greek bronze-casters Pliny notes that Lysippus, working at almost exactly the same time as the sculptor of the Priene head, observed very carefully the *symmetria* of his figures, a term which Pliny himself could not translate into Latin, and which is best put into English as a 'canon of proportions', rather than simply as 'symmetry'.[25] To modern eyes at least the proportions of the Priene head, and of its companion from the Mausoleum, are surely more regular and more handsome than those of the reconstruction. For example, the reconstruction, based on scientific measurements, gives her a chin which seen in profile looks rather weak and flabby – just the kind of feature that both sitter and artist would wish to avoid showing in an idealising, official portrait. The differences between the two faces can readily be explained by the circumstances of their making, the material of which they are made (a version of the reconstruction in a terracotta finish has a much softer appearance than the bronze or coloured resin versions, and has much more in common with the marble heads), and the fact that neither claims to be a true portrait. It might be worth adding too that Carter suggests that the portrait was probably carved during Ada's first period of power when she was still a younger woman, whereas naturally the reconstruction, based on the skull from her grave, shows her at the end of her life: even though she was never a beauty, by now the tautness of youth was gone.

This is perhaps as close as we can come at present to certainty in naming the 'Carian Princess', in the absence of inscriptions from her own tomb or of any human remains from the Mausoleum which might have provided the basis for a DNA comparison. The balance of evidence would seem to be in favour of identifying her as Ada I, and it is as such that she was to be displayed in the Bodrum Museum. We have already touched on the rather dramatic plans that lay behind Dr Alpözen's request for the reconstructions. It was now necessary for us to consider the 'whole body' reconstruction that he required.

It was something we had never attempted before, for two reasons. First, to reconstruct an individual body by the same methods as a head should require the same detailed study of the medical history of every part of that body, which would be enormously time-consuming, and not necessarily very productive in terms of the final product, for in most cases it would presumably be largely concealed by clothing; and second, because the statistical data which, together with the anatomy, form the basis for reconstructing a face on a skull do not exist for the rest of the body, we should lack the essential guidelines. However, what was required in Bodrum was a vehicle for displaying a replica of the silk peplos in which the 'Princess' had been buried, onto which the gold ornaments were to be sewn – a mannequin on which the dress could be hung, but which had the head of the 'Princess' and the visible portions of whose anatomy were those of a lady of around forty-five. The easiest solution was to turn to one of the specialist firms who make mannequins for museum displays. However, the largest figure available 'off the peg' was apparently a size ten, not quite the fuller body which her physical remains suggested was appropriate for Ada. So as ever in such situations, we reached a compromise over our ideal woman: a version of the head was made in coloured resin; hands and feet were cast from those of a colleague of suitable age; then these middle-aged appendages were attached to the slender body that was supplied to us. Since she was to be well and discreetly covered by her clothes, it hardly mattered that our mature princess had the body of a bimbo. After all, no one should ever see her unclothed once the display was complete.

It was necessary to make the head from coloured resin both so that it could easily be attached to the body and so that it would continue to look presentable with the minimum of maintenance, for even if the display was regularly cleaned, it was unlikely that a specialist who could service and remodel a waxwork would be readily available to the museum authorities in Bodrum. Otherwise there is no doubt that a waxwork would have given a more satisfactory and more realistic result, for however much one attempted to soften and temper the finish of the resin, the endproduct still has a rather hard and unsympathetic appearance, which is not helped by the deliberately strong lighting under which she is displayed, and which rather unfairly seems to pass over into the character of the person herself.

This reconstruction 'in fleshy form', as Dr Alpözen put it, now stands in a reconstructed tomb in the 'Axe Tower' of Bodrum castle: not the simple tomb in which the 'Princess' had been found, in which there would have been no room for anything but the sarcophagus, but a replica of 'Andron B', a ritual dining room of the Hecatomnid period from Labraunda near Mylasa, in which are displayed her own grave goods, including the plain sarcophagus in which her skeleton has been reassembled, along with that of an unfortunate mouse which somehow got trapped inside it. Around the sides of the hall are replicas of the appropriate furniture; high up on the wall is painted a frieze of imaginary scenes from her life; and from a niche at the end of the room (which in the original 'Andron' probably held one or more statues, possibly of members of the Hecatomnid family) under strong theatrical lighting the reconstructed 'Carian Princess' dressed in her funeral finery of silk and gold presides over all, as visitors are welcomed to her obsequies by one of

7. *The reconstruction of Ada I, the 'Carian Princess', displayed in Bodrum Museum.*

the museum staff, herself dressed to resemble the 'Princess' (fig. 7).[26] It is undoubtedly a striking and memorable display, and the assumptions which it makes about the status of the dead woman are almost certainly correct. It is of course possible that both she and the marble heads from Priene and the Mausoleum are merely typical members of the early Hellenistic nobility of Caria who by coincidence have a remarkably similar appearance, but we venture to suggest that this is unlikely. As in the first report which we wrote on this piece of work, it is surely appropriate to quote the words attributed by the satirist Lucian to Diogenes the philosopher. When they met in Hades, Diogenes would not allow Mausolus any of the special honours which the great man claimed on the grounds of his wealth and beauty, because, Diogenes said, a judge of beauty would not set greater store by either of their skulls: both were bald, both showed their teeth, both had lost their eyes and noses; the only bonus that Mausolus had was the burden of a heavier tomb to bear.[27] But Diogenes was the founder of the Cynics. He would undoubtedly get a wry pleasure from learning that forensic science would one day upstage him, at least when it came to Mausolus' little sister.

CHAPTER 11

'Who will say "corpse" to his vivid cast?'

Good frend for Iesus sake forbeare
to digg the dust encloased heare:
Blese be yᵉ man yᵗ spares thes stones,
and curst be he yᵗ moves my bones.

For all his ability to portray the innermost workings of other men's minds, William Shakespeare was a very private person. Why he should have placed such a vehement interdict on the opening of his grave is itself a matter for debate in which we need not join here (over a century ago there was already a proposal in the name of portraiture to 'open the grave reverently, have the photographers ready, and the moment the coffin lid is removed...expose the plates, and see what will be the result').[1] What concerns us more is the deeply felt desire that his physical remains should be allowed a decent anonymity and peaceful repose, a desire that is by no means peculiar to a poet buried in a Warwickshire church early in the seventeenth century, and probably holds good of the majority of people, if not always for the same reasons. On the one hand, the academic detachment that goes with both medical and archaeological research tells one that any form of preservation is only an interruption in the natural process of total decay: 'earth to earth, ashes to ashes, dust to dust' is how the Prayer Book puts it. Yet as a fellow human being, one can readily feel intrusive as one seeks out someone's personal details. Is the making of a reconstruction a prying into a person's private life, almost a form of voyeurism?

Writ large, this question can be applied to the study of all human remains, and it comes as no surprise that some peoples and some faiths object to such study on religious and ethical grounds, even sometimes to the retention of human remains in ordinary museum stores, as they may also object to the taking of any kind of likeness of a person. As a scholar, one replies by underlining the importance of learning about our past in order to complete our knowledge of ourselves and our world, and draws attention to the way in which this may also help in improving the lot of those who come after. Hence the stress that we have laid on the reconstructions as three-dimensional research reports – one might here quote again Mortimer Wheeler's dictum that 'Archaeology is digging up people, not things.' If there is any value at all in the study of history and of one's past, then the reconstructions should be seen as an important element in completing the story.

So far we have generally described the reconstructions which we have undertaken in the context of the development of the technique and of the academic research of which they formed part. In assessing their value it is here worth mentioning again the point touched on in discussing the skulls from Mycenae, namely that the actual casts of the skulls can have a role to play as accurate and durable replicas of the fragile bones, surviving when the latter have suffered damage or decay and preserving in three-dimensional form important information that might otherwise be lost. Moving on, one may ask how the physical reconstruction of a human being can be used to help fill in the details of the historical picture in a wider manner and for a wider audience.

At its simplest level, there is the museum diorama, using mannequins – replicas of human figures – to provide an anthropological context for historical artefacts (often themselves replicas or reconstructions) or for physical discoveries about the story of man. Such figures may depict the appropriate physical and ethnic type, and there are of course many levels and many refinements. Whilst they may represent an anthropological 'type' in quite a sophisticated way, they do not make any claim to represent the features or physique of a particular historical individual, although this is not to say that the artist may not have used a specific person as his model. The same will generally be true of two-dimensional reconstructions such as illustrations in books, be they picture books, historical guides or text books.

With the advent of sophisticated radiological techniques such as CT-scans (computed tomography) in combination with the development of computer programs that can process such radiographs into a three-dimensional model of a skull, there has come the possibility of a new form of reconstruction, used in some museum displays such as that at the Jorvik Viking Centre in York. We have described how the milled-out skull created by the computer can be used as the foundation for a normal three-dimensional reconstruction, where muscles and tissue are applied manually to the skull, or for a face generated by computer on the basis of information gleaned exclusively from the remains of the individual in question. This other approach uses the face of another – modern – individual whose skull is reckoned to be of similar form to that generated by the computer, which is scanned into the computer and then applied over the 'ancient' skull. This in turn provides the model for a three-dimensional face created by a sculptor in the traditional manner, without measured flesh-thicknesses or detailed examination of muscle-insertions. The result appears convincing, and certainly fulfils its aim of producing as authentic a face or series of faces as possible in order to populate a realistic and lifelike display. Yet the fact remains that what has been created is not a true and faithful reconstruction of the historical person whose skull formed the basis for the work. Although undoubtedly more realistic in appearance and technically far more advanced, in one sense the philosophy is still that of the traditional replicas of museum dioramas: their features too are generally modelled on modern people, but within each ethnic type man has not changed so much physically over the last five or six millennia that this is of great import except in a display of 'early man' and the hominids. Furthermore, this new approach uses the face of a one individual over the skull of another who may have lived many generations earlier, hence vitiating the notion of physical accuracy: indeed, by doing so it introduces a very significant distortion of historical veracity. A study in which the faces of five recently deceased men were reconstructed on their skulls using this computer-based technique with the scanned faces of living people, and then compared with photographs of the actual faces, has demonstrated that for the present this approach is still flawed and unreliable, in contrast to the controlled reconstructions carried out in Manchester some twenty years ago and described in Chapter 2.[2] The difference from our method is that we build up from the framework of the skull without prejudgement rather than adapting the tissues of a pre-existing face over it, and thus try to present the story of that person, with all its imperfections and blemishes. The fascination in all this work of facial reconstruction, for both the scientist and the layman, is with the appearance and the story of an individual rather than merely of a type, and this the new approach fails truly to achieve.

A third type of reconstruction which might serve to fill out the historical picture, one that would certainly seem to fill the need for depicting an individual and perhaps the most obvious of them all, is the straightforward portrait, painted, carved or modelled by an artist contemporary with the sitter. We have touched on portraiture as it relates both to realism and to facial reconstruction several times in the course of this study. The topic is vast and with a vast literature: the prospect of following it through in relation to our own special approach and technique is enormously attractive, but it would stretch this book out by many more chapters. Portraiture is after all far more than merely the accurate physical representation of a human being. The earliest portraits must be seen in the context of belief in the afterlife. So the skulls from neolithic Jericho with their features recreated in plaster are at the same time the dead person and the image of the dead person. The Egyptians saw portrait-statues as a kind of extension of personality to take the subject into the next world, a simulacrum which the soul could inhabit when even the mummified body had decayed. Therefore the Egyptian artist had no need to be concerned with subtle variations of age or movement or emotion. The Greeks in the Archaic and Classical periods might individualise statues by inscribing on them a name and by giving them attributes appropriate to the age and station of their subject, but as a general rule they set on one side the truly individual and idiosyncratic: for them a portrait depicted not the actuality but the idea of the whole person in a social or religious context, at least until the Hellenistic period. There are of course exceptions, and we have noted some of them, but in western art it was the Etruscans and after them the Romans for whom the quirks and foibles of each face and each person first became a matter of interest and concern. The history of the portrait is much more than the history of an art-form: it is also one of religious beliefs, social attitudes, psychology, and far more yet – David Piper's masterly survey of *The English Face* is but one account of the English obsession with portraiture through the ages. For this reason no portrait can stand on its own as a physically accurate likeness of any individual of the kind which we have been seeking, for it must always be seen in the historical context in which it was created and at least with a sidelong glance at the artist who made it. This makes it no less interesting as a historical document, indeed rather the opposite: but cool, academic impartiality and fidelity need not be one of its attributes.

Portraiture has taken us some way from the generalised mannequin or illustrated historical recreation in attempting to answer the question of how a physical reconstruction of a person might help elucidate a historical picture, and has introduced a number of complicating and not necessarily relevant elements. We should normally assume a portrait to have been made with the subject's knowledge and consent, although this expectation need only apply to the original version in the case of a portrait of which more than one copy exists. It would normally also only apply to the original of a posthumous portrait, since it is equally natural to assume that such an image, if it is to make any claim to realism, is based on a version made during the subject's lifetime. However, such an assumption is founded on relatively modern European notions of realistic portraiture, and cannot be applied for instance to the idealising portraits of the Greeks: to take but one example, Homer lived before the development of sculpture or painting, and none of his portraits can have been made in his lifetime; instead, they depict the idea or ethos of the old, blind singer of tales, but once the 'type' had been conceived it was often repeated in Classical sculpture and is easily recognisable.

With these exceptions, however, it is fair to assume that the subject was normally aware of the making of the portrait. Almost by definition, the subject of a reconstruction can know nothing of it; the only exceptions are likely to be those rare cases where a technique is tested on a living person, such as the experiment described in the Codicil. This in itself raises an ethical question – the matter of voyeurism again. While most scientists, be they of an archaeological or a medical bent, would argue for the benefits to knowledge that can be gained from the study of human remains, and so far only a minority of zealots would resist it at all costs, the matter of the public display of such remains is one that is increasingly preoccupying museum curators. There is the undoubted fascination of seeing real people from the past, as anyone knows who has visited a display of Egyptian mummies, particularly in the company of children; yet this has to be balanced against the respect that is due to the dead: while it is not uncommon for people to leave their bodies to medical research, it is very rare that anyone specifically gives permission for their remains to be put on public display, aside from Jeremy Bentham at University College London and a few others.

On this basis one can readily justify the study of remains of which a reconstruction forms part on the grounds of historical research: it is no different from the work carried out on human and other remains from archaeological excavations everywhere, work which is an essential part of those excavations and without which there is little justification for undertaking the excavation in the first place. On this basis too one can justify the display of the reconstruction, as a report on that research. Indeed, one might well argue that it is better to display the reconstruction than the actual skull, skeleton or body, which had once been given proper burial according to the customs and beliefs of the time, or which in the case of most of the bog bodies had been piously sacrificed (whether one agrees with the practice and the faith that sacrificed them or no).

The impression which a reconstruction makes upon the viewer is of course very important. Even allowing for the detail which we try to achieve, one cannot and must not claim complete accuracy for the result. The reconstruction is not a portrait, and even if made of wax it is not, like the figures in Madame Tussaud's, taken from the life. Equally important is the fact that a human head, separated from the body to which it belongs and seen in isolation, conveys a powerful and sometimes disturbing impression, as any painter knows — contrast for example some of Rembrandt's isolated late self-portraits with those of his earlier flamboyant baroque period. In a 'full-body' portrait or even a bust, the head is seen in the context of the body, the dress and the setting, though naturally the viewer's eye is drawn to the face; an isolated head has no such context, and there can be no such distraction or diversion from the face. This means that the material of which a reconstruction is made becomes very important.

At one end of the spectrum is bland white plaster of Paris, at the other the high-ly realistic coloured waxwork, with real hair and specially made glass eyes. While the effect given by a head done in plaster, lacking any colour or texture, may be too flat and too remote to carry enough conviction, the waxwork is usually too accu-rate and too vivid. As the basis for a photograph or even a film it serves well, because through that secondary medium it is reduced to two dimensions and yet conveys a mass of information, but when faced with a dramatically lifelike head in three dimensions, the viewer often feels uncomfortably close to this personality from the past. One has resisted using the expression 'in the flesh' when describing such heads so far, but that is in fact how some people come to see them. The happy compromise seems to be to use a material that apes a medium with which people are already familiar, such as bronzed resin or 'ferracotta'. The former is both strong and light, but there are those who feel that a reconstruction in this material resem-bles a 'genuine' sculpture in bronze too closely. 'Ferracotta' is a form of plaster of Paris to which iron filings have been added so that it looks like fired clay: it has the drawbacks of plaster of being heavy and fragile, but it is visually less intrusive than most other media. Many of the illustrations in this book are of ferracotta heads, and most of those on display in Manchester are made of this material.

What, then of those reconstructions that have been undertaken primarily or even purely with public display in mind? Of the examples which we have discussed so far, it is really only Ada, the 'Carian Princess', who falls into this category. It is fair to say that her reconstruction was conceived in the first instance to grace the new gallery that was planned for her in the Bodrum Museum, and that much of the historical and medical research that followed was at the outset only secondary. In the upshot one can readily explain the display of the reconstruction, described and illustrated in the previous chapter, in the context not only of the academic publica-tion of the research results, but also of the exhibit itself, which succeeds in its intention of presenting to the public the story of the discovery and excavation, the research that followed and the subsequent reconstruction.

In September 1991 the Verulamium Museum in St Albans reopened after eigh-teen months of planning and modernisation. The new galleries set out to 'bring the story of…one of Roman Britain's major cities vividly to life', and to achieve this the designers combined re-creations of rooms with graphics and displays of objects. As well as a rich merchant's villa and a carpenter's shop, the displays included a num-ber of recent discoveries from cemeteries in the area. In the section 'People of Verulamium' were three skeletons, one of them that of a remarkably well-preserved man of forty-five to fifty from the third century AD excavated in the St Stephen's cemetery complex along Watling Street. He had been buried in a fine lead coffin elaborately decorated with scallop shells – clearly a man of substance. No grave goods were buried with him, although there were traces of textiles over some of the bones. His coffin had been packed with chalk, which probably accounted for the good condition of his remains: indeed, the report of the excavation in *Current Archaeology* commented that they were so well conserved that 'he would be an excellent candidate for the new technique of building up a portrait from the skull'.[3] He stood about 1.73 m (5 ft 8 in) tall; Dr Don Brothwell of the Institute of Archaeology in London University noted slight traces of arthritis, and commented that it was possible from the way the sutures in the skull had opened that he had died after a blow to the side of the head. His teeth were in remarkably good condition

for his age, suggesting a good diet, and our colleague Dr John Lilley at the Manchester Dental School remarked upon some unusual features about his bite which may have caused him a speech impediment. The Museum proposed that this display should be supplemented by a reconstruction in bronzed resin, which we duly made for them (fig. 1). However, in order to bring him further to life, they also commissioned a video-recording for which an actor who resembled the reconstructed head told the Roman's own story, from excavation to museum display. His name is not recorded, but 'Posthumus', as he became known first by the Verulamium Museum staff and then by the visitors to the museum, was the first known 'living' face from Roman Britain.

In contrast to the numerous forensic tasks undertaken for the police, Posthumus was the first such straightforward commission from another museum. In the past we had generally turned down such requests partly through lack of time, since this work has to be fitted into other university commitments, and in part because we believed (and still believe) that as a university team our forte as well as our interest lies in the research and the development of

1. 'Posthumus': the head of a Romano-British man from the third century AD, reconstructed for the Verulamium Museum, St Albans.

the technique. However, we also believe that we do it better than anyone else, and that one can hardly deny to one's colleagues and thus to the general public a service which is provided to the police. Besides, the financial exigencies of British university life at the end of the twentieth century are such that it is no longer enough to develop a new technique; one has literally to sell it as well in order to survive.

Other such commissions followed, and continue to come in when there is time to honour them. Two concern us here, from Colchester and Rochester museums, for they continue the gallery of early British heads.

Just as 'Posthumus' was being completed in 1991, there came a request from the museum in Colchester, another major city of Roman Britain, where a 'face-to-face with the past' display was being prepared of material excavated in the Romano-

British cemetery at Butt Road. In this exhibit they wished to present the image of a person who actually lived in the city in the Roman period. Like the St Stephen's cemetery at St Albans, Butt Road belonged to the later Roman period; it contained a number of fourth-century family groups, which were already the subject of a DNA finger-printing project in Oxford.[4] Three skulls, all female, were thought to be candidates for reconstruction. One of these was selected, a fine and apparently healthy specimen excavated in 1977 who had been laid to rest in a timber coffin next to a man – presumably her husband – around AD 330–50. Because she was a middle-aged lady the file acquired the title 'Colchester Roman matron', for her real name is not known, but this sounded rather formidable and rather impersonal, and she was soon given the name 'Camilla', after Camulodunum, the Roman name for her native city. Roman men in the third and fourth centuries AD had their hair cut short, and Posthumus had been given a plain hairstyle with his locks combed forward, rendered in a rather impressionist manner. Coinage, sculpture and painting show that women of this period wore more elaborate coiffures, sometimes very elaborate indeed; but Camilla was after all only a matron from the northern provinces, not an empress, and so she was treated to long hair, parted in the centre and then brought up over the top of her head in two thick plaits. After some delay the bronzed resin reconstruction was finally finished, and at last she made her way back to her native Camulodunum, to take her place as a star attraction in Colchester Museum (fig. 2).

2. 'Camilla': a middle-aged Romano-British woman who died c.AD 330–350, reconstructed for Colchester Museum Services.

Camilla and Posthumus in effect form a Romano-British couple; in Lindow Man we had reconstructed a head from the end of the Iron Age just as the Romans were arriving in Britain, and if one was seeking for a partner for him, there is the Yde Girl from the Netherlands who must be virtually his contemporary. It was thus appropriate that we should respond to a request from the Guildhall Museum in Rochester to reconstruct the face of a young man from the Bronze Age.[5] He had been buried in a pit towards the side of a ditched enclosure above the Medway at Wouldham, about halfway between Rochester and Maidstone. In the centre of the enclosure was a pit containing an urn, in which had been placed the cremated remains of a woman of between twenty and forty-five years of age, and it seems likely that a low disc barrow had been raised over her. The relationship between the two people is uncertain, but the woman had clearly been buried first. Comparisons with other similar burials, together with the shape of the urn, suggested to the excavators a date around 1500 BC, in the Early Bronze Age. The extent to which the ends of the long bones in his arms and legs had fused, together with the fact that his wisdom teeth were beginning to erupt, made it likely that the man was around nineteen years old when he died. He was 1.74 m (5 ft 8½ in) tall, and apart from a small cavity in the molars of his lower jaw he appeared to have been in good health. There was nothing to show how or why he had died. We have no sure evidence for hairstyles at this period of prehistory, so his hair was shown roughly trimmed at the nape. Bearing in mind that at nineteen he was well into a fully adult life, his final appearance is rather older than a modern youth would look in his late teens. His reconstruction was welcomed home to Kent with much press and television coverage (some of it apparently suitably spooky, as befitted one who had returned from the dead), and the bronzed resin head is now displayed beside his physical remains, mounted on a stand which the visitor can rotate in order to see him from all sides (fig. 3).

At much the same time as the young man from Wouldham was returning to Rochester another Bronze Age Briton from the middle of the second millennium BC was being reconstructed, not in Manchester but at the Department of Illustration of the Newcastle Dental Hospital.[6] This was no southerner, but a Lewisman from the Outer Hebrides in his late thirties, who perhaps as the result of an attack with a club had suffered extensive injuries to the right side of his face, including a severe fracture of the cheek-bone which had become infected and led to further complications. He survived all this, but the movement of his lower jaw was limited as a result, and this in turn led to a restricted diet and to dental problems. It was the man's interesting medical history that led the Scottish archaeologists and their colleagues to propose a facial reconstruction, partly in order to express clearly the results of their research and the discomfort and sheer pain which their man must have suffered, and partly in the 'hope that the reconstruction may also tempt visitors to think further about the people behind the exhibition'. The head currently forms part of an exhibition of material from the Western Isles in the Museum nan Eilean at Stornoway.

3. Young man from Wouldham, Kent, reconstructed for Guildhall Museum, Rochester: Early Bronze Age (c. 1500 BC).

In these remarks lies the key to the reason and the justification for making heads that are primarily intended for public display, and the answer to the question that we posed earlier. The two reconstructions of Ada, the 'Carian Princess', in Bodrum Museum serve to underline the excitement and the splendour of the life and burial of one hereditary dynast of ancient Halicarnassus: they are very much intended to illustrate the life of one particular individual, and one who was not a member of the common people. This is exciting in itself – one scholar has written in the context of ancient portraiture, 'To be brought face to face with the famous personalities of ancient Greece is itself an inspiring experience.'[7] However, the other reconstructions described in this chapter are also of individuals, and throughout the study and the process of reconstruction they have been treated with the respect due to them as individuals. They have painstakingly been given their own faces which tell their own story. In the museums where they are exhibited they are nevertheless also treated at least in part as representatives of their people and their time. The fascination that lies in them is not only that these are the people behind the artefacts, but also that, in the end, they look so very much like people today. They are our own forbears, and they look like us.

An exhibition of bog bodies held at Silkeborg Museum in Denmark in 1996 acknowledged this fact in its title, 'Face to Face with your Past'. One would think that, going round such an exhibition or studying the book that accompanies it,[8] one would indeed meet the faces from the past, perfectly and naturally preserved by the tannin and the acids in the peat. In fact, as even the two bodies illustrated in this book show (pls x and xii), the action of the peat is very variable in its preservative powers, and is counterbalanced by the distorting action of its weight, pressing down on the softened body over many centuries. It takes almost as great a leap of the imagination to connect their crushed and wrinkled faces with the fleshed-out reconstructions as it does in the case of a bare skull. It was in many ways a relief to come across three reconstructions in that exhibition, two from Manchester and one (of the Windeby girl from Schleswig) by Professor Richard Helmer in Bonn.

The bog bodies, like Egyptian mummies, raise more vividly than a dry skeleton the question with which we began this chapter, 'When do human remains become more than mere museum objects?' Expressed in this way the question may appear simplistic, but it sums up the predicament of whether we treat them as people or as mere things. By translating those remains into people and by bringing those people so clearly before our eyes the reconstructions only serve to heighten the dilemma. As scientist, archaeologist, medical artist one tries to remain detached, although of course it is the fascination of finding out about people and of trying to understand them which is the mainspring of one's work. We began this chapter with a poet's concern to maintain the privacy of his earthly remains. Perhaps it takes another poet fully to understand and to interpret the quandary in which we find ourselves. Seamus Heaney, farmer's son from the rich peatlands of Ulster, poet and Nobel Laureate, is sharply aware of the humanity of some of the remains that the bogs have yielded up, both in his native Ireland and across the seas in Denmark and in Germany. He is able to stand before them as they are exhibited to public view and yet understand them for the people they once were, to explain the way in which their bodies can change from expressing a living, personal identity to being an object which shares much with the sculpted heads and statues that are displayed in museums, and which thus speaks across the divide directly to the viewer.[9] Many of his poems about bog bodies address the problem, and the last word should be with him:

> Who will say 'corpse'
> to his vivid cast?
> Who will say 'body'
> to his opaque repose?

Richard Neave Comes Face to Face
with the Truth

Early in 1996 I received an invitation from the Dutch National Association for Oral and Maxillo-Facial Surgeons to give a keynote lecture at their fortieth annual meeting, to be held jointly with the Royal Belgian Association of Stomatology at the beginning of November at Zeist, a small town about six miles from Utrecht. The invitation was in part inspired by the work we had done on the Yde Girl, and I accepted with great pleasure, for it presented an opportunity to meet and discuss many matters of mutual interest with a group of people who are intimately concerned with the heads of living people, and who would have many ideas of great interest to share with us. However, shortly after I had accepted this invitation, it was followed by another from the same organisation, but this time of a rather different nature: although offered in the spirit of collaborative research it was an invitation that presented a challenge. I cannot do better than to quote the letter I received from Dr Wittkampf at Utrecht:

One of the members of the scientific committee of our association has a typically-shaped skull and is willing to go into the CT-scanner, so we are able to make a three-dimensional model of the skull of this colleague. We have the idea that maybe you can play with this skull as you did with the bog-girl [i.e. the Yde Girl] earlier. Maybe it is a challenge for you to create the face of one of the members of the scientific committee without having met him before. Also for the small Dutch community of Oral and Maxillo-Facial Surgeons it may give an extra tension during your lecture when one of our colleagues is created by...Richard Neave.

The idea was very simple, one that we had frequently discussed as being the ideal way to assess the differences and similarities between a reconstruction and the original face: to work on the skull of a living person.

Our Dutch colleagues are people well used to working with three-dimensional milled skulls based on CT-scans of their patients, which give them models on which to assess their surgical procedures in correcting facial malformations. Now the organising committee would arrange for one of their colleagues to be put through the CT-scanner. His identity would be kept secret from us. From the digital data thus gathered a replica of the skull would be milled by the computer in styrene foam and posted to us in England. I was to reconstruct the head on this styrene replica and present the results at the autumn meeting in Holland. There would be no opportunity to check the results beforehand. Under the circumstances there was no question of not taking part in the experiment, but I did so with some trepidation.

We were given the information that the individual was a normal male Caucasian, retired from the post of director of the facio-maxillary unit in Utrecht, and that he did not have much hair. That was all we were told. It turned out later that he had no idea of what was going on, and had been somewhat baffled when his friends had persuaded him to be scanned. The milled skull duly arrived in Manchester, and a very fine model it turned out to be, with a mandible that could be articulated and the details in the nasal aperture and in the orbits very accurately rendered. It was almost as good as the real thing (fig. 1). The head was reconstructed in the normal way, using the measurements produced by Helmer in the range for individuals of sixty years and upwards who are of normal build. It was photographed, and I placed the slides at the end of the set I intended to show to the meeting.

The day before the meeting I travelled to Zeist. I arrived rather late at the

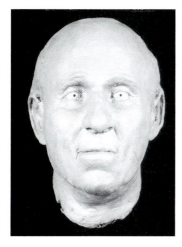

1. The milled skull of the 'unknown Dutchman'.

2. The scanned face of the 'unknown Dutchman'.

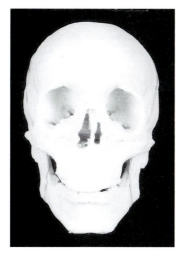

3. The reconstructed head of the 'unknown Dutchman'.

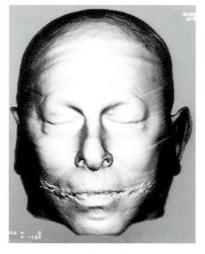

4. Professor Peter Egyedi.

opening reception, and was greeted very warmly and taken to the table around which the organising committee were already eating. After a few words of welcome I was escorted through the now-seated throng to collect my buffet meal. This provided me with an opportunity to observe the heads and faces of many of the delegates amongst whom, I thought, my subject might be sitting. Clutching my laden plate in one hand and a glass in the other I started back through the crowded tables. Ahead, an elderly, rather striking man turned his head to his neighbour in conversation. In contrast to all the other people in the room this man was suddenly very familiar. It was nothing to do with the details of his features, for those were largely hidden in shadow. I turned to my escort and said, 'That is a very familiar-looking face – I hope it is my man.' Shortly afterwards they told me that it was indeed my man. I slept well that night.

The following morning I was shown pictures of the scans of the subject's face (fig.2). Such images have a very different appearance from conventional photographs, but they provide important information on flesh thickness, although there is some apparent distortion caused by the fact that the subject has to lie down to be scanned. I also met my subject, Professor Peter Egyedi, 'face to face'. He was delighted at the prospect of further work being done using the scans as well as specially prepared photographs which he was arranging to have made. The reasons for the differences in the details of some of the morphological features, and the slight deviation from the average norms of soft tissue thickness, will be the subject of a collaborative study between our two institutions over the coming months which we hope will enable reconstructions to be made with even greater accuracy.

Of course the reconstructed face is not exactly the same as Professor Egyedi's – one never claims that the reconstructions are portraits, after all – but it was very similar; similar enough for me to understand what happens when someone recognises the reconstructed face of a person whom he or she knows, even though in my case it was the other way around (pl.xvi and figs 3 and 4).

The wheel seemed to have come full circle. At the outset of this venture into facial reconstruction, things seemed to keep falling into place as we began work on the skull from Vergina all those years ago, the skull that proved to be that of King Philip of Macedon, the skull that set us out on this journey of encounters and meetings. We began then to feel that all this was meant to happen. Nearly twenty years later it is still happening: is it just chance that the meeting in Zeist took place in the very week when this book was finally being completed?

MUSCLES OF THE HEAD

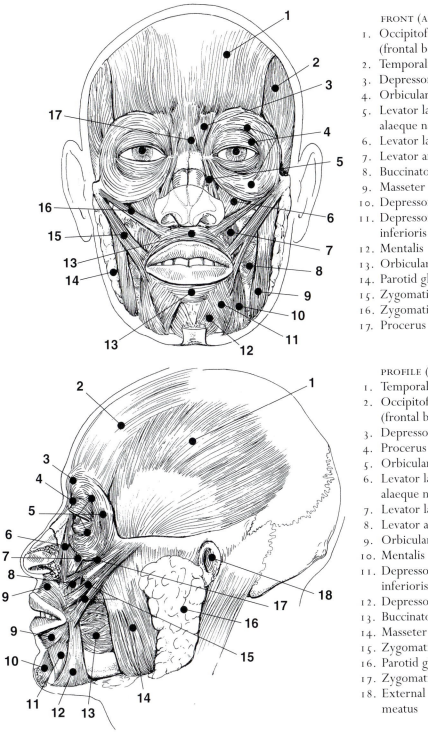

FRONT (AP)
1. Occipitofrontalis (frontal belly)
2. Temporalis
3. Depressor supercilii
4. Orbicularis oculi
5. Levator labii superiorus alaeque nasi
6. Levator labii superiorus
7. Levator anguli oris
8. Buccinator
9. Masseter
10. Depressor anguli oris
11. Depressor labii inferioris
12. Mentalis
13. Orbicularis oris
14. Parotid gland
15. Zygomaticus major
16. Zygomaticus minor
17. Procerus

PROFILE (LAT)
1. Temporalis
2. Occipitofrontalis (frontal belly)
3. Depressor supercilii
4. Procerus
5. Orbicularis oculi
6. Levator labii superiorus alaeque nasi
7. Levator labii superioris
8. Levator anguli oris
9. Orbicularis oris
10. Mentalis
11. Depressor labii inferioris
12. Depressor anguli oris
13. Buccinator
14. Masseter
15. Zygomaticus major
16. Parotid gland
17. Zygomaticus minor
18. External auditory meatus

GAZETTEER

MUSEUMS WHERE THE RECONSTRUCTIONS CAN BE SEEN

Ada (the 'Carian Princess')	Bodrum Museum of Underwater Archaeology, Turkey; and The Manchester Museum, Manchester, England
'Camilla' Romano-British woman from Colchester	Colchester Museum, Colchester, England
Lindow Man	The British Museum (photograph only), London, England
Manchester 1770 and the 'Two Brothers'	The Manchester Museum, Manchester, England
Midas	Museum of Turkish Civilisations, Ankara, Turkey; Cast Gallery, Ashmolean Museum, Oxford, England; University of Pennsylvania Museum of Archaeology and Anthropology, Philadelphia, USA; and The Manchester Museum, Manchester, England
The Minoans (the priest and priestess from Archanes)	Archaeological Museum, Archanes, Crete, and The Manchester Museum, Manchester, England
The Mycenaeans (seven faces from Grave Circle B at Mycenae)	Archaeological Museum, Mycenae, Greece (not yet complete), and The Manchester Museum, Manchester, England
Natsef-Amun	City Museum, Leeds, England
Philip II of Macedon	Archaeological Museum, Thessaloniki, Greece; Cast Gallery, Ashmolean Museum, Oxford, England; and The Manchester Museum, Manchester, England
'Posthumus' Romano-British head from St Albans	Verulamium Museum, St Albans, Herts, England
Rochester Bronze Age youth	Guildhall Museum, Rochester, Kent, England
Seianti	The British Museum, London; and The Manchester Museum, Manchester, England
The Yde girl	Drents Museum, Assen, Netherlands

NOTES

Foreword
1. *Religio Medici* (1643), pt ii, § 2.

Chapter 1
(THE HISTORY OF FACIAL RECONSTRUCTION)

1. On bog bodies, see the further reading list to Chapter 8. On the 'Iceman', see Konrad Spindler, *The Man in the Ice* (London 1994/1995), which has an extensive bibliography to more detailed works. References to mummification will be found in the notes and further reading list of Chapter 3, this volume.

2. Kathleen M. Kenyon, *Archaeology in the Holy Land* (4th edn, London 1979), 34-6, pls 20-1; ead., *Excavations at Jericho* III (London 1981), 77-8, 437, pls 50-9; plastered skull from Pre-Pottery Neolithic A: e.g. Kathleen M. Kenyon, 'Jericho', in Michael Avi-Yonah (ed.), *Encyclopaedia of Archaeological Excavations in the Holy Land* (London 1976), II, especially 556; also Ruth Amiran, 'Myths of the Creation of Man and the Jericho Statues', *Bulletin of the American Schools of Oriental Research* **167** (1962), 23-5. Other plastered skulls have been found at Tell Ramad (south of Damascus), Beisamun at the top of the Jordan valley, and 'Ain Ghazal near Amman: Kenyon, *Archaeology in the Holy Land*, 38-9, pls 22-4; A.H. Simmons et al., 'A Plastered Human Skull from Neolithic 'Ain Ghazal, Jordan', *Journal of Field Archaeology* 17 (1990), 107-9.

3. The 'Ain Ghazal statues, e.g. G.O. Rollefson and A.H. Simmons, 'The Neolithic Settlement at 'Ain Ghazal', in A.N. Garrard and H.G. Gebel, *The Prehistory of Jordan:The State of Research in 1986* II (*British Archaeological Reports International Series* 396 ii) (1988), 393-421, where the skull is also discussed. The Nahal Hemar finds: O. Bar-Yosef, David Alon et al., 'Nahal Hemar Cave', *Atiqot* **18** (1998), 23-7, 59-63. The practice of plastering skulls is also found among other more recent cultures: some references will be found in the *Atiqot* articles (p.63). Other examples of cults of the head in the prehistoric west: e.g. Graham Clark, *The Stone Age Hunters* (London 1967), 116-19 (mesolithic southern Germany); Anne Ross, *The Pagan Celts* (London 1986), especially 50 ff., 121-3; ead., *Pagan Celtic Britain* (London 1967), chapter 2; Miranda Green, *Symbol and Image in Celtic Religion and Art* (London/New York 1989), especially chapters 6 and 7 (Celtic cult of the severed head).

4. Pliny, *Natural History*, xxxv 153. The interpretation of the passage has sometimes been disputed.

5. Galen, *De Anatomicis Administrationibus*, i 2.218; English translation: C. Singer, *Galen on Anatomical Procedure* (Oxford 1956), 2. Lelli's reconstructions are beautifully illustrated in the catalogue of an exhibition held at Bologna University in 1981: M. Armaroli, *Le Cere Anatomiche Bolognesi del Settecento* (Bologna 1981); see also Richard Neave, 'Pictures in the Round: Moulage and Models in Medicine', *Journal of Audiovisual Media in Medicine* **12** (1989), 80-4.

6. The work of His, Welcker, Schaafhausen and others is conveniently summarised with full references to their publications by O. Grüner in the opening pages of 'Identification of Skulls: a Historical Review and Practical Applications', in M.Y. İşcan and R.P. Helmer, *Forensic Analysis of the Skull* (New York 1993), 29-45, and in the Introduction to M.M. Gerasimov, *The Face Finder* (London/Philadelphia 1971); Gerasimov also tells the story of Schiller's remains (177-84). We have ourselves carried out similar work on the skull of Leonello d'Este, Marquis of Ferrara 1441-1450, to assist Mr J. Thomann (then at the Warburg Institute in the University of London) with his research into the portrait of d'Este by Pisanello in comparison with those by other painters: as far as we know Mr Thomann has not published the results.

7. J. Kollman and W. Büchly, 'Die Persistenz der Rassen und die Rekonstruktion der Physiognomie Prähistorischer Schädel', *Archiv für Anthropologie* **25** (1898), 329-59.

8. H. von Eggeling, 'Die Leistungsfähigkeit physiognomischer Rekonstruktionsversuche auf Grundlage des Schädels', *Archiv für Anthropologie* **12** (1913), 44-7; contrast Gerasimov, op. cit., xx-xxi.

9. V. Suk, 'Fallacies of Anthropological Identifications and Reconstructions: a Critique Based on Anatomical Dissections', *Publications of the Faculty of Science, Charles University, Prague*, **207** (1935), 1-18.

10. Gerasimov, op. cit.

11. W.M. Krogman & M.Y. İşcan, *The Human Skeleton in Forensic Medicine* (2nd edn; Springfield, Illinois 1986).

12. M.F.A. Montagu, 'A Study of Man Embracing Error', in *Technology Review* **49** (1947); T.D. Stewart, *Essentials of Forensic Anthropology* (Springfield, Illinois 1979) 255-74;

A.M. Brues 'Identification of Skeletal Remains', *Journal of Criminal Law* **48** (1958), 551-63.

13. T. Suzuki, 'On the thickness of the soft parts of the Japanese face', *Journal of the Anthropological Society of Nippon* **60** (1948), 7-11.

14. B.P Gatliff, 'Facial Sculpture on the Skull for Identification', *American Journal of Forensic Medicine and Pathology* **5** (1984), 327-32.

15. P.C. Caldwell, 'New Questions (and Some Answers) on the Facial Reproduction Techniques', in K. Reichs (ed.), *Forensic Osteology: Advances in the Identification of Human Remains* (Springfield, Illinois 1986), 229-45.

16. Asiatic measurements: G.V. Lebedinskaya, V.S. Stepin, T.S. Surnina, B.A. Fedosyutkin, L.A. Tscherbin, 'The first experience of the application of ultrasound for the study of the thickness of soft facial tissues', *Sovetsakaya Etnografia* **4** (1979), 121-31; G.V. Lebedinskaya, T.S.Balueva and E.V. Veselovskaya, 'Principles of Facial Reconstruction', in M.Y. İşcan and R.P. Helmer (eds), *Forensic Analysis of the Skull* (New York 1993), 183-98. American Afro-Caribbeans and Caucasians: J.S. Rhine amd H.R. Campbell, 'Thickness of Facial Tissues in American Blacks', *Journal of Forensic Sciences* **25** (1982), 847-58; J.S. Rhine and C.E. Moore, 'Reproduction Tables of Facial Tissue Thickness of American Caucasoids', in *Forensic Anthropology, Maxwell Museum Technical Series* **1** (Albuquerque 1984). Helmer's measurements: R.P.Helmer, *Schädelidentifizierung durch Elektronische Bildmischung* (Heidelberg 1984), 60-4. Helmer's 'test': R.P. Helmer, S. Röhricht, D. Petersen and F. Möhr, 'Assessment of the Reliability of Facial Reconstruction', in İşcan and Helmer, op. cit., 229-46: the illustrations to this paper demonstrate very clearly the similarities between the work of different reconstructors, and of their results to the original subject.

17. John Hunter, Charlotte Roberts and Anthony Martin, *Studies in Crime: An Introduction to Forensic Archaeology* (London 1996), especially chapters 7 and 9. The reconstruction of the skull of a Neanderthal child from Gibraltar: 'John Musty's Science Diary', *Current Archaeology* **145** (November 1995), 31, reporting work by Zollikofer et al. at Zürich University in *Nature* 375 (1995), 283.

Chapter 2

(TECHNIQUES AND THE FORENSIC EVIDENCE)

1. H. von Eggeling, 'Die Leistungsfähigkeit physiognomischer Rekonstruktionsversuche auf Grundlage des Schädels', *Archiv für Anthropologie* 12 (1913), 44-7; F. Stadmüller, 'Zur Beurteilung der plastischen Rekonstruktionsmethode der Physiognomie auf dem Schädel', *Zeitschrift Morphol. Anthropologie* **49** (1922), 337-72; F. Diedrich, 'Ein Beitrag zur Prüfung der Leistungsfähigkeit der plastischen Rekonstruktionsmethode...', *Deutsche Zeitschrift der Gesellschaft für Gerichtliche Medizin* 8 (1926) 365-89; M.M. Gerasimov, *The Face Finder* (London/Philadelphia 1971); C.C. Snow, B.P. Gatliff and K.R. McWilliams, 'Reconstruction of Facial Features from the Skull: An Evaluation of its Usefulness in Forensic Anthropology', *American Journal of Physical Anthropology* **49** (1970), 221-8; Richard P. Helmer, S. Röhricht, D. Petersen and F. Möhr, 'Assessment of the Reliability of Facial Reconstruction', in M.Y. İşcan and R.P. Helmer (eds) *Forensic Analysis of the Skull* (New York 1993), 229-46. The work of W.M. Krogman, *The Human Skeleton in Forensic Medicine* (Springfield, Illinois 1962), 244-76, is also important, although she adopted a 'rule of thumb' method for the relationship of the different parts.

2. P. Williams et al. (ed.), *Gray's Anatomy* (38th edn, Edinburgh 1990), 550.

3. Ibid., 550.

4. J. Kollman and W. Büchly, 'Die Persistenz der Rassen und die Rekonstruktion der Physiognomie prähistorischer Schädel', *Archiv für Anthropologie* **25** (1898), 329-59. Japanese: T. Suzuki 'On the thickness of the soft parts of the Japanese face', *Journal of the Anthropological Society of Nippon* **60** (1948), 7-11; Caucasians: J.S. Rhine and C.E. Moore, 'Reproduction Tables of Facial Tissue Thicknesses of American Caucasoids', in *Forensic Anthropology, Maxwell Museum Technical Series* **1** (Albuquerque 1984); Afro-Caribbeans: J.S. Rhine and H.R. Campbell, 'Thickness of facial tissues in American Blacks', *Journal of Forensic Sciences* 25.4 (1980), 847-58; ultrasonic probing: R.P. Helmer, *Schädelidentifizierung duch Elektronische Bildmischung* (Heidelberg 1984), 60-4, and G.V. Lebedinskaya, T.S. Balueva and E.V. Veselovskaya, 'Principles of Facial Reconstruction', in İşcan and Helmer (eds), *Forensic Analysis of the Skull*, 183-98.

5. E.g. R.M.H. McMinn and R.T. Hutchings, *A Colour Atlas of Human Anatomy* (London 1977), 9 ff., especially 34-5; J.A. Gosling, P.F. Harris, J.R. Humpherson, T. Whitmore and P.L.T. Wilson, *Atlas of Human Anatomy* (London 1995), chapter 7, 'The Head and Neck'.

6. Galen, *De Anatomicis Administrationibus*, i 2.218; English translation: C. Singer, *Galen on Anatomical Procedure* (Oxford 1956) 2.

7. J.P. Moss, A.D. Linney, S.R. Grindrod, S.R. Arridge and J.S. Clifton, 'Three-dimensional Visualisation of the Face and Skull Using Computerized Tomography and Laser Scanning

Techniques, *European Journal of Orthodontics* **9** (1987), 247-53; P. Vanezis, R.W. Blowes, A.D. Linney, A.C. Tan, R. Richards and R. Neave, 'Application of 3-D Computer Graphics for Facial Reconstruction and Comparison with Sculpting Techniques', *Forensic Science International* **42** (1989), 69-84. The validity of this technique is put in question by the tests carried out by Susannah M. Addyman, *The Use of Three-Dimensional Laser Imaging for Facial Reconstruction* (unpublished MA Thesis, University of Knoxville, Tennessee 1994): see further Chapter 11, this volume. The principle of computed tomography and its application to facial reconstruction is conveniently summarised by Ian Isherwood and C.W. Hart, 'The Radiological Investigation', in A.R. David and E. Tapp (eds), *The Mummy's Tale* (London 1992), 100 ff., especially 110-11; see also R.A.H. Neave, 'The Facial Reconstruction of Natsef-Amun', 162-7 in the same book.

Chapter 3
(RICHARD NEAVE'S EGYPTIAN ENCOUNTER)
1. R. David and E. Tapp (eds), *Evidence Embalmed: Modern Medicine and the Mummies of Ancient Egypt* (Manchester 1984), 45-157.
2. *Journal of Egyptian Archaeology* **52** (1966), 95-119.
3. The excavation is described by W.M.F. Petrie, *Gizeh and Rifeh* (London 1907), 12, 27, pls xa-e, XIIIe-h; the examination of the mummies, and further details of the tomb and its contents, were published by M.A. Murray, *The Tomb of Two Brothers* (Manchester Museum Handbook, Manchester 1910), from whom the quotation is taken. For a summary, see R. David and E. Tapp (eds), *Evidence Embalmed*, 11-12, 33-6.
4. Richard Neave, 'Reconstruction of the Heads of Three Ancient Egyptian Mummies', *Journal of Audiovisual Media in Medicine* **2** (1979), 156-64; also R.A.H. Neave et al., 'Faces and Fingerprints', in Rosalie David (ed), *Mysteries of the Mummies* (London 1978), 172-5.
5. Rosalie David and Eddie Tapp (eds), *Evidence Embalmed: Modern Medicine and the Mummies of Ancient Egypt* (Manchester 1984): this is an updated version of the earlier collection of papers edited by Dr David, *Mysteries of the Mummies* (London 1978). The detailed account is in A.R. David (ed.), *The Manchester Museum Mummy Project* (Manchester 1979), and papers from the symposia that grew from the project were published under Dr David's editorship as *Science in Egyptology* (Manchester 1986).
6. R.A.H. Neave, 'The Reconstruction of Skulls for Facial Reconstruction Using Radiographic Techniques', in A.R. David (ed.), *Science in Egyptology* (Manchester 1986), 329-33.

7. A.D. Linney, J.P. Moss, R. Richards et al., 'The Use of 3-D Visualisation System in the Planning and Evaluation of Facial Surgery', in R.E. Herron (ed.), *Proceedings of the Biometric Technology and Applications Meeting* (1991), 190-9.
8. W. Osburn, *An Account of an Egyptian Mummy presented to the Museum of the Leeds Philosophical and Literary Society* (Leeds 1828).

Chapter 4
(KING PHILIP II OF MACEDON)
1. The first full account of this reconstruction is A.J.N.W. Prag, J.H. Musgrave and R.A.H. Neave, 'The Skull from Tomb II at Vergina: King Philip II of Macedon', *JHS* **104** (1984), 60-78, and the description of the modification to the eye wound is in A.J.N.W. Prag, 'Reconstructing King Philip II: the "Nice" Version', *AJA* **94** (1990), 237-47. Numerous more popular accounts have also appeared.
2. N.G.L Hammond, *A History of Macedonia* (Oxford 1972), I 156-8. The whole question has recently been reassessed by Panayiotis B. Faklaris, 'Aegae: Determining the Site of the First Capital of the Macedonians', *AJA* **98** (1994), 609-16, where all the references are conveniently gathered together: Faklaris rejects all the previous identifications of Aigai (including Vergina) on literary and topographical grounds, and comes down in favour of a new site by Kopanos near Naousa; while his general topographic arguments in particular are interesting (and we are not qualified to check them), it appears to us that Faklaris does not take sufficient account of the detailed correspondence of the buildings at Vergina with those known to have existed at Aigai, and above all sets aside the identification of the royal tombs and the recent work by Tomlinson and Andronicos on the dating of the barrel-vaulting of 'Macedonian' tombs (n. 36 below). We owe this reference to Dr Vassiliki Vemi.
3. Plutarch, *Pyrrhus*, xxvi 6. M. Andronicos, 'The Royal Tombs at Aigai (Vergina)', in M.B. Hatzopoulos and L.D. Loukopoulos (eds), *Philip of Macedon* (Athens/London 1980/1981), 198 with n. 12 for further references; id., *Vergina: The Royal Tombs and the Ancient City* (Athens 1984), 55 ff. describes the background and the discovery of the tomb. A slightly more detached account is given by Nicholas Hammond, *Philip of Macedon* (London 1994), chapter XVII.
4. Homer, *Iliad*, xxiv 785-99 (Hector's funeral; Patroclus' cremated bones are wrapped in fat rather than wool, ibid. xxiii 236-57); *Odyssey*, xxiv 72-3 (Achilles). The description of the finds is at M. Andronicos, *Vergina: The Royal Tombs*, 55 ff.
5. The discovery produced a flurry of articles

attempting to identify the occupants of the various tombs, often expressed with great passion. The most comprehensive list is given by Alice Swift Riginos, 'The Wounding of Philip II of Macedon', *JHS* 114 (1994), 103 n. 1, to which can be added T.D. Papazoes, *Ston Philippo B' i ston M. Alexandrou anikei o Basilikos Taphos tis Berginas? (Does the Royal Tomb at Vergina Belong to Philip II or Alexander the Great?)* (Thessaloniki 1993).

The age of the bones in the tomb is assessed by N. Xirotiris and F. Langenscheidt, 'The Cremations from the Royal Macedonian Tombs of Vergina', *Archaiologike Ephemeris* (1981), 142-60, especially 153, 158, pls 52-4, with which we have had no reason to disagree, although Dr Musgrave now believes that the man in Tomb II belongs at the middle or the older end of the age bracket, on the basis of the rather 'ragged' ends of the ribs, a sign of ageing: see Norman Hammond, 'Ending a bone of contention', *The Times*, 12 August 1980.

A good summary of the state of play on Alexander's tomb as it stood in 1993 is provided by Robert S. Bianchi, 'Hunting Alexander's Tomb', *Archaeology* 46.4 (July/August 1993), 54-5; aside from the flurry of interest caused by Dr Liana Souvaltzi's short-lived claim to have found the tomb at the Siwa oasis in 1995, the situation has not changed significantly since. The most perceptive (though not the most readily accessible) analysis of the evidence is still that of Alan J.B. Wace, 'The Sarcophagus of Alexander the Great', *Bulletin of the Faculty of Arts, Farouk I University, Alexandria* 4 (1948), 2-16.

On the dating of the salt-cellars and the barrel-vaulting, see nn. 35-6 below.

6. Arrian, *Anabasis*, vii 9.2 ff. (transl. G. Cawkwell). Part 1 of the Prologue to A.B. Bosworth, *Conquest and Empire: the Reign of Alexander the Great* (Cambridge 1988/1993), 'The Legacy of Philip', sums up Philip's achieve-ment and Alexander's debt to his father. There is no ancient life of Philip, but many books about him and assessments of his character and achievements. See Further Reading list to Chapter 4.

7. Arrhidaeus' mental health: Plutarch, *Alexander*, lxxvii 5; as a 'mute guardsman': id., *Moralia* 791e (Loeb edn, transl. E.N. Fowler); cf. ibid. 337d. We discussed Arrhidaeus' abilities and role in the story further in *JHS* 104 (1984), 69-70; Hammond, *Philip of Macedon*, 221 n.9 gives a full list of references. Andronicos put forward his views in *Athens Annals of Archaeology* 13 (1980), 170-3, and again in *Vergina: The Royal Tombs* 226-31. Hammond, op. cit., 40-3 with fig. 5 summarises life at the Macedonian court, and gives a family tree of Philip's wives and descendants.

8. The clearest account (even though we do not agree with him in every particular) is that given by Nicholas Hammond, *Philip of Macedon*, 170-9, which has comprehensive references to both modern and ancient sources. Andronicos' briefer and rather more dramatic rendering is at *Vergina: The Royal Tombs*, 231-3.

9. Achilles' funeral: *Odyssey* xxiv 71-3: by contrast, Achilles himself required divine intervention before Patroclus' funeral pyre would light: *Iliad* xxiii 192 ff. On the Vergina bones, see the comments of J.H. Musgrave in *JHS* 104 (1984), 77-8; for a later more detailed analysis together with a summary of ancient cremation practice, see Musgrave's 'Dust and Damn'd Oblivion: A Study of Cremation in Ancient Greece', *BSA* 85 (1990), 271-99, especially 275-8; this article also describes and illustrates the cremation experiments mentioned in the following paragraphs, and contains a discussion of the identity of the occupants of the different tombs based on a detached medical analysis (with full references to the other aspects of the debate). See also the same author's 'The Skull of Philip II of Macedon', in S.J.W. Lisney and B. Matthews (eds), *Current Topics in Oral Biology* (Bristol 1985), 1-16. On the application of electron spin resonance spectroscopy, see e.g. Don Robins et al. in I.M. Stead, J.B. Bourke and Don Brothwell (eds), *Lindow Man: The Body in the Bog* (London 1986), 140-2.

10. N.I. Xirotiris and F. Langenscheidt, 'The Cremations from the Royal Macedonian Tombs of Vergina', *Archaiologike Ephemeris* (1981), 142-60, especially 153, 158, pls 52-4.

11. Alice Swift Riginos, 'The Wounding of Philip II of Macedon', *JHS* 114 (1994), 103-19.

12. Demosthenes, *De Corona*, xviii 66-7.

13. Didymus Chalcenterus on [Demosthenes], *Philippic*, xi 22, in *Kommentar zu Demosthenes*, H. Diels and W. Schubart (eds) (Berlin 1904), col. 12.43 ff. The other ancient authors are discussed briefly in our article in *JHS* 104 (1984), 74-5, n. 38, along with the exact circumstances of the incident and the language used; the passages are quoted in greater detail by Dr Riginos, op. cit. (n.11). Hammond's comments, along with some telling remarks on the psychological effect of this injury and Philip's surprisingly lenient treatment of the Methonians, are on pp. 257-8 of N.G.L. Hammond and G.T Griffith, *A History of Macedonia* II (Oxford 1979).

14. On the shape of the nose, *JHS* 104 (1984), 68, 76, pl. IV c. On Macedonian royal noses see also R.R.R. Smith, *Hellenistic Royal Portraits* (Oxford 1988), 84-5.

15. G.M.A. Richter, *Portraits of the Greeks* (London 1965), iii 253 gives the ancient references; add to her list Athenaeus xii 591b.

16. On ancient attitudes to physical malformation, whether congenital or acquired, see now Robert Garland, *The Eye of the Beholder: Deformity and Disability in the Graeco-Roman World* (London 1995).

17. Those who would cite one team of 'experts' against another (as for example Alice Swift Riginos, *JHS* **114** [1994], 104 n.3; E.N. Borza, 'The Royal Macedonian Tombs and the Paraphenalia of Alexander the Great', *Phoenix* **41** [1987], 106 with n.5, and elsewhere) should look at Jonathan Musgrave's careful account of his discussion with Professor Xirotiris with the bones before them in 1985: in our minds the evidence is still overwhelmingly in favour of malformation and injury (in S.J.W. Lisney and B. Matthews [eds], *Current Topics in Oral Biology* [Bristol 1985] 15-16; also the other articles cited in n.9 above).

18. The finds are illustrated and described by Andronicos, *Vergina: The Royal Tombs*, 175-97; the greaves are illustrated as fig. 150.

19. Didymus Chalcenterus, op. cit. (n.13), cols 12.64-13.7. The problem is that the surviving manuscript of Didymus is not clear at the point where he describes the second injury (suffered while pursuing Pleuratos of Illyria), and the afflicted part can be read as either *knemen* = lower leg or *klein* = collar bone. Since another ancient commentator on Demosthenes (*De Corona*, xviii 67) says that it was Philip's collar bone that was injured during fighting with the Illyrians, and Didymus himself talks of the spear in the thigh as the third wound that Philip suffered, the balance seems against the calf wound.

Alice Swift Riginos, *JHS* 114 (1994), 115-17 conveniently brings together the evidence and references to earlier discussions: Dr Riginos is perhaps a little cavalier in her treatment of the archaeological and forensic evidence, and appears to overlook the fact that Didymus Chalcenterus mentions *two* injuries to the leg, col. 12.64 (wounded in the lower leg by a spear in battle against the Illyrians) and col. 13.1 (struck in the thigh during an attack on the Triballians). See also Andronicos, *Vergina: The Royal Tombs* 146, 186-8 for his final view of the matter; he suggested a congenital lameness (one of the sets of matching greaves is illustrated on his p.145), while others have postulated club-foot or polio as the cause: Peter Green, 'The Royal Tombs of Vergina: A Historical Analysis', in W.L. Adams and E.N. Borza (eds), *Philip II, Alexander the Great and the Macedonian Heritage* (Washington 1982), 135-6. On the leg bones:

Musgrave, in *Current Topics in Oral Biology* (n.9 above), p. 9 with fig. 6. Lameness does not of course entail legs of different length. It has also been suggested that the unequal greaves were made for an archer who habitually went down on one knee to shoot: but archers rarely if ever wore leg-armour, and the king of Macedon certainly did not fight with bow and arrows.

The right greave from the antechamber is 41.5 cm long (measured internally) and 9.7 cm in diameter, the left 38.2 cm long and 9.0 cm in diameter; the three pairs of greaves from the main chamber measure 42 cm (right), 42.1 cm (left); 42 cm (right), 41.5 cm (left); 40.5 cm (right), 40.5 cm (left).

20. [Demetrius] *De Elocutione*, 293, cited by e.g. Riginos, op. cit., 110.

21. The Assos skeleton: M.D. Grmek, *Diseases in the Ancient World* (transl. M. and L. Muellner) (Baltimore/London 1989), 58-9, fully described by R. Virchow, 'Über die alte Schädel von Assos und Cypern', *Abhandlung K. Preuss. Akad. Wiss. zu Berlin: Phys.-Math. Cl.* **24** (1884), II 25. References to the literature (which we owe to Dr Christine Salazar, along with much valuable help in the matter of ancient eye wounds) will be found in *AJA* **94** (1990), 240 n.10. In noting that only the wounded men remained in a fort which he captured during the Civil War, Julius Caesar does not describe any of their injuries except for those received by four centurions, who had lost their eyes (he does not say if both eyes or only one) (*Civil War*, iii 53): does this seemingly casual reference conceal the fact that he was surprised to find them alive?

22. Thomas Leland, *The History of the Life and Reign of Philip of Macedon; the Father of Alexander* (London 1758), I, 135-7 (we owe this reference to Catherine Bankes). The passage in Pliny was pointed out to us by Dr Christopher Ehrhardt of Otago University in New Zealand, who chanced most opportunely to be on sabbatical leave in Manchester at the time: he deserves our warm thanks.

23. A.J.N.W. Prag, 'Reconstructing King Philip II: The "Nice" Version', *AJA* **94** (1990), 237-47, where full references to both ancient and modern literature are given. The translated collection of Hippocratic surgical cases by G. Majno, *The Healing Hand: Man and Wound in the Ancient World* (Cambridge, Mass. 1975), is of particular value for anyone wanting to pursue this somewhat gruesome topic in greater detail.

24. Celsus, *De Medicina*, VII 5.2C (Wellman, frag. 191 [p.206]) = Loeb edition, vol. III 318. This passage leads into Celsus' very complicated description of the spoon of Diokles – but the Loeb translation is cumbersome and probably

wrong in several places: cf. *AJA* **94** (1990), 241 for a corrected version. Künzl's demolition of the example alleged to be from Ephesus is in E. Künzl, 'Die archäologischen Objekte der Sammlung Meyer-Steineg in Jena', in C. Habrich (ed.), *Theodor Meyer-Steineg (1873-1936) – Arzt, Historiker, Sammler. Kataloge des Deutschen Medizinhistorischen Museums Ingolstadt* **11** (Ingolstadt 1991), 26-7, 40, nos 10, 10a; id., 'Die Instrumente aus Ephesos und Kos', in S. Zimmermann and E. Künzl, 'Die Antiken der Sammlung Meyer-Steineg in Jena I', *Jahrbuch des Römisch-Germanischen Zentralmuseums Mainz* **38.2** (1991), 521, 522-4, 529, nos 10, 10a, pls 41-2. Such forgeries of Greek and Roman medical instruments are being identified in growing numbers.

25. The full account of this treatment, described in *AJA* **94** (1990), 243, is based on John Scarborough's analysis of *On Wounds*, 'Theoretical Assumptions in Hippocratic Pharmacology', in F. Lasserre and P. Mudry, *Formes de Pensée dans la Collection Hippocratique Actes du IVe Colloque International Hippocratique, Lausanne, 1981 (Université de Lausanne, Publications de la Faculté des Lettres* **26**) (Geneva 1983), 318-23. Our heartfelt thanks are due to Professor Scarborough for sharing with us his knowledge of ancient medicine when we came to this part of our study.

26. E.J. Edelstein and J. Edelstein, *Asclepius. A Collection and Interpretation of the Testimonies* I (Baltimore 1945), 423 nos 32, 40 (pp. 227-8).

27. Like everything else in this story, the portraits have been argued over with ever-growing sharpness since the discoveries at Vergina. In our original publication in the *JHS* **104** (1984), 68-77, pls VI-VII, we discussed and illustrated those where we felt that the identification is reasonably certain, and the likeness relevant to our own particular quest, and considered too those pieces which do not seem to carry sufficient weight to be included in the list; see also *AJA* **94** (1990), 247 and fig. 6. Nothing that has been written since has persuaded us to change our minds. G.M.A. Richter, *Portraits of the Greeks* (London 1965), iii 253 has the list of ancient references; the Baalbek mosaic of the birth of Alexander is her fig. 1707a-b; see now also R.R.R. Smith, *Hellenistic Royal Portraits* (Oxford 1988), 148 Appendix III (his no. 39, pl. 28.3-4 was at one stage also mooted as portraying Philip II, but that notion has been – rightly – dismissed). The ivory head has been discussed in most of the literature on Vergina: for a recent and detached view, N. Spivey, *Understanding Greek Sculpture: Ancient Meanings, Modern Readings* (London 1996), 198.

28. We owe a very great debt of gratitude to the late Dr Martin Price not only for showing us his photographs of this coin, which is in a private collection, and for discussing it with us, but for showing such faith in our work from the outset. It was an important thing to have won the confidence of such a distinguished Macedonian scholar from the very start. His publication of the coin is to be found in *Praktika tou XII Diethnous Synedriou Klasikis Archaiologias, Athina...1983* (Athens 1985), I 243-7. On the coinage of Macedonia see G. Le Rider, *Le Monnayage d'Argent et d'Or de Philippe II Frappé en Macédoine de 359 à 294* (Paris 1977), especially 364-6 on the type showing Philip on horseback. Dr Price also drew our attention, with some hesitation as to its conclusions, to the article by Maria Regina Kaiser-Raiss, 'Philipp II. und Kyzikos', *Schweizerische Numismatische Rundschau* **63** (1984), 27-43 (especially 35), which suggests that a portrait head of Philip is also to be found on electrum staters of Cyzicus on the Sea of Marmara. Although the head is surely intended as a portrait, as is proposed in the British Museum *Guide to the Principal Coins of the Greeks* (1960), no. III A 8-9, pl. 18, it is the idealised portrait of a powerful kingly figure, and the face is not that of Philip: the eyes are smaller, the forehead larger, and though masked by the beard, the chin is smaller and the distance between chin and nose shorter than for instance on the Vergina ivory; the line of the jaw seen in profile is less square, while the face is altogether more fleshy. It is, however, interesting that once again we are shown the left profile. Cleopatra's goitre, and other bumps and swellings, are discussed by G.D. Hart, 'The Diagnosis of Disease from Ancient Coins', *Archaeology* **26** (1973), 123-7 – an article to which Professor J.F. Healy kindly drew our attention.

29. The Tarsus medallion: *JHS* **104** (1984), 71 with n. 27, pl. VI c; also M.B. Hatzopoulos and L.D. Loukopoulos (eds), *Philip of Macedon* (Athens/London 1980/1981), fig. 91 (colour); the rider on the fresco: Andronicos, *Vergina: the Royal Tombs*, 116, fig. 71; also Hammond, *Philip of Macedon*, 181, fig. 10.

30. Copenhagen, Ny Carlsberg Glyptotek, no. 2466. V. von Graeve, 'Zum Herrscherbild Philipps II und Philipps III von Makedonien', *Archäologischer Anzeiger* (1973), 244-59, discusses the sculpted portraits of both Philip II and Philip III Arrhidaeus, including the 'Alcibiades' type of Philip II as philosopher-king; they are considered more briefly by ourselves in *JHS* **104** (1984), 69-74, pls VC-VII.

31. See R.W. Hartle, 'The Search for Alexander's Portrait' in W.L. Adams and E.N. Borza (eds), *Philip II, Alexander the Great and the*

Macedonian Heritage (Washington 1982), 153-76.
32. E.g. E.N. Borza, 'A Macedonian Skull',
Association of Ancient Historians, Newsletter **36** (April
1985) and elsewhere. Several of the portraits
show Philip apparently wearing a narrow band
of cloth around his head, which is interpreted as
the *diadema* of cloth bound around the head that
was the symbol of Macedonian royalty at least
from the time of Alexander who, the ancient
authors tell us, took it over from the Persians.
The exact nature of this diadem has been much
debated, together with the question of whether
it already existed and had the same significance
before the time of Alexander. The issue is
complicated by the finding in Tomb II of an
adjustable silver-gilt tubular ring incised with a
diamond pattern thought to represent strips of
cloth, which has been interpreted as a version of
the diadem in precious metal. Those who hold
that no royal diadem existed in Macedonia before
Alexander take the presence of the diadem on
most of the portraits as clear evidence that they
cannot show Philip II, or were made
posthumously. The argument is in the end a little
irrelevant, for there were many other forms of
headband, hatband and hair-ribbon worn by men
as well as women and known by the general name
of *tainiai*. There is an extensive and sometimes
contentious literature on the topic: the earlier
references are collected in *JHS* **104** (1984), 72
n.32; to these should be added H. Ritter, 'Zum
sogennanten Diadem des Philippsgrabes', *AA*
(1984), 105-11; M. Andronicos, *Vergina*, 171,
174-5 (includes illustrations); C. Rolley, 'Une
couronne et un diadème sur la tête d'Alexandre',
in K. Gschwantler and A. Bernard-Walcher
(eds), *Griechische und Römische Statuetten und
Großbronzen: Akten der 9. Tagung über Antike
Bronzen...1986* (Vienna 1988), 92-3; E.N. Borza,
In the Shadow of Olympus: The Emergence of Macedon
(Princeton 1990), 263-4 with earlier references;
R.R.R. Smith, *Hellenistic Royal Portraits* (Oxford
1988), 34-8.
33. Dr Musgrave's articles are cited in n. 9
above. Peter Green gives a very useful table of
all the potential candidates for Tombs I-III on
pp. 140-1 of 'The Royal Tombs of Vergina: A
Historical Analysis', in W.L. Adams and E.N.
Borza (eds), *Philip II, Alexander the Great and the
Macedonian Heritage* (Washington 1982).
34. Eugene N. Borza, *In the Shadow of Olympus:
The Emergence of Macedon* (Princeton 1990),
chapter 11 and appendix C.
35. Susan I. Rotroff, 'Spool Salt-Cellars in the
Athenian Agora', *Hesperia* **53** (1984), 343-54:
this article was already in press at the time our
work appeared, but Dr Rotroff discussed its
implications with us, and agreed that it was in

fact perfectly possible that the black-glazed 'salt-
cellars' of the type found in Tomb II might well
have had a longer life than she at first thought,
and that they might have reached Macedonia as
early as 340 BC: a minority of pots from the three
wells which yielded the comparative material on
which the dating was based already belong to
the years 350-325 BC. It is noteworthy that the
undersides of these and other similar pieces in
the tomb were quite unmarked, showing that
they were brand new when they were buried. It
is worth mentioning that just after the first
publication of the reconstruction, amid all the
stir and scepticism which it provoked, we
discussed this pottery with Dr John Hayes, then
on the staff of the Royal Ontario Museum and
one of the world's acknowledged experts on
later Greek and Roman pottery: having listened
to the evidence of the bones, he agreed without
hesitation that it would entail an updating of the
black-glazed pottery.
36. R.A. Tomlinson, 'The Architectural Context
of the Macedonian Vaulted Tombs', *BSA* **82**
(1987), 305-12. This article should be read
together with M. Andronicos, 'Some Reflections
on the Macedonian Tombs', pp. 1-16 of the same
volume, who put forward very similar arguments.
At the time Tomb II was discovered the latest
study of barrel-vaults was that of T.D. Boyd,
published as 'The Arch and the Vault in Greek
Architecture', *AJA* **82** (1978), 83 ff., but based
on research carried out before the discovery not
only of the Vergina tombs but also of other early
vaults such as the entrance to the stadium at
Nemea. The Panathenaic sherd: e.g. Hammond,
Philip of Macedon, 179 (with references).

Chapter 5

(KING MIDAS HAS ASS'S EARS?)
1. For a detailed account of the study of the
skull from the Midas Mound, see A.J.N.W.
Prag, 'Reconstructing King Midas: a First
Report', *Anatolian Studies* **39** (1989), 159-65.
2. Herodotus, *Histories*, vii 73, viii 138; for a
fuller discussion see S. Eitrem, 'Midas', in *Real
Encyclopädie*, XV.2 1526.
3. Homer, *Iliad*, iii 184 ff.
4. Ovid, *Metamorphoses*, xi 146 ff., especially
180-93 (transl. Mary M. Innes; Harmondsworth
1955); for other ancient accounts, Aristophanes,
Plutus, 287-8; Hyginus, *Fabulae*, 191; also Eitrem,
op. cit., 1526-36, and (for a list) e.g. Margaret
C. Miller, 'Midas as the Great King in Attic
Fifth-Century Vase-Painting', *Antike Kunst* **31**
(1988), 79 n.1.
5. Arrian, *Anabasis*, ii 3; G. and A. Koerte,
*Gordion: Ergebnisse der Ausgrabung im Jahre 1900.
Jahrbuch des Deutschen Archäologischen Instituts,*

Erganzungsheft 5 (1904), 12-15; Eitrem, op. cit., 1536-8.

6. The problem has been much discussed: see e.g. Lynn E. Roller, 'Midas and the Gordian Knot', *Classical Antiquity* **3** (1984), 256-72, who gives further references; also Oscar White Muscarella, 'King Midas of Phrygia and the Greeks' in K. Emre et al. (eds), *Anatolia and the Ancient Near East: Studies in Honor of Tahsin Özgüç* (Ankara 1989), 333 – but contrast his remarks at 334.

7. Eusebius, *Chron.* (Armenian version) canon, year 1321 after birth of Abraham. See further e.g. J. D. Hawkins, 'Mita' in *Reallexikon der Assyriologie*, VIII. 3/4 (Miete-Moab) (Berlin/New York 1994), 271-3; Machteld J. Mellink, 'Mita, Mushki and Phrygians', *Anadolu Araçtırmaları = Jahrbuch fur kleinasiatische Forschung* is (1965), 317-20; Muscarella, op. cit., 333 for further references.

8. The throne: Herodotus, *Histories*, i 14; see further on the whole question of Midas' relations with Greece, Muscarella, op. cit., 333-44. Herodotus' story of Croesus' researches into numerous oracles before selecting the one he wished to consult on a weighty question shows how seriously another eastern monarch took the matter (*Histories* i 47 ff.). Midas' marriage: Aristotle, frag. 611, 37 (Rose); Pollux, *Onomastikon*, ix 83. Some argue that the princess' husband was a later Midas, on the grounds that Aristotle adds that she struck the earliest coinage for her native city: on the received view coinage was not reckoned to have reached the Ionian Greeks much before 600 BC. However, this evidence has been reassessed, and a date around 700 BC seems acceptable – see Muscarella, op. cit., 334-5.

9. K. DeVries, 'Greeks and Phrygians in the Early Iron Age', in K. DeVries (ed.), *From Athens to Gordion* (Philadelphia 1980), 33-50, who discusses the whole question of Phrygian-Greek relations at this period with admirable detail and conciseness. On Greek finds from Phrygia and Phrygian finds from Greece, John Boardman, *The Greeks Overseas* (4th edn, London 1980), 87-91; Muscarella, op. cit., 336-42; Greek sherds from Gordion: K. Sams, 'Patterns of Trade in First Millennium Gordion', *Archaeological News* VIII 2/3 (1979), 47.

10. Muscarella, op. cit., 337; Seton Lloyd, *Ancient Turkey: A Traveller's History of Anatolia* (London 1989), 66; the comment on the Phrygian alphabet is by R.D. Barnett in *Cambridge Ancient History* (3rd edn), ii pt 2, *The Middle East and the Aegean Region c.1380-1000 BC* (Cambridge 1975), 433-4; Boardman, op. cit., 88, with n. 228 for further references; other references at

DeVries, op. cit., 34 n.6.

11. Strabo, *Geography*, i 61. On the toxic qualities of bull's blood see R.J. Lenardon, *The Saga of Themistocles* (London 1978), 194-8 and 239 nn. 306-7, quoting the toxicologist Dr Emmerich von Haam.

12. G. and A. Koerte, *Gordion: Ergebnisse der Ausgrabung im Jahre 1900. Jahrbuch des Deutschen Archäologischen Instituts*, Erganzungsheft 5 (1904). Site, excavation and finds are described briefly in the site guide (R.S. Young, *Gordion: A Guide to the Excavations and Museum* [Ankara 1975]), and much more fully in the first American excavation report by Young, *Three Great Early Tumuli: Gordion I (Pennsylvania University Museum Monograph* **43**; Philadelphia 1981), especially 79-190. Seton Lloyd gives a brilliantly vivid summary in *Ancient Turkey*, 61-5.

13. E.g. A. Steinberg and W.J. Young in R.S. Young, *Three Great Early Tumuli: Gordion* I, 288-9 with n.33; cf. Young's own comments, ibid., 248 with n.128, and Muscarella's review in *The Quarterly Review of Archaeology* (Dec. 1982), 7.

14. Elizabeth Simpson, '"Midas' Bed" and a Royal Phrygian Funeral', *Journal of Field Archaeology* **17** (1990), 69-87, summarised in DeVries, 'The Gordion Excavation Seasons of 1969-1973 and Subsequent Research', *AJA* **94** (1990), 371-406.

15. Young, *Gordion: A Guide*, 50-1; id., *Three Great Early Tumuli: Gordion I*, 102: for example, he noted that a bronze situla (bucket) in the form of a lion's head was identical to situlae shown in relief on the gateway of Sargon II's palace at Khorsabad (constructed 713-707 BC), while fibulae similar to those found in the Midas Mound are carved on the same reliefs, and on a relief of King Urpallu at Ivriz near Konya, which must be dated before 738 BC when Urpallu became a vassal of the Assyrians. References to other articles by Young on the problem are in Prag, *Anatolian Studies* **39** (1989), 159 n.3; further arguments are put forward by Muscarella in *The Quarterly Review of Archaeology*, (Dec. 1982), 9 and elsewhere.

16. Machteld Mellink in Young, *Three Great Early Tumuli: Gordion I*, 271: this report on the excavations was published posthumously in Young's name but with further contributions.

17. Also expressed by DeVries and Mellink in Young, *Three Great Early Tumuli: Gordion I*, 271-2, and by DeVries in *AJA* **94** (1990), 388-9. It is worth adding that the date of the Khorsabad palace, where Young found parallels for the metalwork, is as close to Midas' recorded dying date as to that of Gordios.

18. Peter Ian Kuniholm, Bernd Kromer, Sturt Manning, Maryanne Newton, Christine E. Latini and Mary Jaye Bruce, 'Anatolian tree rings and the absolute chronology of the eastern Mediterranean, 2220-718 BC', *Nature* **381** (27 June 1996), 780-3; see also Colin Renfrew, 'Kings, tree-rings and the Old World', 733-4 of the same issue. This new dating, which Kuniholm and his colleagues link to a major climatic disaster in 1628 and connect with the eruption of the volcano on Thera, supersedes Kuniholm's earlier work, *Dendrochronology at Gordion and on the Anatolian Plateau* (University Microfilms, Ann Arbor 1977), 3 and 45-53. We are most grateful to Professor Kuniholm for discussing the dating with us as his work progressed, and to Dr S.R. Edwards for drawing our attention to the articles in *Nature*.

19. Young, *Three Great Early Tumuli: Gordion I*, 101.

20. J.G. Frazer, *Pausanias' Description of Greece* (London 1913), II 74 on Pausanias i 4.5 for a list of other versions, with bibliography; the Irish version in e.g. J. Grimm, *Household Tales* (transl. M. Hunt; London 1892), II 498.

21. J. Grimm, *Kleinere Schriften IV: Recensionen und Vermischte Aufsätze* (Berlin 1869), I 216-17.

22. J.G. Frazer, *The Golden Bough III: Taboo and the Perils of the Soul* (London 1936), 258 ff. with n.1.

23. E.g. F. Brommer, 'Mythologische Darstellungen auf Vasenfragmenten', *Antike Kunst*, Beiheft 7 (1970), 56-7, and Eitrem, op. cit., 1531; contrast Lynn E. Roller, 'The Legend of Midas', *Classical Antiquity* **2** (1983), 308 n. 67; F. Bömer, *P. Ovidius Naso, Metamorphosen: Kommentar* (Heidelberg 1980), V 284-5; cf. ibid., V 261-2.

24. Tyrtaeus, frag. 12, l.6; Herodotus, *Histories*, viii 138. Roller, op. cit., 302 ff. gives an excellent account of the story of Midas in Greek literature and art; Eitrem, op. cit., 1526-38 has a detailed discussion, incorporating ethnographic connections and parallels.

25. No. E447. The other two vases are a cup in the Vatican Museum, no. 16585, and a krater in Syracuse, no. 4322B.

26. It must be added that contrary to the evidence of the sculptures, Plutarch comments that Pericles' personal appearance was flawless (*Pericles*, ii 2-4). For further discussion and references to historical events on Greek vases, see e.g. A.J.N.W. Prag, *The Oresteia: Iconographic and Narrative Tradition* (Warminster / Chicago 1985), 102-5 with 128, n.64.

27. *Iliad* ii 862-03, iii 185-7, x 431.

28. Lynn E. Roller, *Classical Antiquity* **2** (1983), 308; Eitrem, 'Midas', in *Real Encyclopädie*, XV.2 1531; F. Bömer, *P. Ovidius Naso, Metamorphosen: Kommentar*, V 260-2, for fuller discussions and references.

29. R. Ruggles Gates and T.N. Bhaduri, 'The inheritance of hairy ear-rims', *Mankind Monographs* i (*The Mankind Quarterly*; Edinburgh 1961); C. Pianetta, 'Un caso di ipertricosi in alienato', *Archivo de Psichiatria, Antropologia Criminale e Scienze Penale* **22** (1901), 454-7; E. Thurston and K. Rangachari, *Castes and Tribes of Southern India* (Madras 1909), vii 121.

30. Young, *Three Great Early Tumuli: Gordion I*, 101.

31. Young, ibid., 101, 156, 168 ff., 187, pl. 41A-43A; Elizabeth Simpson, '"Midas' Bed" and a Royal Phrygian Funeral', *Journal of Field Archaeology* **17** (1990), 69-87; S. Lloyd, *Ancient Turkey*, 64.

32. This account is a summary of that prepared by Danaë Thimme and published in *Anatolian Studies* **39** (1989), 164-5.

33. See e.g. O. Acar and S. Mazur, 'The Dig that is Shaking Ancient History', *Connoisseur*, December 1989, 151. Professor Alpagut's report on the skull is as follows:

UPPER FACIAL HEIGHT	71 mm
UPPER FACIAL WIDTH	112 mm
UPPER FACIAL INDEX (H/W)	long face
NASAL HEIGHT	53 mm
NASAL WIDTH (APERTURE WIDTH)	25 mm
NASAL INDEX (W/H)	middle width nose
ORBIT HEIGHT (LEFT)	35 mm
ORBIT WIDTH	40 mm
ORBITAL INDEX (H/W)	high eye-socket
CRANIAL INDEX	long-headed
CRANIAL HEIGHT (BA-BRG)	118 mm
CRANIAL BREADTH	132 mm
CRANIAL LENGTH	181 mm
CRANIAL LENGTH-HEIGHT INDEX	low head from lateral aspect

Therefore according to the anthropological measurements this skull is long-headed with a low head, long-faced (upper face), has a medium nose and high eye-sockets.

34. E.g. K. Dortluk et al., *Antalya Museum* (Ankara 1988), no. 41; Acar and Mazur, op. cit., 151.

35. Ezekiel xxvii 13, with Machteld J. Mellink, 'Mita, Mushki and Phrygians', *Anadolu Araçtırmaları = Jahrbuch fur kleinasiatische For.s hung* 2 (1965), 319-20.

36. K. DeVries, 'Greeks and Phrygians in the Early Iron Age', in K. DeVries (ed.), *From Athens to Gordion* (Philadelphia 1980), 34-7.

Chapter 6
(GRAVE CIRCLE B AT MYCENAE)

1. The work described in this chapter could not even have got off the ground without the encouragement, support and sometimes good-natured criticism of our colleague Dr Elizabeth French: indeed, the suggestion came from her in

the first place. Many other people gave crucial help too – rather than invidiously select a few here, we have named them all in the Acknowledgements. The reconstruction of the Mycenaean faces has been described in detail in J.H. Musgrave, R.A.H. Neave and A.J.N.W. Prag, 'Seven Faces from Grave Circle B at Mycenae', *BSA* **90** (1995), 107-36, with a detailed bibliography.

There are many easily accessible accounts of the story of Mycenaean civilisation: aside from those mentioned elsewhere in this chapter, see the Further Reading list to Chapter 6. On Alexander's tomb, see Chapter 4 n.5

2. Pausanias, *Guide to Greece*, ii 16.6-7.

3. The passage quoted is taken from Schliemann's manuscript *Tagebuch*, preserved in the Gennadeion Library in Athens. Most of his letters and draft newspaper reports on Mycenae are reproduced in William M. Calder III and David A. Traill (eds), *Myth, Scandal, and History* (Detroit 1986) (the passage quoted appears on p. 254). Compare the account in H. Schliemann, *Mycenae* (London 1878), 296-7. A further selection of Schliemann's letters is published by E. Meyer, *Heinrich Schliemann: Briefwechsel* (Berlin 1958), with a supplement in *Journal of Hellenic Studies* lxxxii (1962), 75-105. Schliemann's identification of the modern village with Pausanias' description (ii 16.6-7): e.g. *Mycenae*, 333 ff.; Meyer, *Briefwechsel*, II 62 (letter of 27 November 1876). Calder and Traill's investigation sets out to question Schliemann's veracity and reliability; in a similar vein is David Traill, *Schliemann of Troy* (London 1995). The most readable and unprejudiced account of his work is probably chapter 2 of Michael Wood's *In Search of the Trojan War* (London 1985/1987), a book which also has a perceptive analysis of the chronology of the Late Bronze Age, and of the nature of Agamemnon's 'empire'; alongside this should now be set pp. 53-94 of the beautifully illustrated *The Discovery of the Greek Bronze Age* by J. Lesley Fitton (London 1995). On the 'Agamemnon' mask, e.g O.T.P.K. Dickinson, 'Schliemann and the Shaft Graves' in *Greece and Rome* **23** (1976), 164 with nn. 19-20; Calder and Traill, op. cit., 234 no. 14. The exact number and sex of each of the bodies found by Schliemann is a little confused: see O.T.P.K. Dickinson, *The Origins of Mycenaean Civilisation (Studies in Mediterranean Archaeology* **49**; Göteborg 1977), 48.

4. Dickinson, *The Origins of Mycenaean Civilisation*, 50-1; Elizabeth French, '"Dynamis" in the Archaeological Record at Mycenae', in M.M. Mackenzie and C. Roueché (eds), *Images of Authority: Papers Presented to Joyce Reynolds (Cambridge Philological Society Supplement* **16**,

1989), 123. Since both these authors wrote, a wooden bowl from Shaft Grave V has been dated to 1619 ± 37 BC by dendrochronology, but because the bowl is a carved piece and does not have the bark layer we do not know when the tree was cut, nor how long it had been in use before being put into the grave, so the date cannot be regarded as absolute yet: P.I. Kuniholm, 'A Date-list for Bronze Age and Iron Age Monuments Based on Combined Dendrochronological and Radiocarbon Evidence', in *Aspects of Art and Iconography: Anatolia and its Neighbours – Studies in Honor of Nimet Özgüç* (Ankara 1993), 2. On the new chronology described in Chapter 5 n.18, this date can now presumably be narrowed down to 1580 BC.

5. G.E. Mylonas, *Mycenae Rich in Gold* (Athens 1983), 46-61, describes the discovery and context of Grave Circle B; the full report, in Greek with an English summary and containing the report on the skulls in English by J.L. Angel, is G.E. Mylonas, *O Taphikos Kyklos B ton Mykenon (Grave Circle B at Mycenae)* (Athens 1973). The burials have been recently reanalysed by Imma Kilian-Dirlmeier, 'Beobachtungen zu den Schachtgräbern von Mykenai und zu den Schmuckbeigaben mykenischen Männer', in *Jahrbuch des Römisch-Germanischen Zentralmuseums* **33** (1986), 159-86, and by S. Dietz, *The Argolid at the Transition to the Mycenaean Age* (Copenhagen 1991), 106-132. The summary and reassessment by Dickinson, op. cit., 39-46 is both clear and crucial to an understanding of this circle and the later one. G.E. Mylonas, *Mycenae and the Mycenaean Age* (Princeton 1966), 132 discusses the reuse of the graves.

6. Michael Wood, *In Search of the Trojan War* (London 1985), 225 ff., especially 230-41: Wood's argument hinges on identifying 'Homer's Troy' with Troy VIh rather than the traditionally accepted Troy VIIa.

7. Pausanias ii 16.3 ff.; Apollodorus *Library* ii 4.4 ff.; *Epitome* ii 11; told in Mylonas, *Mycenae Rich in Gold,* 13-14; cf. also e.g. Wood, op. cit., 157.

8. This much simplified account is based particularly on the admirable – but opposing – summaries by Dickinson and French, op. cit., n. 4, but the significance and role of the two circles continues to occupy archaeologists: see for example the references cited by French.

9. The most comprehensive publication is still G. Karo, *Die Schachtgräber von Mykenai* (Munich 1930-3), nos 27-8, 36, 75, pls xxvii, xxx, but this is very hard to find, and illustrations of selections of Schliemann's finds appear in most books about Mycenae and the Mycenaean Age: the pieces mentioned here can be found in e.g.

Mylonas, *Mycenae Rich in Gold*, figs 18, 26, 29-31, 203. The Lion Hunt Dagger is also illustrated by e.g. M.S.F. Hood, *The Arts in Prehistoric Greece* (Pelican History of Art; Harmondsworth 1978), fig. 178; S. Marinatos and M. Hirmer, *Crete and Mycenae* (London 1960), pl. XXXVI; Oliver Dickinson, *The Aegean Bronze Age*, 100 pl. 5.1.

10. C.T. Newton, *Essays on Art and Archaeology* (London 1880), 271-2.

11. The arguments for and against the 'portraiture' theory are conveniently collected by Günter Kopcke, 'Zum Stil der Schachtgräbermasken' in *Athenische Mitteilungen* **91** (1976), 1-13. The comments of Angel, who sees the problem from an anthropologist's point of view, are interesting: Mylonas, *Grave Circle B*, 390.

12. G.E. Mylonas, in *Archaiologike Ephemeris* (1969), 125-42 (English summary 141-2); also id., *Mycenae Rich in Gold*, 59; the arguments against the Egyptian connection put forward by Dickinson, *The Origins of Mycenaean Civilisation*, 57-8, seem more convincing; compare also e.g his pp. 36-7 and 101-6, or Emily Townsend Vermeule, *The Art of the Shaft Graves at Mycenae* (Cincinnati 1975), on the paucity of Mycenaean contact with the world beyond the Aegean at this time: at pp. 8-9, fig. 7, she reproduces the highly imaginative 'Egyptian' reconstruction proposed by M. Meurer, 'Der Goldschmuck der Mykenischen Schachtgräber', in *Jahrbuch des Deutschen Archäologischen Instituts* 27 (1912), 208-27, pl. XII.

13. Traill seeks to cast doubt on the authenticity of this mask, but largely on the flimsy grounds that it is different from the others: Calder and Traill, *Myth, Scandal and History*, 134-5.

14. Letter to *The Times* dated 25 November 1876: Meyer, *Briefwechsel*, II 61.

15. Mylonas, *Grave Circle B*, 384, pl. 247.

16. Personal communication from its rediscoverer, Professor Spyridon Iakovidis; also Mylonas, *Archaiologike Ephemeris* (1969), 142.

17. Calder and Traill, *Myth, Scandal and History*, 255; repeated at Schliemann, *Mycenae*, 298. Schliemann's notebooks are now in the Gennadeion Library in Athens.

18. The burials are all illustrated and described in Mylonas, *Grave Circle B* (with a summary in Mylonas, *Mycenae Rich in Gold*, 46-61); see also n.5. Angel's analyses and discussions of the skeletons are on pp. 379-97, pls 244-9. For a further analysis see also Dickinson, *The Origins of Mycenaean Civilisation*, 40-6.

19. We located the following skulls together with their skeletons (the letters refer to the graves, but the numbering is Angel's and simply reflects the order in which he happened to work on them): Gamma 51, Beta 52, Pi 53, Eta 54, Gamma 55, Xi$_1$ 57, Gamma 58, Zeta 59, Delta 61, Alpha 62, Alpha 64? (the number on the skull is indistinct, but the long bones marked 64 are medieval), Nu 66, Nu 66a, 67 (a child, labelled 'from Foundation tower near Lion Gate, LH III'), Iota 68, Sigma 131, Upsilon 132, Lambda$_2$ 133. We also found the following fragmentary skeletons without distinguishable skulls: Lambda$_1$ 56, Theta 63, 65, Alpha$_1$ 69, Kappa 70, Lambda 70a, and Lambda$_2$ 134, and two unnumbered skeletons, one of which may be the missing fourth body from Grave Gamma. This does not correspond exactly with Angel's list: he also studied Delta 60 ('unmeasurable fragments of an adult of about 40'), but does not mention the skull Alpha 64? or 67. A fuller account of the skeletal material is published in our report in *BSA* **90** (1995), 111-12, 131-6.

20. Angel in Mylonas, *Grave Circle B*, 380, with references to other trephinations; also K. Manchester, *The Archaeology of Disease* (Bradford 1983), 62-3; M.D. Grmek, *Diseases in the Ancient World* (Baltimore/London 1989), 63-5; Hippocrates, *On Wounds in the Head*, ii 30-1, in E. Littré, *Oeuvres Complètes d'Hippocrate* (Paris 1849, repr. Amsterdam 1969), iii 182-260.

21. So e.g. Kopcke, *Athenische Mitteilungen* 91 (1976), 1-13.

22. The sculpted stela from Shaft Grave V shows a charioteer and a figure on foot, both of whom seem to be short-haired and clean-shaven, although the carving is not very detailed. The Late Helladic III silver shallow cup from chamber tomb 24 at Mycenae shows long-haired men with neat beards but no moustache, as do the niello plaques of the same date found at Pylos; these are both rather later than our people (thirteenth century BC), and seem to reflect a time when the clean-shaven upper lip was the general fashion. Ivories from the Shaft Grave period show men completely clean-shaven, but a beard with clean upper lip appears on the contemporary amethyst seal from Grave Gamma. These pieces are illustrated by e.g. Mylonas, *Mycenae Rich in Gold*, figs 18, 29, 30, 32, 114, 124, 181; niello plaques: Marinatos and Hirmer, *Crete and Mycenae*, pl. 204, also M.S.F. Hood, *The Arts in Prehistoric Greece*, figs 115, 118, 121, 164B; for references to the lion-hunt dagger and rings, see n.9. The suggestion that hair length indicates social status was put forward by S. Marinatos, 'Minoische Porträts', in D. Ahrens (ed.). *Festschrift Max Wegner* (Münster 1962), 9-12, with further references. We discussed the problems in greater detail in in *BSA* **90** (1995), 122-5.

23. M.D. Grmek, *Diseases in the Ancient World*, 60.

24. Angel in Mylonas, *Grave Circle B*, 380-1, 389; Dickinson, *The Origins of Mycenaean Civilisation*, 45.

25. See n.9 above.

26. The gold plaques, n.9 above; fresco-paintings of women's hair: cf. also the women in the Procession Fresco from Tiryns, Marinatos and Hirmer, *Crete and Mycenae*, pls XL and 226; the 'stephane' head-dress: e.g. the priestess from the Shrine at Mycenae, Mylonas, *Mycenae Rich in Gold*, fig. 113; terracotta 'idols': Mylonas, op. cit., fig. 110; C. Renfrew et al., *The Archaeology of Cult* (*BSA* Supplementary vol. 18, 1985), 214-15, nos SF 2660, 2691, fig. 6.4, pls 31-33a. The fashion with the single pony-tail is also clearly illustrated on a thirteenth-century ivory box lid from Minet el-Beida in Syria which though probably Syrian work, shows strong Mycenaean influence: Mylonas, op. cit., fig. 208. The Theran fashions: C. Doumas, *The Wall-paintings of Thera* (Athens 1992), passim, especially 154-63. For further references see *BSA* **90** (1995), 125 n.28.

27. Lucian, *Dialogues of the Dead*, xviii (transl. H.W. and F.G. Fowler); quoted in part by Mylonas, *Mycenae Rich in Gold*, **61**.

28. For example, the lively frieze of soldiers with their impossibly long noses on the Late Helladic IIIc 'Warrior Vase' (*c.* 1100 BC) (Mylonas, op. cit., fig. 117), or the eccentric-seeming idols from the shrines at Mycenae, Tiryns and Phylakopi (n.26 above).

29. See n.5: the discussion by Imma Kilian-Dirlmeier, in *Jahrbuch des Römisch-Germanischen Zentralmuseums* **33** (1986), 159-86 is important.

30. See e.g. Terence A. Brown and Keri A. Brown, 'Ancient DNA and the Archaeologist', *Antiquity* 66 (1992), 10-23, which has a full bibliography.

Chapter 7

(THE PRIEST AND PRIESTESS)

1. The best English account of Archanes and the sites nearby, including the discovery at Anemospilia, is now J. and E. Sakellarakis, *Archanes* (Athens 1991), especially 148-56, with full bibliography. First reports of the discovery: H.W. Catling, 'Archaeology in Greece 1979-80', *Archaeological Reports* (hereafter *AR*) **26** (1979-80), 50-1; id., 'Archaeology in Greece 1980-1', *AR* **27** (1980-1), 42; the full report (in Greek) by J.A. and E. Sakellarakis, appeared in *Praktika tes en Athinais Archaiologikes Etaireias* (1979), 347-72 (the finding of the skeletons: pp. 386-90, pl. 184.2). For a dramatic reconstruction of the event, Yannis Sakellarakis and Efi Sapouna-Sakellaraki, 'Drama of Death in a Minoan Temple', *National Geographic* **169** (February 1981), 204-22. We have published the detailed account of the reconstruction, with the full anatomical notes, in J.H. Musgrave, R.A.H. Neave, A.J.N.W. Prag, E. Sakellarakis and J. Sakellarakis, 'The Priest and Priestess from Archanes-Anemospilia', *BSA* **89** (1994), 89-100.

2. Theseus and the Minotaur: Plutarch, *Theseus*, xv 1; funeral of Patroclus: Homer, *Iliad*, xxiii 173-83; Iphigeneia and Polyxena: A.J.N.W. Prag, *The Oresteia: Iconographic and Narrative Tradition* (Warminster 1985), 61-7; Themistocles at Salamis: Plutarch, *Themistocles*, xiii 2. The possible instances of human sacrifice are summarised in J. and E. Sakellarakis, *Archanes* (Athens 1991), 155-6. Oliver Dickinson, *The Aegean Bronze Age* (Cambridge 1994), 264 ff., especially 265-6, gives a detached account of Minoan religion.

3. P.M. Warren, 'Knossos: Stratigraphical Museum Excavations 1978-80', *AR* **27** (1980-1), 89-93.

4. E.g. at Eleutherna in Crete (Early Iron Age): N.C. Stambolidis, *Eleutherna* (Rethymno 1994), especially 26-8. For a sceptical view, Dennis D. Hughes, *Human Sacrifice in Ancient Greece* (London/New York 1991).

5. E.g. S. Marinatos, 'Minoische Porträts', in D. Ahrens (ed.), *Festschrift Max Wegner* (Münster 1962), 9-12, with further references. Marinatos also has some very interesting comments on Minoan hairstyles, including the suggestion of a half-length cut for officials. The 'Chanting Priest' is illustrated by e.g. M.S.F. Hood, *The Arts in Prehistoric Greece* (Pelican History of Art; Harmondsworth 1978), 224-5, fig. 227.

6. P.J.P. McGeorge, 'Minoan Health and Diet', in R.E. Jones and H.W. Catling (eds), *New Aspects of Archaeological Science in Greece* (Fitch Laboratory Occasional Paper **3**, British School at Athens 1988), 52-3.

7. See further M.D. Grmek's encyclopaedic account, *Diseases in the Ancient Greek World* (trans. by M. Muellner and L. Muellner; Baltimore and London 1989), which contains further references; others will be found in J.H. Musgrave et al., *BSA* **89** (1994), 91 n.3. For an excellent discussion of current thinking on congenital versus acquired anaemia, see P.L. Stuart-Macadam, *Nutrition and Anaemia in Past Human Populations* (Chacmool 1988), 284-87; id., 'Nutritional deficiency diseases: a survey of scurvy, rickets, and iron-deficiency anaemia', in M.Y. İçcan and K.A.R. Kennedy (eds), *Reconstruction of Life from the Skeleton* (New York 1989), 201-22.

8. 'La Parisienne': e.g. J.H. Musgrave et al., *BSA* 89 (1994), 95 fig.7; M.S.F. Hood, *The Arts of Prehistoric Greece*, fig.51; Hood's fig.52 illustrates a galaxy of Minoan faces and hairstyles.

9. The sistrum player on the 'Harvester Vase': e.g. J. and E. Sakellarakis, *Archanes*, fig. 98; S. Marinatos and M. Hirmer, *Crete and Mycenae*

(London 1960), pls 104-5 show the whole riotous crowd of faces on this vase.

10. The 'Snake Goddess' figurines: e.g. M.S.F. Hood, op. cit., 133 fig. 123; Oliver Dickinson, *The Aegean Bronze Age*, 100 pl. 5.1.

11. J. and E. Sakellarakis, *Archanes* (Athens 1991), 94; report of the excavation (in Greek): *Ergon* 1987, 132-8, figs 111-18.

Chapter 8

(BODIES FROM THE BOG)

1. Pitiscus, 'Etwas von den Eigenschaften des Torfmoors, insonderheit Mumien zu bereiten, über die antiseptischen Heilkräfte desselben, und über die Kunst, Leder darin zu Gerben', *Blätter vermischten Inhalts* **4** (1791), 52-72: had he put his proposal into practice, Pitiscus would have anticipated the first scientific reconstructions by about a century.

2. The best and most accessible general introduction to bog bodies in general remains P.V. Glob, *The Bog People* (London 1969/1977), although parts of this are now rather dated and superseded by Wijnand van der Sanden, *Through Nature to Eternity: The Bog Bodies of North-West Europe* (Amsterdam 1996). The papers comprising the detailed study of Lindow Man are collected in I.M. Stead, J.B. Bourke and Don Brothwell (eds), *Lindow Man: The Body in the Bog* (London 1986), in which the reconstruction is described on pp. 42-4, R.A.H. Neave and R. Quinn, 'Reconstruction of the Skull and the Soft Tissues of the Head and Face of Lindow Man'; see also R.A.H. Neave, 'Reconstruction of the Skull and the Soft Tissues of the Head and Face of "Lindow Man"', *Canadian Society of Forensic Science Journal* **22.1** (1989) 43-53. Don Brothwell, *The Bogman and the Archaeology of People* (London 1986) is a thoroughly readable account of the discovery, setting it in the context of other preserved bodies. More recent research on Lindow Man appears in R.C. Turner and R.G. Scaife (eds), *Bog Bodies: New Discoveries and New Perspectives* (London 1995). The background evidence for this chapter will be found in these works even if we do not always give specific references.

3. See the gazetteer compiled by R.C. Turner and R. Ó Floinn in Turner and Scaife, *Bog Bodies*, 205-34, and the more summary one of van der Sanden, *Through Nature to Eternity,* 189-95 together with his chapter 6.

4. On the different parts of the different bodies, D. Brothwell and J.B. Bourke, 'The Human Remains from Lindow Moss 1987-8', in Turner and Scaife, *Bog Bodies* 52-8 (especially fig. 18), and the useful summary by Rick Turner himself on pp. 188-9 of the same volume.

5. The causes of death of bog bodies have been much discussed: see for example P.V. Glob, *The Bog People, passim* but especially chapter VI; Anne Ross, 'Lindow Man and the Celtic Tradition', in Stead et al., *Lindow Man,* 162-9; van der Sanden, *Through Nature to Eternity*, chapter 11; and for an iconoclastic view C.S. Briggs, 'Did They Fall or Were They Pushed?' in Turner and Scaife, *Bog Bodies,* 168-82.

6. Don Brothwell and Keith Dobney, 'Studies on the Hair and Nails of Lindow Man...', in Stead et al., *Lindow Man,* 66-8; Brothwell, *The Bog Man,* 37.

7. Brothwell, *The Bog Man,* chapter 6; Stead et al., *Lindow Man,* chapters 26-7, 29 and 31 (papers by T.G. Holden, R.G. Scaife, Don Robins et al., and Anne Ross); T.G. Holden, 'The Last Meals of the Lindow Bog Men', in Turner and Scaife, *Bog Bodies,* especially 79, 83; van der Sanden, *Through Nature to Eternity*, chapter 8, especially 116-18. The passage from Pliny, *Natural History*, xvi 95 is cited in full by Anne Ross, op. cit., 167.

8. On the variety and nature of peat bogs as they affect the preservation of human remains, e.g. van der Sanden, *Through Nature to Eternity*, chapters 1-2.

9. R.A.H. Neave, 'The Reconstruction of Skulls for Facial Reconstruction Using Radiographic Techniques', in A.R. David (ed.), *Science in Egyptology* (Manchester 1986) 329-33. At the time we did not know of the work of Richard Helmer in reconstructing the Windeby Girl, found in the bogs of Schleswig ('Die Moorleiche von Windeby. Versuch einer plastischen Rekonstruktion der Weichteile des Gesichtes auf dem Schädel', *Offa* **40** [1983] 345-52, summarised in van der Sanden, *Through Nature to Eternity,* 149-50, fig. 207): like Lindow Man, Windeby Girl's skull was both difficult of access and deformed by the peat, and parts of it had shrunk. Helmer dealt with this problem by using a cast made from a modern skull which resembled that of Windeby Girl very closely in sex, age and form, modified in accordance with information retrieved from CT-scans. He does not mention the fact that the sex of this body is not certain (see van der Sanden in Turner and Scaife, *Bog Bodies,* 149).

10. E.g. Anne Ross, 'Lindow Man and the Celtic Tradition', in Stead et al., *Lindow Man,* 162-9; the idea of the 'anti-Roman' sacrifice is put forward – in somewhat fanciful form – by Anne Ross and Don Robins, *The Life and Death of a Druid Prince* (London 1989); for a more detached view, R.C. Turner, 'Boggarts, Bogles and Sir Gawain...', in Stead et al., *Lindow Man,* 170-6; id., 'The Lindow Man Phenomenon:

Ancient and Modern', in Turner and Scaife, *Bog Bodies*, 188-204, and also J.R. Magilton, 'Lindow Man: the Celtic Tradition and Beyond', ibid., 183-7 (though the parallel he suggests with the death of Agamemnon [p. 185] is not based on any Greek source). On the problem of the radiocarbon dating of Lindow Man, J.A.J. Gowlett, R.E.M. Hedges and I.A. Law, 'Radiocarbon accelerator (AMS) dating of Lindow Man', *Antiquity* **63** (1989), 71-9.

On the nature and wealth of sacrifices in bogs, e.g. van der Sanden, *Through Nature to Eternity*, chapter 12, who illustrates some of the Danish displays.

11. Van der Sanden, *Through Nature to Eternity*: chapters 4 and especially 5 and 6 assess the earlier evidence, notably the work of Dieck.

12. Unfortunately for English readers the fullest accounts of the discovery and early history of the Yde Girl are both in Dutch: Wijnand van der Sanden (ed.), *Mens en Moeras* (Drents Museum, Assen 1990); id., *Het Meisje van Yde* (Drents Museum, Assen 1994); however, much information on the history and research on this body set in the context of other bog bodies are to be found in the same author's *Through Nature to Eternity, passim*.

Chapter 9
(SEIANTI HANUNIA TLESNASA)

1. This chapter relies heavily on the work of our collaborators in this Etruscan phase of our work, notably Professor Marshall Becker, Dr Birgitte Ginge and Dr R.W. Stoddart. At the time of writing the detailed report of this reconstruction has not yet been published: it is planned as a joint monograph under the editorship of Judith Swaddling and John Prag with contributions from all those mentioned in this chapter, to be published in 1998. In the meantime preliminary reports on the authenticity, analysis and identification of the skeleton and the coffin by M.J. Becker and B. Ginge have appeared in *Antropologia Contemporanea* **13.4** (1990), 359-69. Becker has also analysed the skeleton in G. Maetzke (ed.), *La Civiltà di Chiusi e del suo Territorio* (Florence 1993), 397-410. There are numerous general introductions to the Etruscans apart from Heurgon's: see the Further Reading list to Chapter 9. Also, the two volumes of George Dennis, *The Cities and Cemeteries of Etruria* (London 1848/1878) though naturally very dated still make entertaining and interesting reading.

2. British Museum GRA 1887.4-2.1 = H.B. Walters, *BMC Terracottas* (1903), D786 (sarcophagus) and GRA 1887.4-2.2 (skeleton). The silver: GRA 1887.4-2.1-7 = Walters, *BMC*

Silver Plate (1921), pl. 4.9. The discovery: L.A. Milani, 'Sarcofago di terracotta policroma, scoperto a Poggio Cantarello, presso Chiusi', *Notizie degi Scavi* (1886), 353-6; W. Helbig, 'Viaggio nell' Etruria e nell' Umbria', *Römische Mitteilungen* **1** (1886), 217-19. The sarcophagus is described in detail by Maria Donatella Gentili, *I Sarcofagi Etruschi in Terracotta di Età Recente* (Rome 1994), 68 (no. A69), also 183 ff.; there is a full early bibliography in R. Bianchi-Bandinelli, 'Clusium…', *Monumenti Antichi* **30.2** (1925), 307 n.1.

3. The sarcophagus of Larthia Seianti and the tomb-complex are described by Gentili, op. cit., 64-7, no. A66; also R. Bianchi-Bandinelli, op. cit., 303, 305-8. A much simpler ash-urn of the second century BC also from Chiusi, without portrait-sculpture but bearing the name of Seianti Cumerunia, daughter of Frunei and wife of Cicu, is in the collections of the Danish National Museum in Copenhagen (inv. no. 3677).

4. There appears to have been a second inscription painted on a layer of plaster applied over the first one, giving a slightly different combination of names: this will be discussed further by Dr Ginge in the full report.

5. Illustrated e.g. H. Salskov Roberts, 'Later Etruscan Mirrors: Evidence for Dating from Recent Excavations', *Analecta Romana* **12** (1983), 52, fig. 42 (who also discusses the mirrors held by the two Seianti women, pp. 49-52).

6. Helbig, *Römische Mitteilungen* **1** (1886), 217-18, thought that her face was shown paler than her neck and arms, and therefore suggested that she was wearing the thick (and poisonous) white-lead make-up known to the Greeks as psimythion and to the Romans as cerussa, but Dr Swaddling has compared the colouring of the face and the arms for us with this in mind, and reckons that there is no significant difference between the two.

7. On the discovery, see n. 2. The following section rests heavily on the investigations and deductions of our medical colleagues, notably Professor M.J. Becker, Dr Jonathan Musgrave, Dr R.W. Stoddart and Dr D.K. Whittaker. Indeed the study of Seianti could not have progressed as far nor become as interesting as it did without them. That we are grateful to them goes without saying, although the responsibility for the conclusions here presented is of course our own.

8. The method is described by T. Solheim, 'Dental Root Translucency as an Indicator of Age', *Scandinavian Journal of Dental Research* **97** (1989), 189-97; Whittaker's modified method is summarised in G. Thomas, D.K. Whittaker, G. Embery and M. Hill, 'Sclerotic Apical Dentine in Vital and Non-Vital Teeth', *Journal of Dental*

Research **71** (1992), 573, and Thomas' further development in G.J. Thomas, 'A Comparative Study of Translucent Apical Dentine in Vital and Non-Vital Human Teeth', *Archs. Oral Biology* **39** (1994), 29-34. The 'Gustafson Technique' for ageing teeth and its development is described (with further references) in John Hunter, Charlotte Roberts and Anthony Martin, *Studies in Crime: An Introduction to Forensic Archaeology* (London 1996), 112-13.

9. Larissa Bonfante, 'Daily Life and Afterlife', in Larissa Bonfante (ed.), *Etruscan Life and Afterlife* (Detroit/ Warminster 1986), 250-1, fig. VIII-28. There are several articles on dental appliances by Marshall Becker: see for example 'Etruscan Gold Dental Appliances: Origins and Functions as Indicated by an Example from Orvieto...' *Journal of Palaeopathology* **6.2** (1994), 69-92. Luigi Capasso, 'Dental Pathology and Alimentary Habits: Reconstruction of Etruscan Population' (sic), *Studi Etruschi* **53** (1987), 177-91 is a study of the dental history of some of Seianti's contemporaries from the area of Chiusi.

10. Jacques Heurgon, *Daily Life of the Etruscans* (London 1964), 120-1, where further references are given; G.E.W. Wolstenholme and C.M. O'Connor (eds), *A CIBA Foundation Symposium on Medical Biology and Etruscan Origins (London 1958)*, (London 1959). M.J. Becker, 'Human Skeletons from Tarquinia', *Studi Etruschi* **58** (1992), 211-48; for other references to Becker's work see nn. 1 and 9; E. Pacciani, 'Resti scheletrici umani de insediamenti Etruschi: Repertorio della collezione giacente presso la Soprintendenza Archeologica per la Toscana', *Studi Etruschi* **55** (1989), 221-6.

11. Otto J. Brendel, *Etruscan Art* (New Haven/London 1995), 106-9; also ibid. 129-31 (with further bibliography).

12. J.D. Beazley, *Etruscan Vase-Painting* (Oxford 1947), 10, 128-9, pl. XXIX 7-10; also Brendel, op. cit., 393 with n. 20 for further references, fig. 303.

13. Brendel, op. cit., 393-4, fig. 304; G. Hafner, 'Frauen- und Mädchenbilder aus Terracotta im Museo Gregoriano Etrusco', *Römische Mitteilungen* **62** (1965), 41-61; id. 'Männer- und Jünglingsbilder...', *Römische Mitteilungen* **63-4** (1966/7), 29-52; and on Etruscan terracotta heads in general, e.g. P.J. Riis, *Etruscan Types of Heads. A Revised Chronology of the Archaic and Classical Terracottas of Etruscan Campania and Central Italy* (Copenhagen 1981).

14. Brian A. Sparkes, *So Few People Look Like Themselves* (Inaugural lecture: Southampton 1988), 26. This publication provides an admirable – and concise – summary of the nature of portraiture in Classical art.

15. Filippo Balduccini, *Vocabulario toscano dell'Arte del Disegno* (Florence 1681), 137, quoted in R. Bianchi-Bandinelli, 'Ritratto', in *Enciclopedia dell'Arte Antica* VI, 695-738. On the definition of portraiture see also e.g. Brendel, op. cit., 392 ff. with n.19 for further references.

16. Catullus xxxix 11; Vergil uses the world 'pinguis', 'fat', to describe Etruscans (*Georgics* ii 193). On the fleshiness of the figures, Brendel, op. cit., 323, and in a more cynical and light-hearted vein, Heurgon, *Daily Life of the Etruscans*, 23-5, who refers to some rather surprising racist theories put forward in Germany during the last war, which saw the obesity of the Etruscans as proof of their eastern origins (E. Bux, in *Klio* **35** [1942], 17-59).

17. Brendel, op. cit., 396, 393.

18. For example, links have been found between the wreathed head painted on a red-figure krater of the type described above (Florence, Museo Archeologico 11.245) and that of the young man carved on the lid of a cinerary urn of tufo in Volterra (Museo Guarnacci 676), with further connections among bronzes depicting Apollo from further afield in Etruria; while what is sometimes called the 'central Italian portrait' of a young man with his hair carved in a mass rather than individual locks, of the late fourth and third centuries, has been traced through the various Etruscan workshops back to portraits of the rulers of Pergamum in Asia Minor: A. Maggiani, *Artigianato Artistico in Etruria* (Milan 1985), 89-90.

19. M. Cristofani, *The Etruscans* (London 1979), 96-7.

20. Marie-Françoise Briguet, 'Art', in Larissa Bonfante, op. cit., 125, fig. IV-45 (Volterra, Museo Guarnacci inv. 613); Marjatta Nielsen, 'Portrait of a Marriage: The Old Etruscan Couple from Volterra', *Acta Hyperborea* **4** (1992), 89-140: this article only came to our notice when this chapter was complete, but it provides a perceptive and scholarly analysis of the urn and of the place of 'realism' in Etruscan funerary art (especially pp. 100-15).

21. Laris Pulena: Tarquinia, Museo Nazionale: M. Cristofani, *The Etruscans* (London 1979), 78-9; the Copenhagen figure: Ny Carlsberg Glyptotek H.I.N. 429: Mette Moltesen and Marjatta Nielsen, *Ny Carlsberg Glyptotek Catalogue: Etruria and Central Italy 450-30 BC* (Copenhagen 1996), 60-1 no. 14. No. 42 (I.N. 1261) in the Ny Carlsberg catalogue is a terracotta ash-urn of a bearded man, remarkable for his emaciated physique.

22. Brendel, op. cit., 421-3; he singles out (and illustrates) the urn of Arnth Velimnas from Perugia as typical of Late Hellenistic male

sarcophagi. Aphrodite of Melos (alias 'Venus de Milo'): e.g R. Lullies and M. Hirmer, *Greek Sculpture* (London 1957), pl. 270; G.M.A. Hanfmann, *Classical Sculpture* (London 1967), pl. 256.

23. Maria Donatella Gentili, *I Sarcofagi Etruschi in Terracotta di Età Recente*, especially 171-83, 'Analisi artistica: il problema del ritratto'.

24. Gentili, op. cit., 43-52 (nos A25-44), 150, 180, pls 7-21; her suggestion of a connection between the female lid no. A40 from the Treptie tomb at Tuscania and Seianti can be no more than a stylistic similarity, for the two are made in different centres, and are of quite different quality.

25. R.P. Helmer, *Schädelidentifizierung durch Elektronische Bildmischung* (Heidelberg 1984), 60-4.

26. Oscar Wilde, 'Intentions' (in *Complete Works* [London 1966] 989, cited by B.A. Sparkes, *So Few People Look Like Themselves* (Southampton 1988), 39.

Chapter 10
(THE CASE OF THE CARIAN PRINCESS)

1. We have published the detailed account of this reconstruction as 'Who is the Carian Princess?' in Jacob Isager (ed.), *Hecatomnid Caria and the Ionian Renaissance = Halicarnassian Studies* **1** (Odense 1994), 97-109 (with appendices on the teeth and the pathology by D.K. Whittaker and R.W. Stoddart respectively); in the same volume is the report on the excavation, M. Aykut Özet, 'The Tomb of a Noble Woman from the Hekatomnid period', with full illustrations of her jewellery (pp. 88-96); and an account of the philosophy behind the display of the reconstruction, Oÿuz Alpözen, 'Ada I Revived in the Bodrum Museum of Underwater Archaeology. Some Museological Considerations' (pp. 110-14).

Many of the nicer points concerning this lady, her story, the finds from her grave, and especially the sculpture depicting her family (if it is indeed her family) arise from comments made at a seminar which we gave at the Institute of Classical Studies of the University London in 1993: one cannot acknowledge them individually as they have been absorbed into this chapter, but especially valuable were those of Dr Dyfri Williams and above all of Professor Geoffrey Waywell, whose interest and initiative set this particularly entertaining chapter in our story going.

2. Op. cit. (in J. Isager [ed.], *Hecatomnid Caria...*), 88.

3. T. Molleson, M. Cox, A.H. Waldron and D.K. Whittaker, *The Spitalfields Report II: The Anthropology – the Middling Sort (CBA Research Report* **86**) (1993), 135 with table 9.6.

4. C.T. Newton, *A History of Discoveries at Halicarnassus, Cnidus and Branchidae* (London 1862), II.1 1, 333-41. In footnote 3 to our first publication of the reconstruction (see n.1 above) we charged Newton with having confused the Mindus and Mylasa gates in his report on the tombs; in fact we ourselves were confused, for Newton of course knew the site far better than we do, and had got it right: we apologise unreservedly to his shade. For a plan of the city of Halicarnassus marking the essential details, see e.g. Poul Pedersen, 'The Ionian Renaissance...', in J. Isager (ed.), *Hecatomnid Caria...*, 14, fig. 2.

5. Simon Hornblower, *Mausolus* (Oxford 1982), 278; Geoffrey B. Waywell, 'The Ada, Zeus and Idrieus Relief from Tegea in the British Museum', in O. Palagia and W. Coulson (eds), *Sculpture from Arcadia and Laconia* (Oxford 1993), 81; Idrieus' dedicatory inscriptions, listed by Hornblower, are to be found in J. Crampa, *Labraunda, Swedish Excavations and Researches* iii: *The Greek Inscriptions* (Stockholm 1972), part 2, nos 15-19; see also his p. 6 on the respective relationships and building activities of Mausolus and Idrieus at Mylasa.

6. Simon Hornblower, *Mausolus* (Oxford 1982) is the best account of the history of Caria, and of the Hecatomnid dynasty in particular. His chapter ii gives as succinct and clear an account as is possible of the complicated and often conflicting evidence for the history of the Hecatomnids, while chapter ix assesses the political and psychological significance of the Mausoleum in contemporary thought. The joint reign of Idrieus and Ada is also discussed by Waywell in Palagia and Coulson (eds), *Sculpture from Arcadia and Laconia* 79-85, and by J. Crampa, *Labraunda*, iii.2, 5-8, 11-18, 193.

7. Alexander's progress through Caria: Hornblower, op. cit., 314; G.E. Bean, *Turkey Beyond the Maeander* (2nd edn, London/New York 1980), 161-8. Ada's maternal concern: Plutarch, *Alexander*, xxii 7-10 (transl. Bernadotte Perrin, Loeb edn); also Arrian, *Anabasis*, i 23.7-8; Diodorus xvii 24-7.

8. The siege of Halicarnassus, see Hornblower, op. cit., 102-3, 105; on Ada's end and successor, ibid. 51: Hornblower rightly dismisses the possibility that another and better-known Philoxenos, one of Alexander's financial officers, became satrap in her stead, for neither dates nor circumstances fit.

9. B.A. Sparkes and L. Talcott, *The Athenian Agora XII: Black and Plain Pottery* (Princeton 1970), 60, 244 no. 104, pl. 5; full references are given in A.J.N.W. Prag and R.A.H. Neave, 'Who is the

Carian Princess?' (n.1 above), 108 n.5.
10. The flowers, pendants and terminals echo those on a necklace from Taranto in southern Italy, now in the British Museum: *BMC Jewellery* no. 1952; R.A. Higgins, *Greek and Roman Jewellery* (2nd edn, London 1961), 127, pl. 28; Dyfri Williams and Jack Ogden, *Greek Gold* (London 1994), 204-5, no. 135; compare also e.g. Indiana University Art Museum 70.105.4 (Burton Y. Berry collection): *The Search for Alexander: An Exhibition* (Greek Ministry of Culture and Sciences/New York Graphic Society, Boston 1981), 131 no. 56; also Dallas Museum: *Search for Alexander* 133 no. 62; and British Museum: *BMC Jewellery* no. 1947; Williams and Ogden, op. cit., 68-9, no.22; Higgins, op. cit. 128, 168, pls 29, 49 and colour plate C (all from the eastern Mediterranean). There are especially close parallels with necklaces from the Great Bliznitza mound in the Taman Peninsula opposite the Crimea (330-300 BC): Williams and Ogden, op. cit., 180 ff., especially nos 117, 121, 123, 125-6.
11. Cf. John Boardman, *Greek Gems and Finger Rings* (London 1970), chapter VI, especially 312 ff.: his pl. 926, a blue chalcedony scaraboid from the Cambridge Group showing a Persian spearing a boar, is very close (Louvre A1241), but the single figure and the fall of the soft Persian cap is more typical of gems in the Pendants Group (e.g. fig. 294, once Arndt collection, and pl. 884, Cambridge unnumbered). Our comments on the two gems owe much to the knowledge and the generous help of Professor Sir John Boardman and Dr Dominique Collon, but of course the way in which we have deployed them is entirely our own responsibilty. The head on the agate was at first described as that of Apollo, a god to whom Mausolus was especiallly devoted, but the hairstyle, earrings and necklace all point to its being a woman.
12. Persian warriors on gems, e.g. Boardman, op. cit., figs 289, 297, pls 525, 532, 876, 884; the 'Hellenistic Ruler': e.g. M. Robertson, *A History of Greek Art* (Cambridge 1975), 520-1, fig. 163c; also R.R.R. Smith, *Hellenistic Royal Portraits* (Oxford 1988), 32-3, 84-5, 164 no.44, pl. 32, with a full discussion of the type; the 'Idrieus': G.B. Waywell, *The Free-Standing Sculptures of the Mausoleum at Halicarnassus* (London 1978), 105 no. 29, pl. 16 (British Museum 1857.12-20.236); see also his comments on the Idrieus on the relief from Tegea, referred to again below (p. 214), in Palagia and Coulson (eds), *Sculpture from Arcadia and Laconia*, 81 with fig. 4 (British Museum 1914.7-14.1). The significance of the pose of the Persian warrior, and the implications for

interpreting the two rings, were first pointed out to us by Professor Waywell, who has also drawn our attention to another fragmentary sculpture of heroic size from the Mausoleum, this time actually in Persian dress, which might well have come from a figure similar to that on the gem (Waywell, op. cit., 114 no. 44, pl. 19; *BMC Sculpture* 1049).
13. See Prag and Neave in J.Isager (ed.), *Hecatomnid Caria...*, 99 and Appendix 1 (pp. 106-7) for David Whittaker's report. For references to the technique, see Chapter 9 n.8.
14. Strabo, *Geography*, 656.
15. Hornblower, *Mausolus*, 362-3.
16. Dr Stoddart's report appears in full as Appendix 2 (p. 107) to our report in J.Isager (ed.), *Hecatomnid Caria....*
17. *BMC Sculpture* nos. 1051 (Mausoleum), 1151 (Priene). On the Hecatomnids and Priene: J.C. Carter, *The Sculpture from the Sanctuary of Athena Polias at Priene (Research Report of the Society of Antiquaries of London* XLII, 1983), 25-31; Hornblower, op. cit., 323-6 is less certain.
18. G.B. Waywell, *The Free-Standing Sculptures of the Mausoleum*, 106-7 no. 30; Carter, op. cit. 264-6 on the identity of the head and its Roman companions, and 271-6 no. 85, especially 274, for a detailed analysis of the Priene head and its context.
19. *BMC Sculpture* no. 1153; Carter, op. cit. 277-9 no. 86, pls XL c-e, XLVII b.
20. O. Alpözen, 'Ada I Revived', in J. Isager (ed.), *Hecatomnid Caria...*, 110.
21. Tegea relief: British Museum 1914.7-14.1: Waywell in Palagia and Coulson (eds), *Sculpture from Arcadia and Laconia* 79-86, especially fig. 1; other (lost) statues of Ada are also discussed in this article. Deidameia at Olympia: e.g B. Ashmole and N. Yialouris, *Olympia: The Sculptures of the Temple of Zeus* (London 1967), pls 112-14.
22. Artemisia: *BMC Sculpture* no. 1001; Waywell, *The Free-Standing Sculptures of the Mausoleum* 103-5 no. 27, pl. 13. On the significance of the triple curls and of the sakkos, and for a list of the other heads from Priene, Waywell, op. cit., 41, 71-2. The *tettix*: Carter, op. cit. 273, following a suggestion by F. Hauser, 'Tettix', *Österreichische Jahreshefte* IX (1906), 75-130, especially 75-8. The gilded locks: British Museum GRA 1870.3-20.311, Carter, op. cit., 304, no. 107. Our awareness of the significance of the hairstyle, and the treatment of the curls on the reconstruction, owes much to discussions with Professor Waywell; of course the responsibility for the final rendering is ours alone.
23. Carter's frontispiece (op. cit.) reconstructs this patterning very clearly; see also his pp. 273-

4, pl. XLVII a,d.

24. Ian Jenkins and Dyfri Williams, 'Sprang Hair Nets: Their Manufacture and Use in Ancient Greece', *AJA* **89** (1985), 411-8, pls 44-6; id., 'A Bronze Portrait Head and its Hair Net', *Record of the Art Museum*, Princeton University **46**.2 (1987), 8-15.

25. Pliny, *Natural History* XXXIV 65 (O.1508); cf. the comments of Martin Robertson, *A History of Greek Art* (Cambridge 1975), 464.

26. O. Alpözen, 'Ada I Revived in the Bodrum Museum of Underwater Archaeology', in J. Isager (ed.), *Hecatomnid Caria...*, 110-14, gives a full account of the thinking behind the display. On the use of the niches, Waywell in Palagia and Coulson, op. cit., 81-3, citing P. Hellström (references ad loc.).

27. Lucian, *Dialogues of the Dead*, 24.2.

Chapter 11

(WHO WILL SAY "CORPSE" TO HIS VIVID CAST?)

1. J. Parker Norris, *American Bibliophilist*, April 1876, quoted by e.g. Ian Wilson, *Shakespeare: The Evidence* (London 1993), 409. On p. 394 Wilson draws attention to the fact that despite its famous minatory inscription the tomb nowhere carries Shakespeare's name.

2. Susannah M. Addyman, *The Use of Three-Dimensional Laser Imaging for Facial Reconstruction*, MA Thesis (unpub.) (University of Tennessee, Knoxville 1994): we are most grateful to Miss Addyman for lending us a copy of her thesis, and for discussing the problem with us.

3. 'Verulamium', *Current Archaeology* **120** (June 1990), 413-16. The final report on the skeleton will form part of the report on the excavations in St Stephen's cemetery by Rosalind Niblett (forthcoming).

4. N.C. Crummy et al., *Excavations of Roman and Later Cemeteries, Churches and Monastic Sites in Colchester, 1971-88 (Colchester Archaeological Report no. 9*; Colchester 1993), 8, 111-14, 275: 'Camilla' is grave G395 in the vault CF55 in this report.

5. R.J. Cruse and A.C. Harrison, 'Excavation at Hill Road, Wouldham', *Archaeologia Cantiana* **99** (1983), 81-104, especially pp. 84-5, 100-2: the skeleton of the young man in his grave is illustrated on plate VI.

6. Ian MacLeod and Trevor Cowie, 'A Face from the Past', *Current Archaeology* **147** (April 1996), 100-1.

7. G.M.A. Richter, *The Portraits of the Greeks* (London 1965), p.i.

8. W.J. van der Sanden, *Through Nature to Eternity: The Bog Bodies of North-West Europe* (Amsterdam 1996).

9. E.g. 'The Tollund Man', 'Viking Dublin: Trial Pieces', 'Bone Dreams', 'Bog Queen', 'The Grauballe Man', 'Punishment', 'Strange Fruit': these poems can all be found in Seamus Heaney, *New Selected Poems, 1966-1987* (London 1990); 'The Tollund Man' was first published in *Wintering Out* (London 1972); the other poems come from *North* (London 1975). The quotation is from 'The Grauballe Man'.

FURTHER READING

This is a summary list only: detailed bibliographies will be found in the notes to each chapter.

Abbreviations

AA   *Archäologischer Anzeiger*
AJA   *American Journal of Archaeology*
BMC   *Catalogue of...in the Department of Greek and Roman Antiquities in the British Museum (subject follows)*
BSA   *Annual of the British School at Athens*
JHS   *Journal of Hellenic Studies*

Chapter 1

(THE HISTORY OF FACIAL RECONSTRUCTION)

The only general account is M.M. Gerasimov, *The Face Finder* (London/Philadelphia 1971), now rather dated and somewhat idiosyncratic in approach. A recent collection of papers by specialists is M.Y.İşcan and R.P. Helmer (eds), *Forensic Analysis of the Skull* (New York 1993).

Chapter 2

(TECHNIQUES AND THE FORENSIC EVIDENCE)

See chapter 1.

Chapter 3

(RICHARD NEAVE'S EGYPTIAN ENCOUNTER)

The Two Brothers and Mummy Manchester 1770: Rosalie David and Eddie Tapp (eds), *Evidence Embalmed: Modern Medicine and the Mummies of Ancient Egypt* (Manchester 1984).

This is an updated version of A.R. David, *Mysteries of the Mummies* (London 1978). For a detailed account, A.R. David (ed.), *The Manchester Museum Mummy Project* (Manchester 1979).

Natsef-Amun: A.R. David and E. Tapp (eds), The Mummy's Tale (London 1992).

Chapter 4

(KING PHILIP II OF MACEDON)
The life of Philip: among the many books about Philip we have consulted the following: G.L. Cawkwell, *Philip of Macedon* (London 1978); J.R. Ellis, *Philip II and Macedonian Imperialism* (London 1976); N.G.L. Hammond and G.T. Griffith, *A History of Macedonia* II (Oxford 1979); M.B. Hatzopoulos and L.D. Loukopoulos (eds), *Philip of Macedon* (Athens/London 1980/1981); Nicholas Hammond, *Philip of Macedon* (London 1994), which has a good and selective bibliography. A.B. Bosworth, *Conquest and Empire: The Reign of Alexander the Great* (Cambridge 1988/1993), Prologue, part 1, summarises Philip's achievement and Alexander's debt to him.

The site and the excavation: M. Andronicos, *Vergina: The Royal Tombs and the Ancient City* (Athens 1984), with further references; many articles have been written discussing the identity of the occupants of the tomb, often with great passion: the most comprehensive list is given by Alice Swift Riginos, 'The Wounding of Philip II of Macedon', *JHS* **114** (1994), 103 n. 1.

The reconstruction: A.J.N.W. Prag, J.H. Musgrave and R.A.H. Neave, 'The Skull from Tomb II at Vergina: King Philip II of Macedon', *JHS* **104** (1984) 60-78; the modification to the eye wound: A.J.N.W. Prag, 'Reconstructing King Philip II: the "Nice" Version', *AJA* **94** (1990), 237-47.

Chapter 5

(KING MIDAS HAS ASS'S EARS?)
Midas and the Phrygian kingdom: Seton Lloyd, *Ancient Turkey: A Traveller's History of Anatolia* (London 1989) chapter 6, 'The Kingdom of Midas', who also summarises the excavation; the full account of the latter is by R.S. Young (ed.), *Three Great Early Tumuli: Gordion I (Pennsylvania University Museum*

Monograph 43; Philadelphia 1981), especially 79-190, described more briefly by the same author in the site guide, *Gordion: A Guide to the Excavations and Museum* (Ankara 1975).

The legend is told most vividly by Ovid, *Metamorphoses*, xi 146 ff., especially 180-93 (transl. Mary M. Innes; Harmondsworth 1955), and discussed in greatest detail by S. Eitrem, 'Midas', in *Real Encyclopädie*, XV. 2 1526-36 (in German).

The reconstruction: A.J.N.W. Prag, 'Reconstructing King Midas: A First Report'. *Anatolian Studies* **39** (1989), 159-65.

Chapter 6

(GRAVE CIRCLE B AT MYCENAE)
Mycenaean civilisation: e.g. Oliver Dickinson, *The Aegean Bronze Age* (Cambridge 1994) – comprehensive and with a good bibliography; Peter Warren, *The Aegean Civilizations* (Oxford 1975) is more popular; also Lord William Taylour, *The Mycenaeans* (2nd edn, London 1983), by the director of the post-war British excavations at the site.

The most readable and unprejudiced accounts of Schliemann's excavation of Grave Circle A are Michael Wood, *In Search of the Trojan War* (London 1985/1987), chapter 2 (who also gives a perceptive analysis of the chronology of the Late Bronze Age), and J. Lesley Fitton, *The Discovery of the Greek Bronze Age* (London 1995), 53-94. Grave Circle B: G.E. Mylonas, *Mycenae Rich in Gold* (Athens 1983), 46-61; the full report (in Greek, with English summary and containing the report on the skulls by J.L. Angel) is G.E. Mylonas, *O Taphikos Kyklos B ton Mykenon (Grave Circle B at Mycenae)* (Athens 1973). The Grave Circles are analysed by O.T.P.K. Dickinson, *The Origins of Mycenaean Civilisation (Studies in Mediterranean Archaeology* 49: Göteborg 1977).

The reconstruction: J.H. Musgrave, R.A.H. Neave and A.J.N.W. Prag, 'Seven Faces from Grave Circle B at Mycenae', *BSA* **90** (1995), 107-36, with a full bibliography.

Chapter 7

(THE PRIEST AND PRIESTESS)
The books by Dickinson and Warren listed under the previous chapter also describe the Minoan civilisation. The best English account

of the sites in the Archanes area is J. and E. Sakellarakis, *Archanes* (Athens 1991), with full bibliography.

Disease in the ancient Aegean: M.D. Grmek, *Diseases in the Ancient Greek World* (trans. M. Müllner and L. Müllner; Baltimore and London 1989).

The reconstruction, with full anatomical notes: J.H. Musgrave, R.A.H. Neave, A.J.N.W. Prag, E. Sakellarakis and J. Sakellarakis, 'The Priest and Priestess from Archanes-Anemospilia', *BSA* **89** (1994), 89-J252.

Chapter 8
(BODIES FROM THE BOG)
The best-known and still the most readable book on bog bodies is P.V. Glob, *The Bog People* (London 1969/1977), but there have been numerous more recent publications, such as Don Brothwell, *The Bogman and the Archaeology of People* (London 1986); R.C. Turner and R.G. Scaife, *Bog Bodies: New Discoveries and New Perspectives* (London 1995) and most recently, Wijnand van der Sanden, *Through Nature to Eternity: The Bog Bodies of North-West Europe* (Amsterdam 1996).

Lindow Man: I.M. Stead, J.B. Bourke, and D. Brothwell (eds), *Lindow Man: The Body in the Bog* (London 1986).

Chapter 9
(SEIANTI HANUNIA TLESNASA)
There are many general introductions to the Etruscans: e.g. Ellen MacNamara, *The Etruscans* (London 1990); M. Cristofani, *The Etruscans* (London 1980); Larissa Bonfante (ed.), *Etruscan Life and Afterlife* (Detroit/Warminster 1986); M. Pallottino, *The Etruscans* (2nd edn, Harmondsworth

1975/1978); id., *A History of Earliest Italy* (Ann Arbor/London 1991). Otto Brendel, *Etruscan Art*, revised by Francesca R. Serra Ridgway (New Haven/London 1995) covers much more than its title suggests; the bibliography is excellent.

Whittaker's 'Gustafson Technique' for ageing teeth: in John Hunter, Charlotte Roberts and Anthony Martin, *Studies in Crime: An Introduction to Forensic Archaeology* (London 1996) 112-13 (with further references).

The detailed report on the reconstruction is planned as a joint monograph under the editorship of Judith Swaddling and John Prag to be published in 1998.

Chapter 10
(THE CASE OF THE CARIAN PRINCESS)
The history of Caria and of the Hecatomnid dynasty: Simon Hornblower, *Mausolus* (Oxford 1982), especially chapter ii.

The excavation, reconstruction and display are all discussed in papers published in Jacob Isager (ed.), *Hecatomnid Caria and the Ionian Renaissance = Halicarnassian Studies* **1** (Odense 1994).

Chapter 11
('WHO WILL SAY "CORPSE" TO HIS VIVID CAST?')
'Posthumus': 'Verulamium', Current Archaeology 120 (June 1990), 413-16; 'Camilla': N.C. Crummy et al., *Excavations of Roman and Later Cemeteries, Churches and Monastic Sites in Colchester, 1971-88* (Colchester Archaeological Report no. 9; Colchester, 1993), 8, 111-14, 275 (vault CF55, grave G395); the Rochester head: R.J. Cruse and A.C. Harrison, 'Excavation at Hill Road, Wouldham', *Archaeologia Cantiana* **99** (1983), 81-104.

INDEX